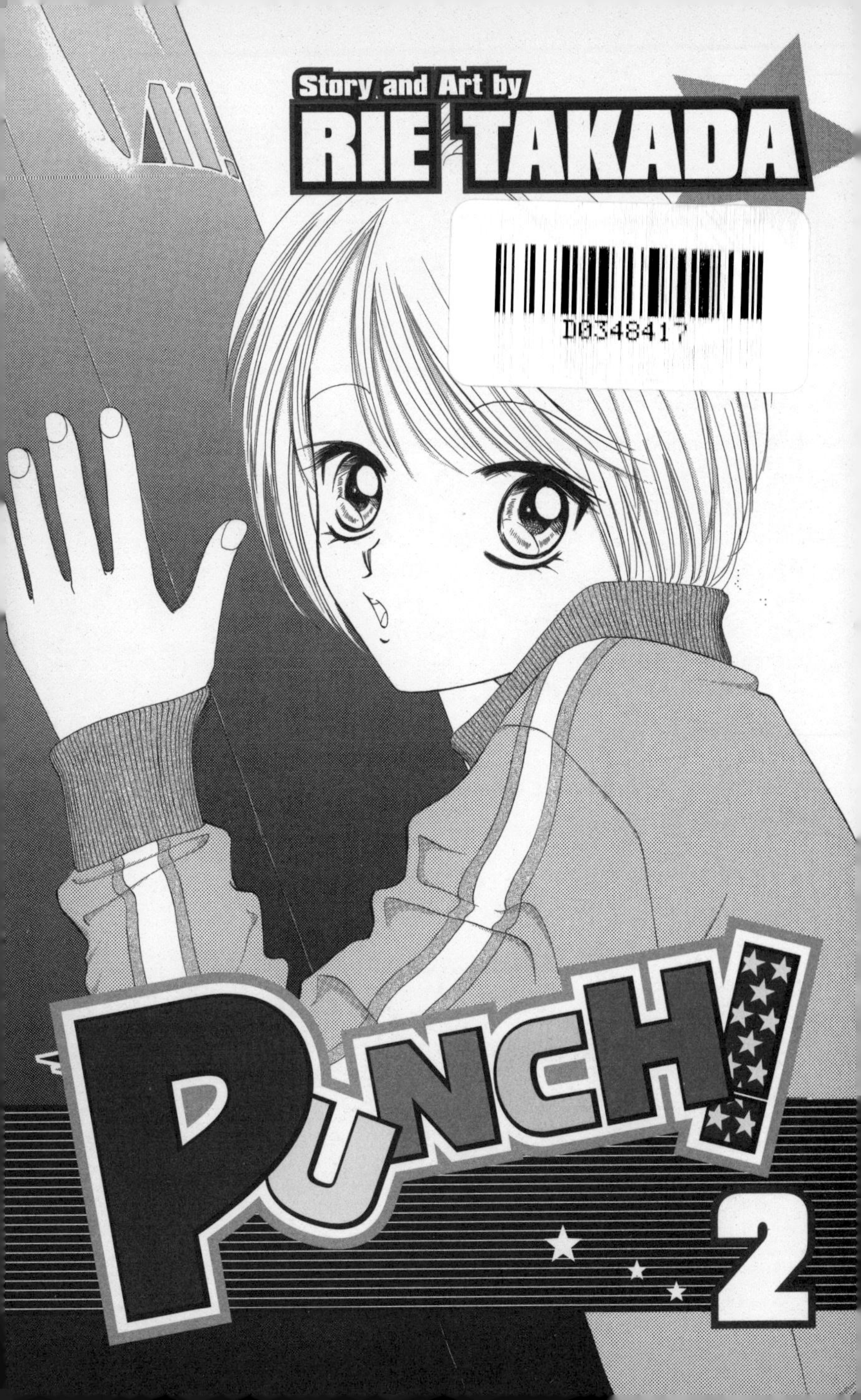
Story and Art by
RIE TAKADA
PUNCH!
2

PUNCH! 2

STORY ★

Elle lives with her grandpa in his martial arts gym, surrounded by grunting guys, stinky sweatsuits and the constant sounds of punching and pummeling. Worse yet, she's also stuck in an arranged engagement to Ruo, the grandson of her grandpa's dearest friend.

Then one day Elle meets Kazuki Shindo—and her world turns upside down! At first, Kazuki just agrees to pose as her boyfriend to help her get away from Ruo. Before long, he has moved into the gym and enrolled at Elle's school.

Will their make-believe relationship turn into the real deal? Elle sure hopes so! ♥

But Ruo won't give her up without a fight, and now he's picked their school hallway for his own private boxing ring…

CHARACTERS ★

GIGI NAGAHARA

Elle's grandpa. Former kickboxing champion and present owner of Nagahara Martial Arts Gym.

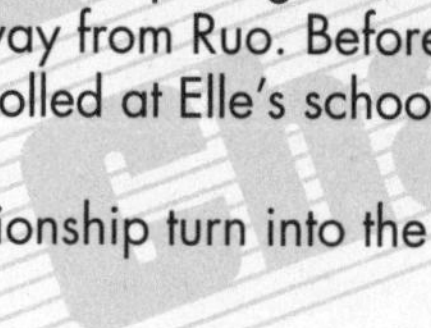

Elle Nagahara

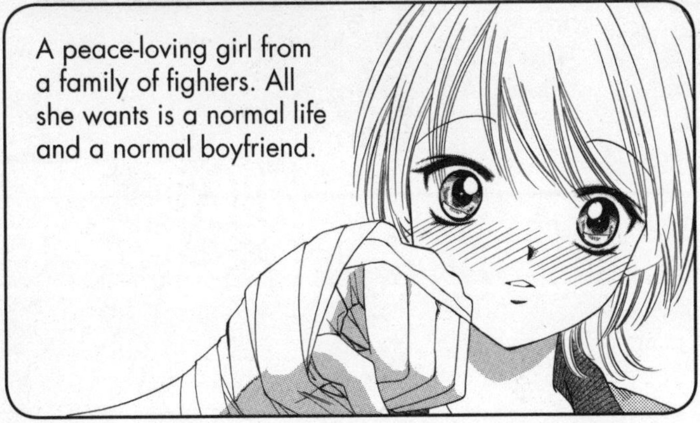

A peace-loving girl from a family of fighters. All she wants is a normal life and a normal boyfriend.

Ruo M. Eschuck

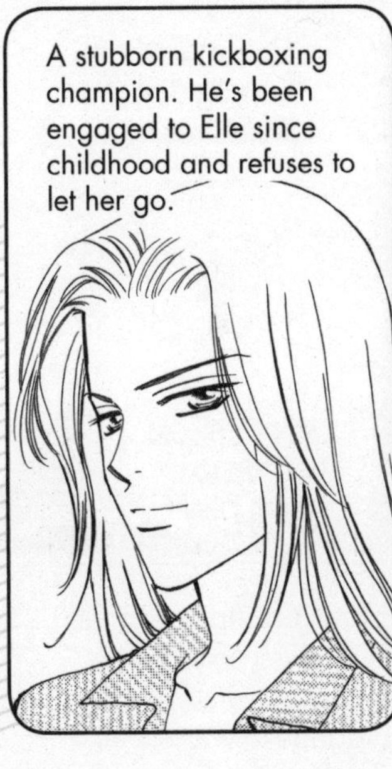

A stubborn kickboxing champion. He's been engaged to Elle since childhood and refuses to let her go.

Kazuki Shindo

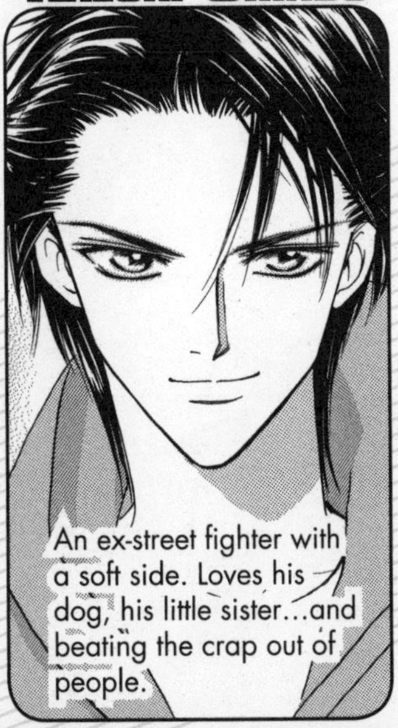

An ex-street fighter with a soft side. Loves his dog, his little sister...and beating the crap out of people.

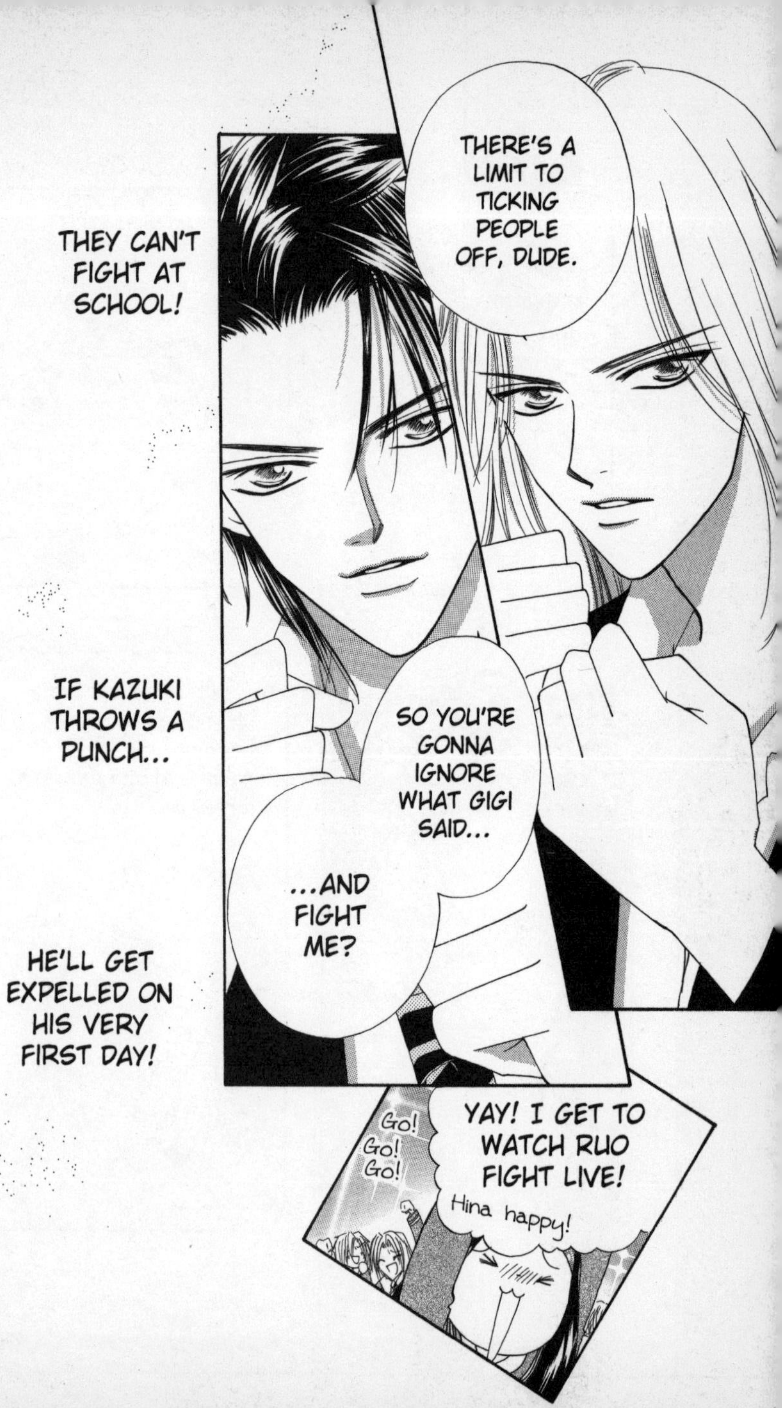
THERE'S A LIMIT TO TICKING PEOPLE OFF, DUDE.
THEY CAN'T FIGHT AT SCHOOL!
SO YOU'RE GONNA IGNORE WHAT GIGI SAID...
...AND FIGHT ME?
IF KAZUKI THROWS A PUNCH...
HE'LL GET EXPELLED ON HIS VERY FIRST DAY!
YAY! I GET TO WATCH RUO FIGHT LIVE!
Hina happy!
Go! Go! Go!

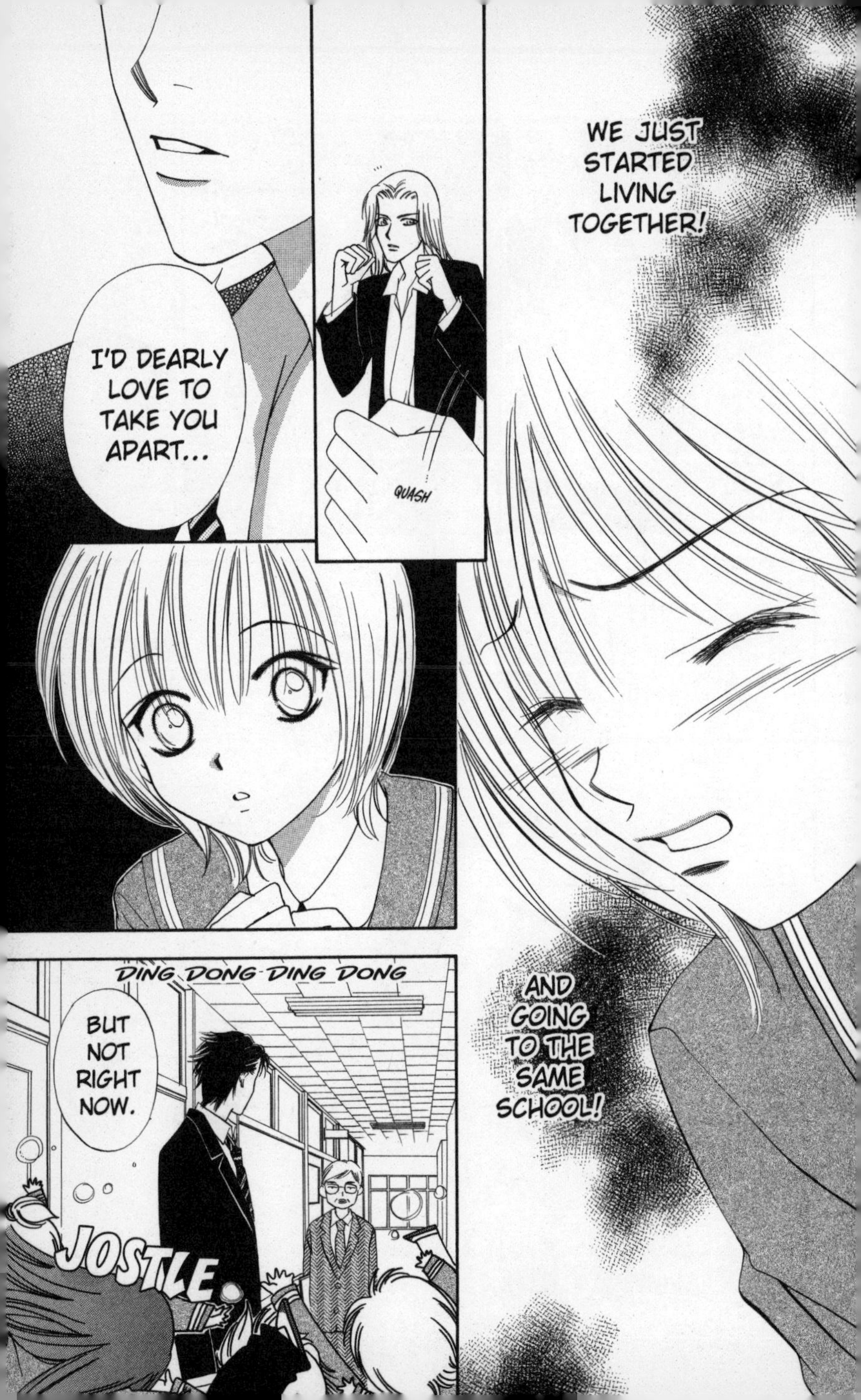
WE JUST STARTED LIVING TOGETHER!
AND GOING TO THE SAME SCHOOL!
QUASH
I'D DEARLY LOVE TO TAKE YOU APART...
DING DONG DING DONG
BUT NOT RIGHT NOW.
JOSTLE

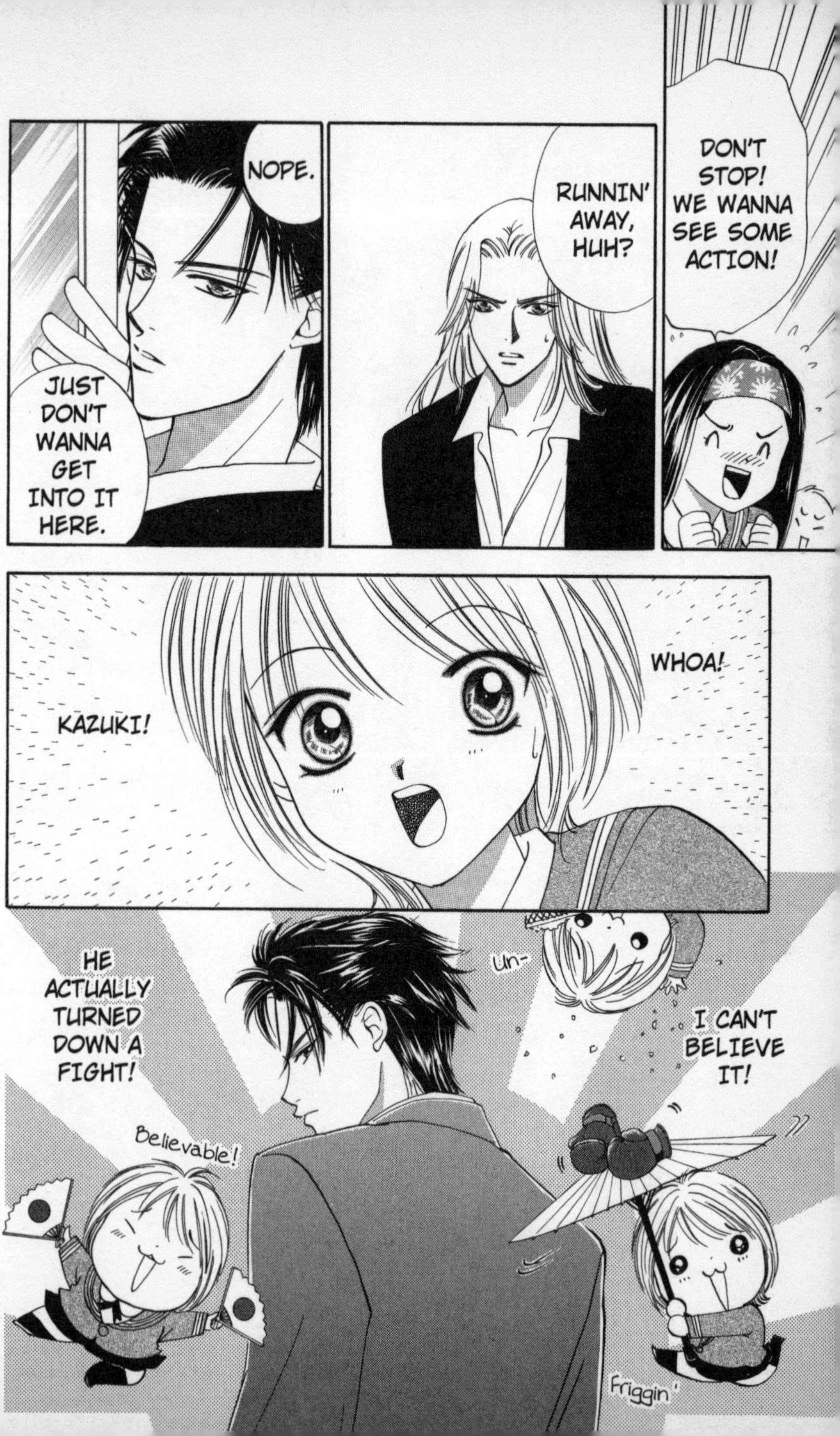
DON'T STOP! WE WANNA SEE SOME ACTION!
RUNNIN' AWAY, HUH?
NOPE.
JUST DON'T WANNA GET INTO IT HERE.
WHOA!
KAZUKI!
Un-
I CAN'T BELIEVE IT!
HE ACTUALLY TURNED DOWN A FIGHT!
Friggin'
Believable!

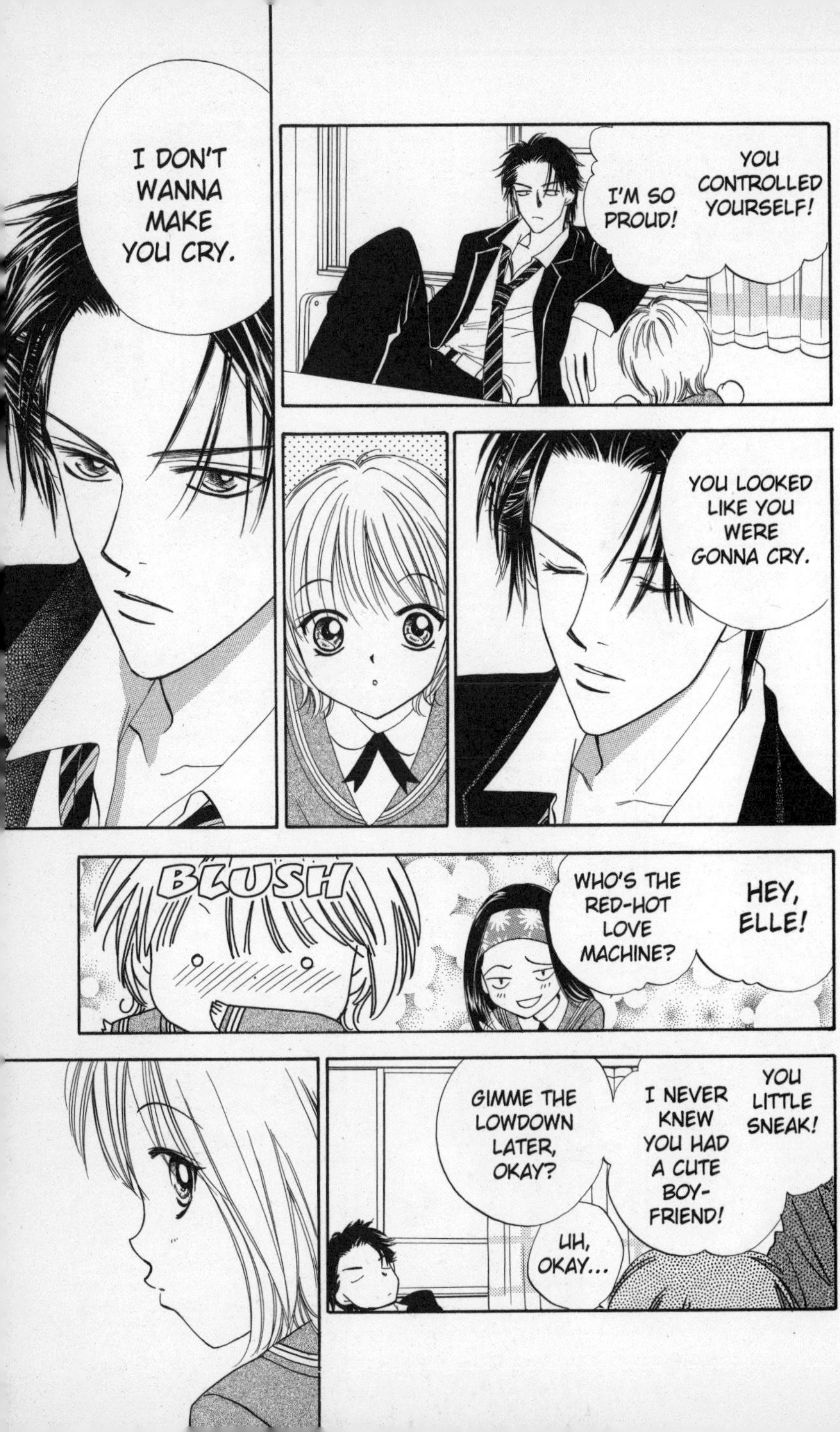
YOU CONTROLLED YOURSELF!
I'M SO PROUD!
YOU LOOKED LIKE YOU WERE GONNA CRY.
I DON'T WANNA MAKE YOU CRY.
HEY, ELLE!
WHO'S THE RED-HOT LOVE MACHINE?
BLUSH
YOU LITTLE SNEAK!
I NEVER KNEW YOU HAD A CUTE BOY-FRIEND!
GIMME THE LOWDOWN LATER, OKAY?
UH, OKAY...

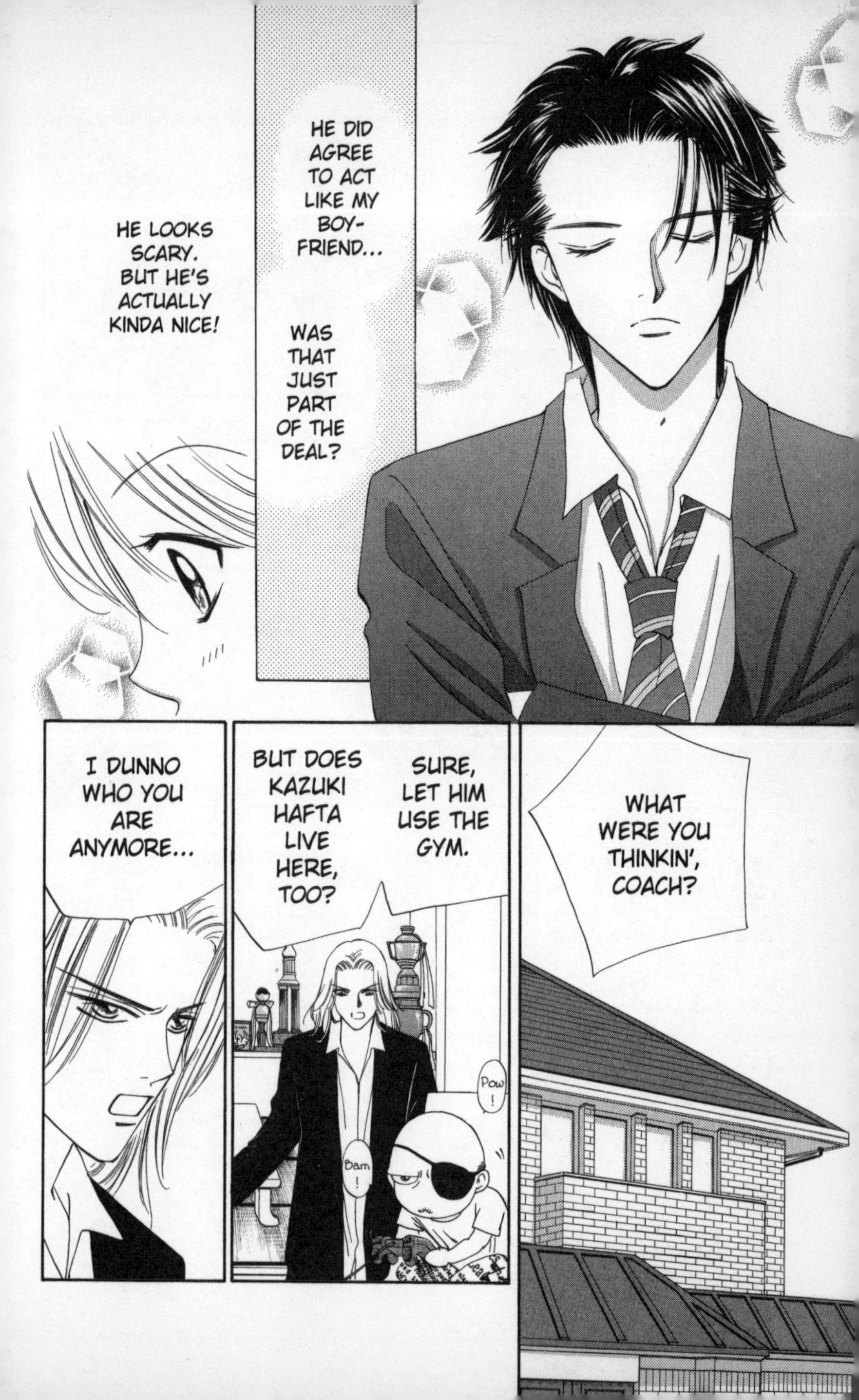
HE DID AGREE TO ACT LIKE MY BOY-FRIEND...
WAS THAT JUST PART OF THE DEAL?
HE LOOKS SCARY. BUT HE'S ACTUALLY KINDA NICE!
WHAT WERE YOU THINKIN', COACH?
SURE, LET HIM USE THE GYM.
BUT DOES KAZUKI HAFTA LIVE HERE, TOO?
Pow!
Bam!
I DUNNO WHO YOU ARE ANYMORE...

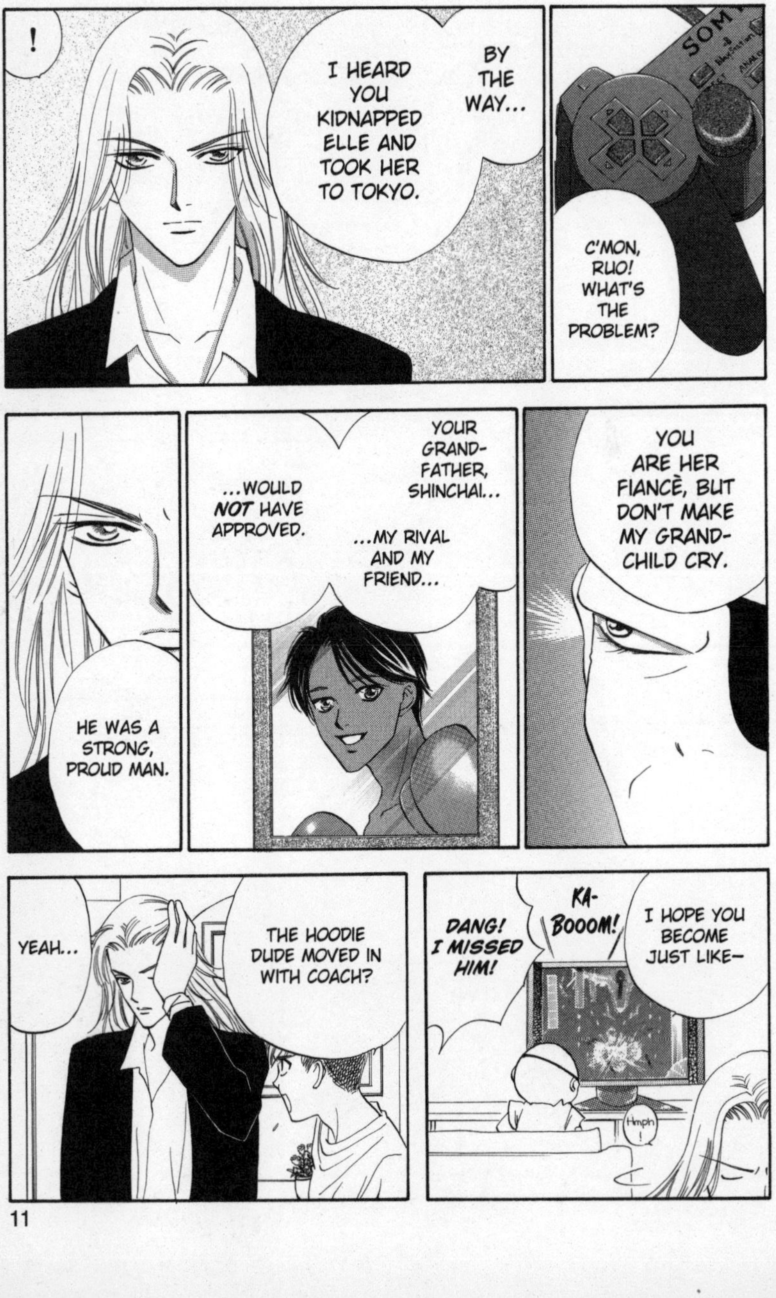
C'MON, RUO! WHAT'S THE PROBLEM?
BY THE WAY...
I HEARD YOU KIDNAPPED ELLE AND TOOK HER TO TOKYO.
!
YOU ARE HER FIANCÈ, BUT DON'T MAKE MY GRAND-CHILD CRY.
YOUR GRAND-FATHER, SHINCHAI...
...MY RIVAL AND MY FRIEND...
...WOULD ***NOT*** HAVE APPROVED.
HE WAS A STRONG, PROUD MAN.
I HOPE YOU BECOME JUST LIKE—
KA-BOOOM!
DANG! I MISSED HIM!
Hmph!
THE HOODIE DUDE MOVED IN WITH COACH?
YEAH...

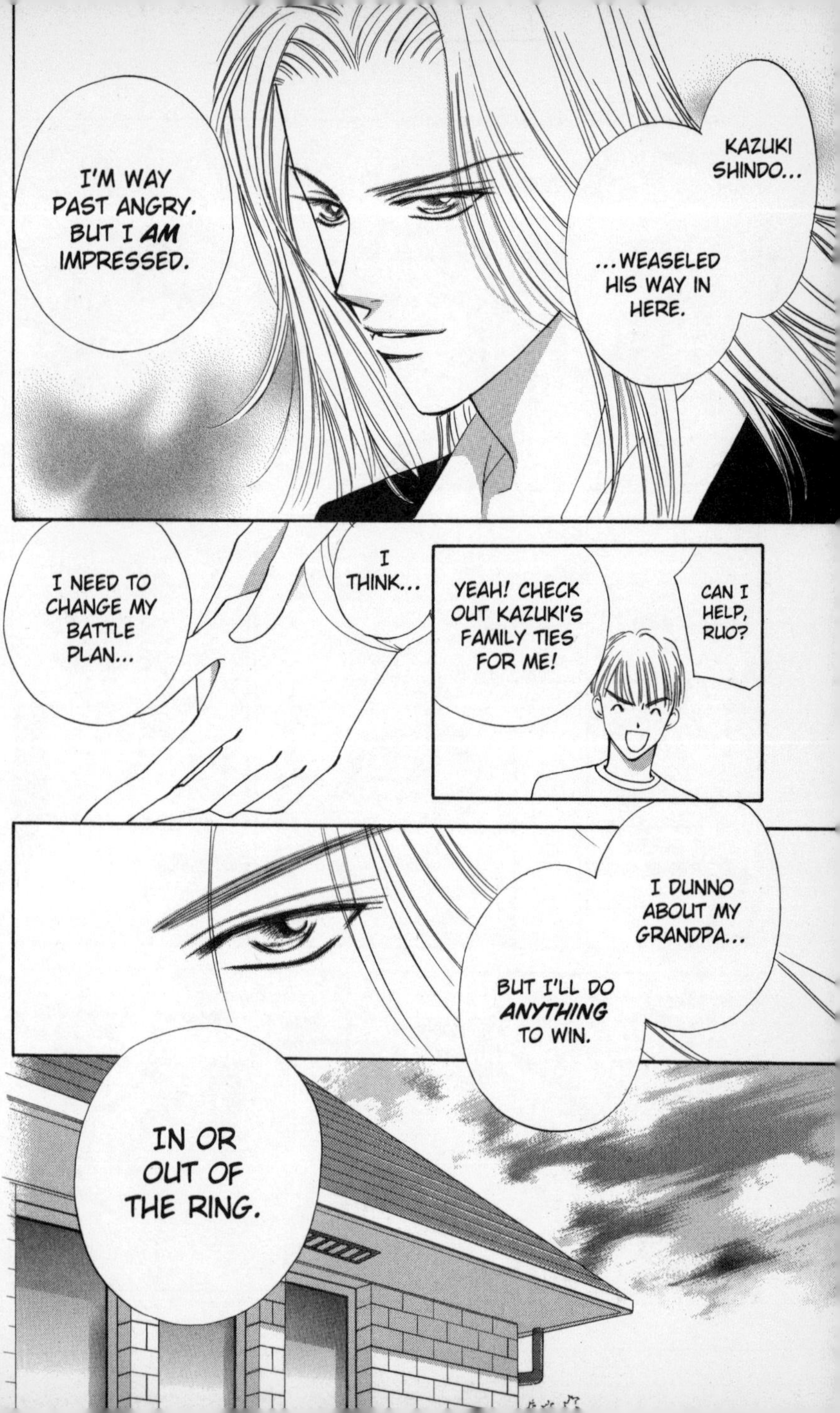
KAZUKI SHINDO... ...WEASELED HIS WAY IN HERE.
I'M WAY PAST ANGRY. BUT I *AM* IMPRESSED.
CAN I HELP, RUO?
YEAH! CHECK OUT KAZUKI'S FAMILY TIES FOR ME!
I THINK...
I NEED TO CHANGE MY BATTLE PLAN...
I DUNNO ABOUT MY GRANDPA...
BUT I'LL DO *ANYTHING* TO WIN.
IN OR OUT OF THE RING.

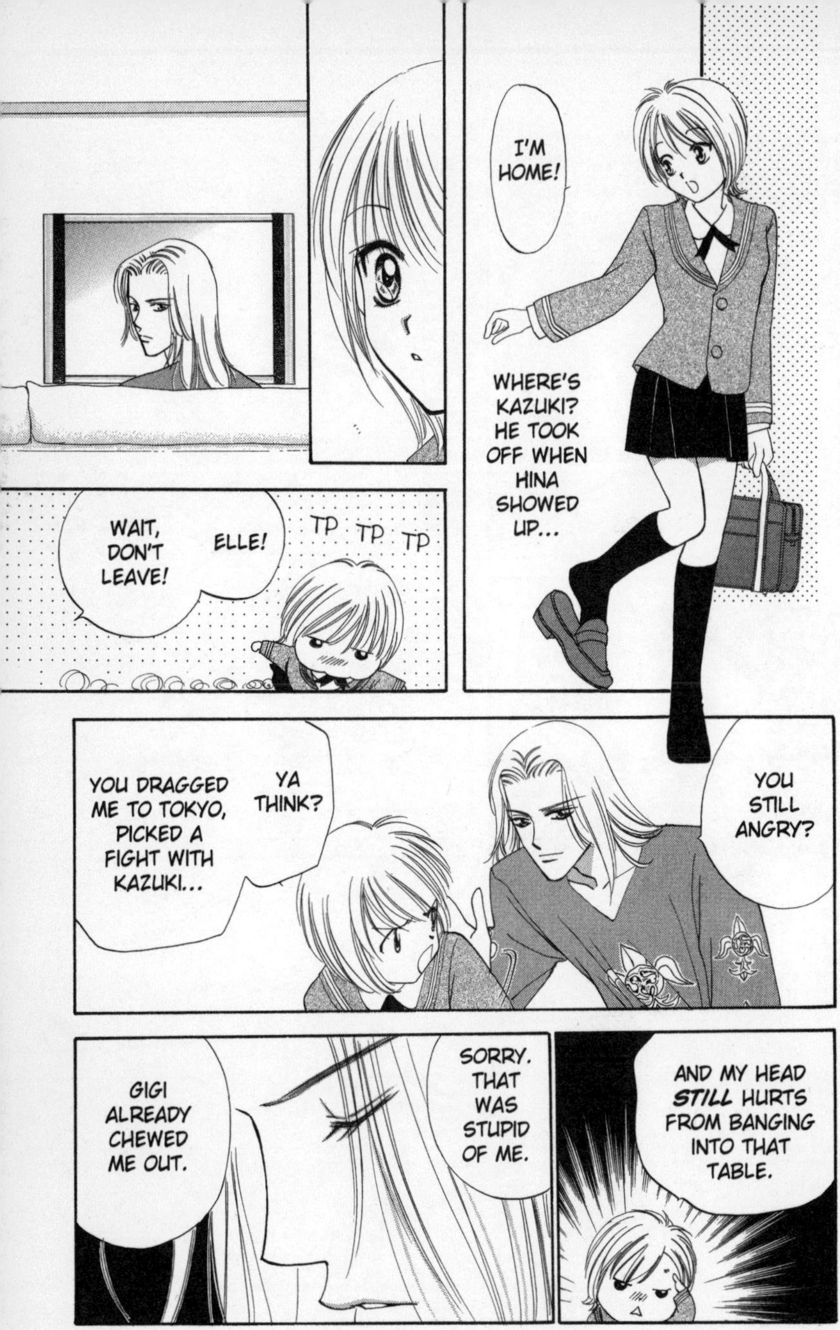
I'M HOME!
WHERE'S KAZUKI? HE TOOK OFF WHEN HINA SHOWED UP...
WAIT, DON'T LEAVE!
ELLE!
TP TP TP
YOU STILL ANGRY?
YA THINK?
YOU DRAGGED ME TO TOKYO, PICKED A FIGHT WITH KAZUKI...
AND MY HEAD STILL HURTS FROM BANGING INTO THAT TABLE.
SORRY. THAT WAS STUPID OF ME.
GIGI ALREADY CHEWED ME OUT.

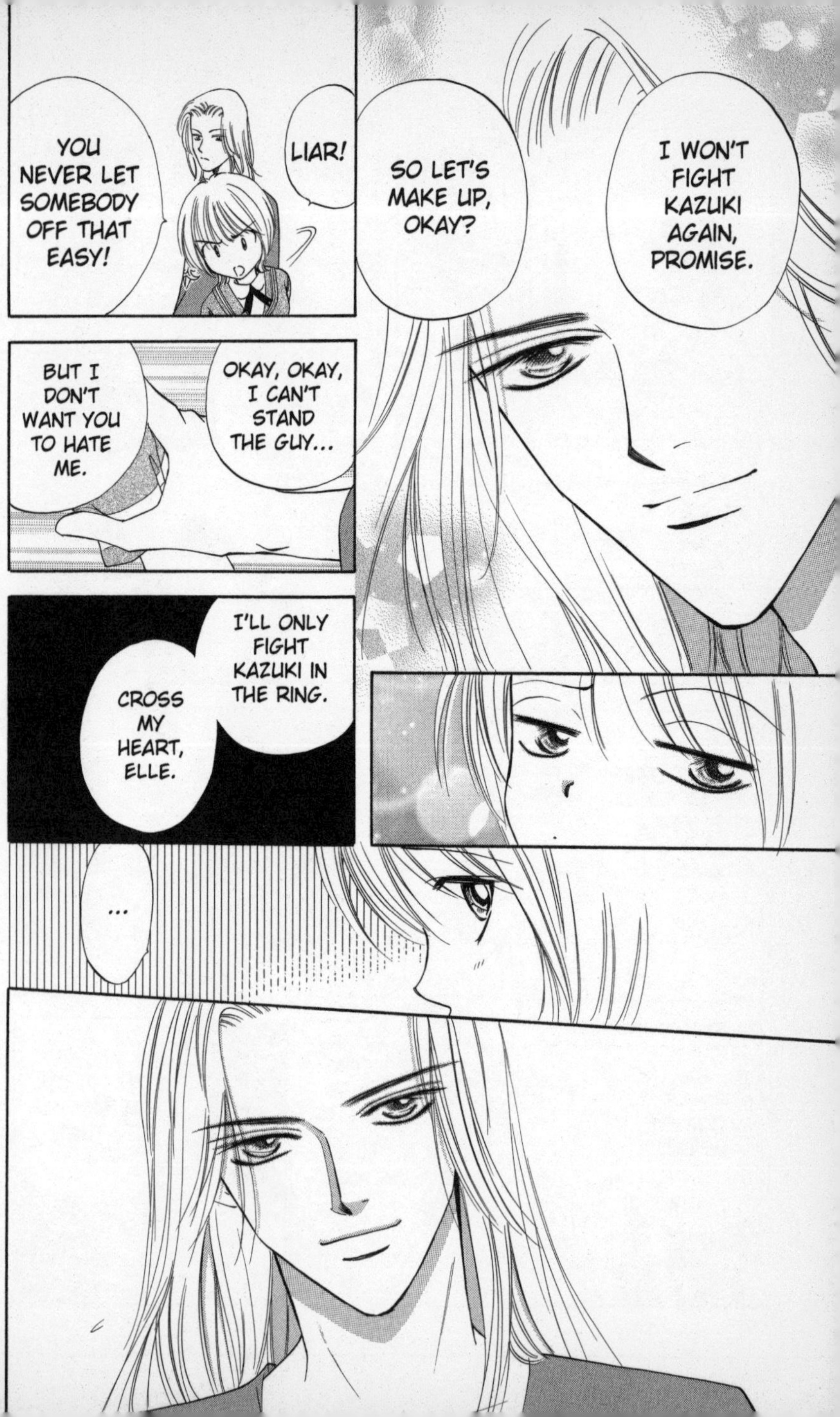
I WON'T FIGHT KAZUKI AGAIN, PROMISE.
SO LET'S MAKE UP, OKAY?
LIAR!
YOU NEVER LET SOMEBODY OFF THAT EASY!
OKAY, OKAY, I CAN'T STAND THE GUY...
BUT I DON'T WANT YOU TO HATE ME.
I'LL ONLY FIGHT KAZUKI IN THE RING.
CROSS MY HEART, ELLE.
...

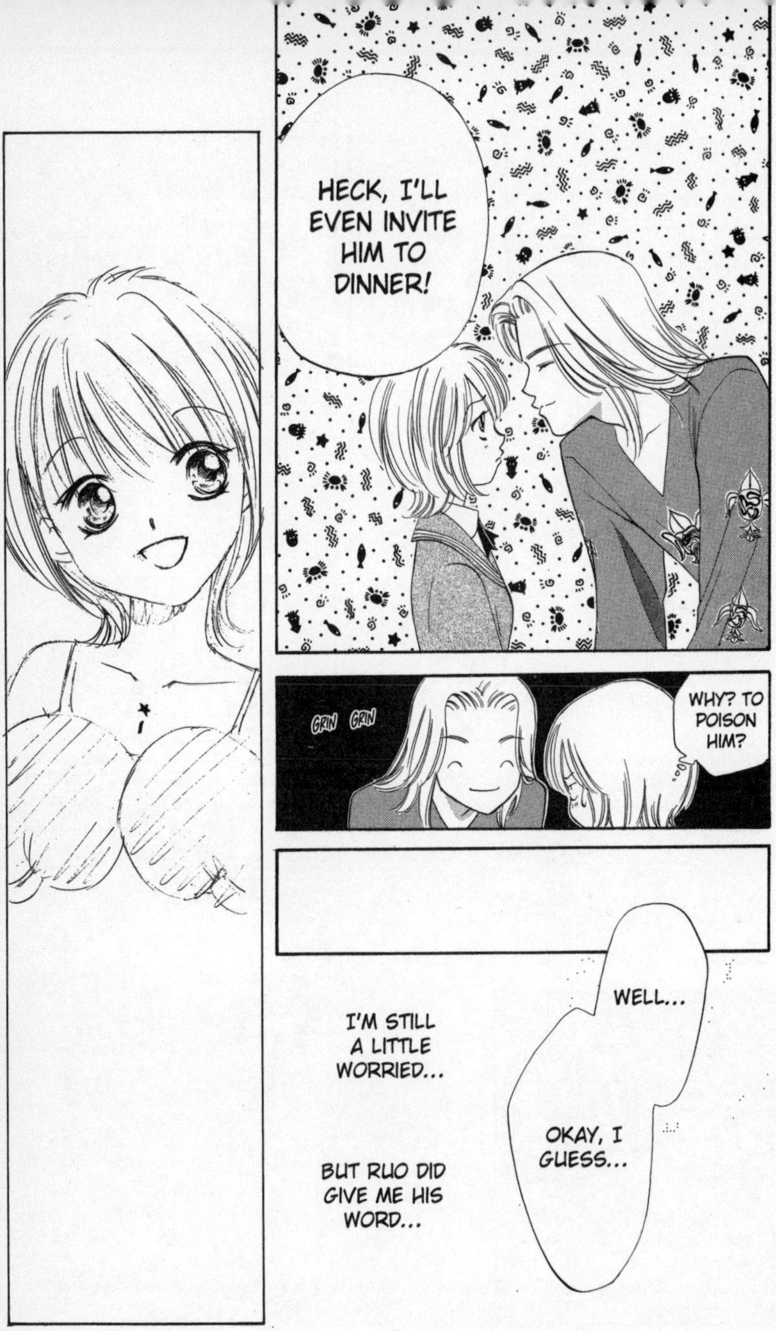
HECK, I'LL EVEN INVITE HIM TO DINNER!
WHY? TO POISON HIM?
GRIN GRIN
WELL...
OKAY, I GUESS...
I'M STILL A LITTLE WORRIED...
BUT RUO DID GIVE ME HIS WORD...

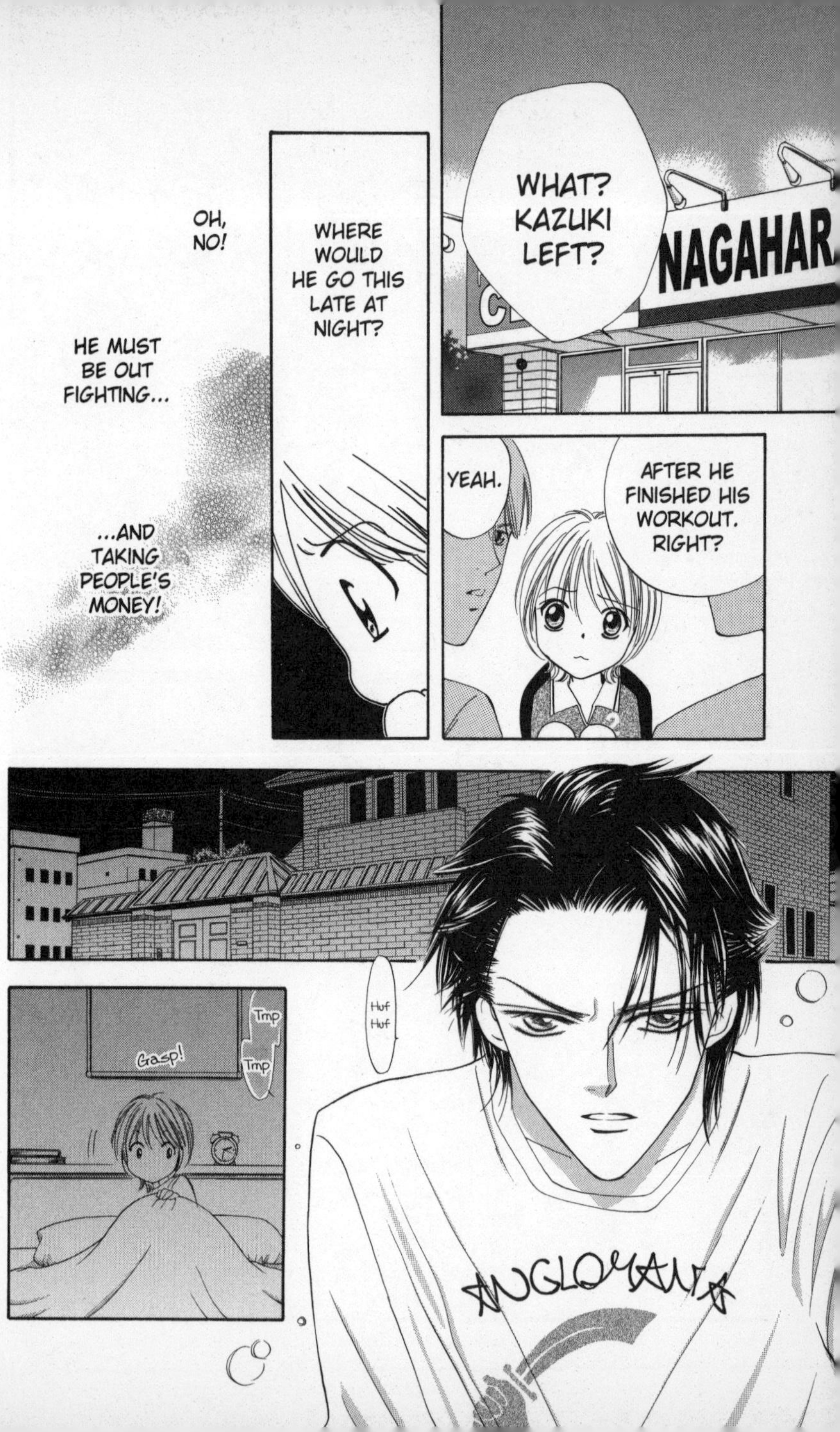
NAGAHAR
WHAT? KAZUKI LEFT?
AFTER HE FINISHED HIS WORKOUT. RIGHT?
YEAH.
WHERE WOULD HE GO THIS LATE AT NIGHT?
OH, NO!
HE MUST BE OUT FIGHTING...
...AND TAKING PEOPLE'S MONEY!
Huf Huf
Tmp
Tmp
Gasp!

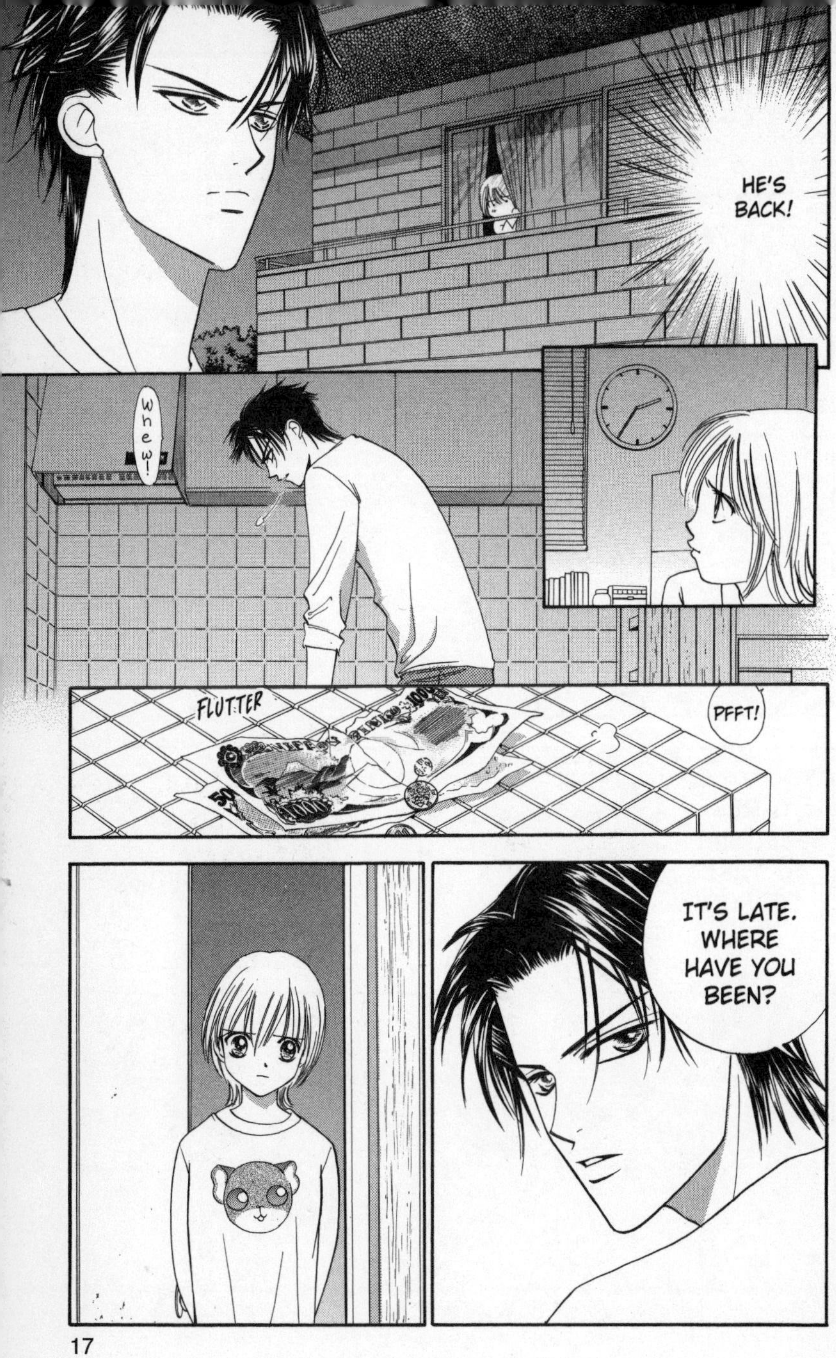
HE'S BACK!
Whew!
PFFT!
FLUTTER
IT'S LATE. WHERE HAVE YOU BEEN?

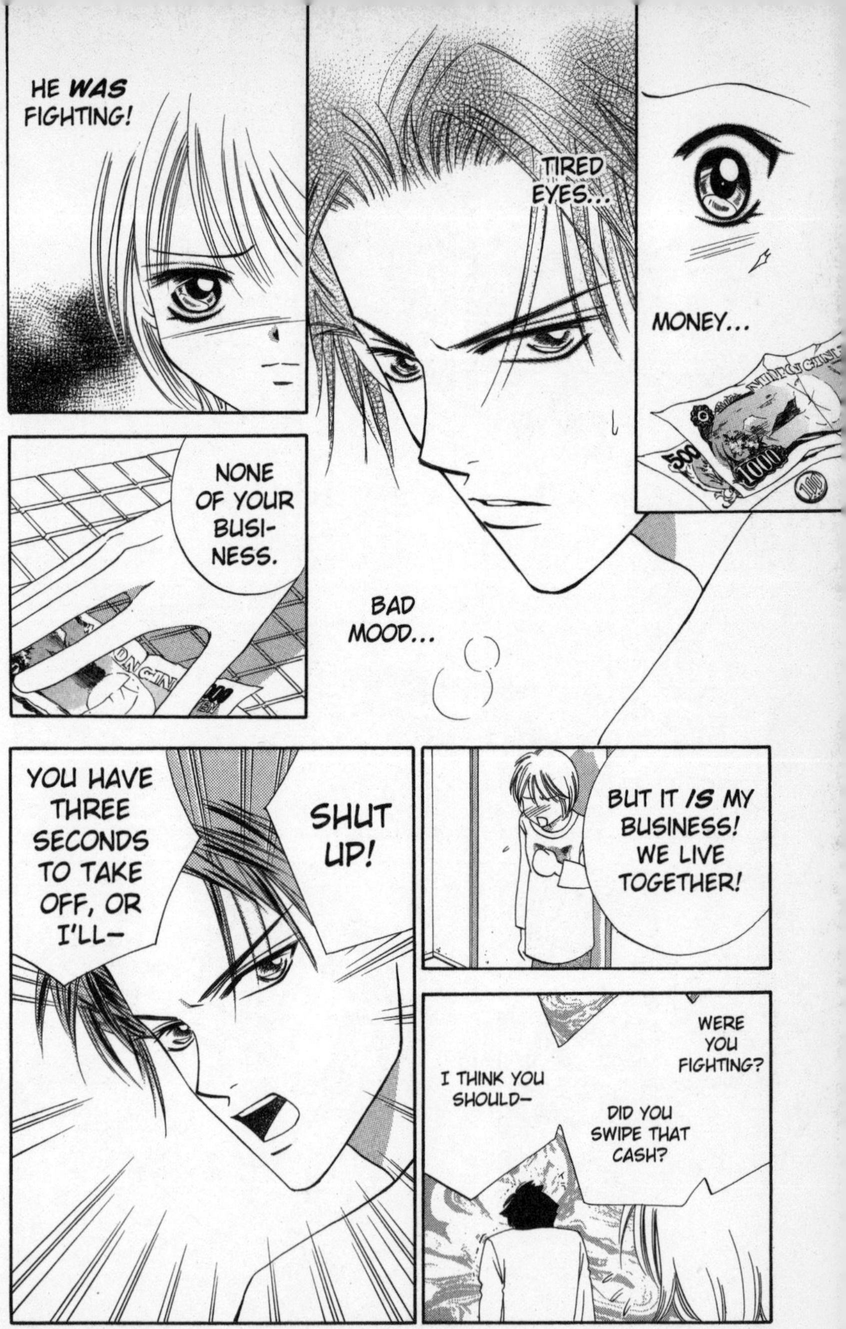
MONEY...
TIRED EYES...
BAD MOOD...
HE *WAS* FIGHTING!
NONE OF YOUR BUSI-NESS.
BUT IT *IS* MY BUSINESS! WE LIVE TOGETHER!
WERE YOU FIGHTING?
DID YOU SWIPE THAT CASH?
I THINK YOU SHOULD—
SHUT UP!
YOU HAVE THREE SECONDS TO TAKE OFF, OR I'LL—

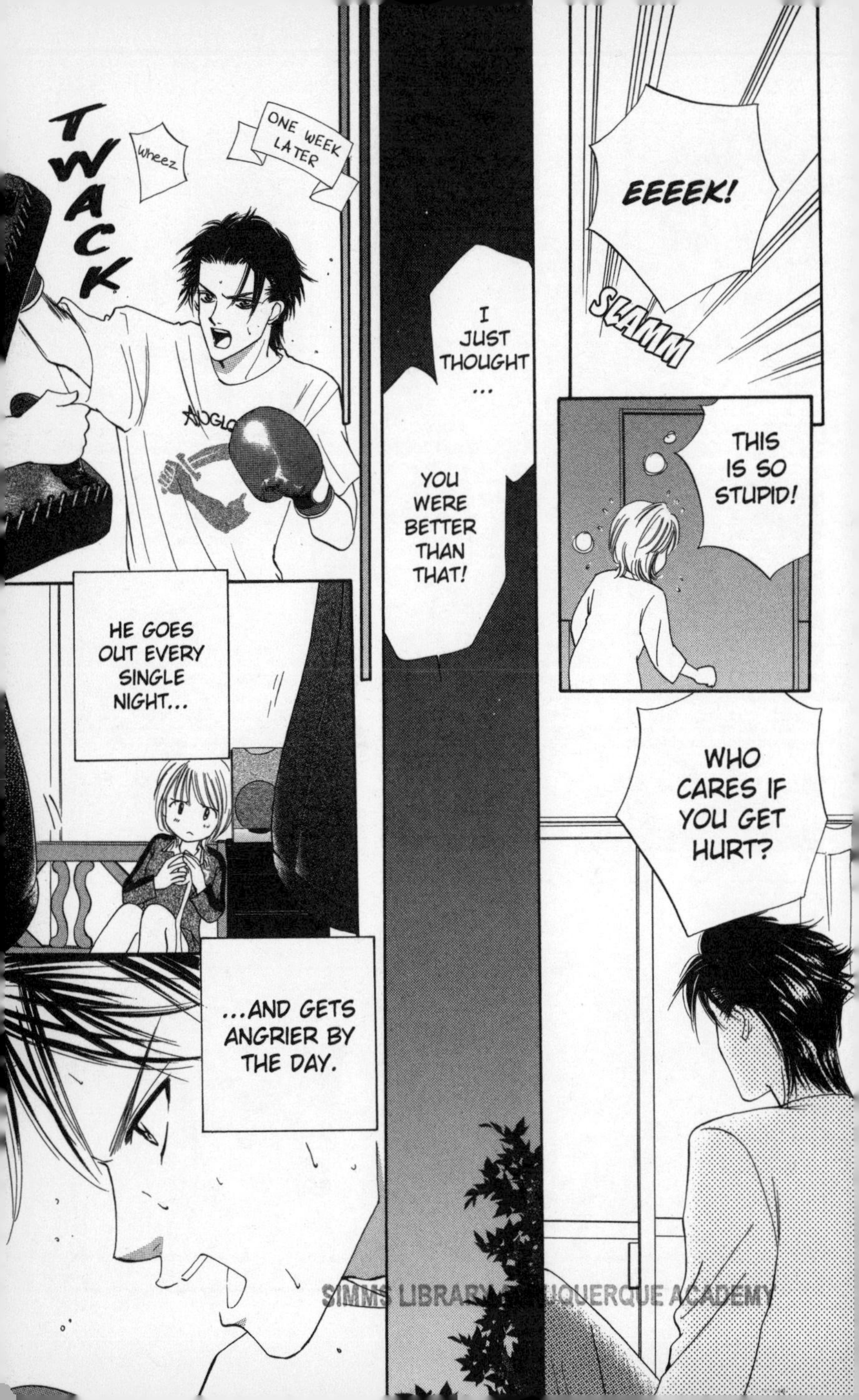
EEEEK!
SLAMM
THIS IS SO STUPID!
WHO CARES IF YOU GET HURT?
I JUST THOUGHT...
YOU WERE BETTER THAN THAT!
ONE WEEK LATER
TWACK
Wheez
HE GOES OUT EVERY SINGLE NIGHT...
...AND GETS ANGRIER BY THE DAY.

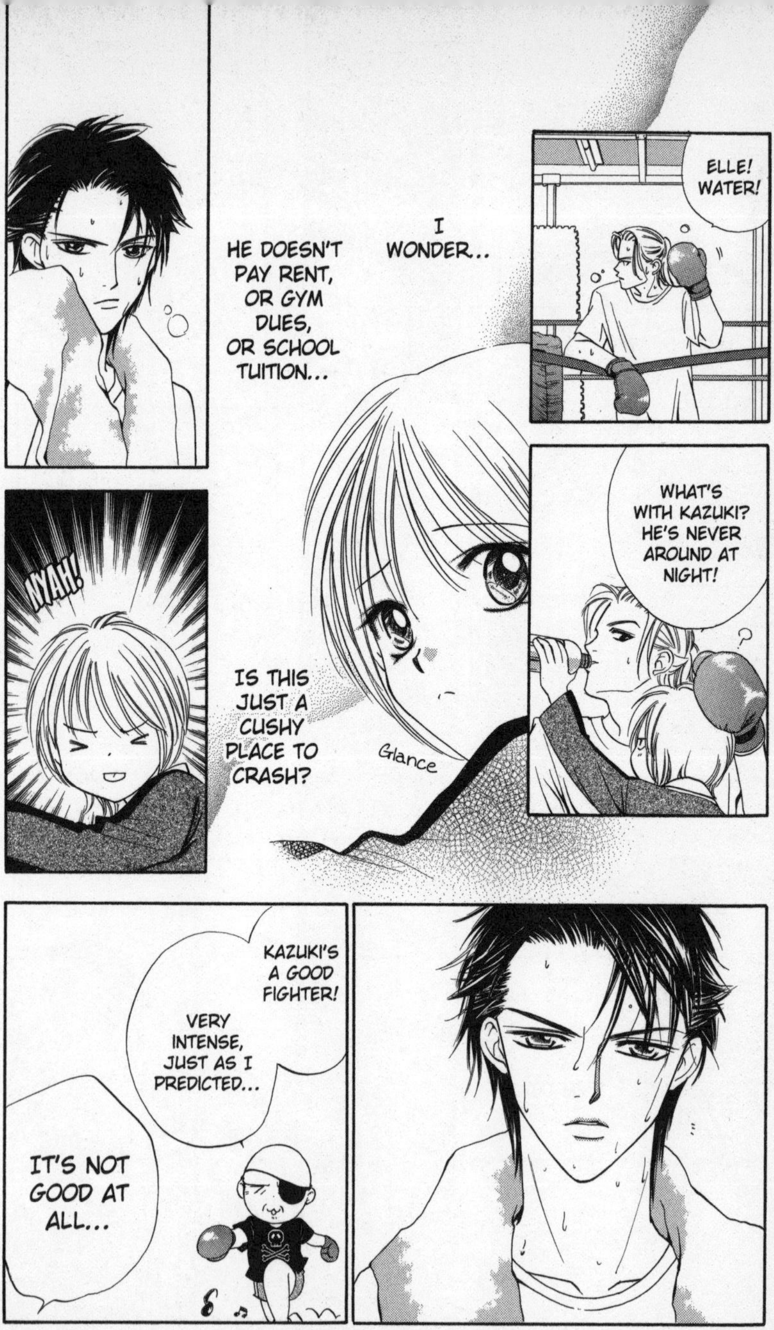
ELLE! WATER!
WHAT'S WITH KAZUKI? HE'S NEVER AROUND AT NIGHT!
I WONDER...
HE DOESN'T PAY RENT, OR GYM DUES, OR SCHOOL TUITION...
IS THIS JUST A CUSHY PLACE TO CRASH?
Glance
NYAH!
KAZUKI'S A GOOD FIGHTER!
VERY INTENSE, JUST AS I PREDICTED...
IT'S NOT GOOD AT ALL...

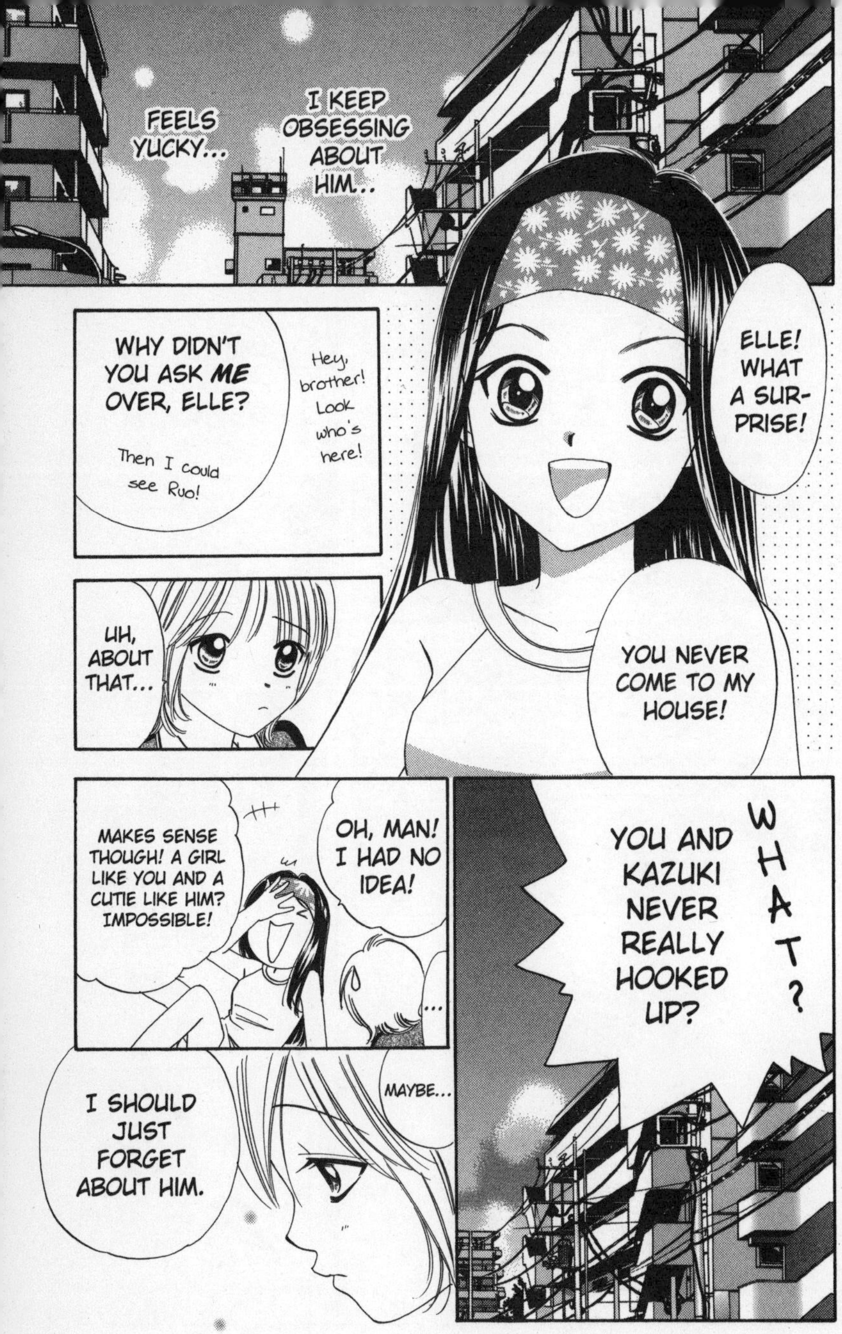
I KEEP OBSESSING ABOUT HIM...
FEELS YUCKY...
ELLE! WHAT A SURPRISE!
YOU NEVER COME TO MY HOUSE!
Hey, brother! Look who's here!
WHY DIDN'T YOU ASK *ME* OVER, ELLE?
Then I could see Ruo!
UH, ABOUT THAT...
WHAT?
YOU AND KAZUKI NEVER REALLY HOOKED UP?
OH, MAN! I HAD NO IDEA!
MAKES SENSE THOUGH! A GIRL LIKE YOU AND A CUTIE LIKE HIM? IMPOSSIBLE!
...
MAYBE...
I SHOULD JUST FORGET ABOUT HIM.

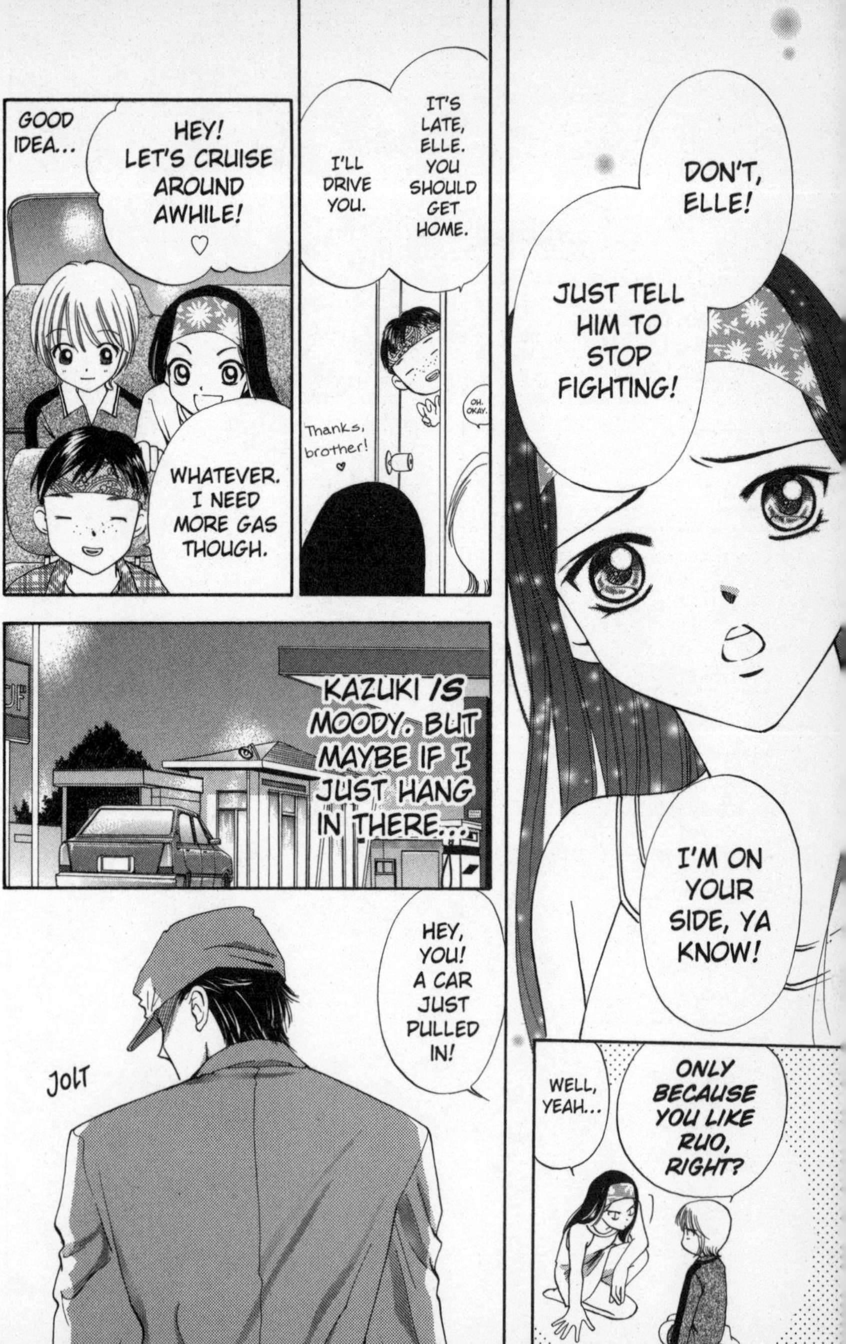
DON'T, ELLE!
JUST TELL HIM TO STOP FIGHTING!
I'M ON YOUR SIDE, YA KNOW!
ONLY BECAUSE YOU LIKE RUO, RIGHT?
WELL, YEAH...
IT'S LATE, ELLE. YOU SHOULD GET HOME.
I'LL DRIVE YOU.
OH. OKAY.
Thanks, brother! ♡
HEY! LET'S CRUISE AROUND AWHILE! ♡
GOOD IDEA...
WHATEVER. I NEED MORE GAS THOUGH.
KAZUKI IS MOODY. BUT MAYBE IF I JUST HANG IN THERE...
HEY, YOU! A CAR JUST PULLED IN!
JOLT

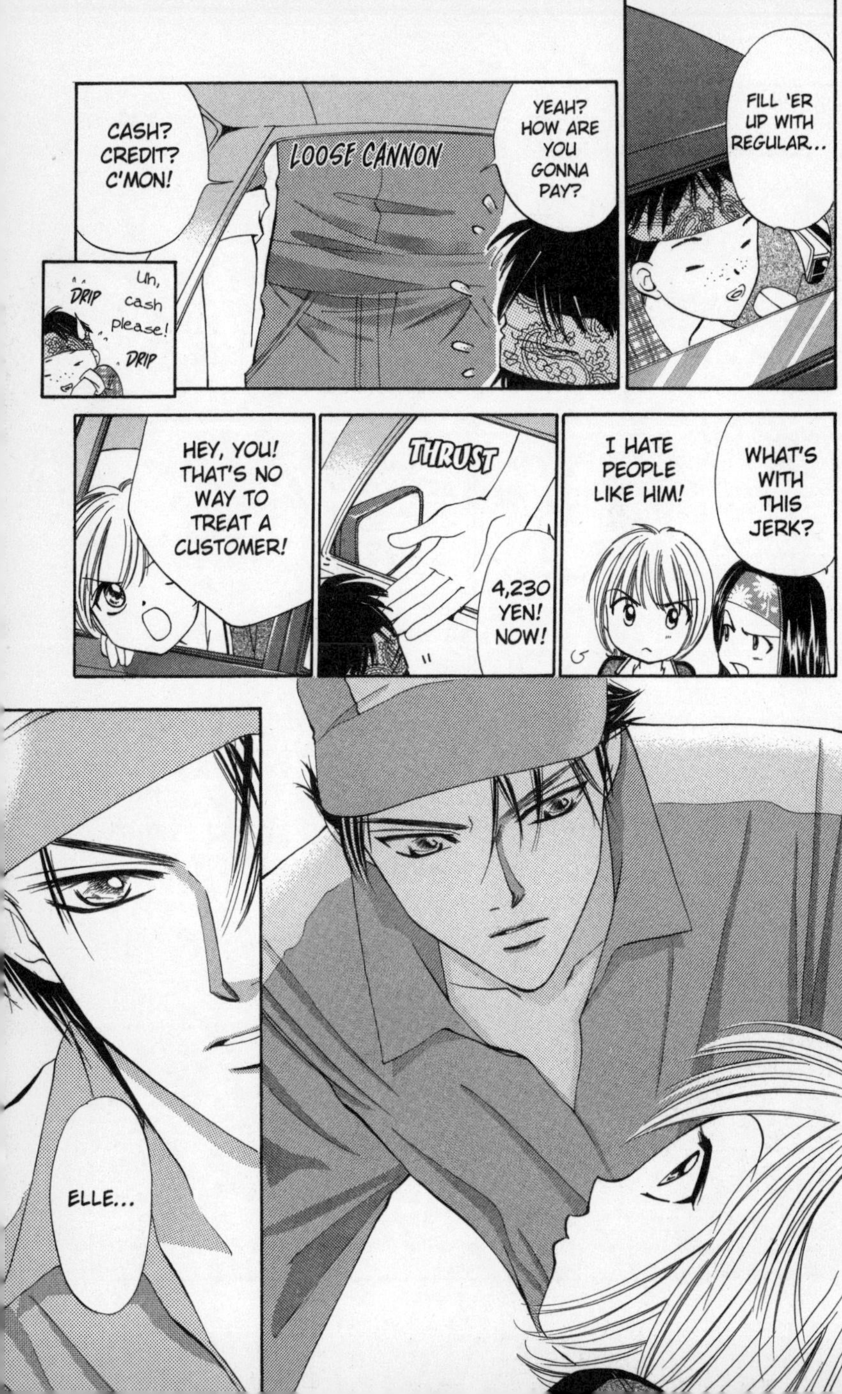
FILL 'ER UP WITH REGULAR...
YEAH? HOW ARE YOU GONNA PAY?
LOOSE CANNON
CASH? CREDIT? C'MON!
DRIP
Uh, cash please!
DRIP
WHAT'S WITH THIS JERK?
I HATE PEOPLE LIKE HIM!
THRUST
4,230 YEN! NOW!
HEY, YOU! THAT'S NO WAY TO TREAT A CUSTOMER!
ELLE...

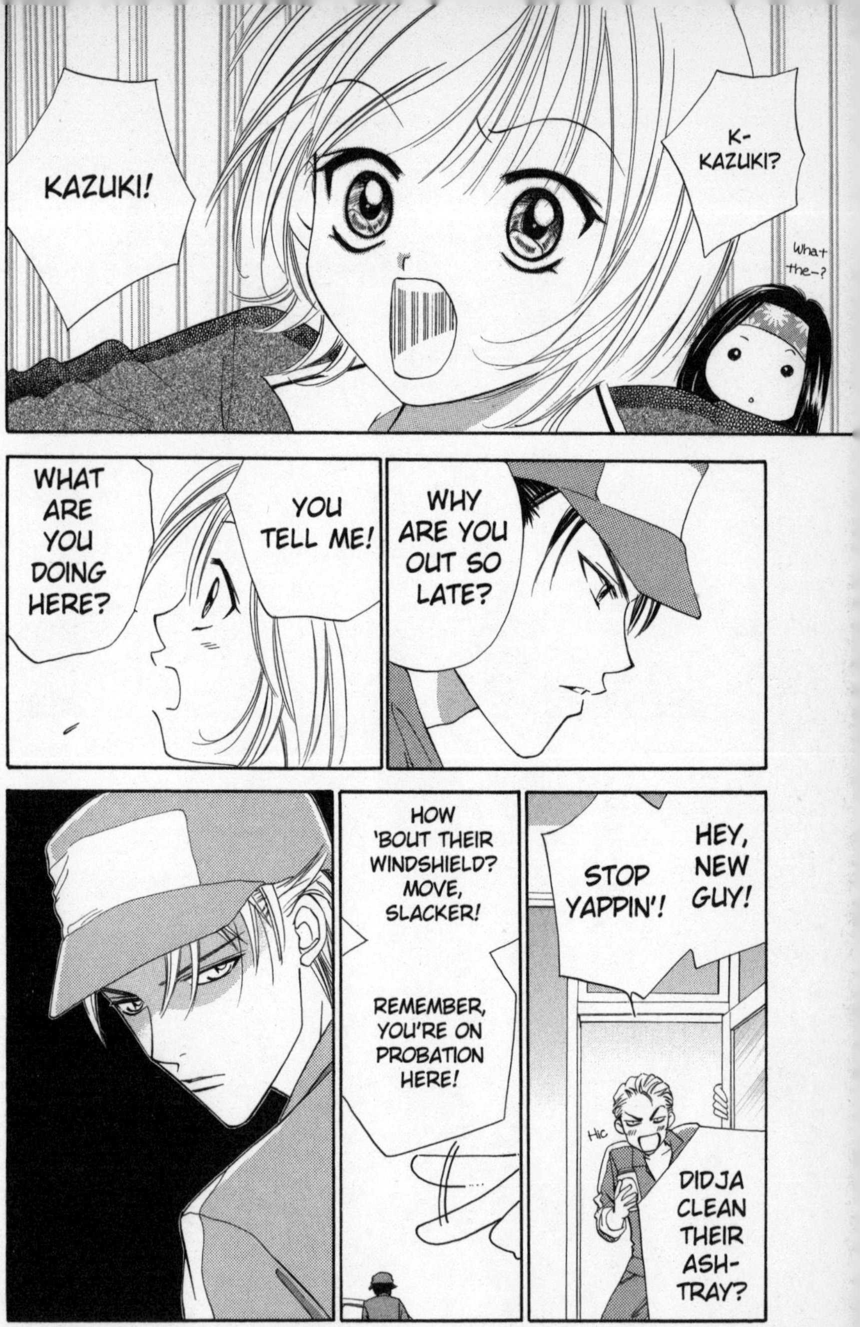
K-KAZUKI?
What the-?
KAZUKI!
WHY ARE YOU OUT SO LATE?
YOU TELL ME!
WHAT ARE YOU DOING HERE?
HEY, NEW GUY!
STOP YAPPIN'!
Hic
DIDJA CLEAN THEIR ASH-TRAY?
HOW 'BOUT THEIR WINDSHIELD? MOVE, SLACKER!
REMEMBER, YOU'RE ON PROBATION HERE!
...

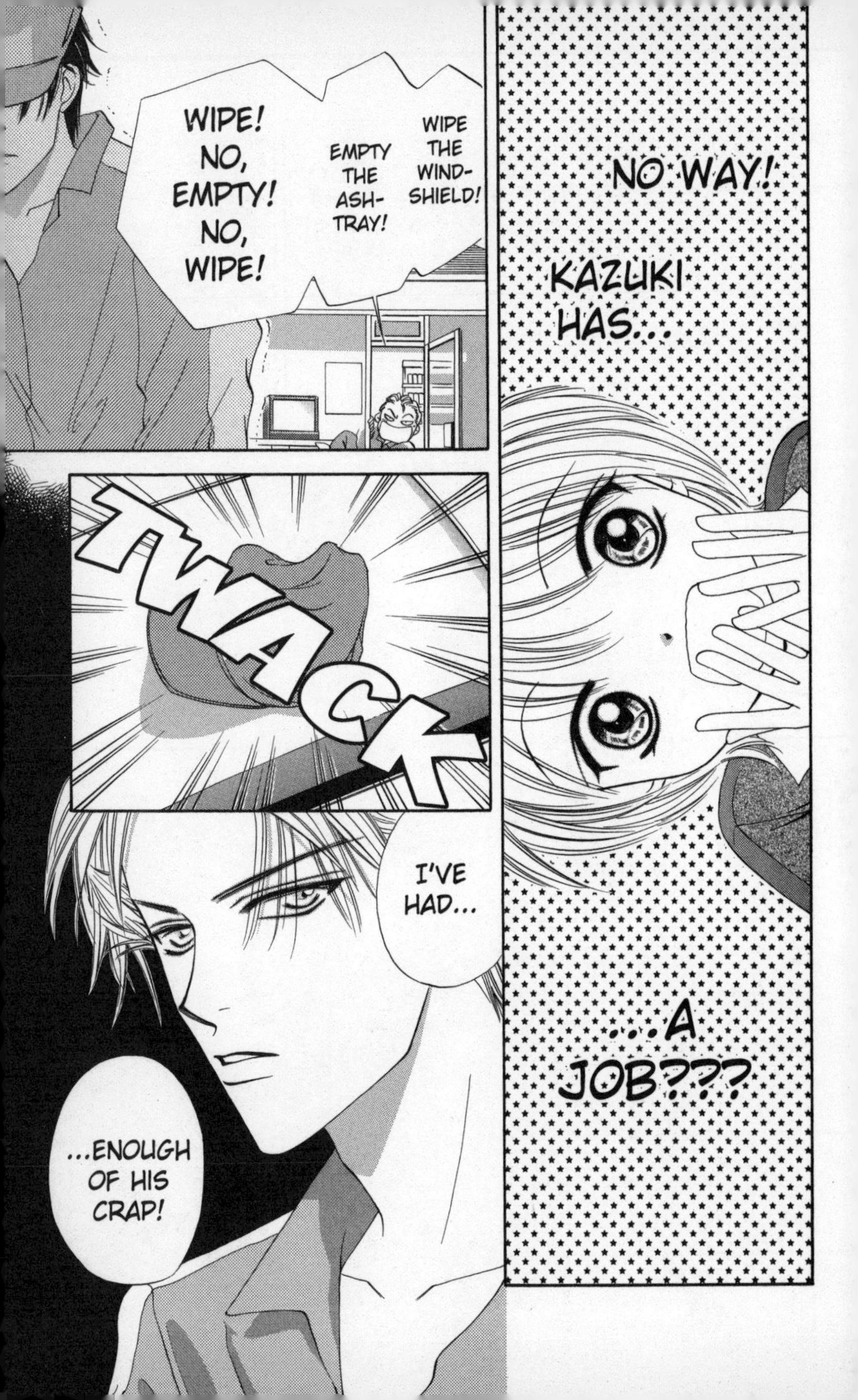
NO WAY!
KAZUKI HAS...
...A JOB???
WIPE THE WINDSHIELD!
EMPTY THE ASHTRAY!
WIPE! NO, EMPTY! NO, WIPE!
TWACK
I'VE HAD...
...ENOUGH OF HIS CRAP!

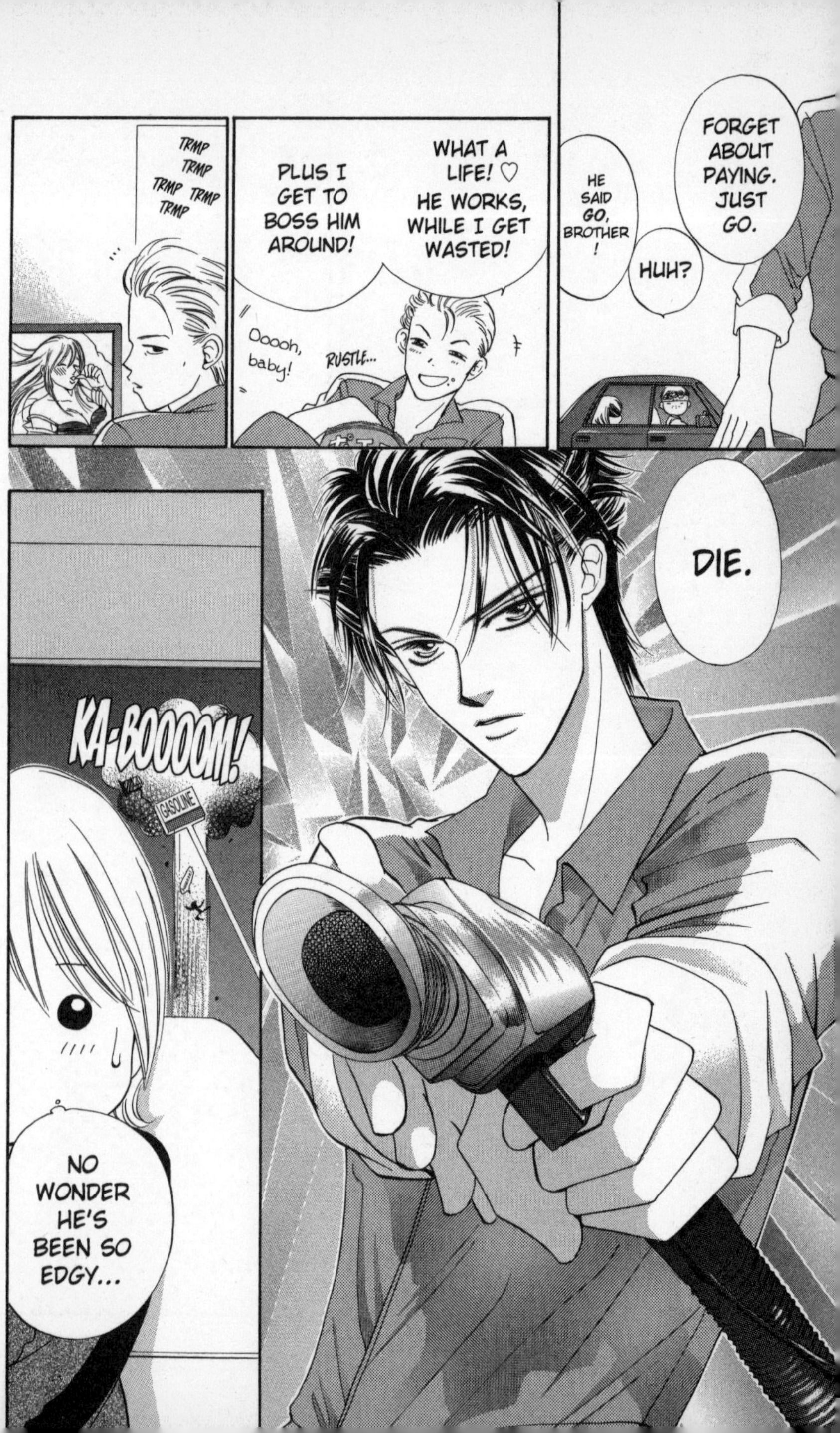
FORGET ABOUT PAYING. JUST GO.
HUH?
HE SAID GO, BROTHER!
WHAT A LIFE! ♡ HE WORKS, WHILE I GET WASTED!
PLUS I GET TO BOSS HIM AROUND!
RUSTLE...
Ooooh, baby!
TRMP TRMP TRMP TRMP TRMP
...
DIE.
KA-BOOOOM!
GASOLINE
NO WONDER HE'S BEEN SO EDGY...

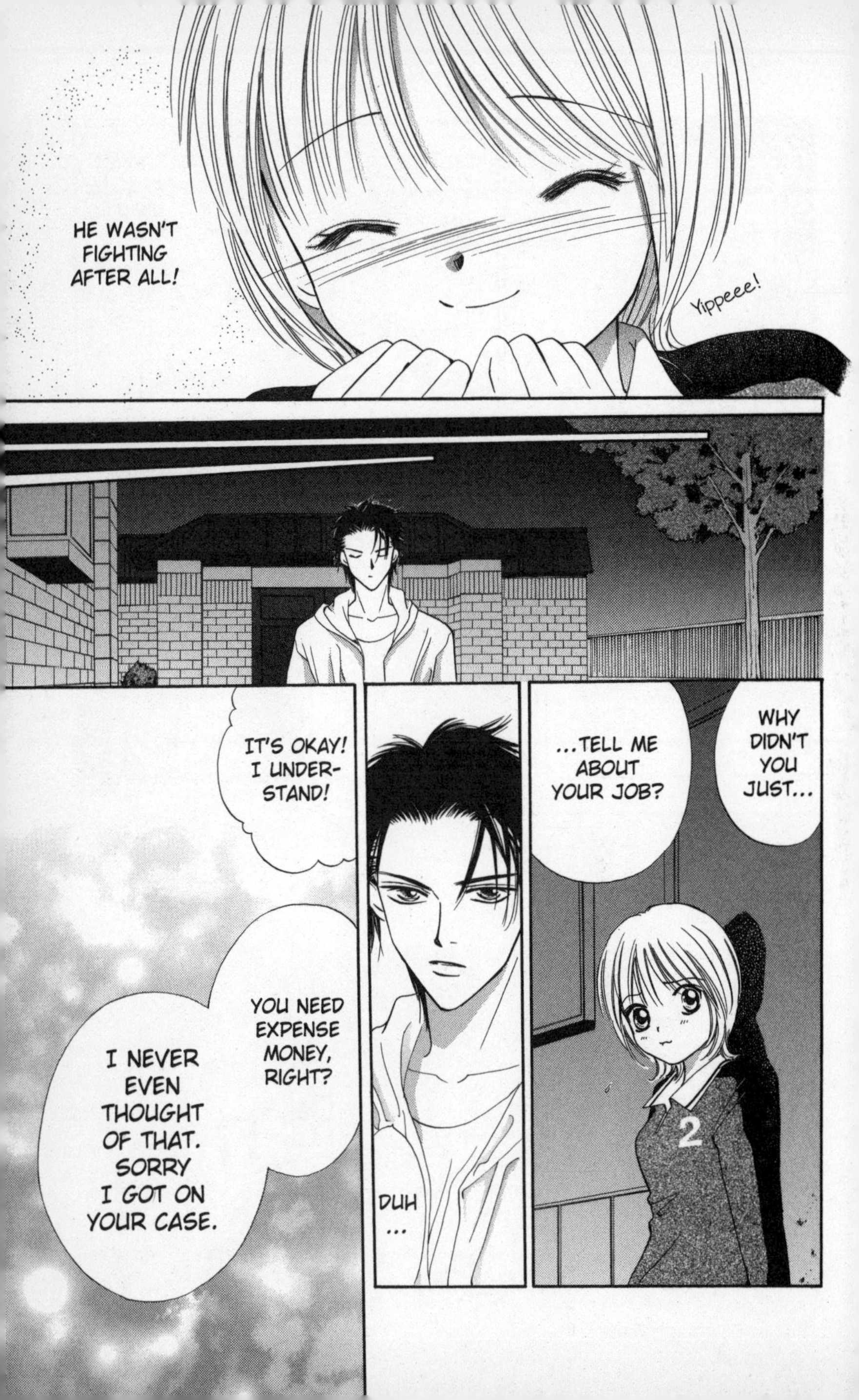
HE WASN'T FIGHTING AFTER ALL!
Yippeee!
WHY DIDN'T YOU JUST...
...TELL ME ABOUT YOUR JOB?
IT'S OKAY! I UNDER-STAND!
YOU NEED EXPENSE MONEY, RIGHT?
I NEVER EVEN THOUGHT OF THAT. SORRY I GOT ON YOUR CASE.
DUH...

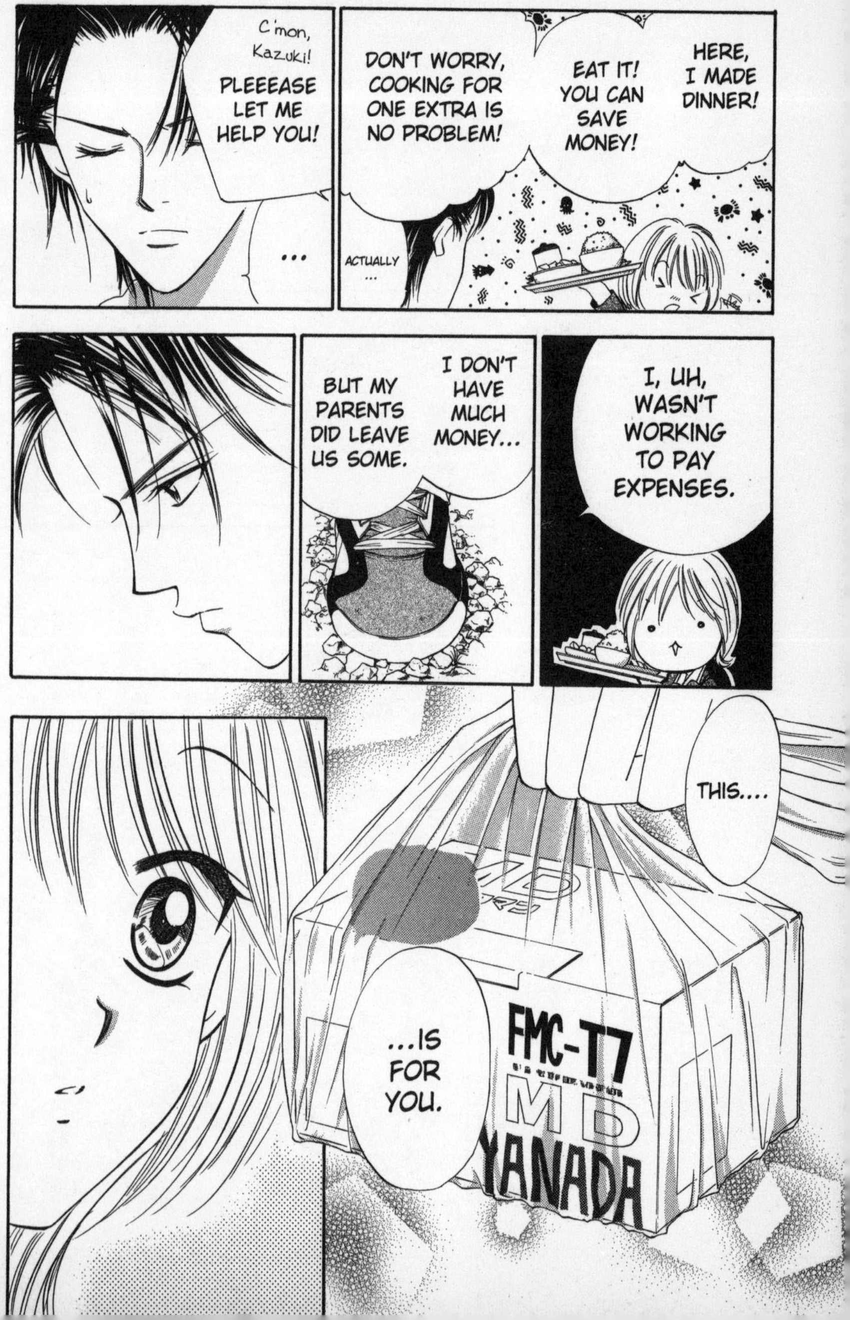
HERE, I MADE DINNER!
EAT IT! YOU CAN SAVE MONEY!
DON'T WORRY, COOKING FOR ONE EXTRA IS NO PROBLEM!
ACTUALLY ...
C'mon, Kazuki! PLEEEASE LET ME HELP YOU!
...
I, UH, WASN'T WORKING TO PAY EXPENSES.
I DON'T HAVE MUCH MONEY...
BUT MY PARENTS DID LEAVE US SOME.
THIS....
...IS FOR YOU.
FMC-T7
MD
YANADA

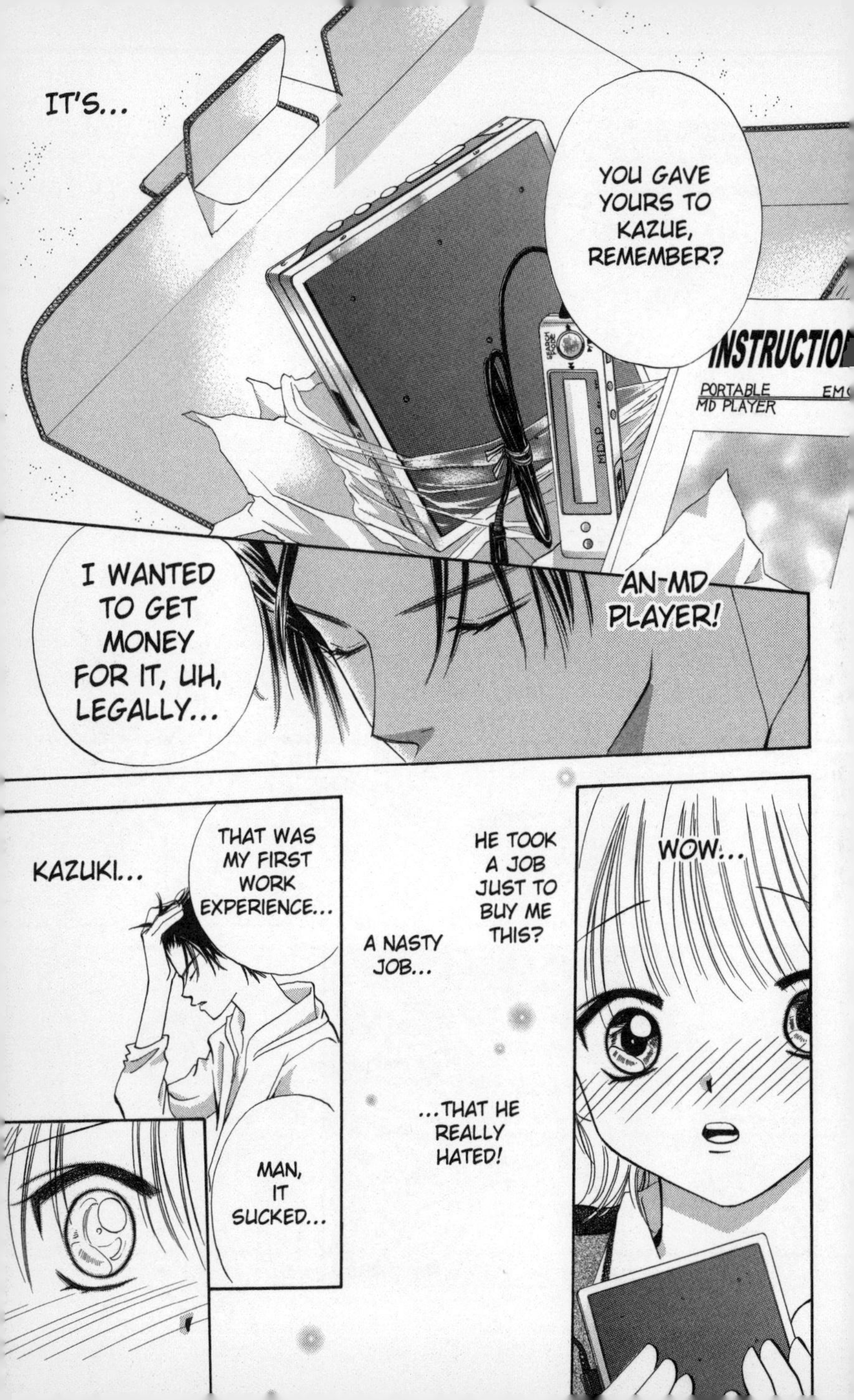
YOU GAVE YOURS TO KAZUE, REMEMBER?
IT'S...
PORTABLE MD PLAYER
AN MD PLAYER!
I WANTED TO GET MONEY FOR IT, UH, LEGALLY...
WOW...
HE TOOK A JOB JUST TO BUY ME THIS?
A NASTY JOB...
...THAT HE REALLY HATED!
THAT WAS MY FIRST WORK EXPERIENCE...
KAZUKI...
MAN, IT SUCKED...

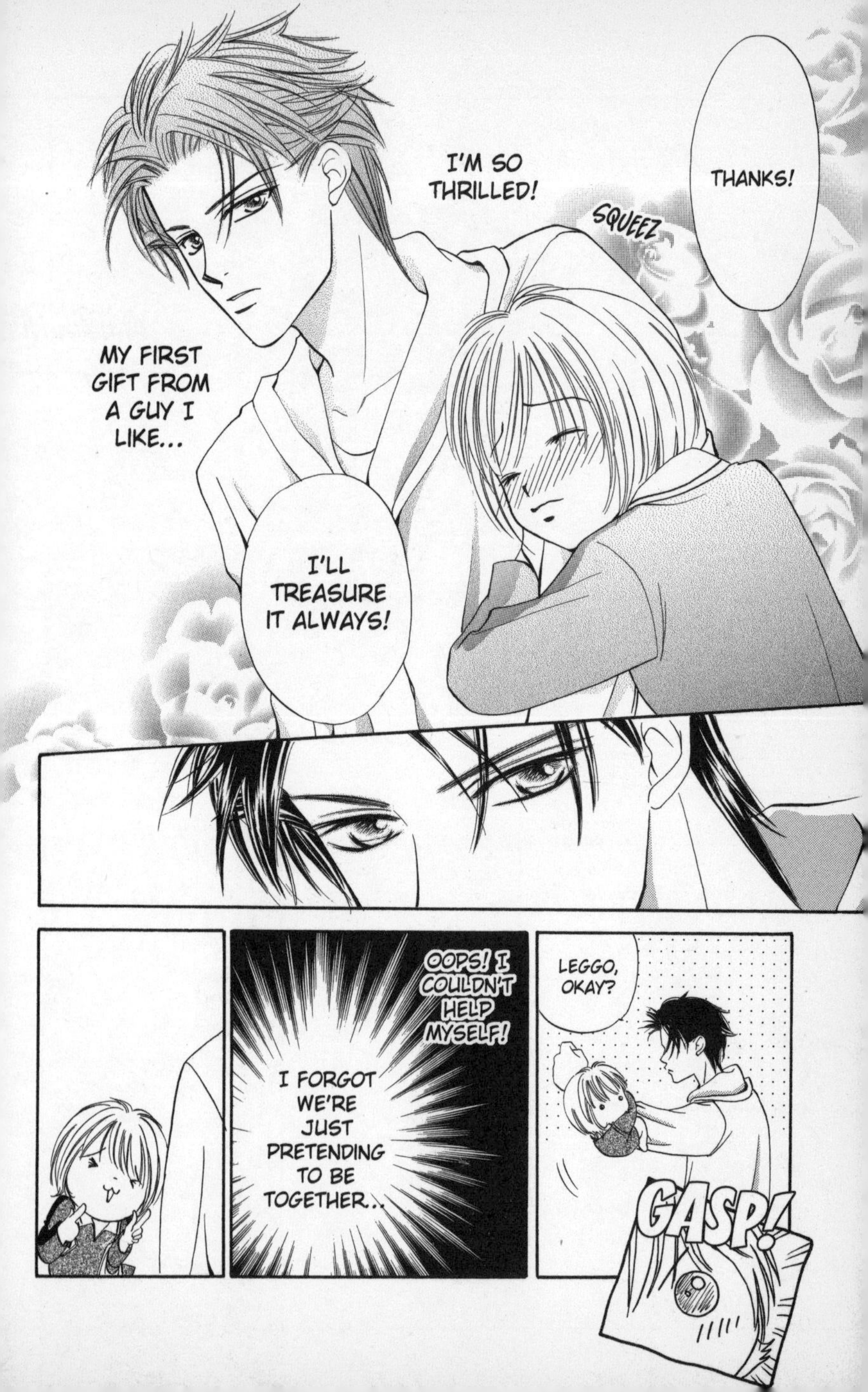
THANKS!
SQUEEZ
I'M SO THRILLED!
MY FIRST GIFT FROM A GUY I LIKE...
I'LL TREASURE IT ALWAYS!
LEGGO, OKAY?
GASP!
OOPS! I COULDN'T HELP MYSELF!
I FORGOT WE'RE JUST PRETENDING TO BE TOGETHER...

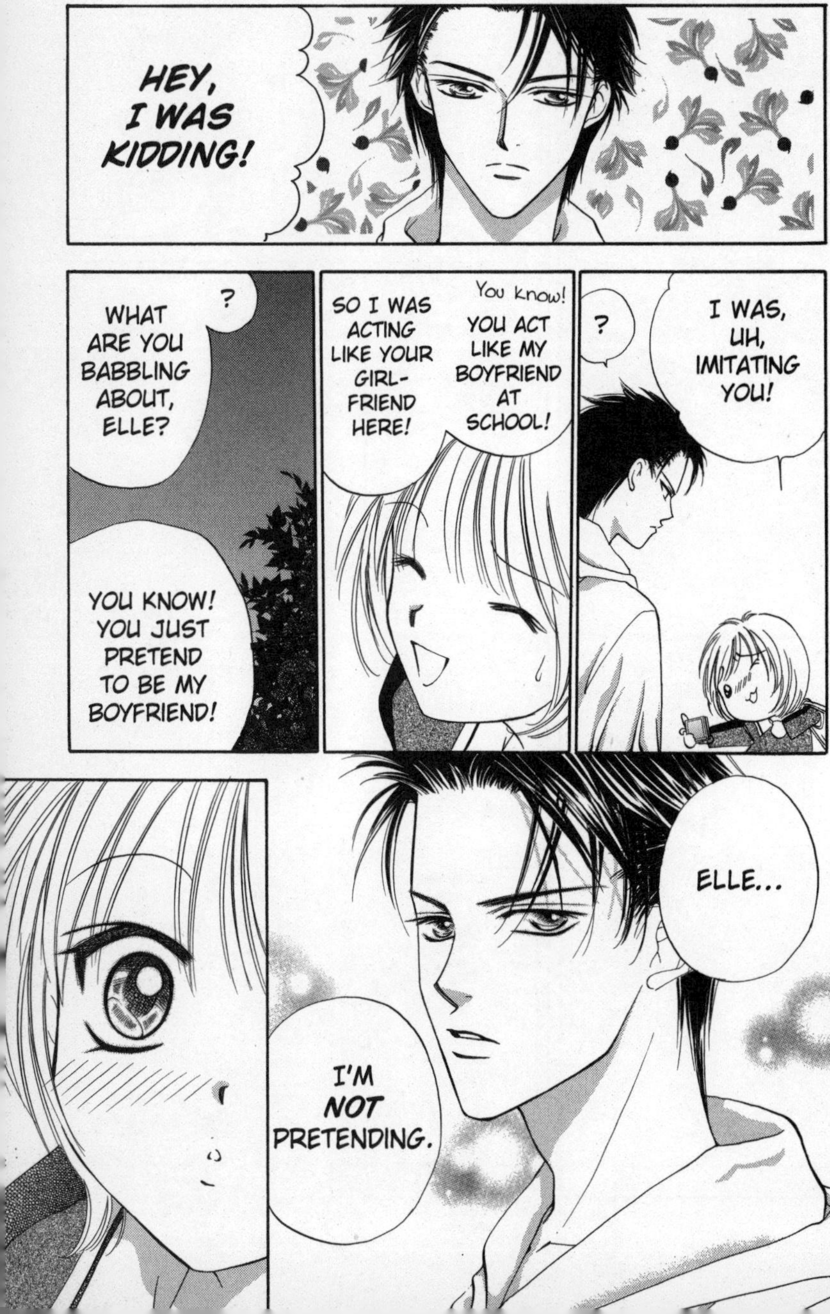
HEY, I WAS KIDDING!
I WAS, UH, IMITATING YOU!
?
You know!
YOU ACT LIKE MY BOYFRIEND AT SCHOOL!
SO I WAS ACTING LIKE YOUR GIRL-FRIEND HERE!
?
WHAT ARE YOU BABBLING ABOUT, ELLE?
YOU KNOW! YOU JUST PRETEND TO BE MY BOYFRIEND!
ELLE...
I'M *NOT* PRETENDING.

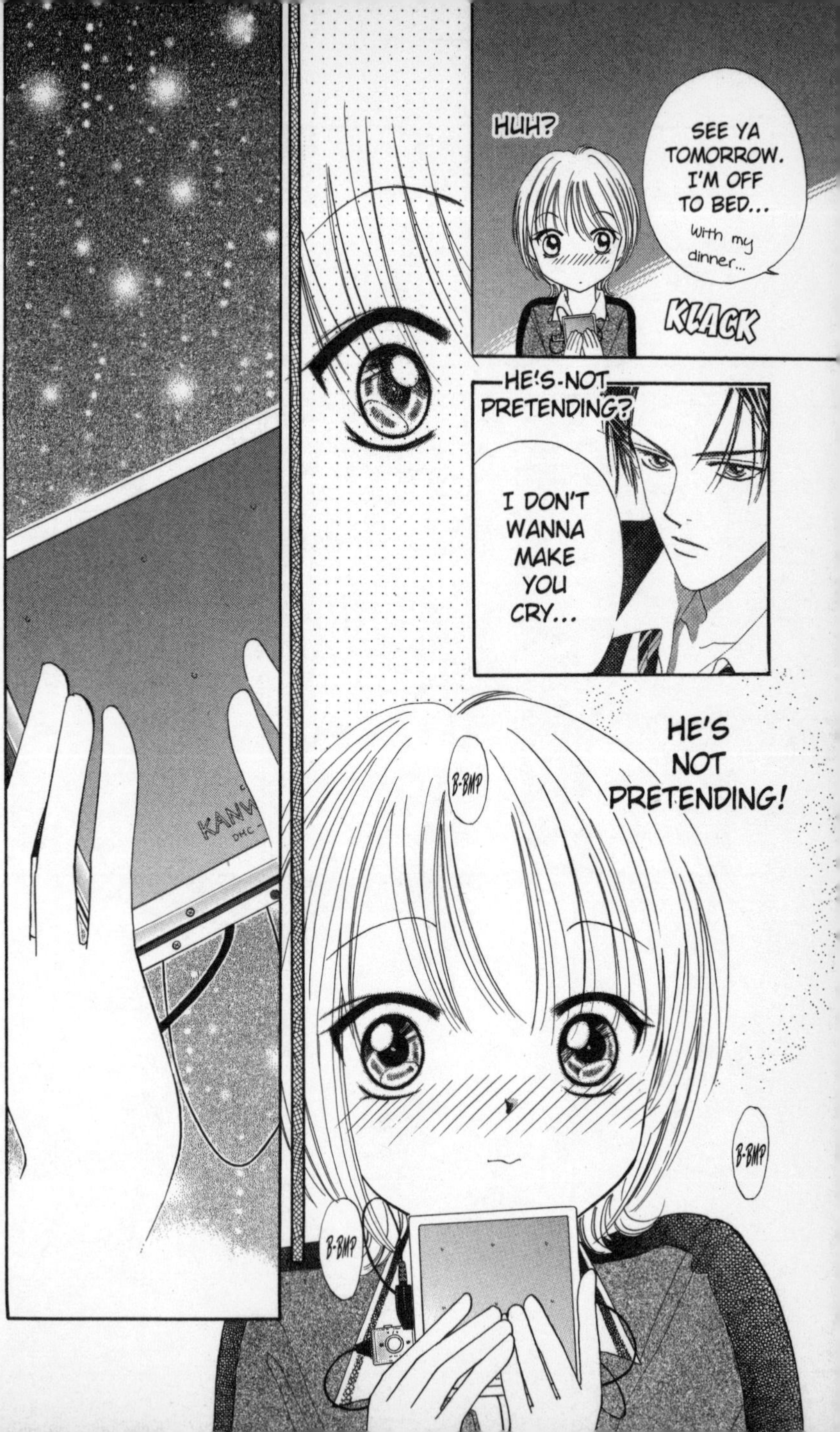
SEE YA TOMORROW. I'M OFF TO BED... With my dinner...
HUH?
KLACK
HE'S NOT PRETENDING?
I DON'T WANNA MAKE YOU CRY...
HE'S NOT PRETENDING!
B-BMP
B-BMP
B-BMP

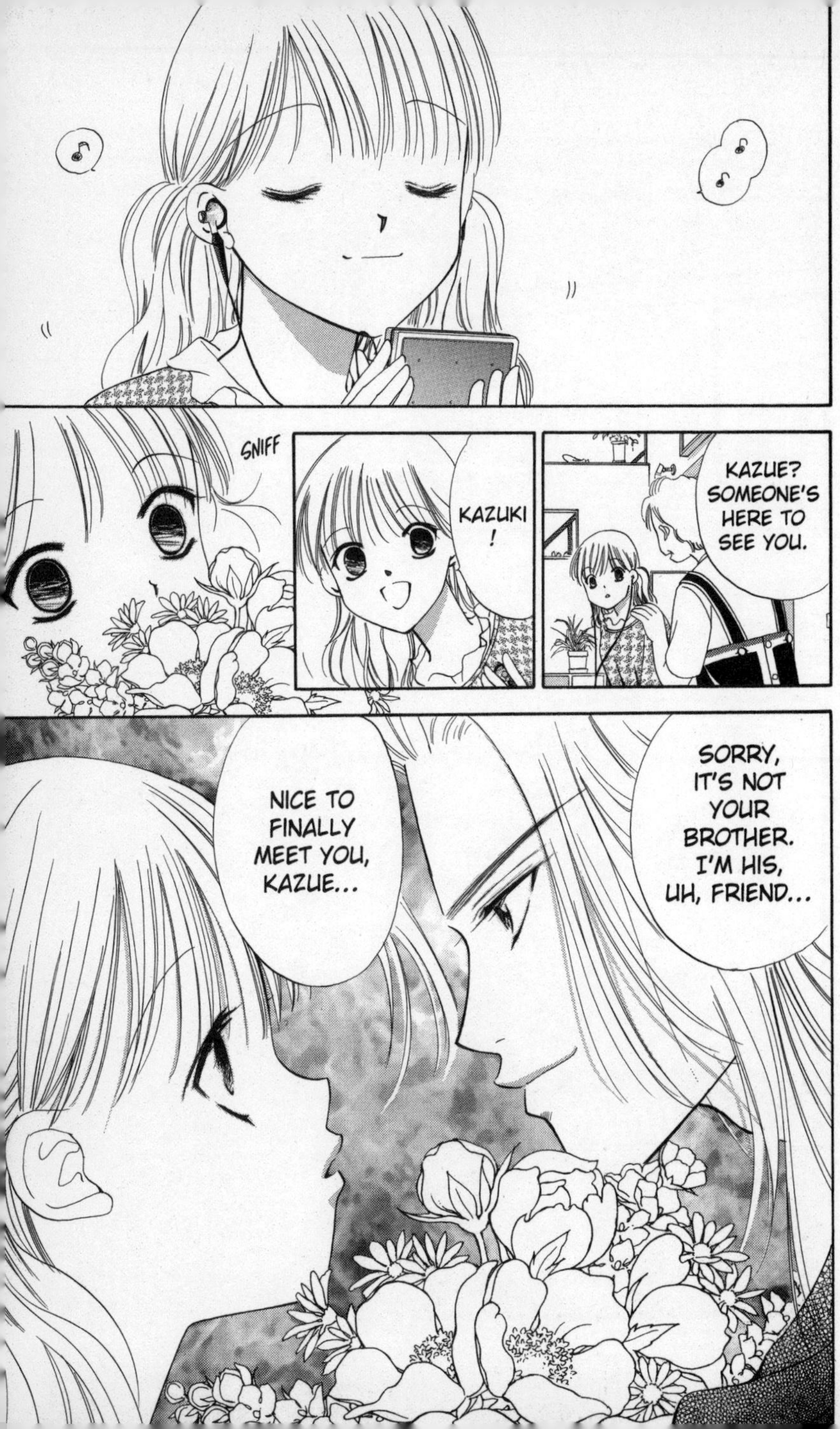
KAZUE? SOMEONE'S HERE TO SEE YOU.
KAZUKI!
SNIFF
SORRY, IT'S NOT YOUR BROTHER. I'M HIS, UH, FRIEND...
NICE TO FINALLY MEET YOU, KAZUE...

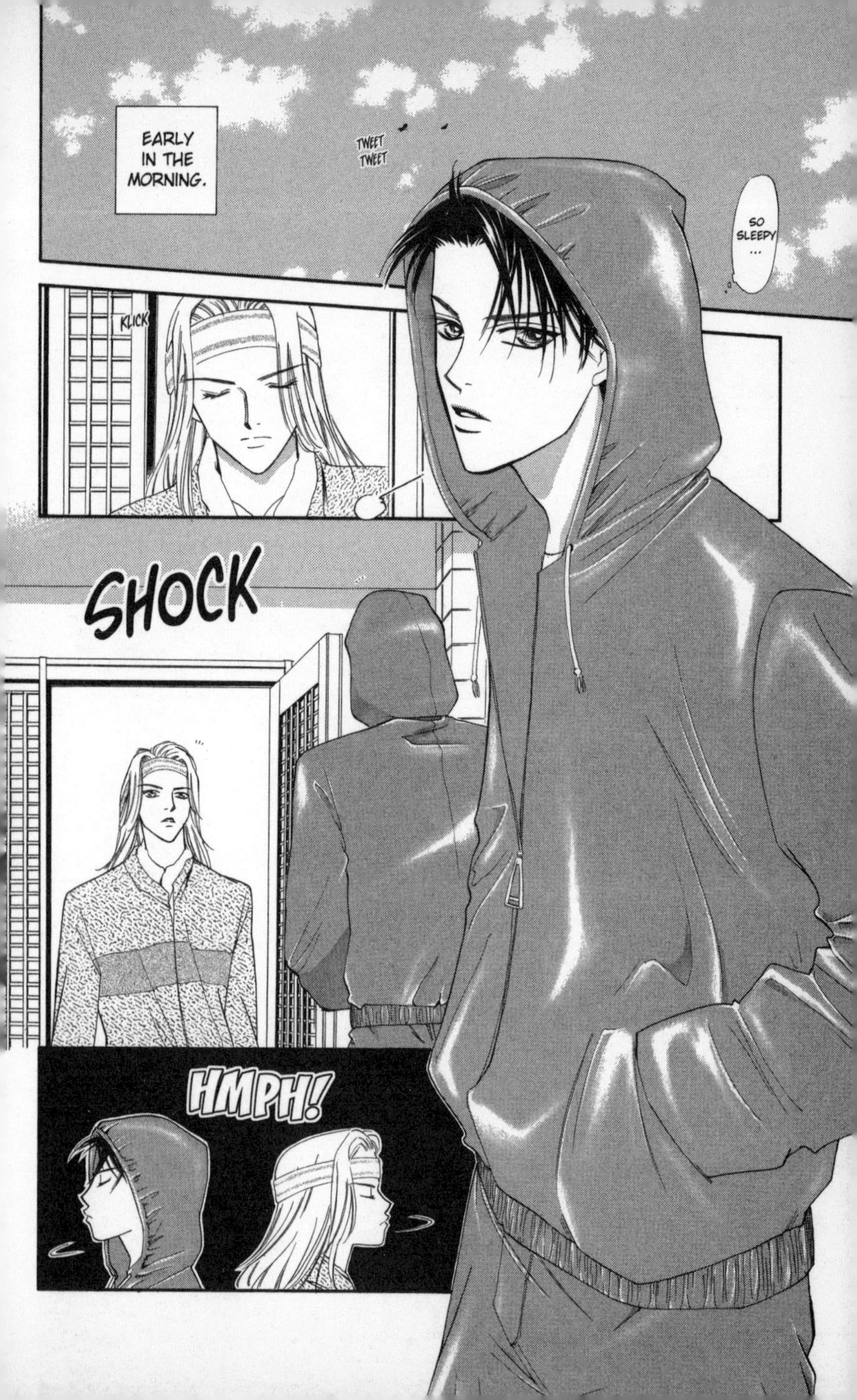
TWEET TWEET
EARLY IN THE MORNING.
SO SLEEPY ...
KLICK
SHOCK
HMPH!

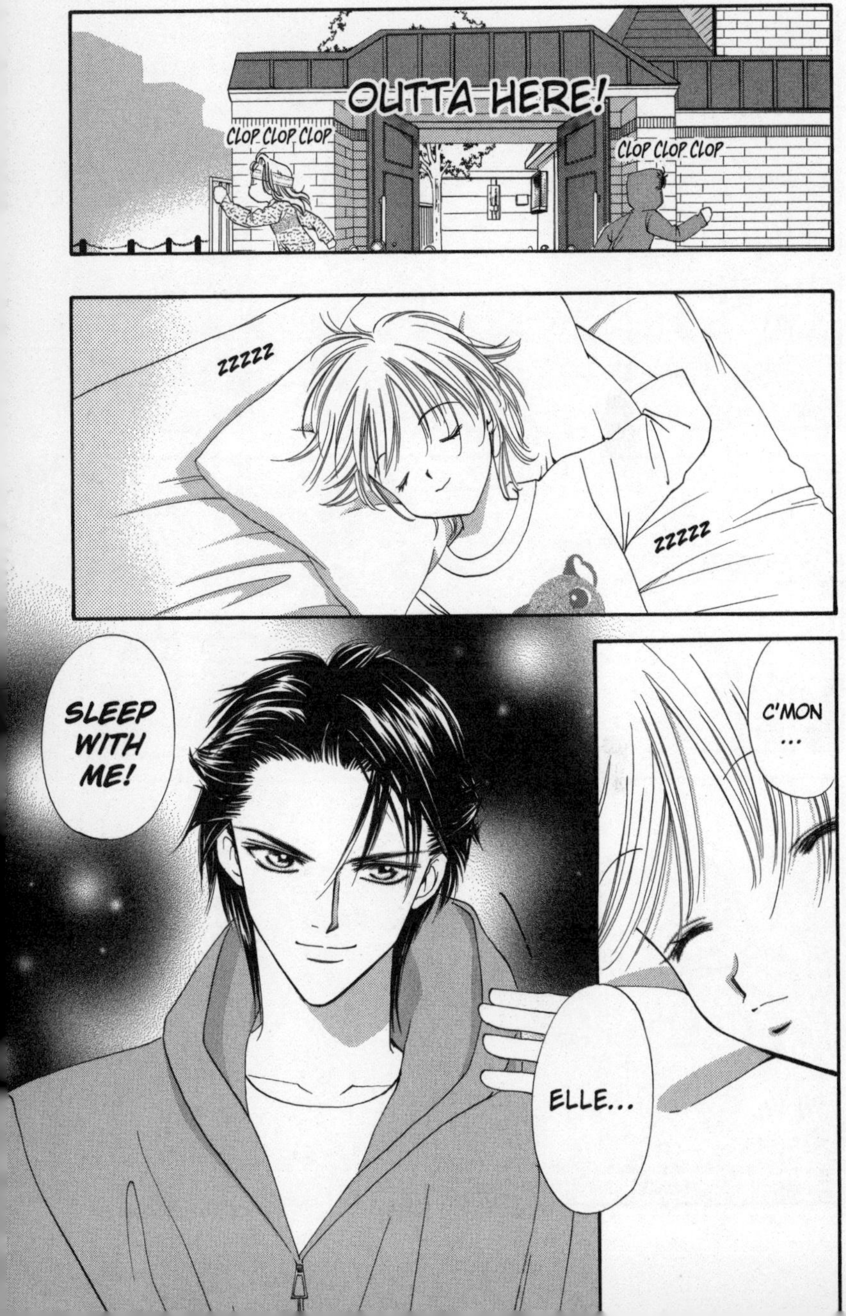
OUTTA HERE!
CLOP CLOP CLOP
CLOP CLOP CLOP
ZZZZZ
ZZZZZ
C'MON ...
ELLE...
SLEEP WITH ME!

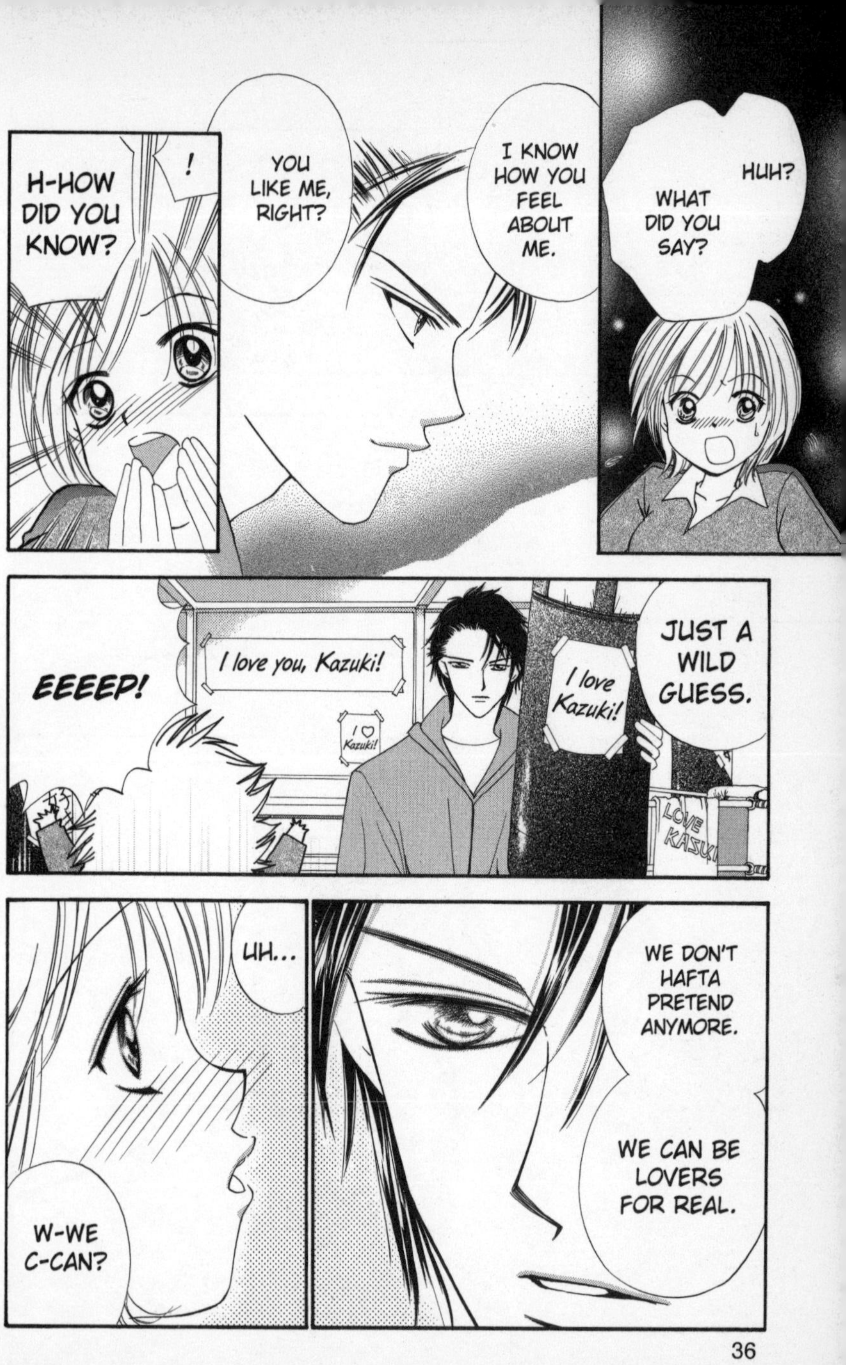
HUH?
WHAT DID YOU SAY?
I KNOW HOW YOU FEEL ABOUT ME.
YOU LIKE ME, RIGHT?
!
H-HOW DID YOU KNOW?
JUST A WILD GUESS.
I love Kazuki!
I love you, Kazuki!
I ♡ Kazuki!
LOVE KASUKI
EEEEP!
WE DON'T HAFTA PRETEND ANYMORE.
WE CAN BE LOVERS FOR REAL.
UH...
W-WE C-CAN?

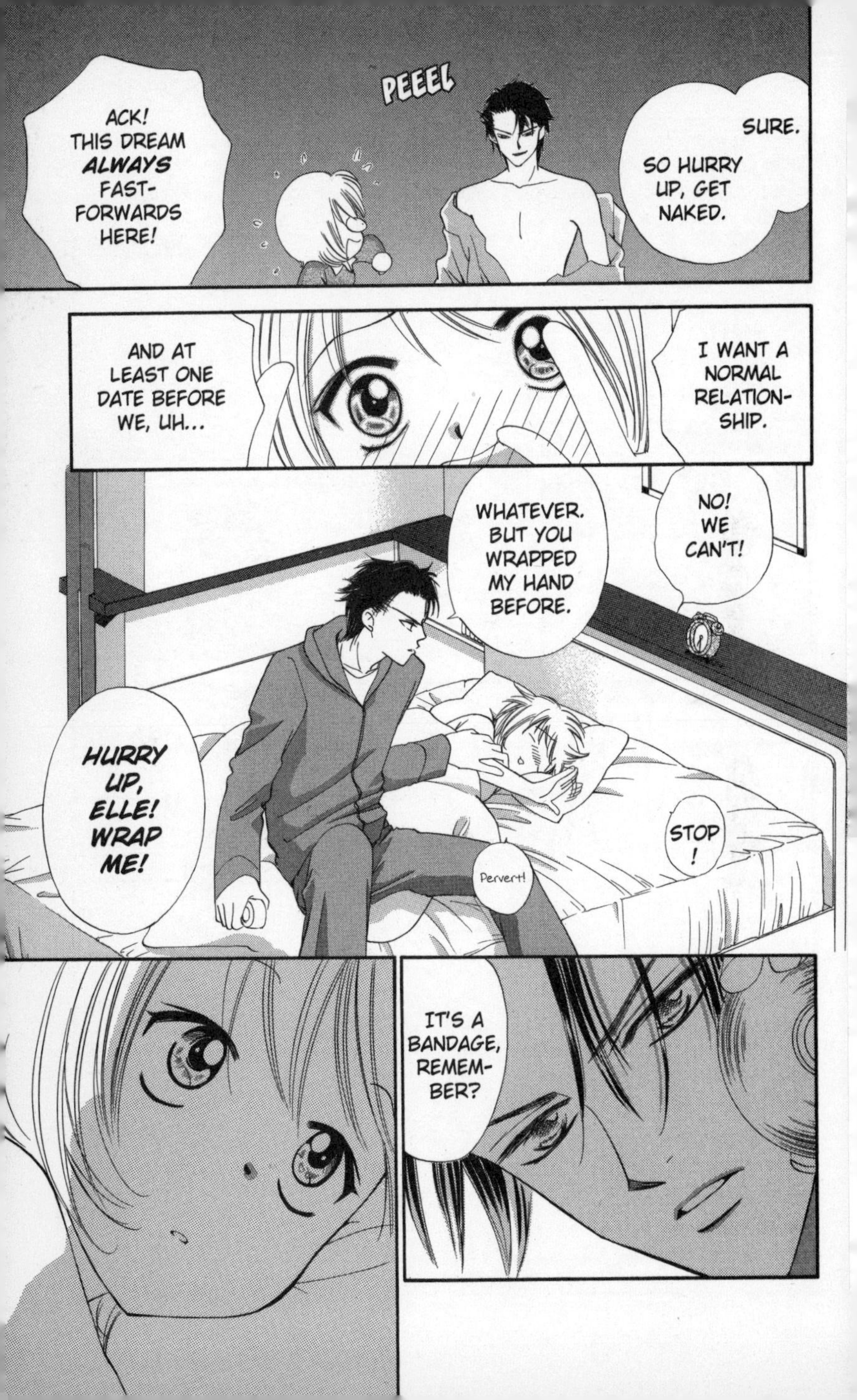
SURE. SO HURRY UP, GET NAKED.
PEEEL
ACK! THIS DREAM ALWAYS FAST-FORWARDS HERE!
I WANT A NORMAL RELATIONSHIP.
AND AT LEAST ONE DATE BEFORE WE, UH...
NO! WE CAN'T!
WHATEVER. BUT YOU WRAPPED MY HAND BEFORE.
HURRY UP, ELLE! WRAP ME!
STOP!
Pervert!
IT'S A BANDAGE, REMEMBER?

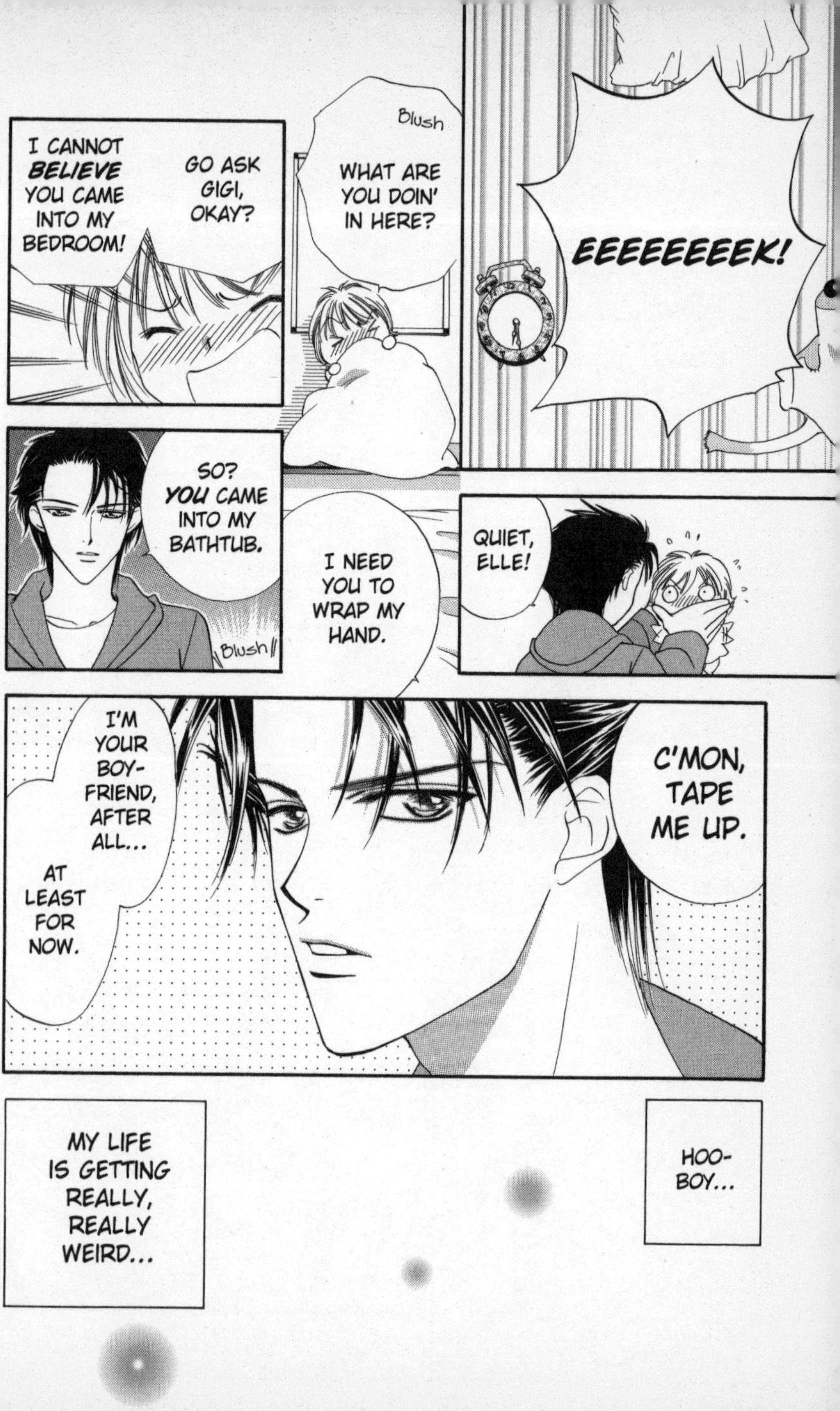
EEEEEEEEK!
Blush
WHAT ARE YOU DOIN' IN HERE?
GO ASK GIGI, OKAY?
I CANNOT BELIEVE YOU CAME INTO MY BEDROOM!
QUIET, ELLE!
I NEED YOU TO WRAP MY HAND.
SO? YOU CAME INTO MY BATHTUB.
Blush
C'MON, TAPE ME UP.
I'M YOUR BOY-FRIEND, AFTER ALL...
AT LEAST FOR NOW.
HOO-BOY...
MY LIFE IS GETTING REALLY, REALLY WEIRD...

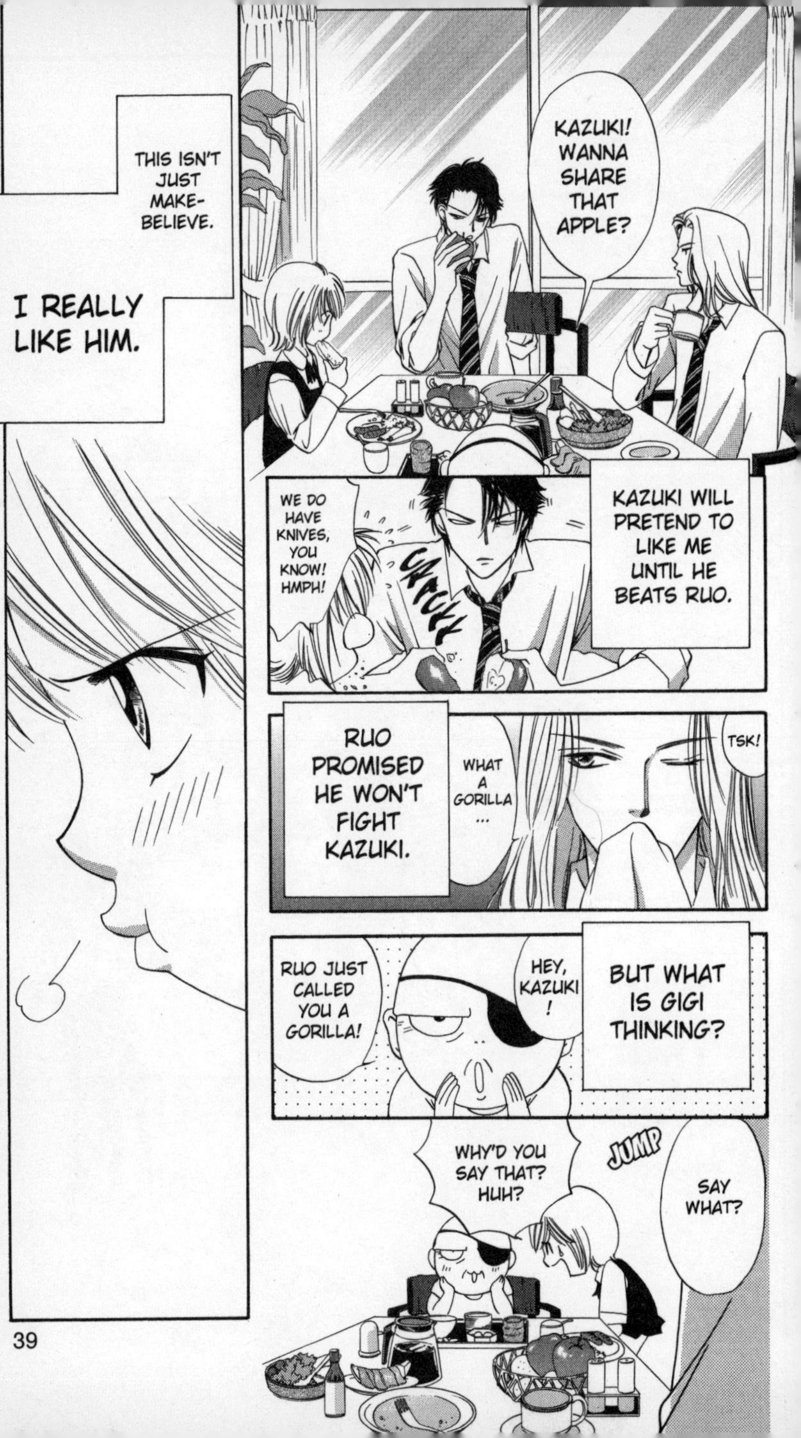
KAZUKI! WANNA SHARE THAT APPLE?
KAZUKI WILL PRETEND TO LIKE ME UNTIL HE BEATS RUO.
CRACK
WE DO HAVE KNIVES, YOU KNOW! HMPH!
TSK!
WHAT A GORILLA...
RUO PROMISED HE WON'T FIGHT KAZUKI.
BUT WHAT IS GIGI THINKING?
HEY, KAZUKI!
RUO JUST CALLED YOU A GORILLA!
SAY WHAT?
JUMP
WHY'D YOU SAY THAT? HUH?
THIS ISN'T JUST MAKE-BELIEVE.
I REALLY LIKE HIM.

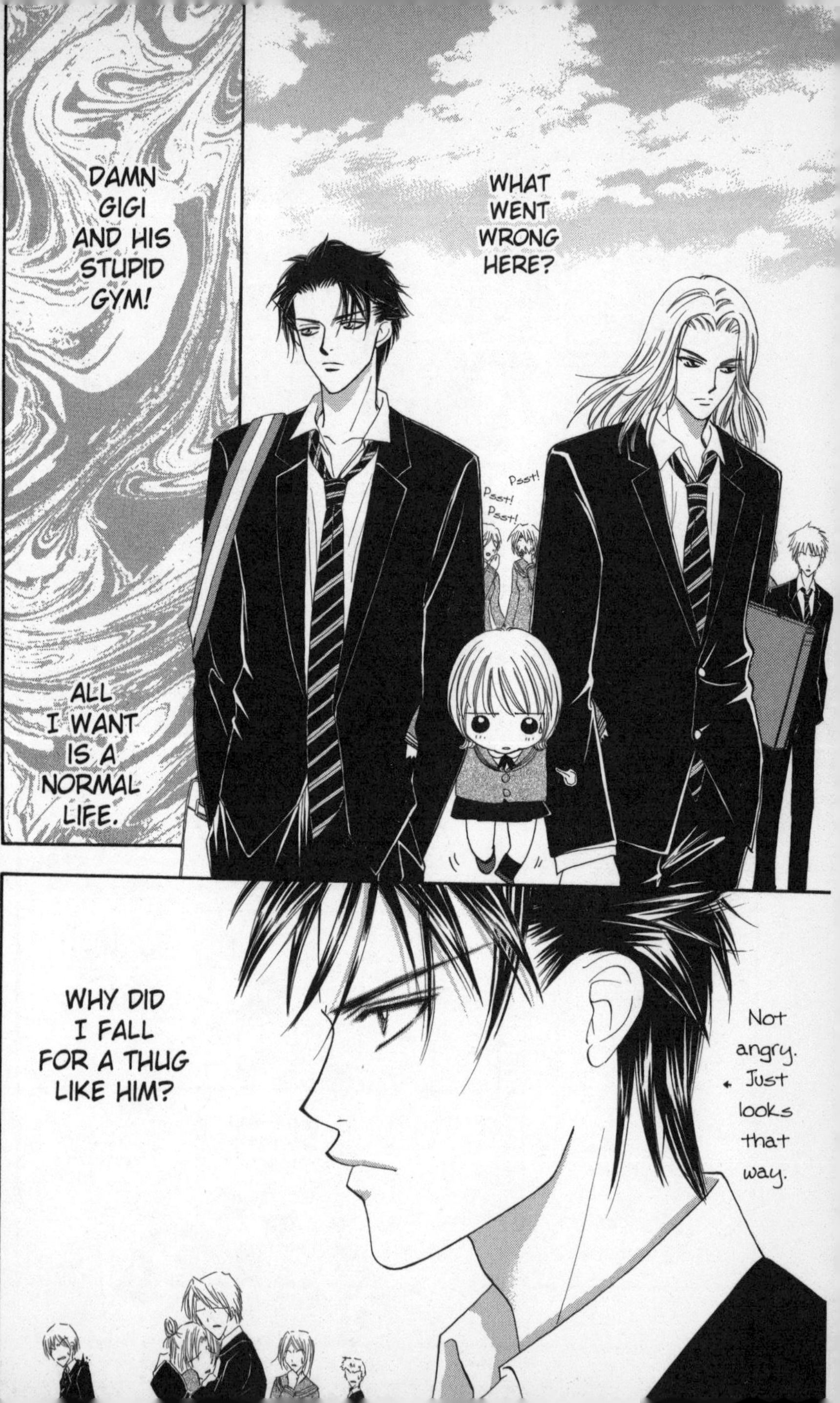
WHAT WENT WRONG HERE?
Psst!
Psst!
Psst!
DAMN GIGI AND HIS STUPID GYM!
ALL I WANT IS A NORMAL LIFE.
Not angry. Just looks that way.
WHY DID I FALL FOR A THUG LIKE HIM?

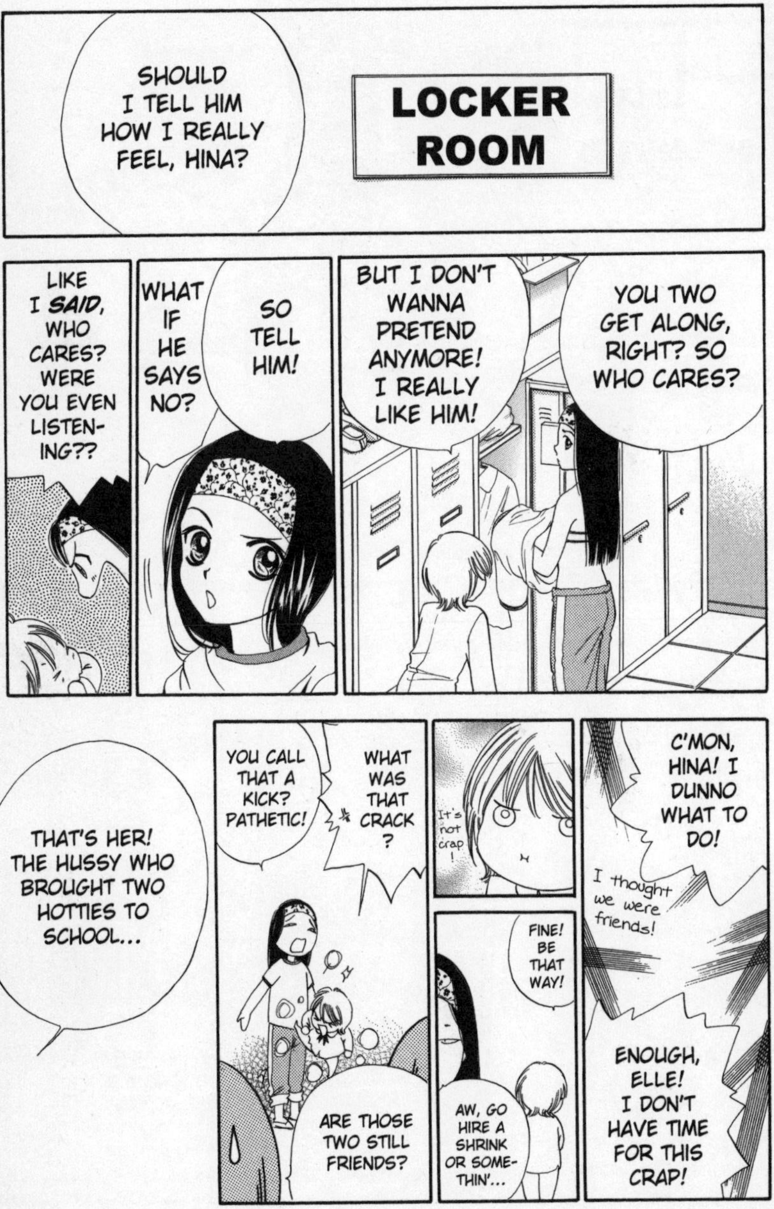
LOCKER ROOM
SHOULD I TELL HIM HOW I REALLY FEEL, HINA?
YOU TWO GET ALONG, RIGHT? SO WHO CARES?
BUT I DON'T WANNA PRETEND ANYMORE! I REALLY LIKE HIM!
SO TELL HIM!
WHAT IF HE SAYS NO?
LIKE I *SAID*, WHO CARES? WERE YOU EVEN LISTEN-ING??
C'MON, HINA! I DUNNO WHAT TO DO!
I thought we were friends!
ENOUGH, ELLE! I DON'T HAVE TIME FOR THIS CRAP!
It's not crap!
FINE! BE THAT WAY!
AW, GO HIRE A SHRINK OR SOME-THIN'...
WHAT WAS THAT CRACK?
YOU CALL THAT A KICK? PATHETIC!
ARE THOSE TWO STILL FRIENDS?
THAT'S HER! THE HUSSY WHO BROUGHT TWO HOTTIES TO SCHOOL...

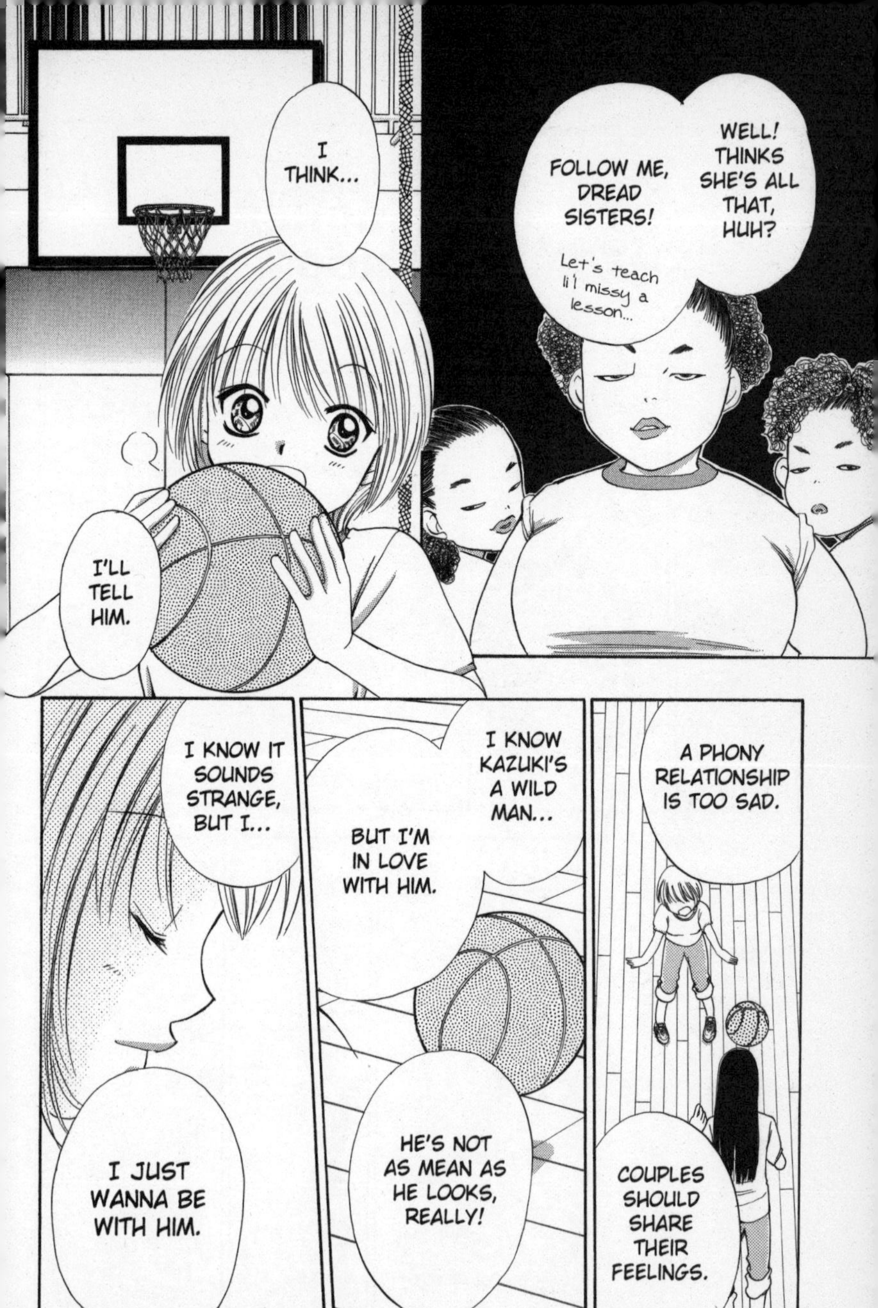
WELL! THINKS SHE'S ALL THAT, HUH?
FOLLOW ME, DREAD SISTERS!
Let's teach li'l missy a lesson...
I THINK...
I'LL TELL HIM.
A PHONY RELATIONSHIP IS TOO SAD.
COUPLES SHOULD SHARE THEIR FEELINGS.
I KNOW KAZUKI'S A WILD MAN...
BUT I'M IN LOVE WITH HIM.
HE'S NOT AS MEAN AS HE LOOKS, REALLY!
I KNOW IT SOUNDS STRANGE, BUT I...
I JUST WANNA BE WITH HIM.

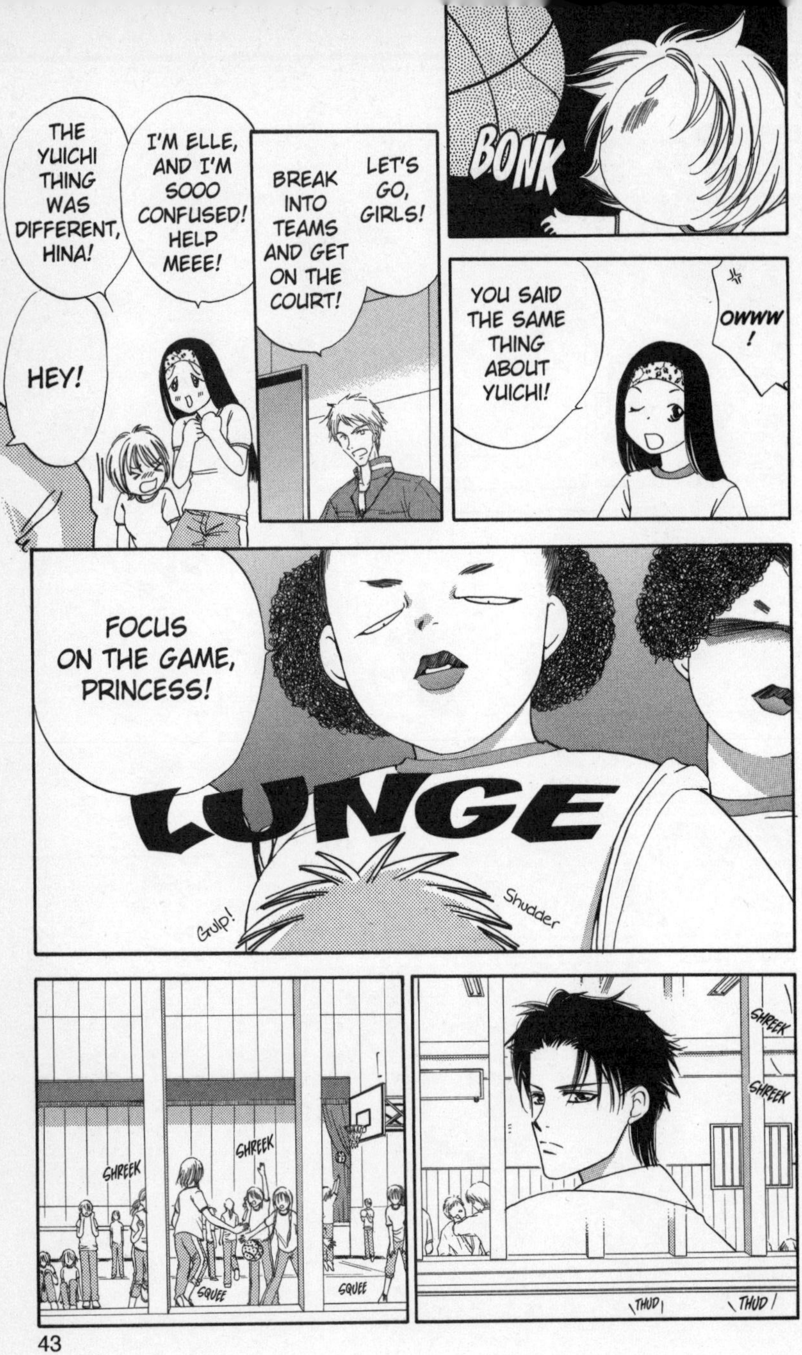
BONK
OWWW!
YOU SAID THE SAME THING ABOUT YUICHI!
LET'S GO, GIRLS!
BREAK INTO TEAMS AND GET ON THE COURT!
I'M ELLE, AND I'M SOOO CONFUSED! HELP MEEE!
THE YUICHI THING WAS DIFFERENT, HINA!
HEY!
FOCUS ON THE GAME, PRINCESS!
LUNGE
Shudder
Gulp!
SHREEK
SHREEK
THUD
THUD
SHREEK
SHREEK
SQUEE
SQUEE

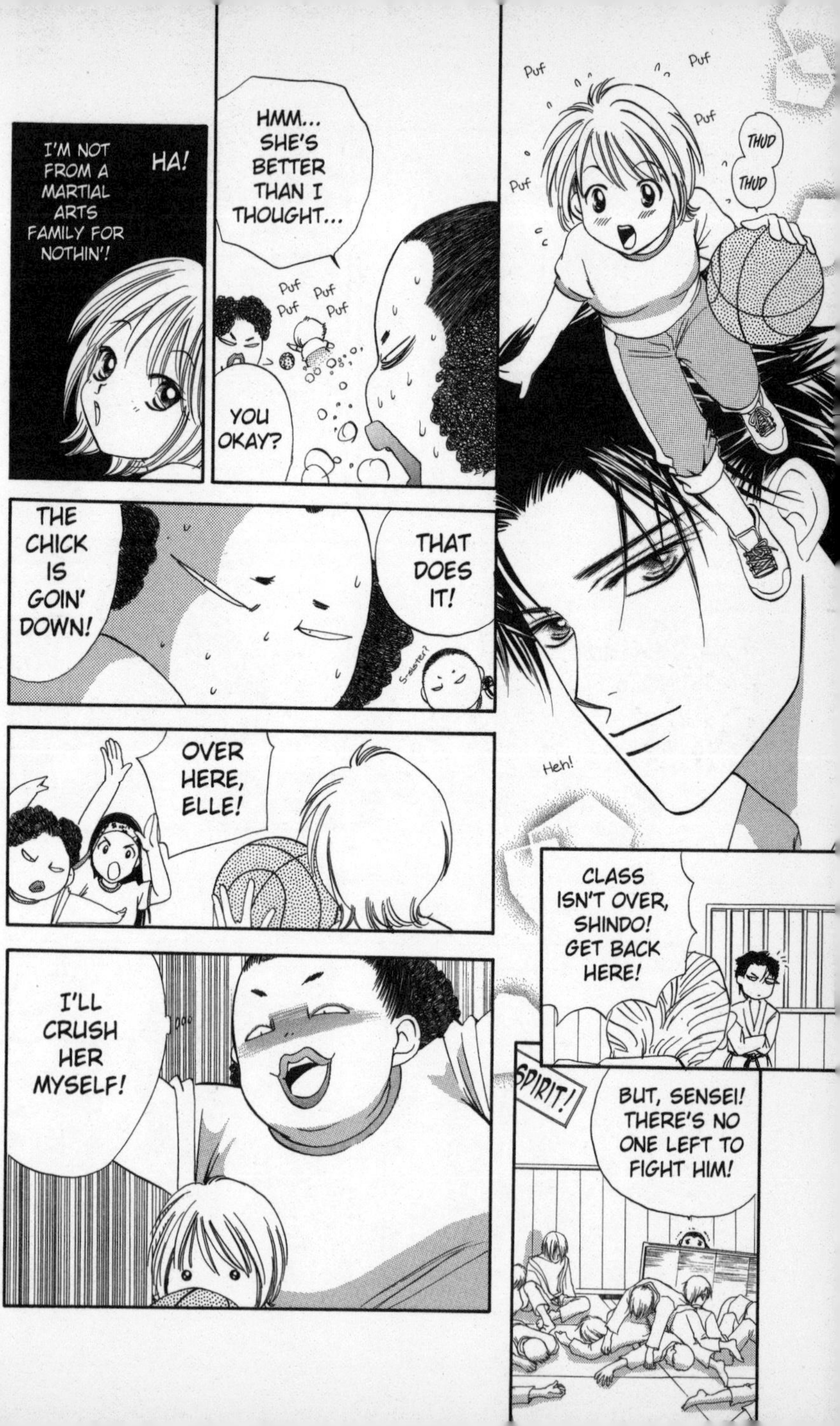
Puf
Puf
Puf
THUD THUD
Puf
Heh!
HMM... SHE'S BETTER THAN I THOUGHT...
YOU OKAY?
Puf Puf
Puf Puf
HA!
I'M NOT FROM A MARTIAL ARTS FAMILY FOR NOTHIN'!
THAT DOES IT!
S-sister?
THE CHICK IS GOIN' DOWN!
OVER HERE, ELLE!
I'LL CRUSH HER MYSELF!
CLASS ISN'T OVER, SHINDO! GET BACK HERE!
SPIRIT!
BUT, SENSEI! THERE'S NO ONE LEFT TO FIGHT HIM!

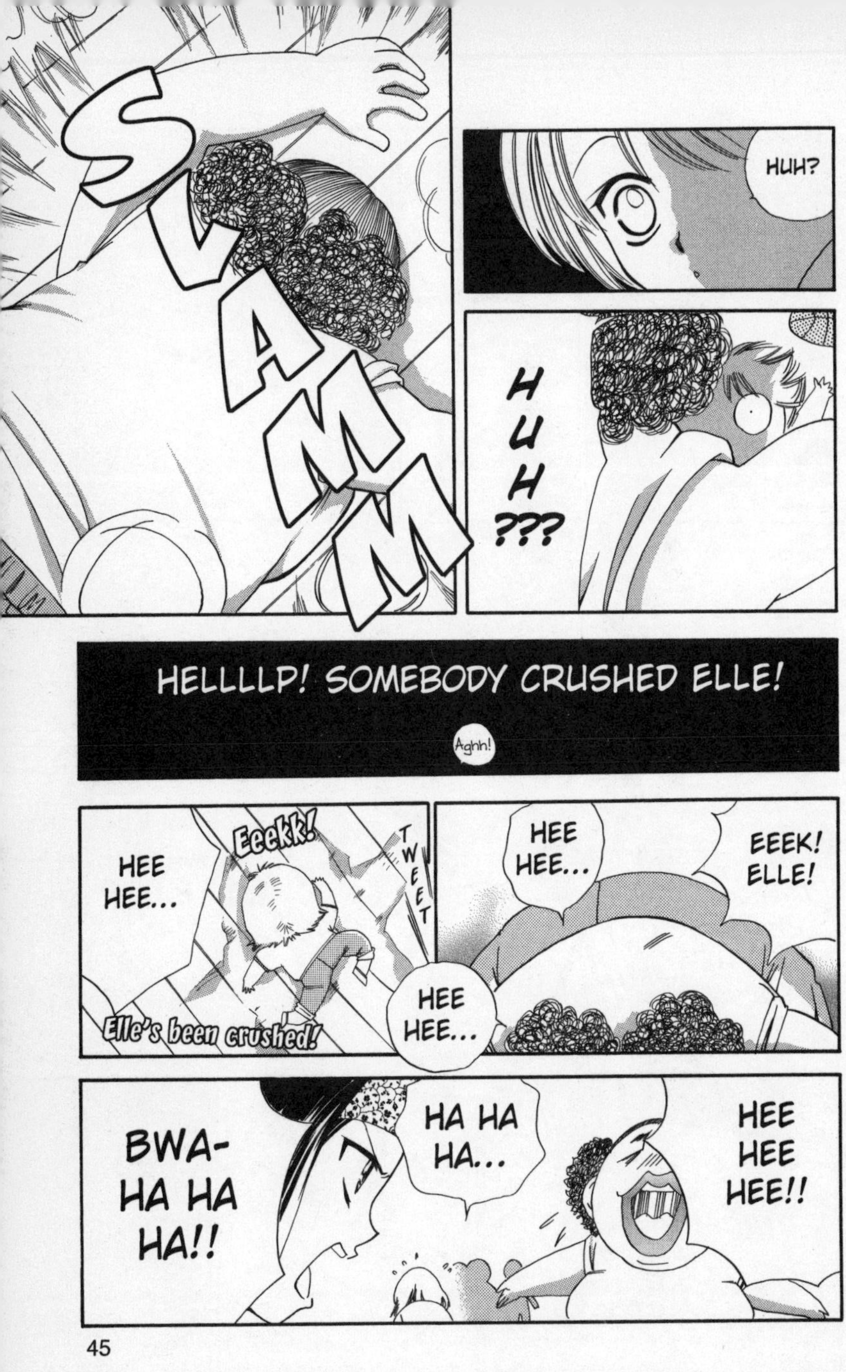
HUH?
HUH???
SVAMM
HELLLLP! SOMEBODY CRUSHED ELLE!
Aghh!
EEEK! ELLE!
HEE HEE...
HEE HEE...
Eeekk!
TWEET
HEE HEE...
Elle's been crushed!
HEE HEE HEE!!
HA HA HA...
BWA-HA HA HA!!

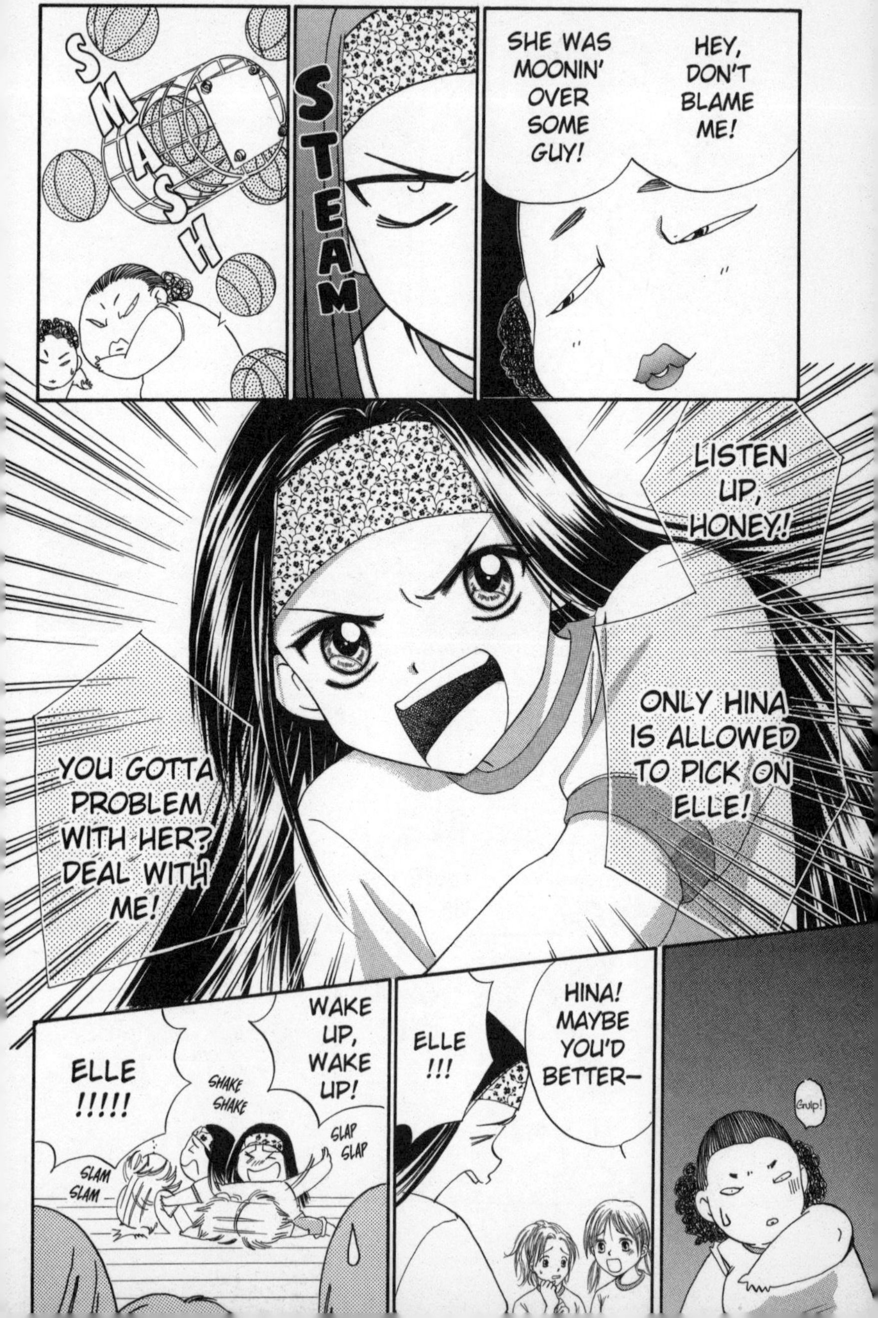
HEY, DON'T BLAME ME!
SHE WAS MOONIN' OVER SOME GUY!
STEAM
SMASH
LISTEN UP, HONEY!
ONLY HINA IS ALLOWED TO PICK ON ELLE!
YOU GOTTA PROBLEM WITH HER? DEAL WITH ME!
Gulp!
HINA! MAYBE YOU'D BETTER—
ELLE !!!
WAKE UP, WAKE UP!
ELLE !!!!!
SHAKE SHAKE
SLAP SLAP
SLAM SLAM

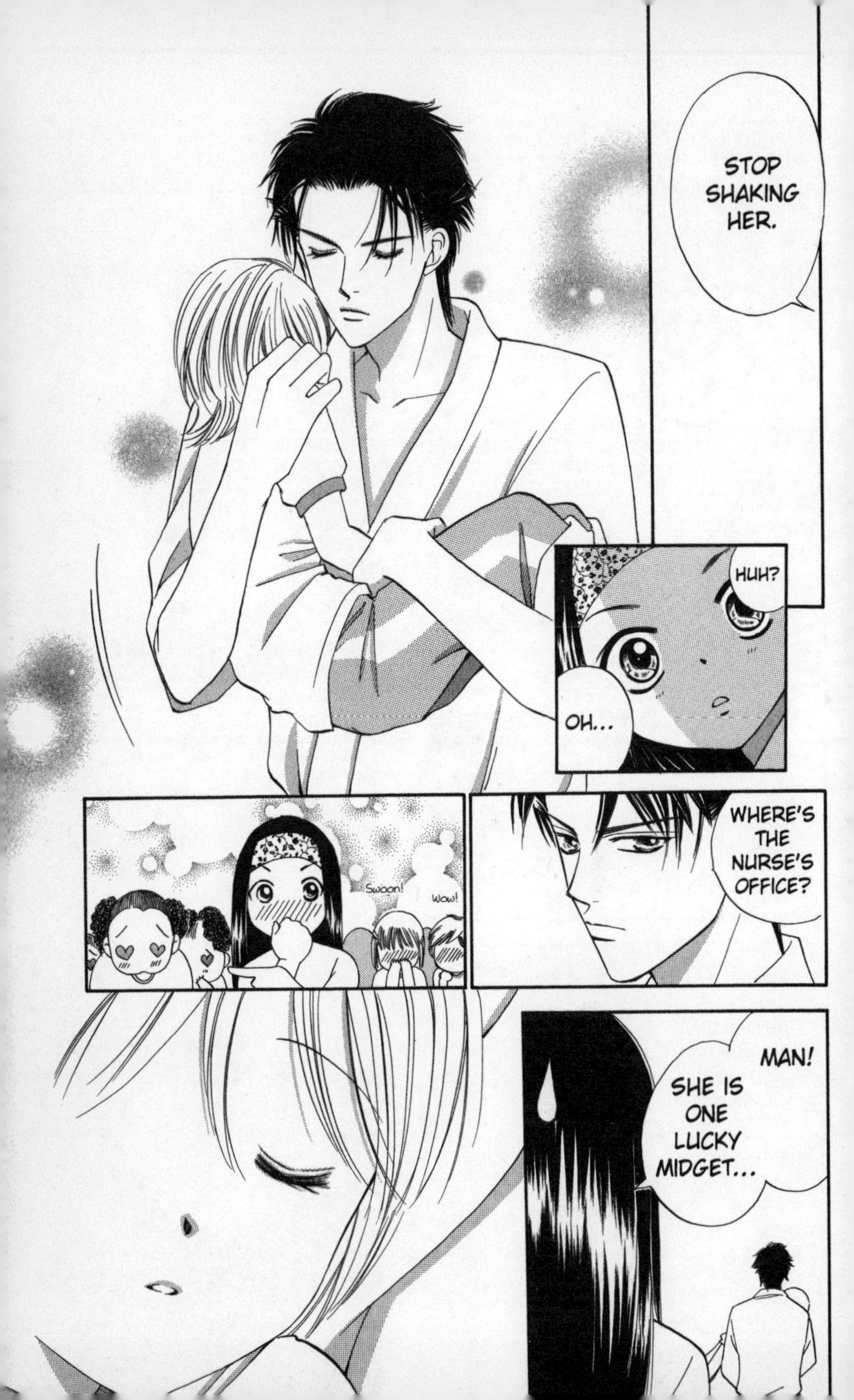
STOP SHAKING HER.
HUH?
OH...
WHERE'S THE NURSE'S OFFICE?
Wow!
Swoon!
MAN!
SHE IS ONE LUCKY MIDGET...

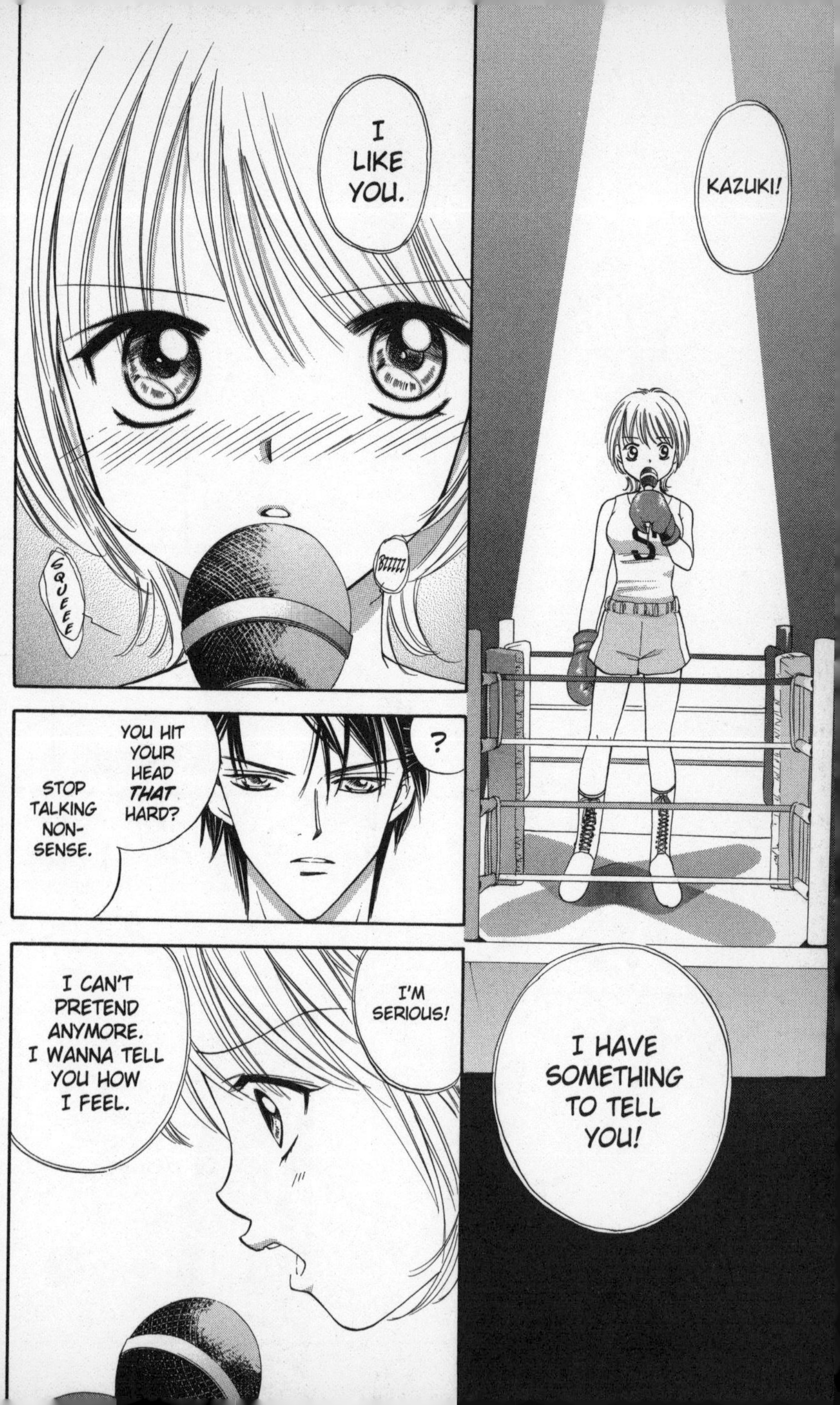
KAZUKI!
I HAVE SOMETHING TO TELL YOU!
I LIKE YOU.
SQUEEE
?
YOU HIT YOUR HEAD *THAT* HARD?
STOP TALKING NONSENSE.
I'M SERIOUS!
I CAN'T PRETEND ANYMORE. I WANNA TELL YOU HOW I FEEL.

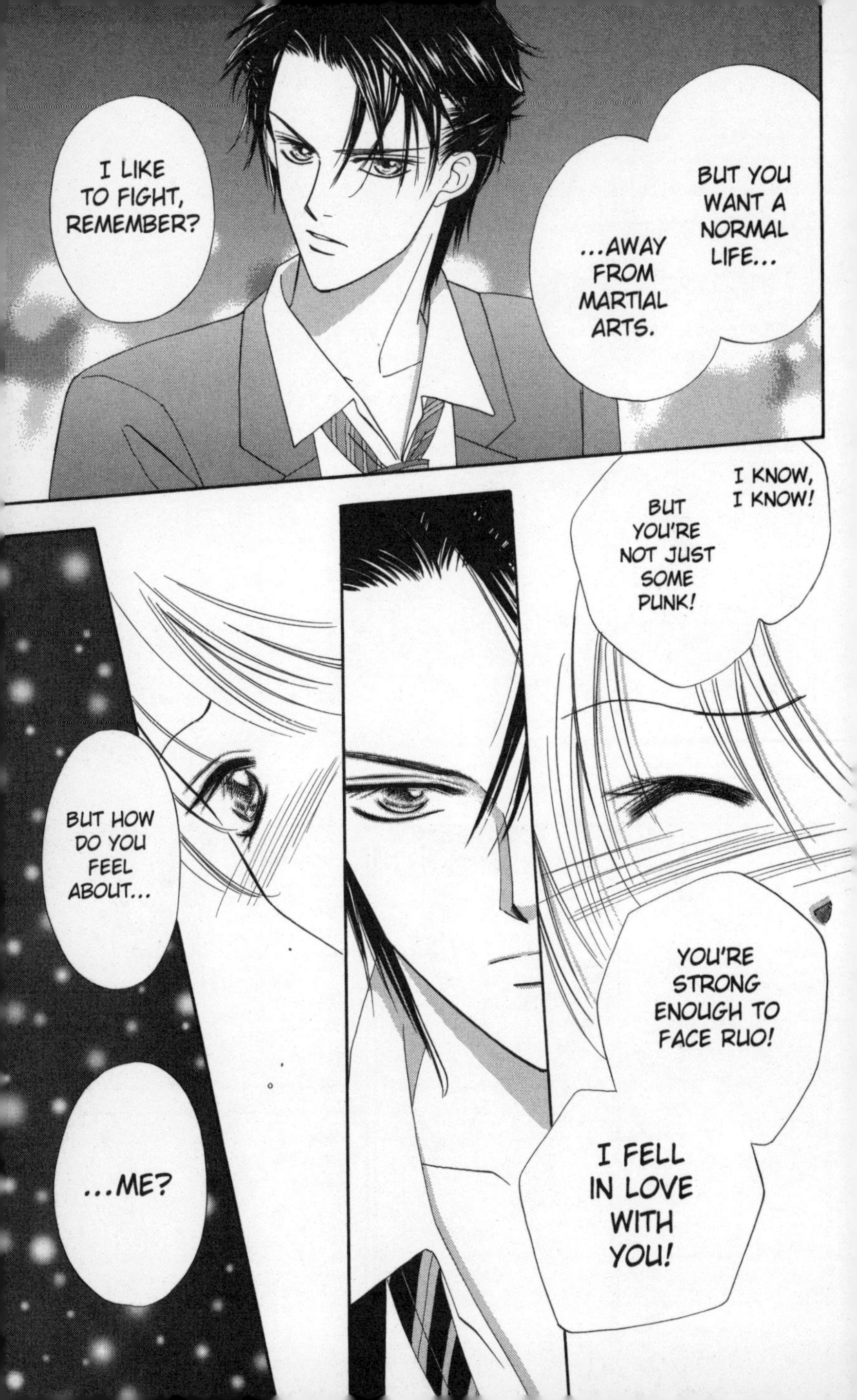
BUT YOU WANT A NORMAL LIFE...
...AWAY FROM MARTIAL ARTS.
I LIKE TO FIGHT, REMEMBER?
I KNOW, I KNOW!
BUT YOU'RE NOT JUST SOME PUNK!
YOU'RE STRONG ENOUGH TO FACE RUO!
I FELL IN LOVE WITH YOU!
BUT HOW DO YOU FEEL ABOUT...
...ME?

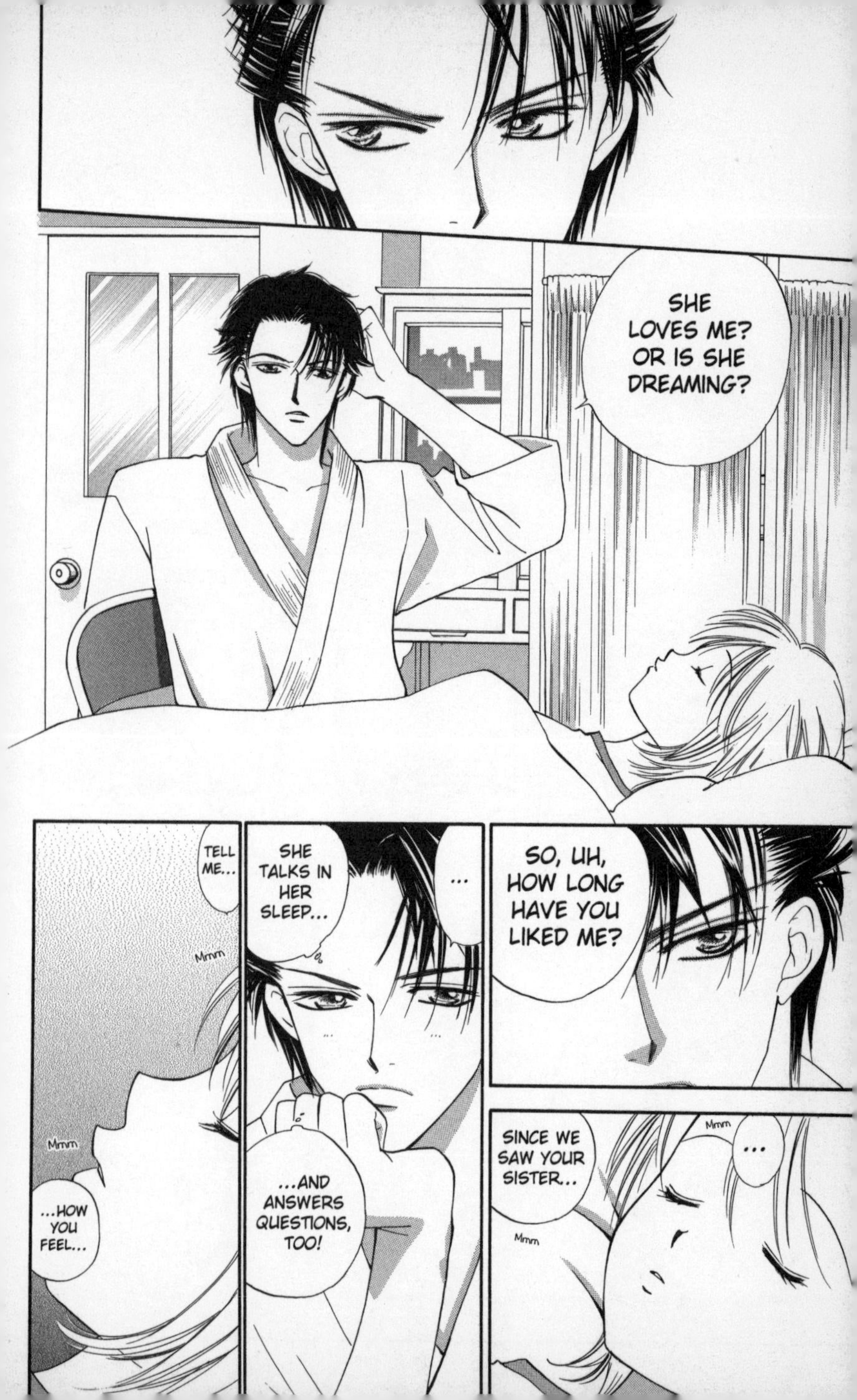
SHE LOVES ME? OR IS SHE DREAMING?
SO, UH, HOW LONG HAVE YOU LIKED ME?
Mmm
...
SINCE WE SAW YOUR SISTER...
Mmm
...
SHE TALKS IN HER SLEEP...
...AND ANSWERS QUESTIONS, TOO!
TELL ME...
Mmm
Mmm
...HOW YOU FEEL...

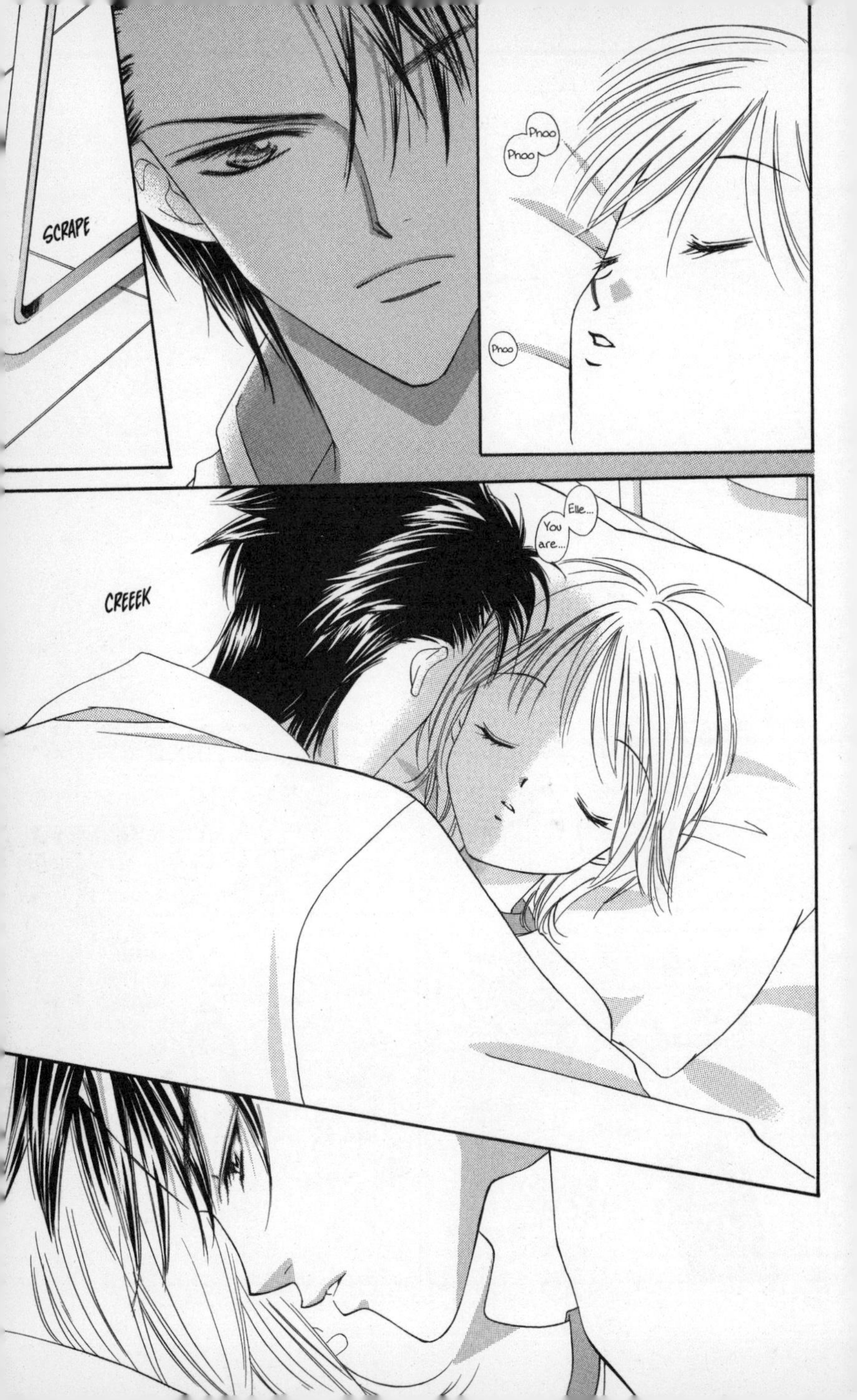
Phoo
Phoo
Phoo
SCRAPE
Elle...
You are...
CREEEK

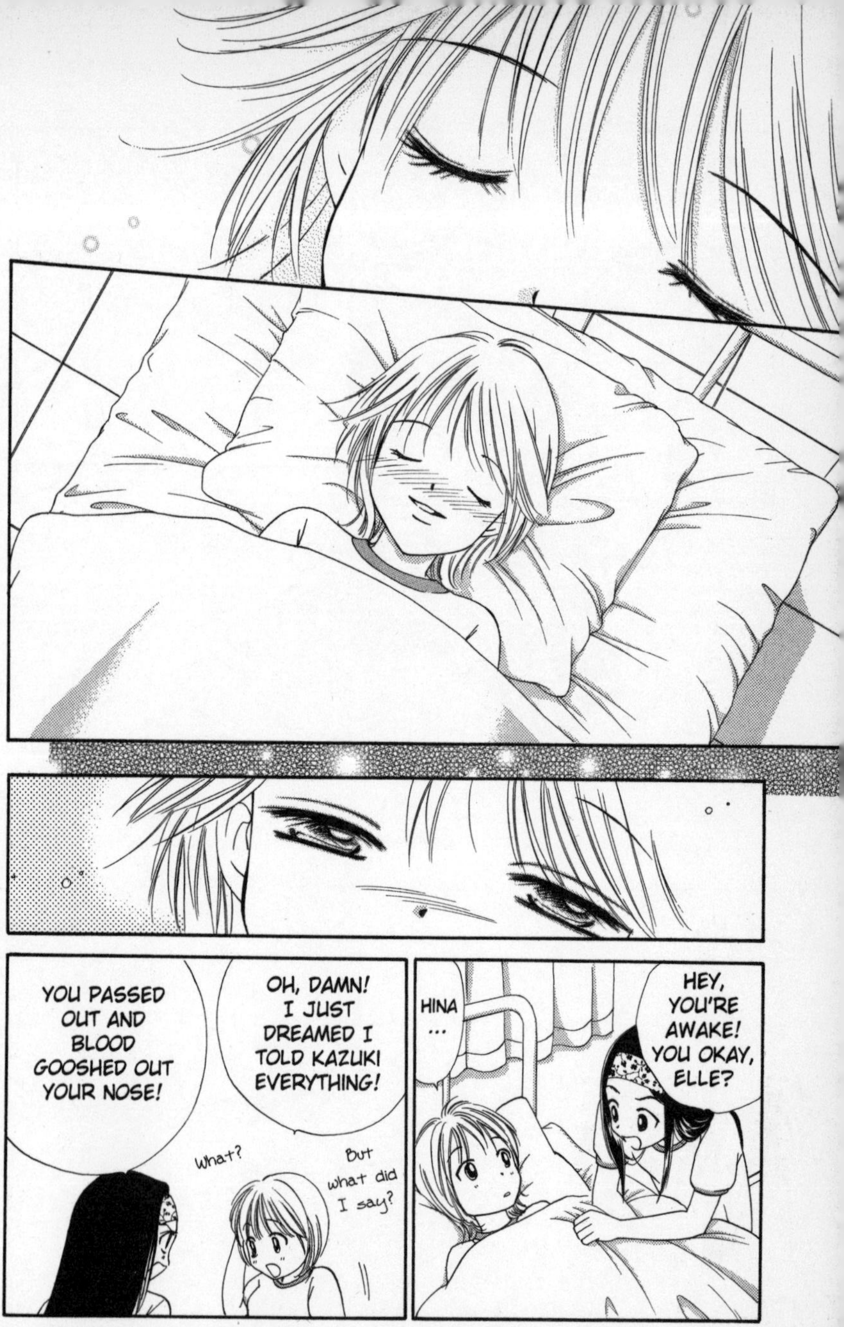
HEY, YOU'RE AWAKE! YOU OKAY, ELLE?
HINA ...
OH, DAMN! I JUST DREAMED I TOLD KAZUKI EVERYTHING!
But what did I say?
YOU PASSED OUT AND BLOOD GOOSHED OUT YOUR NOSE!
What?

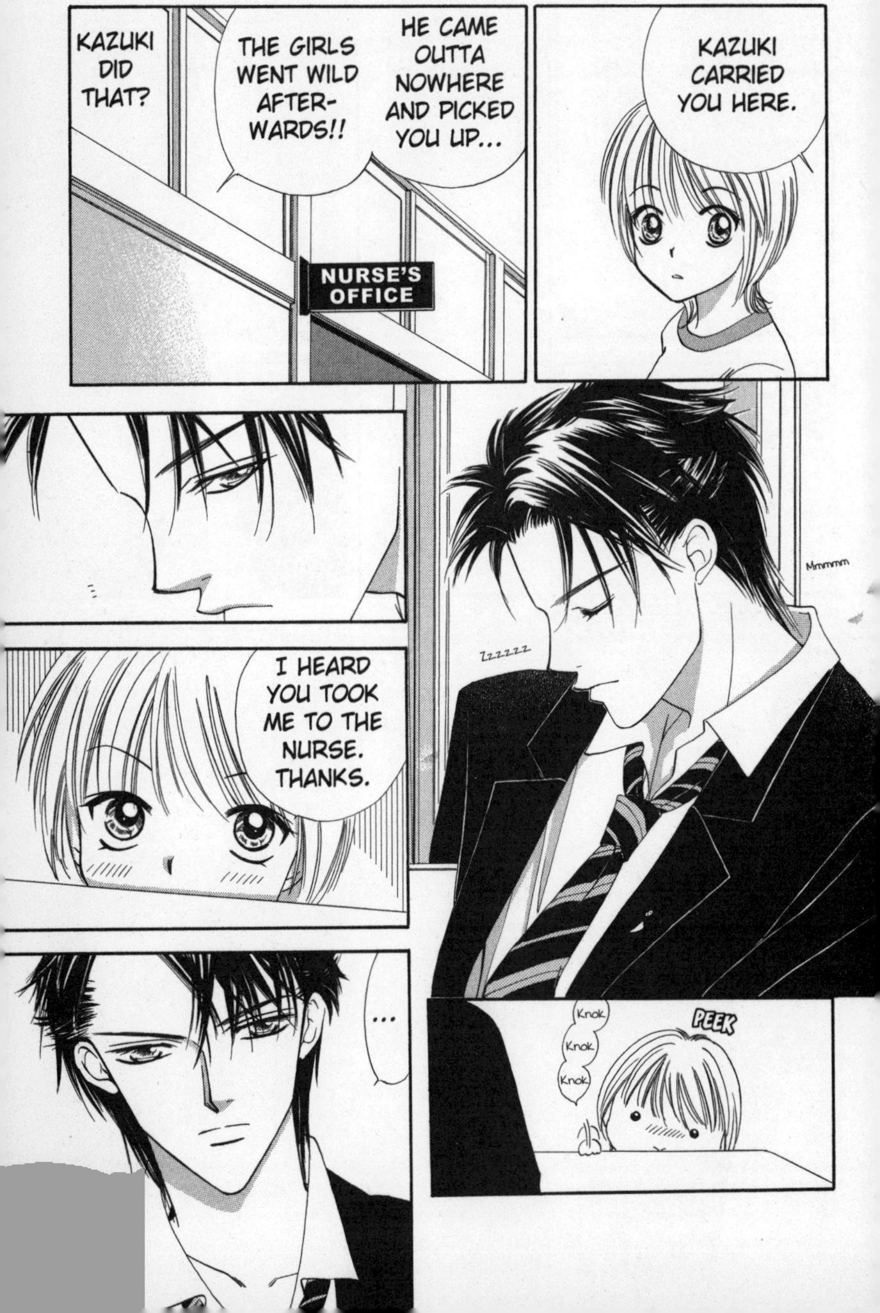
KAZUKI CARRIED YOU HERE.
HE CAME OUTTA NOWHERE AND PICKED YOU UP...
THE GIRLS WENT WILD AFTER-WARDS!!
NURSE'S OFFICE
KAZUKI DID THAT?
Mmmmm
Zzzzzz
PEEK
Knok
Knok
Knok
I HEARD YOU TOOK ME TO THE NURSE. THANKS.
...

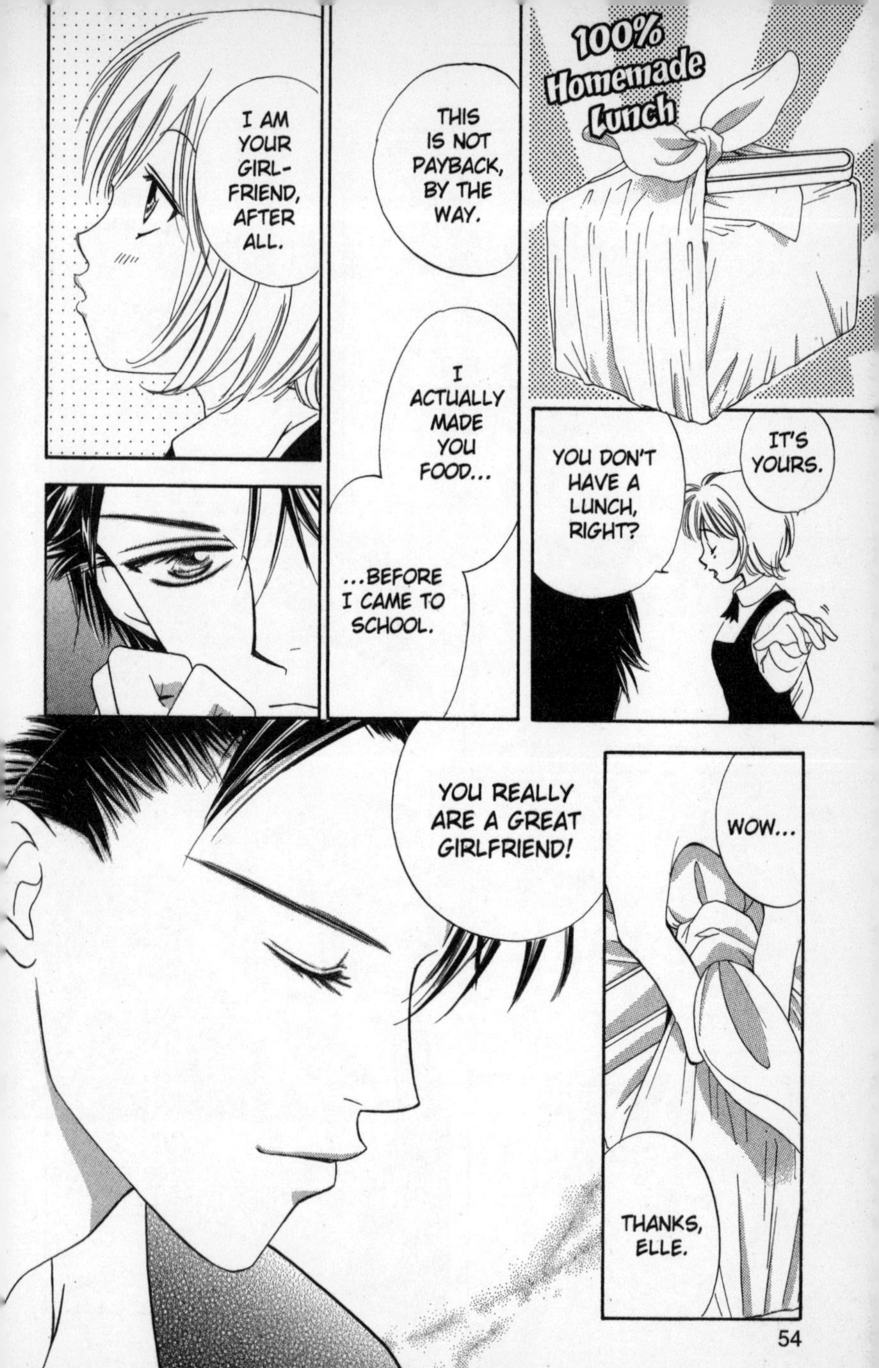
100% Homemade Lunch
IT'S YOURS.
YOU DON'T HAVE A LUNCH, RIGHT?
THIS IS NOT PAYBACK, BY THE WAY.
I ACTUALLY MADE YOU FOOD...
...BEFORE I CAME TO SCHOOL.
I AM YOUR GIRL-FRIEND, AFTER ALL.
WOW...
THANKS, ELLE.
YOU REALLY ARE A GREAT GIRLFRIEND!

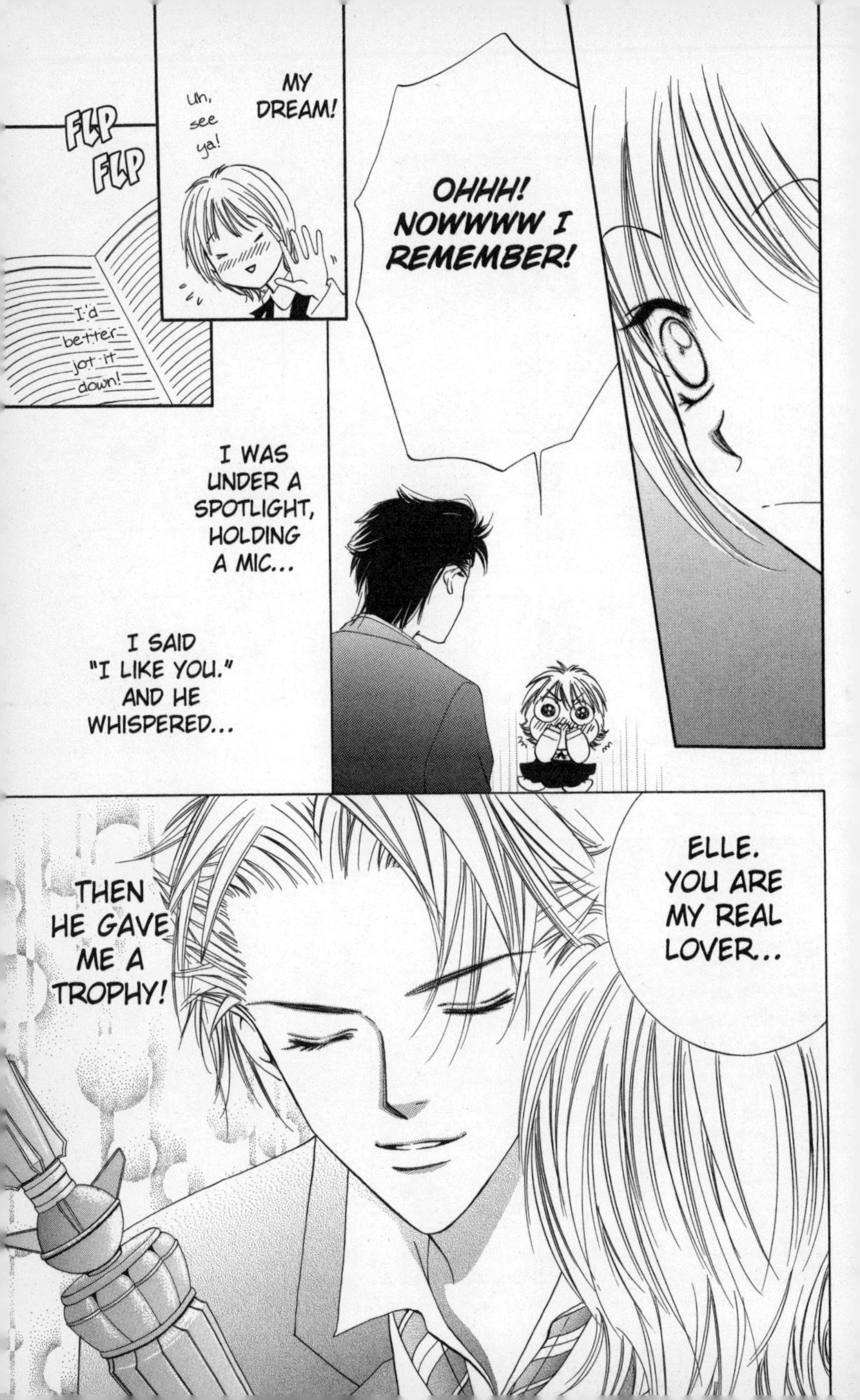
OHHH! NOWWWW I REMEMBER!
MY DREAM!
Uh, see ya!
FLP FLP
I'd better jot it down!
I WAS UNDER A SPOTLIGHT, HOLDING A MIC...
I SAID "I LIKE YOU." AND HE WHISPERED...
ELLE. YOU ARE MY REAL LOVER...
THEN HE GAVE ME A TROPHY!

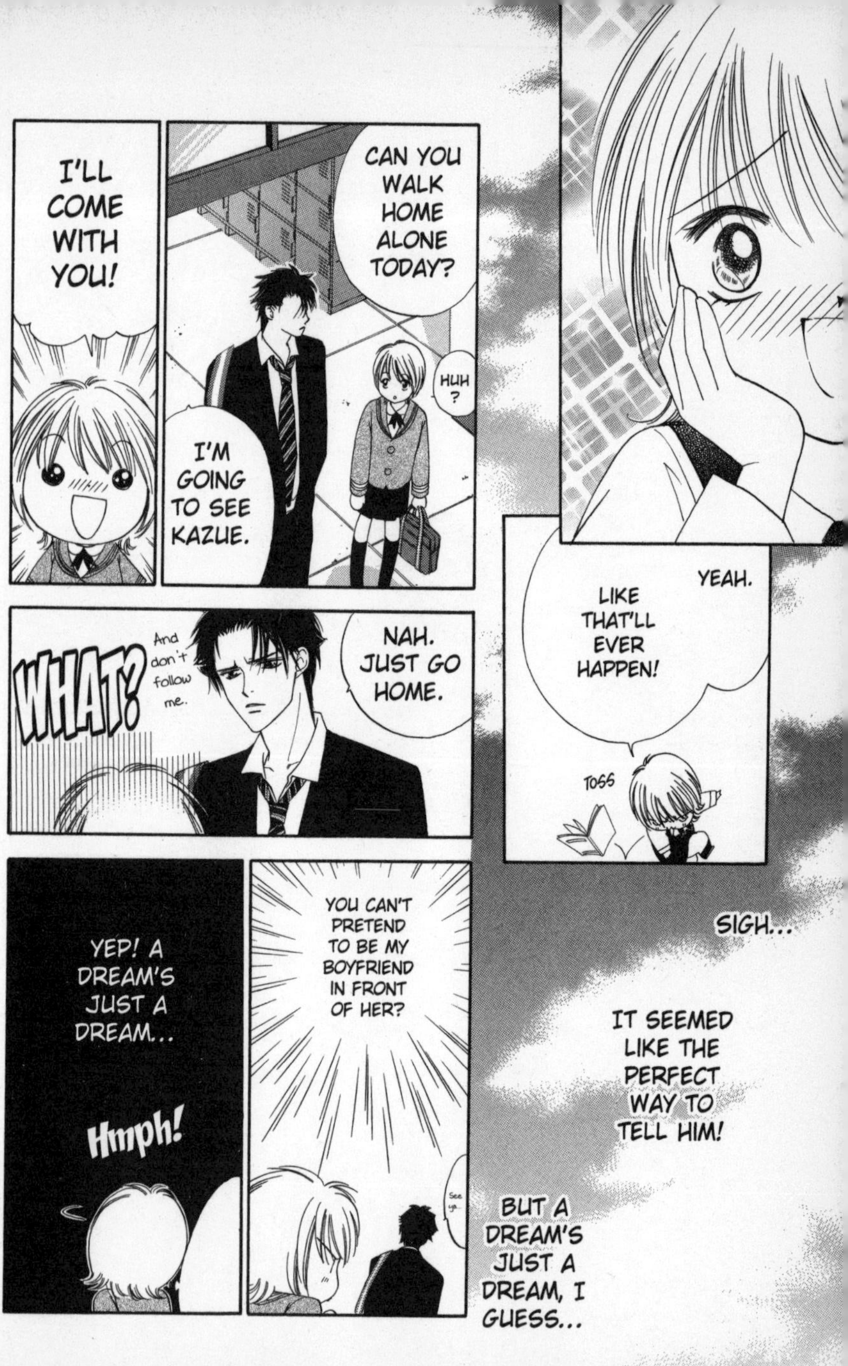
YEAH.
LIKE THAT'LL EVER HAPPEN!
TOSS
SIGH...
IT SEEMED LIKE THE PERFECT WAY TO TELL HIM!
BUT A DREAM'S JUST A DREAM, I GUESS...
CAN YOU WALK HOME ALONE TODAY?
HUH?
I'M GOING TO SEE KAZUE.
I'LL COME WITH YOU!
NAH. JUST GO HOME.
And don't follow me.
WHAT?
YOU CAN'T PRETEND TO BE MY BOYFRIEND IN FRONT OF HER?
See ya.
YEP! A DREAM'S JUST A DREAM...
Hmph!

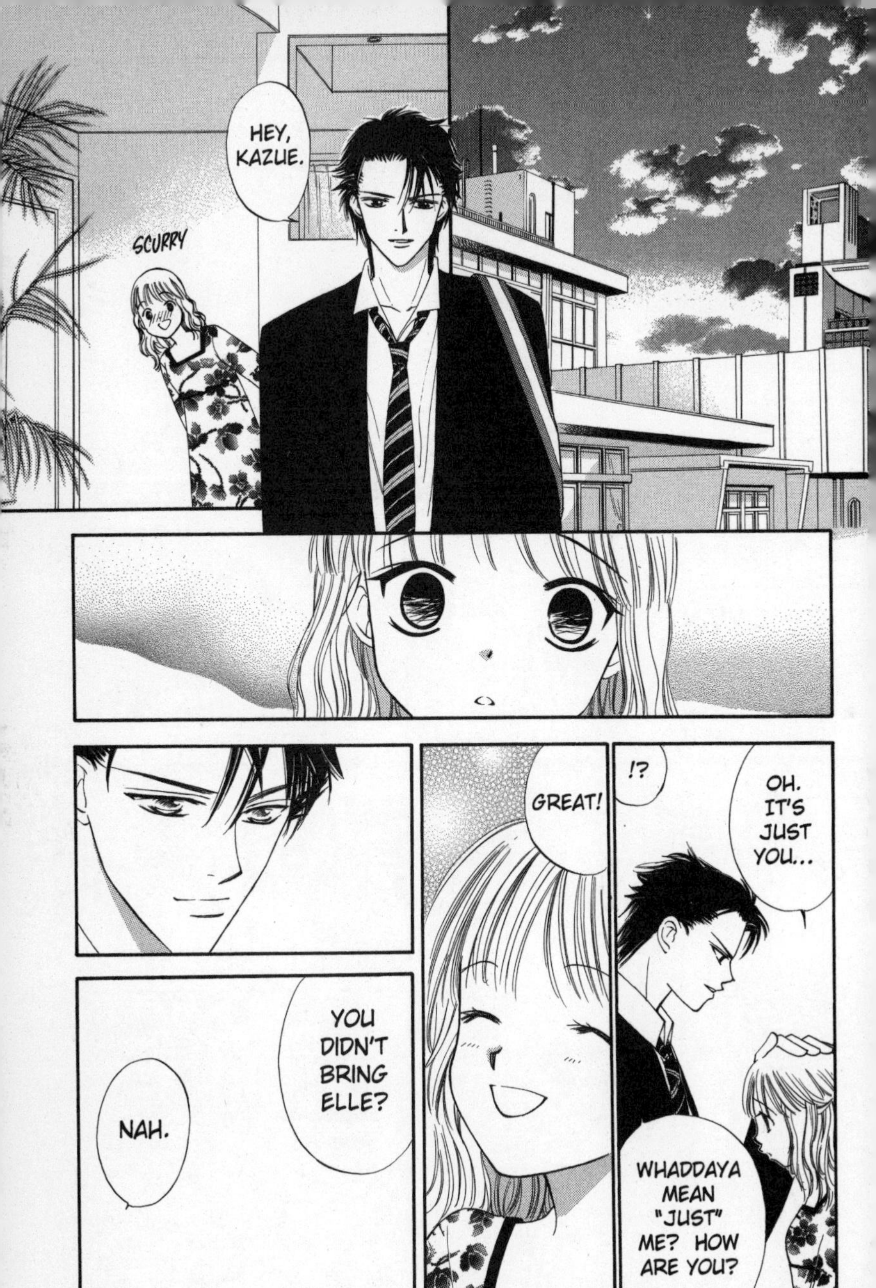
HEY, KAZUE.
SCURRY
OH. IT'S JUST YOU...
!?
WHADDAYA MEAN "JUST" ME? HOW ARE YOU?
GREAT!
YOU DIDN'T BRING ELLE?
NAH.

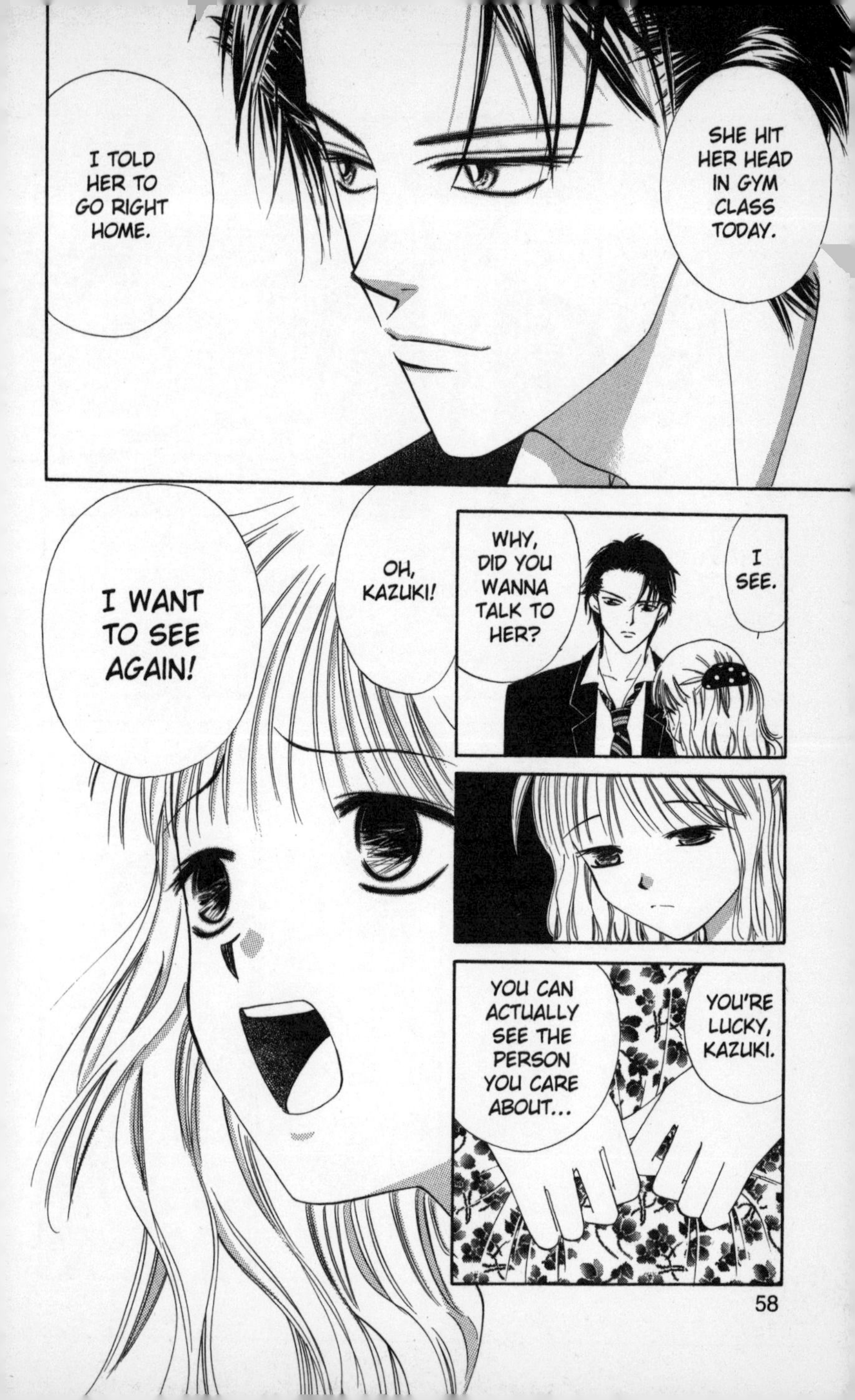
SHE HIT HER HEAD IN GYM CLASS TODAY.
I TOLD HER TO GO RIGHT HOME.
I SEE.
WHY, DID YOU WANNA TALK TO HER?
YOU'RE LUCKY, KAZUKI.
YOU CAN ACTUALLY SEE THE PERSON YOU CARE ABOUT...
OH, KAZUKI!
I WANT TO SEE AGAIN!

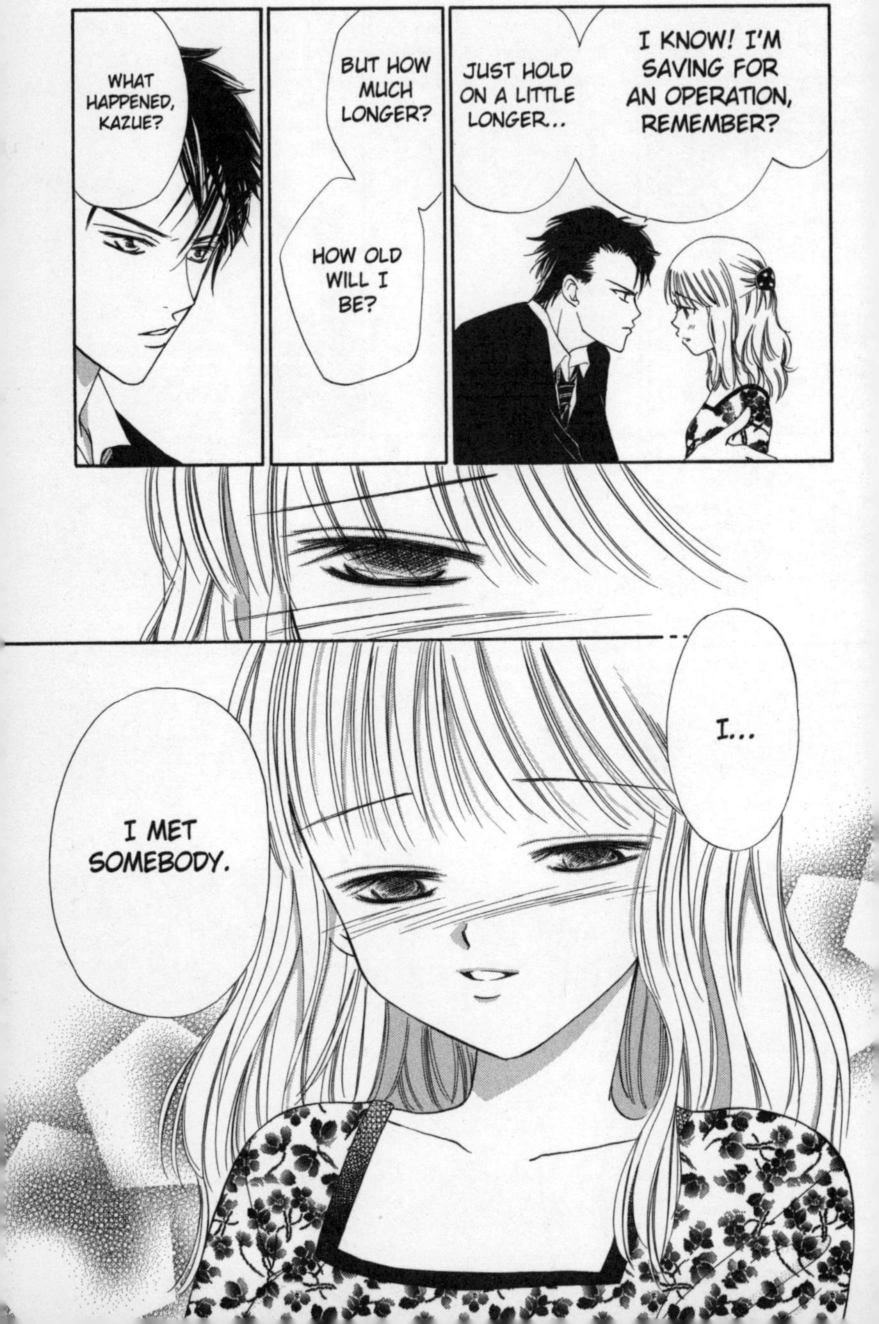
I KNOW! I'M SAVING FOR AN OPERATION, REMEMBER?
JUST HOLD ON A LITTLE LONGER...
BUT HOW MUCH LONGER?
HOW OLD WILL I BE?
WHAT HAPPENED, KAZUE?
I...
I MET SOMEBODY.

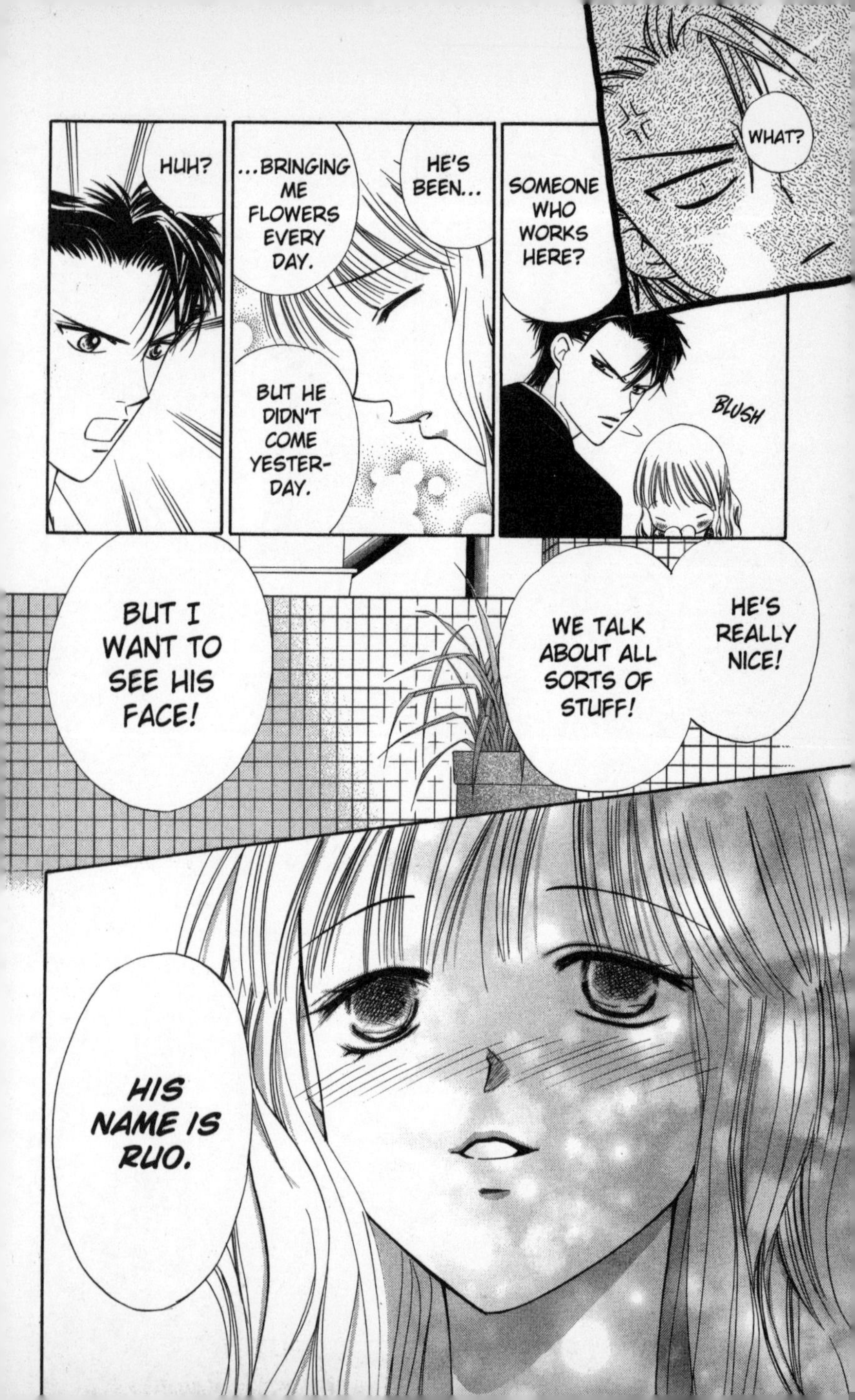
WHAT?
SOMEONE WHO WORKS HERE?
BLUSH
HE'S BEEN...
...BRINGING ME FLOWERS EVERY DAY.
BUT HE DIDN'T COME YESTER-DAY.
HUH?
HE'S REALLY NICE!
WE TALK ABOUT ALL SORTS OF STUFF!
BUT I WANT TO SEE HIS FACE!
HIS NAME IS RUO.

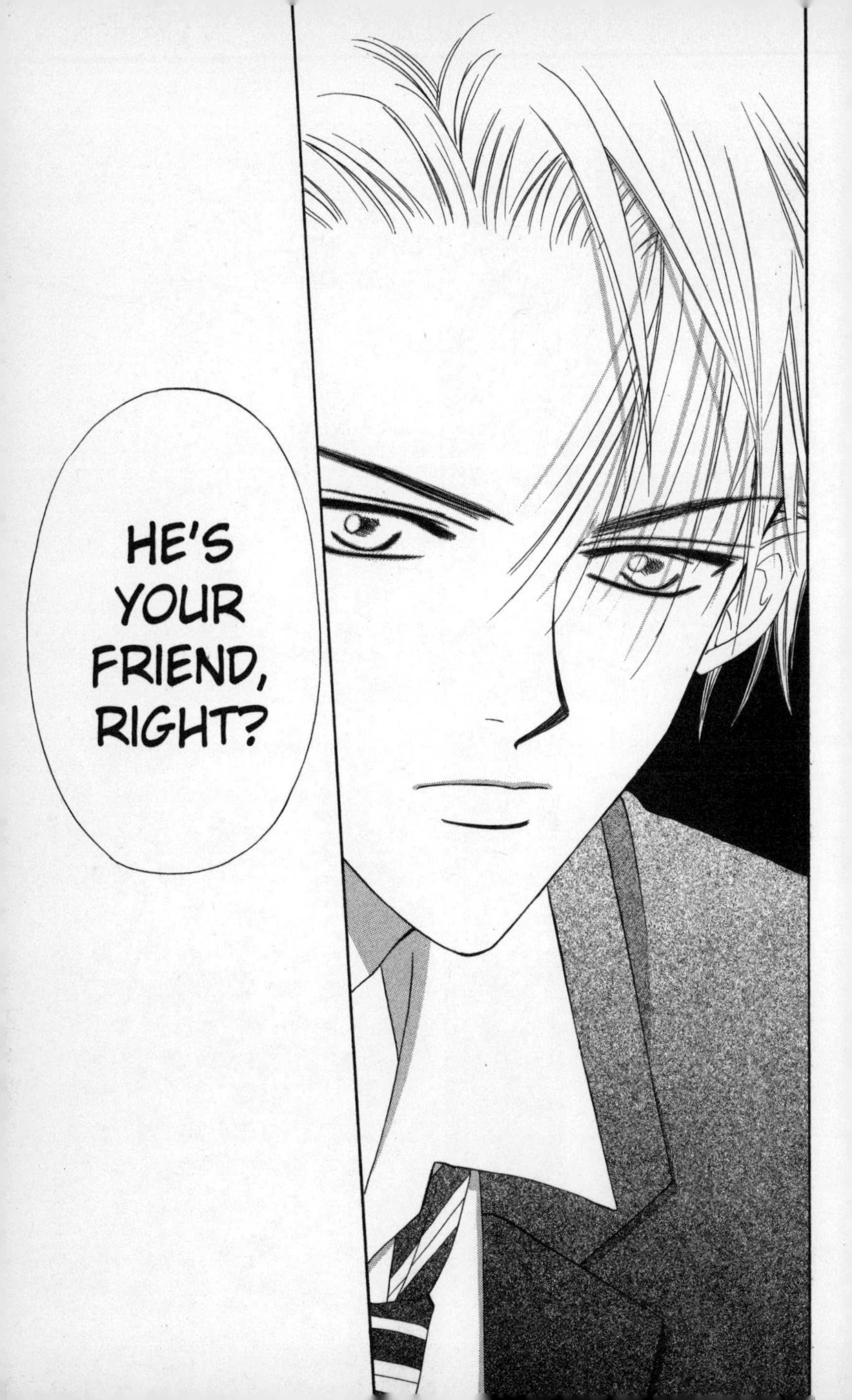
HE'S YOUR FRIEND, RIGHT?

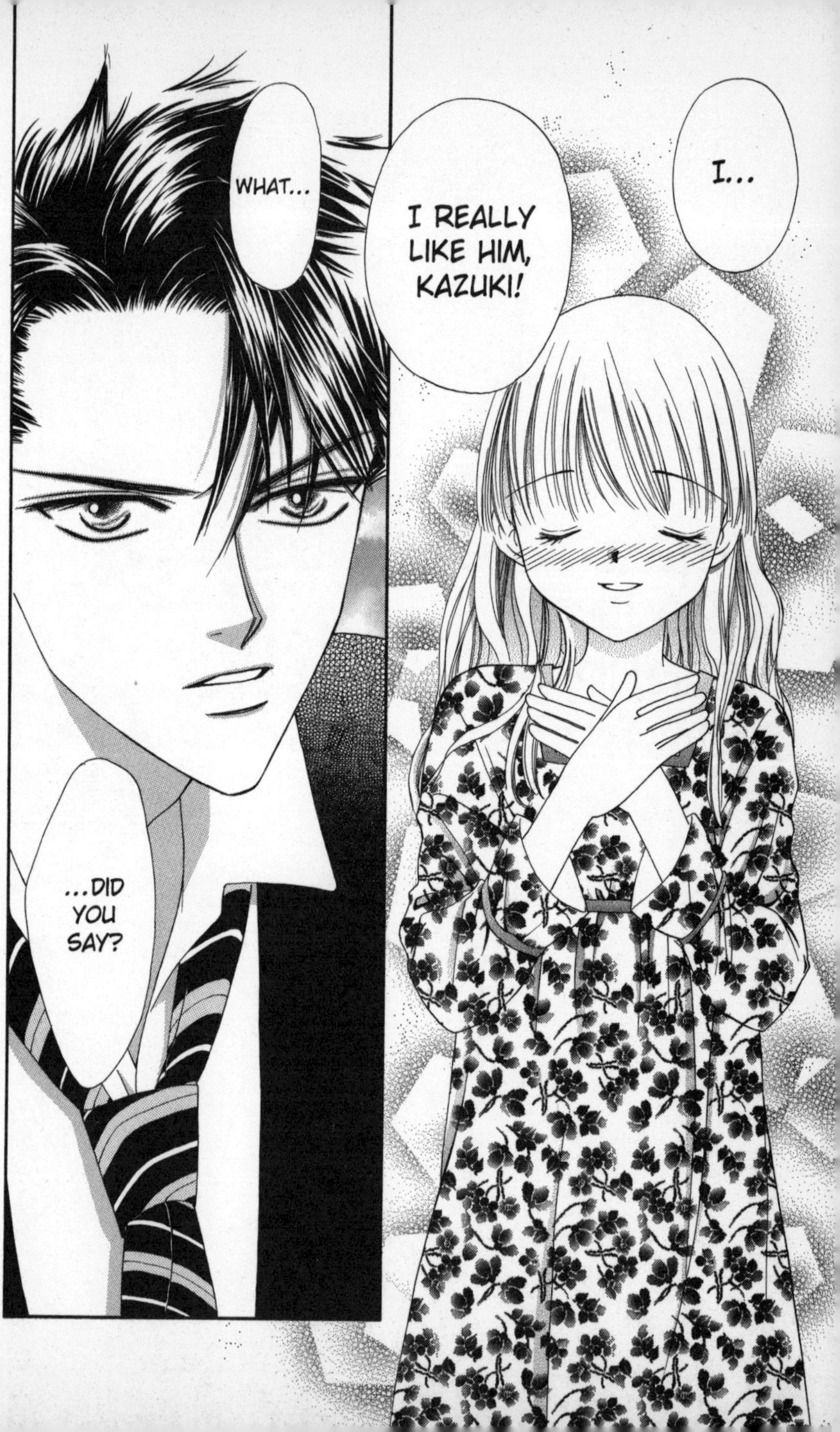
I...
I REALLY LIKE HIM, KAZUKI!
WHAT...
...DID YOU SAY?

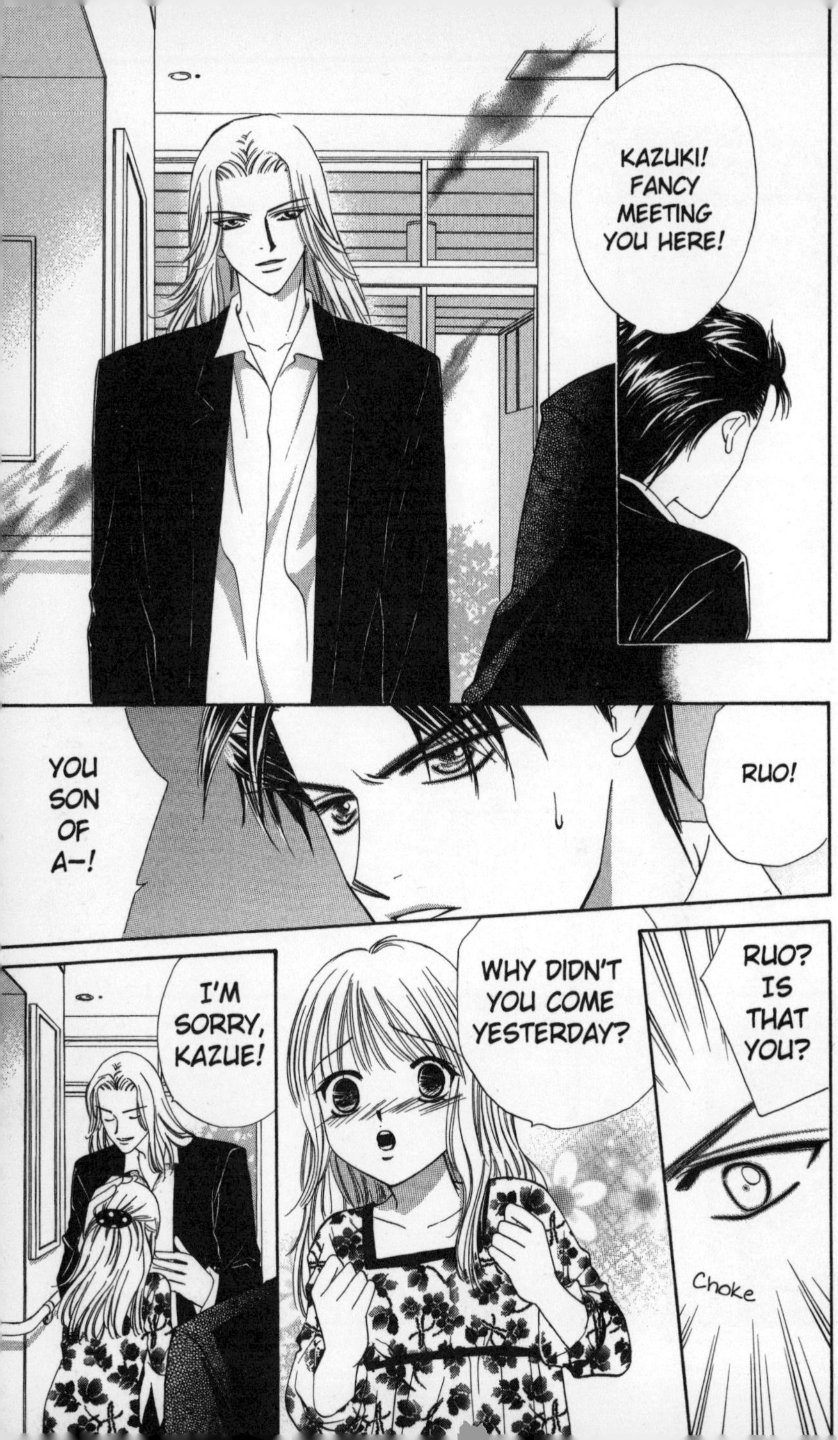
KAZUKI! FANCY MEETING YOU HERE!
RUO!
YOU SON OF A—!
RUO? IS THAT YOU?
Choke
WHY DIDN'T YOU COME YESTERDAY?
I'M SORRY, KAZUE!

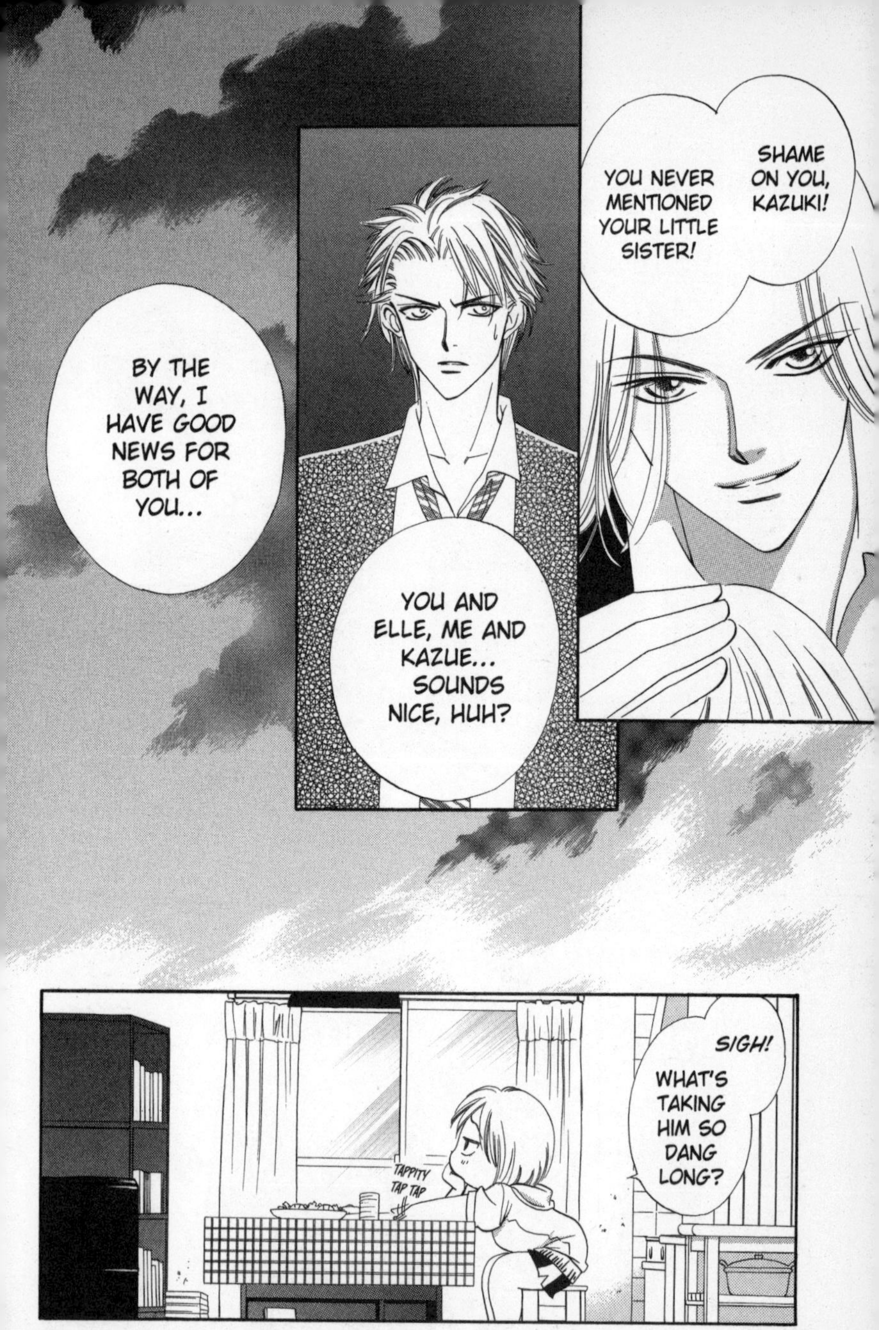
SHAME ON YOU, KAZUKI!
YOU NEVER MENTIONED YOUR LITTLE SISTER!
BY THE WAY, I HAVE GOOD NEWS FOR BOTH OF YOU...
YOU AND ELLE, ME AND KAZUE... SOUNDS NICE, HUH?
SIGH!
WHAT'S TAKING HIM SO DANG LONG?
TAPPITY TAP TAP

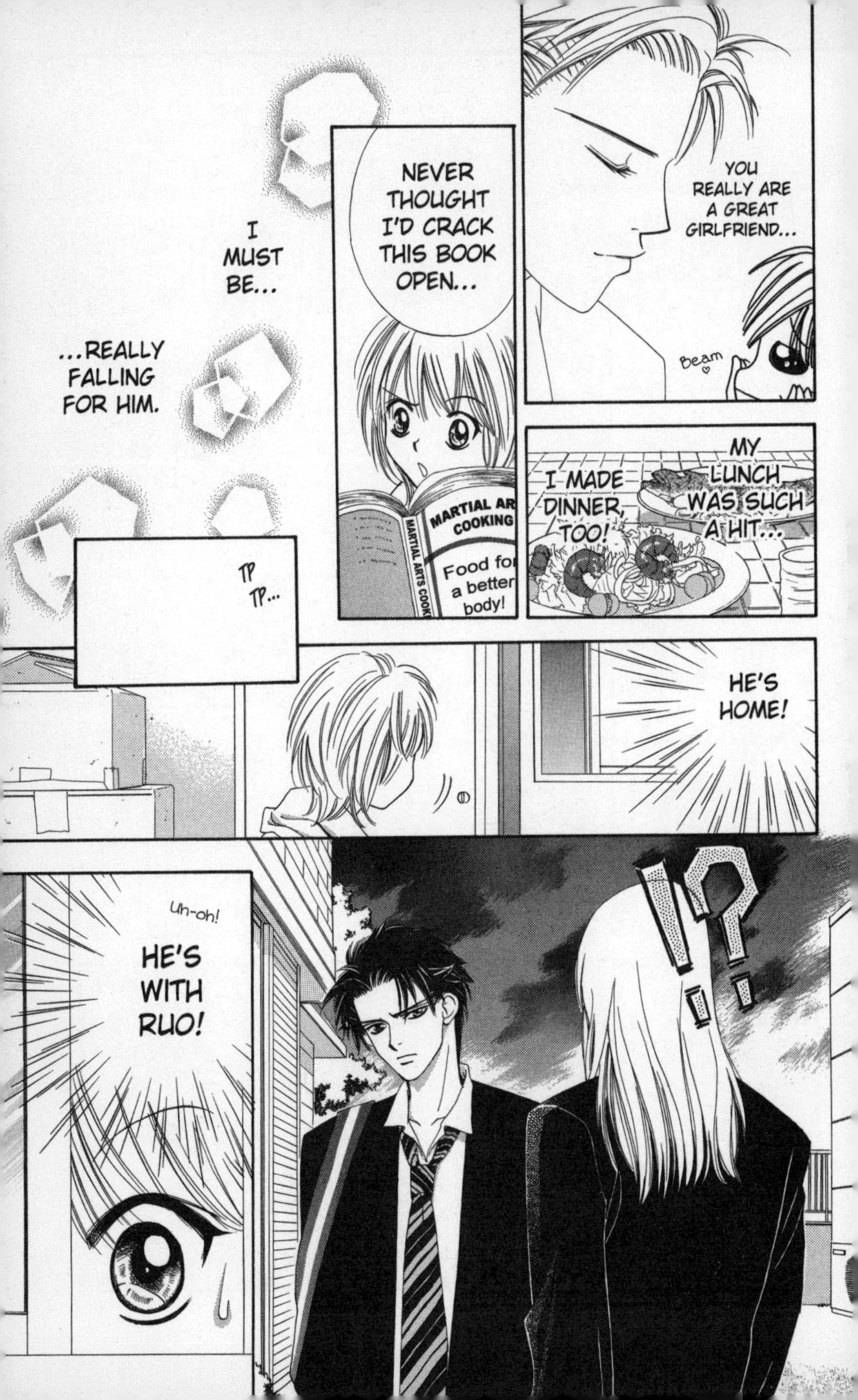

YOU REALLY ARE A GREAT GIRLFRIEND...
Beam
MY LUNCH WAS SUCH A HIT...
I MADE DINNER, TOO!
NEVER THOUGHT I'D CRACK THIS BOOK OPEN...
MARTIAL AR COOKING
Food fo a better body!
MARTIAL ARTS COOK
I MUST BE...
...REALLY FALLING FOR HIM.
TP TP...
HE'S HOME!
!?
Uh-oh!
HE'S WITH RUO!

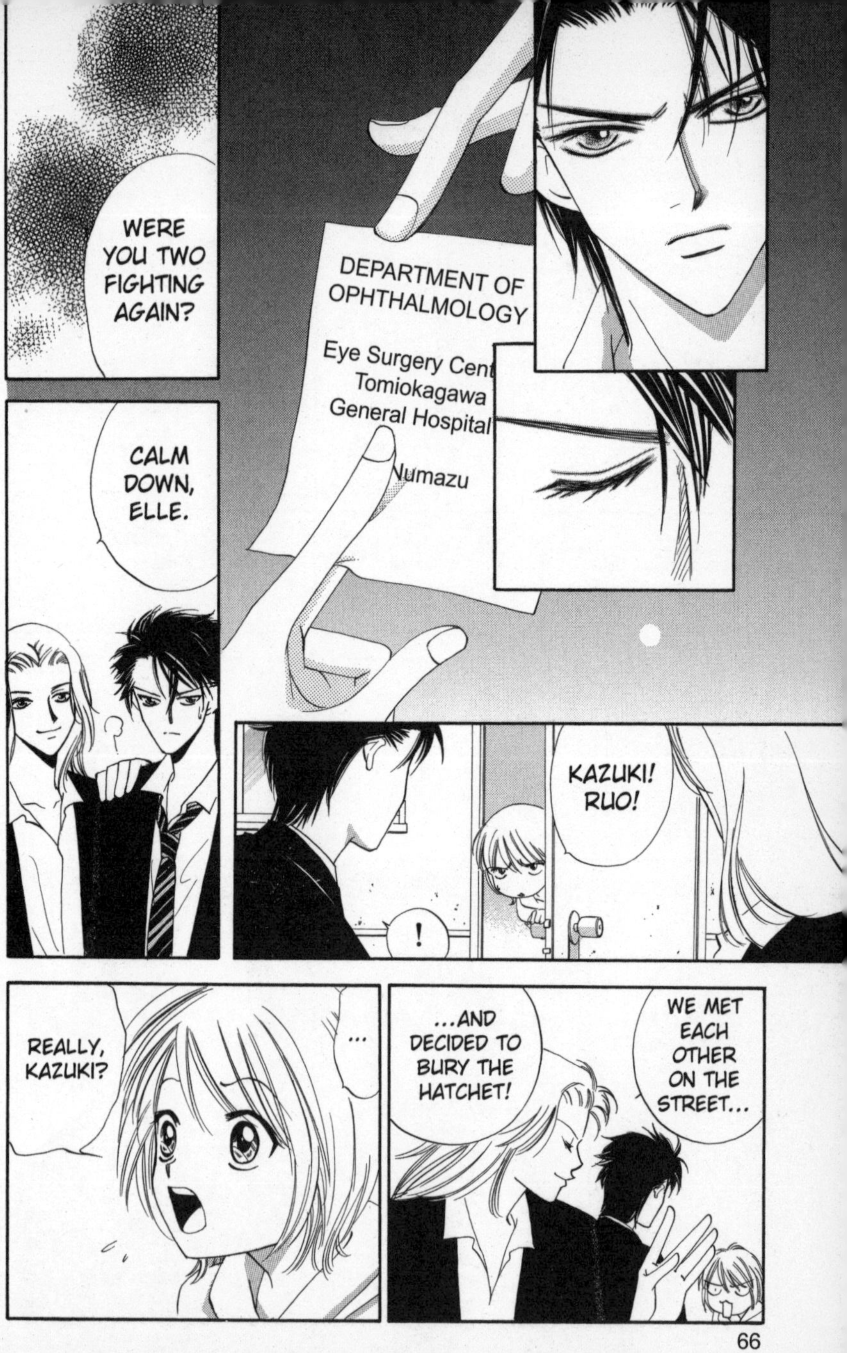
DEPARTMENT OF OPHTHALMOLOGY
Eye Surgery Cent
Tomiokagawa
General Hospital
Numazu
KAZUKI! RUO!
!
WERE YOU TWO FIGHTING AGAIN?
CALM DOWN, ELLE.
WE MET EACH OTHER ON THE STREET...
...AND DECIDED TO BURY THE HATCHET!
...
REALLY, KAZUKI?

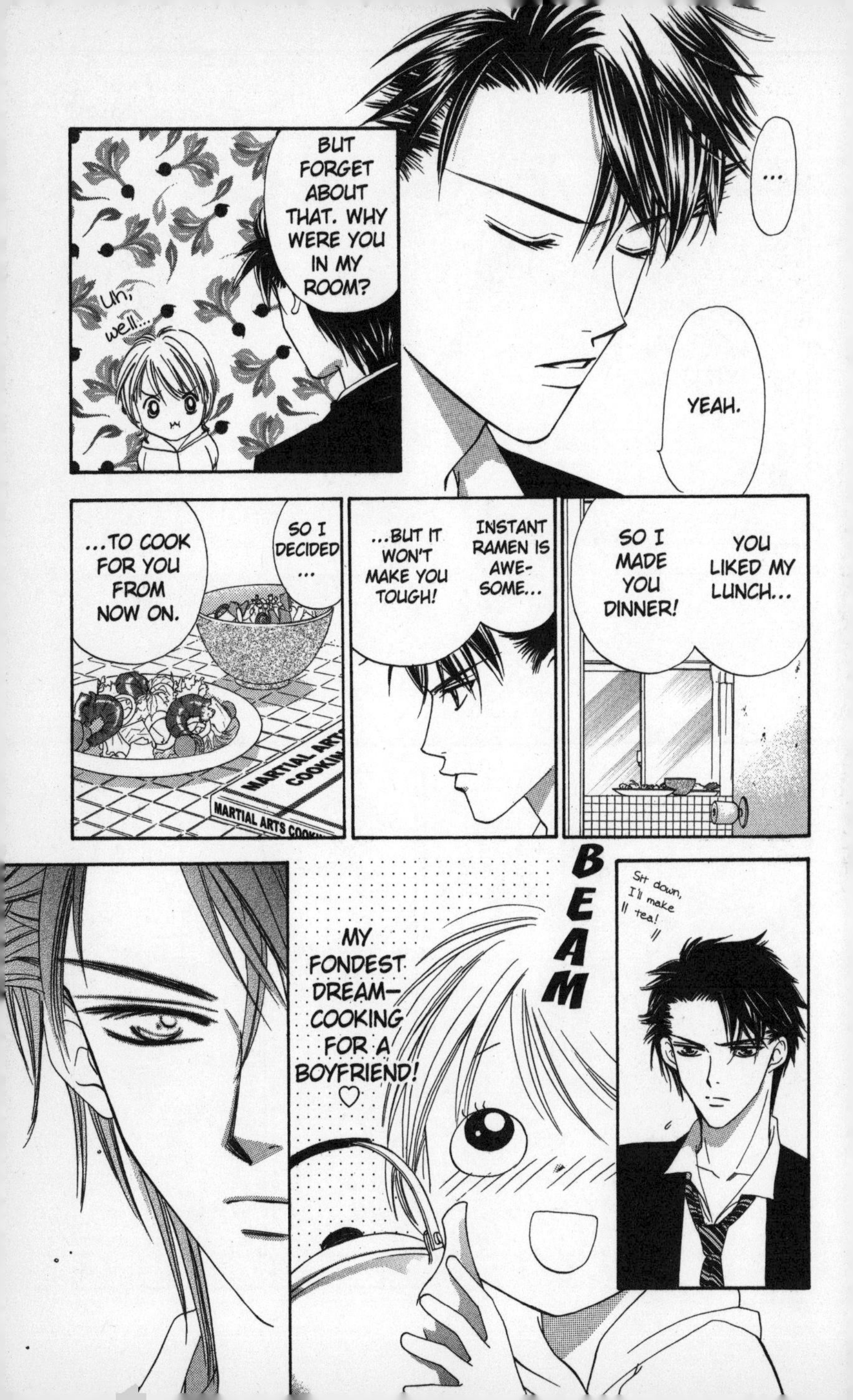
...
YEAH.
BUT FORGET ABOUT THAT. WHY WERE YOU IN MY ROOM?
Uh, well...
YOU LIKED MY LUNCH...
SO I MADE YOU DINNER!
INSTANT RAMEN IS AWESOME...
...BUT IT WON'T MAKE YOU TOUGH!
SO I DECIDED...
...TO COOK FOR YOU FROM NOW ON.
MARTIAL ARTS COOKING
MARTIAL ARTS COOKIN
Sit down, I'll make tea!
BEAM
MY FONDEST DREAM—COOKING FOR A BOYFRIEND! ♡

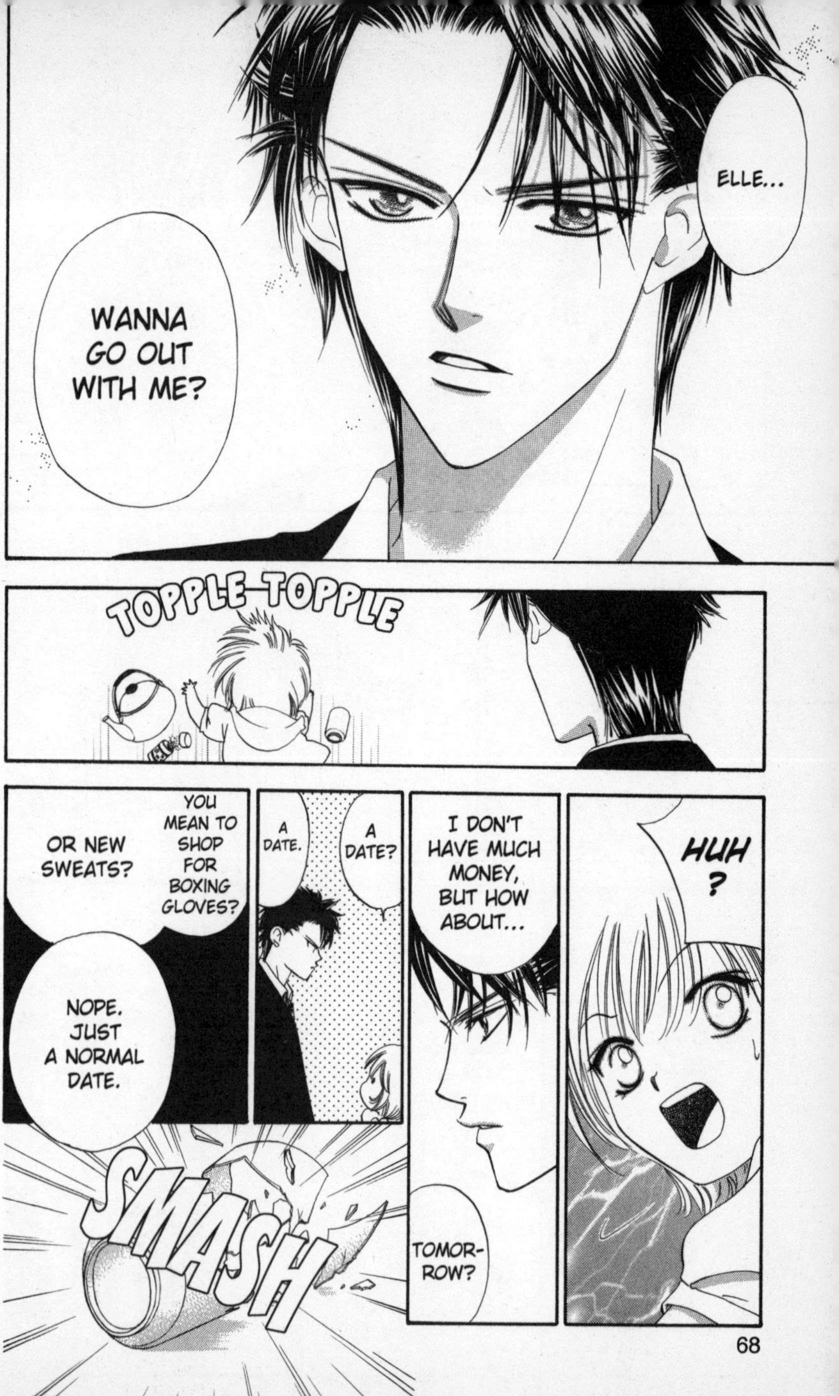
ELLE...
WANNA GO OUT WITH ME?
TOPPLE TOPPLE
HUH ?
I DON'T HAVE MUCH MONEY, BUT HOW ABOUT...
TOMOR-ROW?
A DATE?
A DATE.
YOU MEAN TO SHOP FOR BOXING GLOVES?
OR NEW SWEATS?
NOPE. JUST A NORMAL DATE.
SMASH

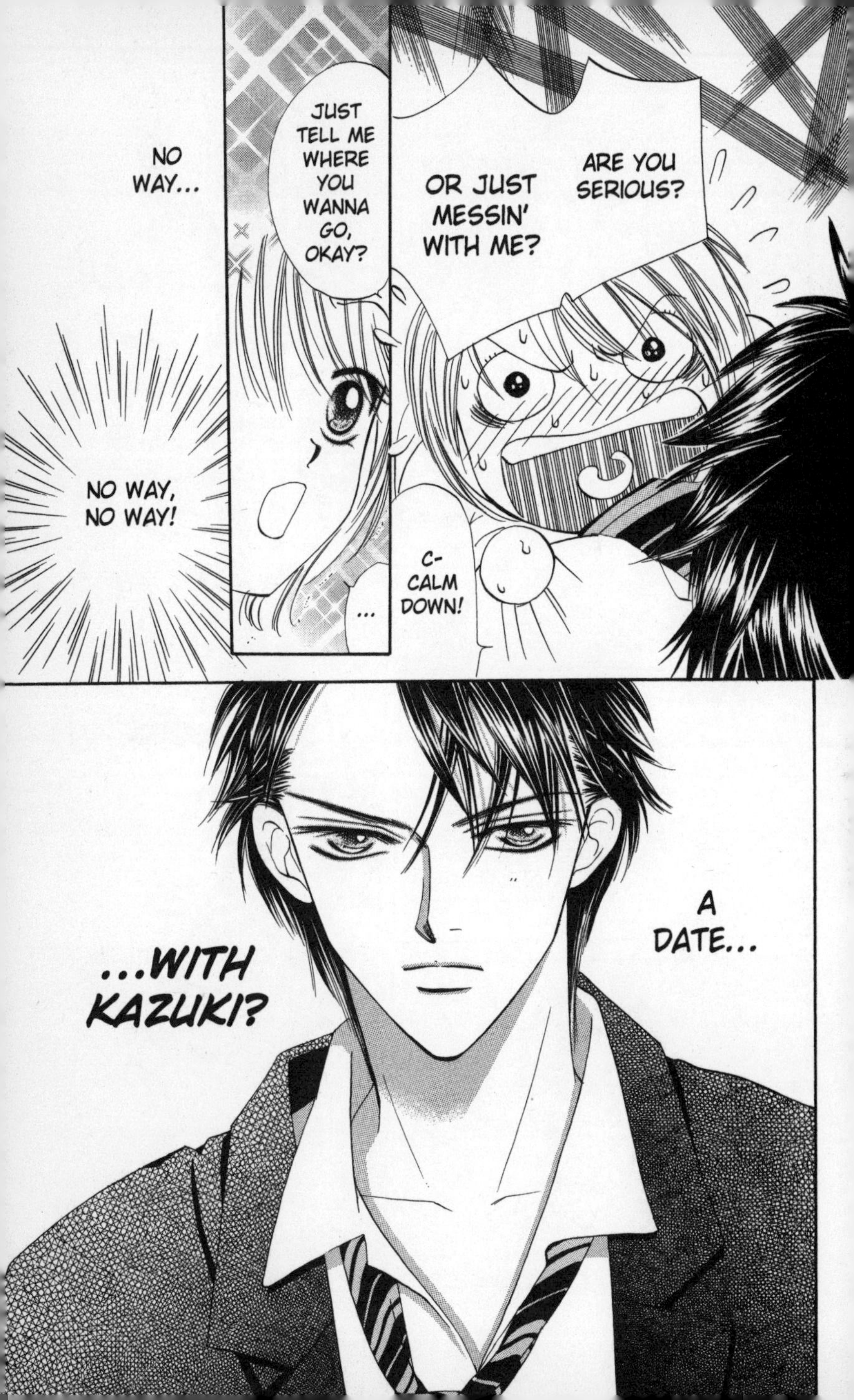
ARE YOU SERIOUS?
OR JUST MESSIN' WITH ME?
C-CALM DOWN!
JUST TELL ME WHERE YOU WANNA GO, OKAY?
...
NO WAY...
NO WAY, NO WAY!
A DATE...
...WITH KAZUKI?

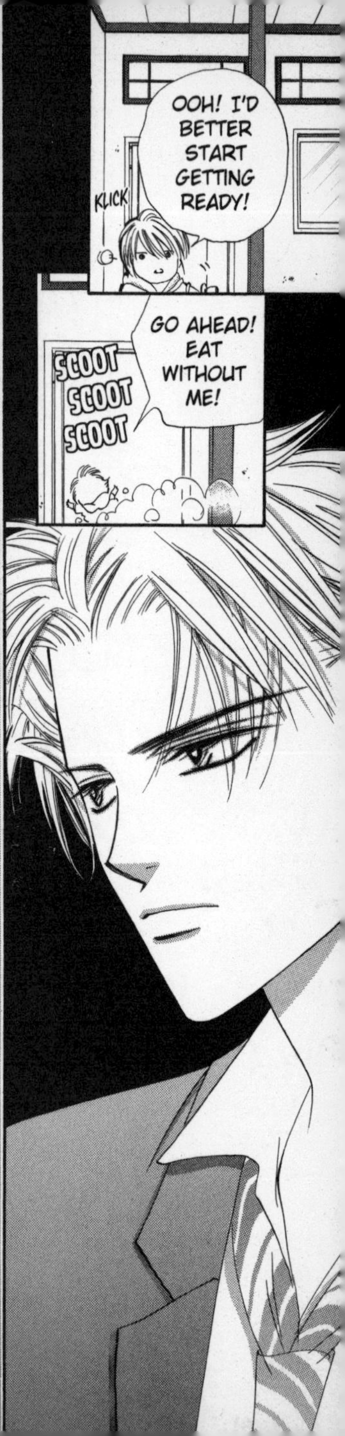
OOH! I'D BETTER START GETTING READY!
KLICK
GO AHEAD! EAT WITHOUT ME!
SCOOT SCOOT SCOOT

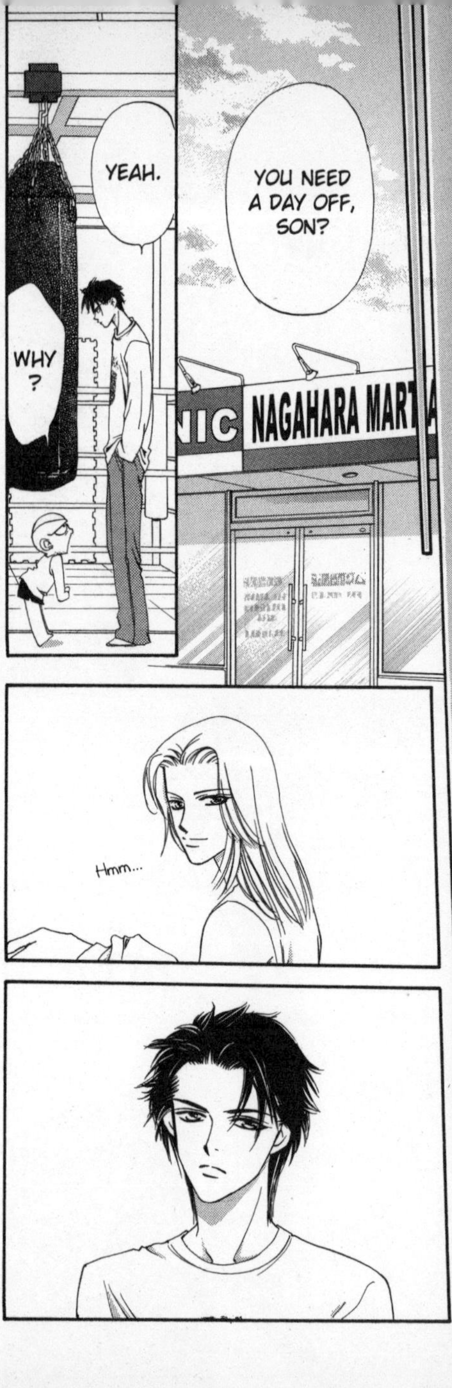
YOU NEED A DAY OFF, SON?
NIC
NAGAHARA MART
YEAH.
WHY ?
Hmm...

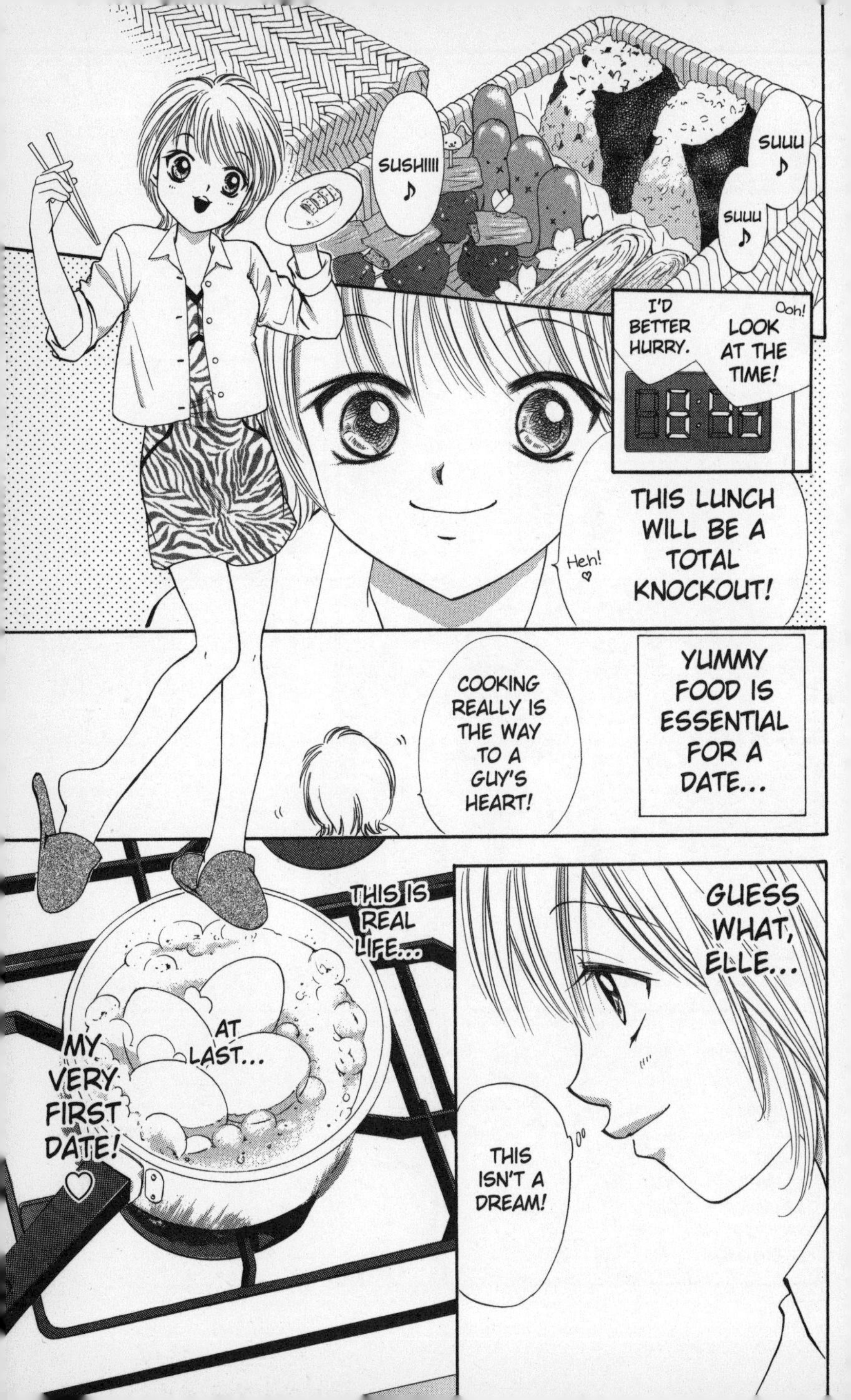
suuu ♪
suuu ♪
SUSHIIII ♪
Ooh! LOOK AT THE TIME!
I'D BETTER HURRY.
THIS LUNCH WILL BE A TOTAL KNOCKOUT!
Heh! ♡
YUMMY FOOD IS ESSENTIAL FOR A DATE...
COOKING REALLY IS THE WAY TO A GUY'S HEART!
GUESS WHAT, ELLE...
THIS ISN'T A DREAM!
THIS IS REAL LIFE...
AT LAST...
MY VERY FIRST DATE! ♡

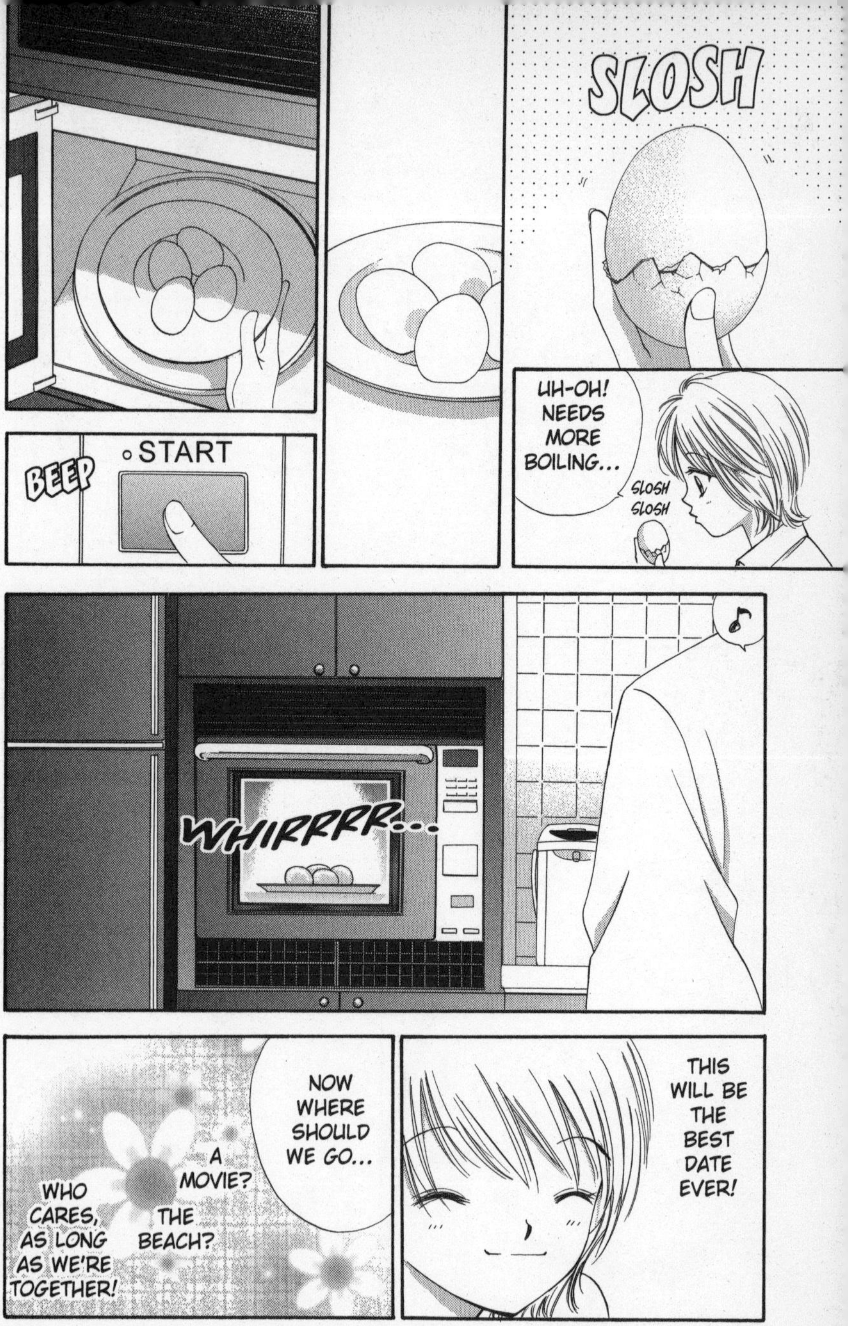
SLOSH
UH-OH! NEEDS MORE BOILING...
SLOSH SLOSH
BEEP
START
♪
WHIRRRR...
THIS WILL BE THE BEST DATE EVER!
NOW WHERE SHOULD WE GO...
A MOVIE?
THE BEACH?
WHO CARES, AS LONG AS WE'RE TOGETHER!

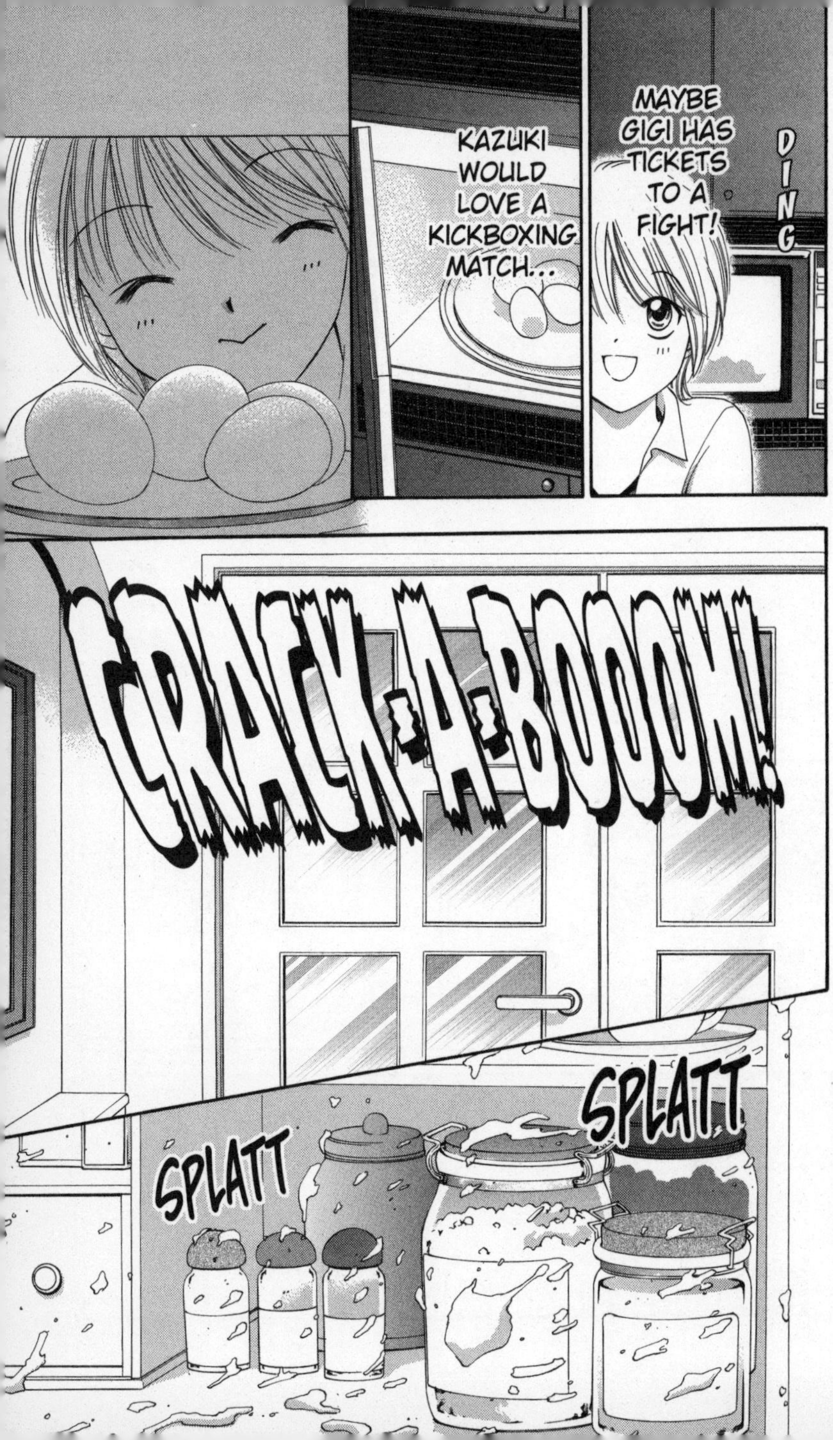
MAYBE GIGI HAS TICKETS TO A FIGHT!
DING
KAZUKI WOULD LOVE A KICKBOXING MATCH...
CRACK-A-BOOOOM!
SPLATT
SPLATT

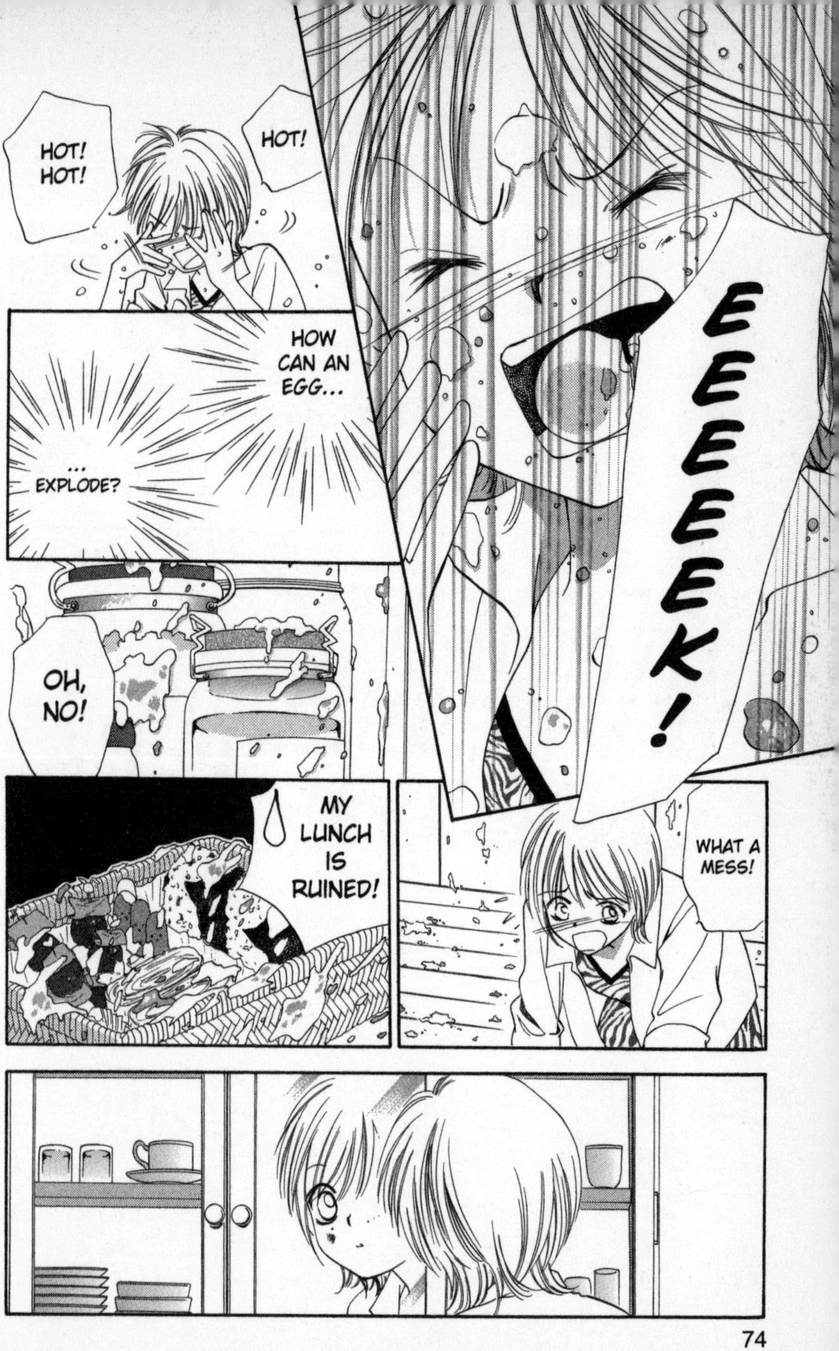
EEEEEEK!
HOT!
HOT! HOT!
HOW CAN AN EGG...
...EXPLODE?
OH, NO!
WHAT A MESS!
MY LUNCH IS RUINED!

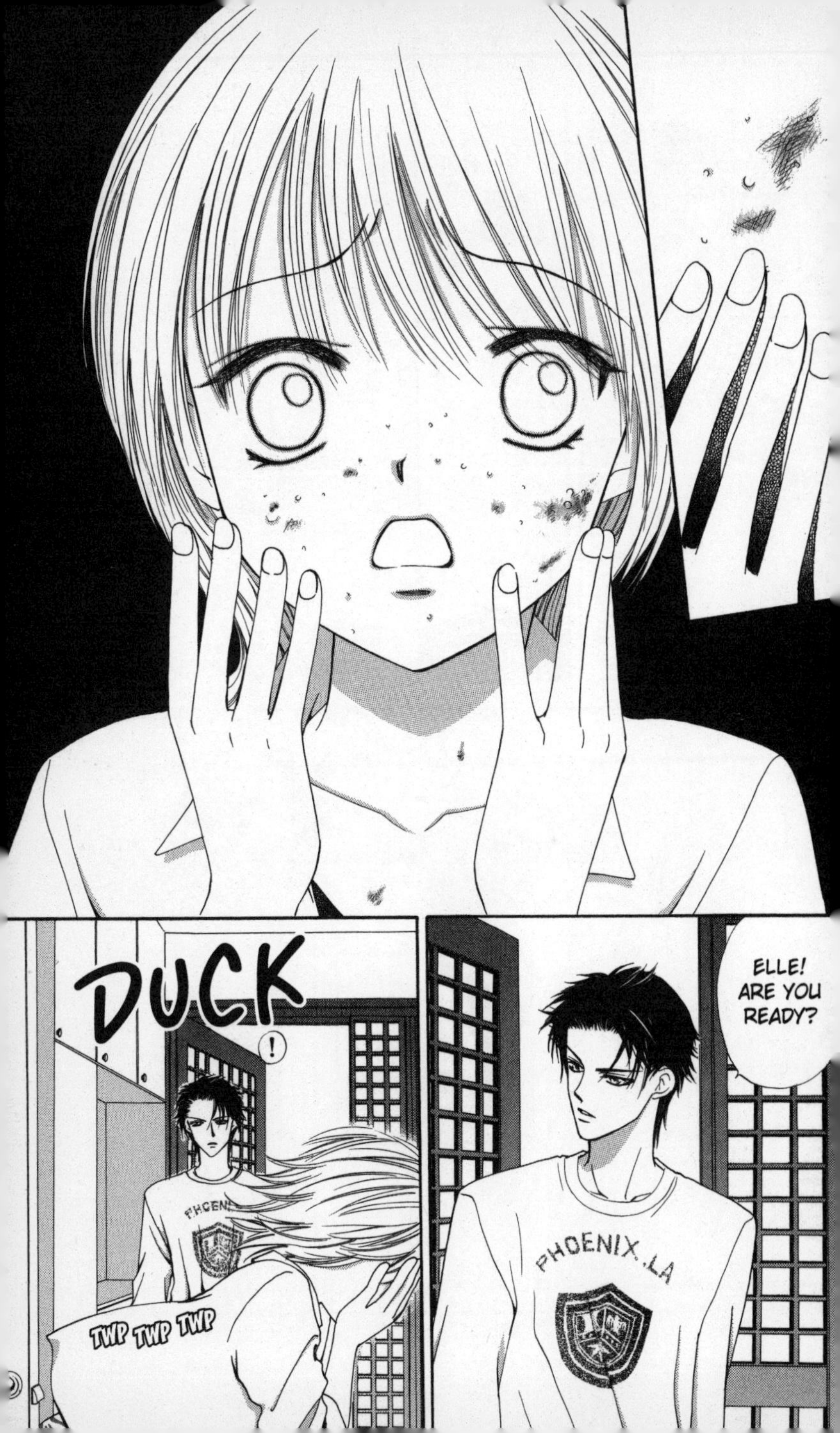
ELLE! ARE YOU READY?
DUCK
!
TWP TWP TWP
PHOENIX.LA

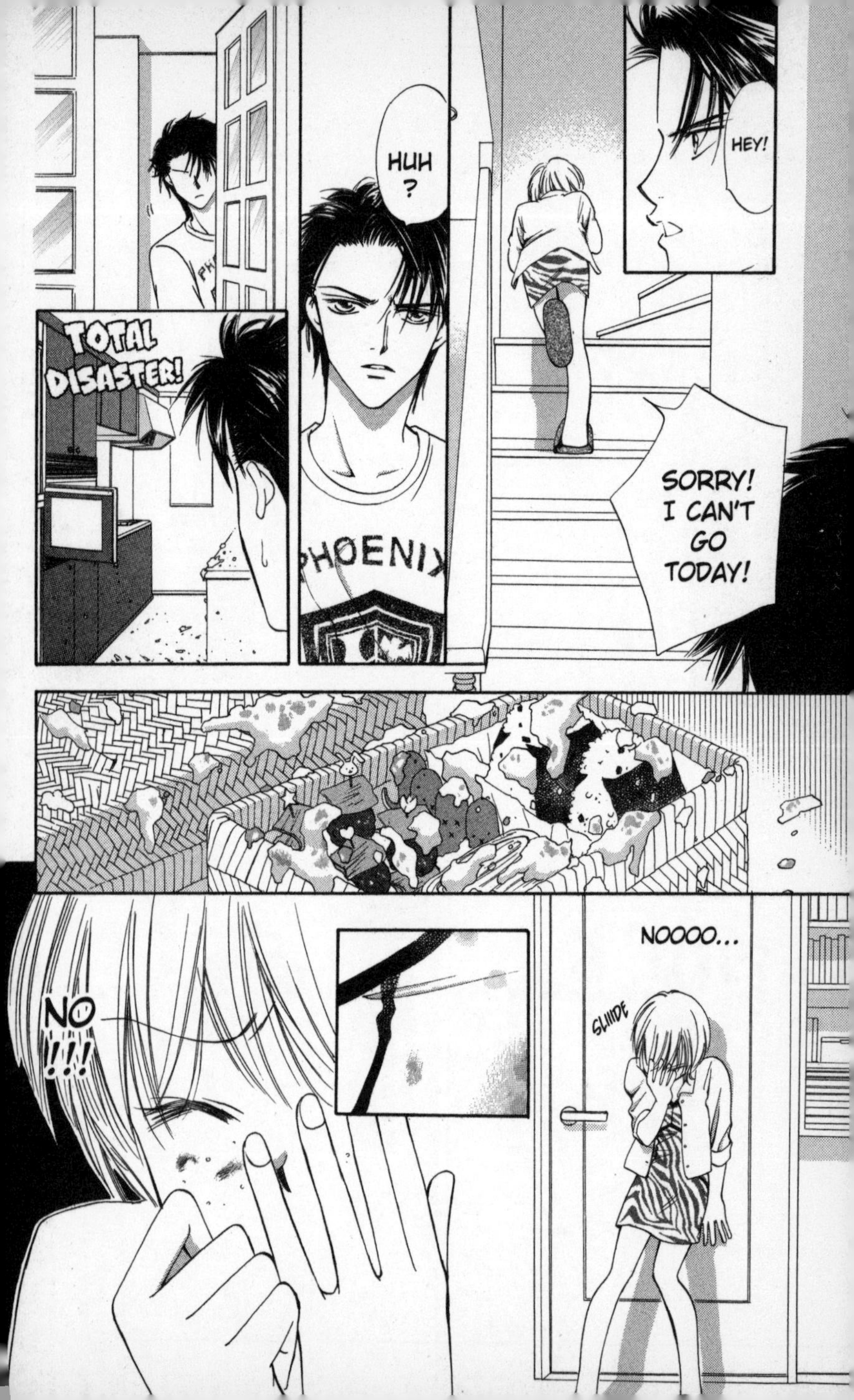
HEY!
SORRY! I CAN'T GO TODAY!
HUH ?
TOTAL DISASTER!
NOOOO...
SLIIDE
NO !!!

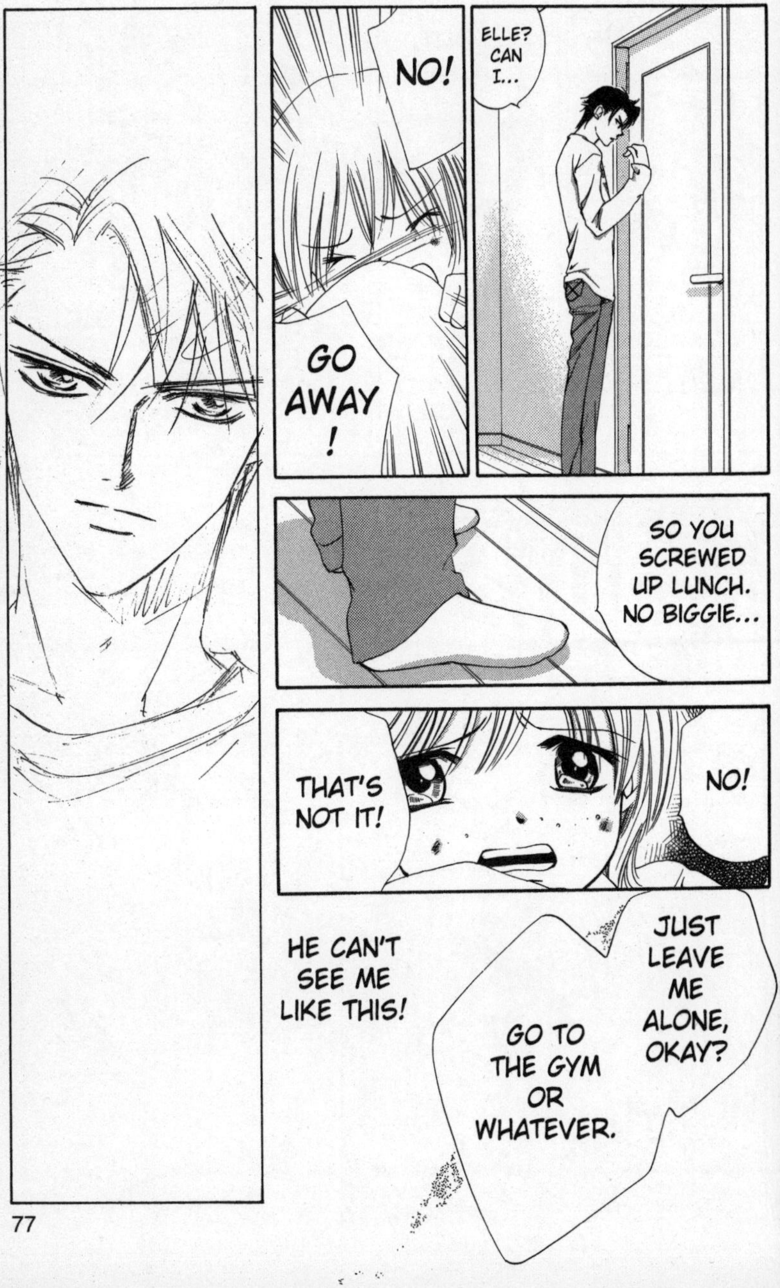
ELLE? CAN I...
NO!
GO AWAY!
SO YOU SCREWED UP LUNCH. NO BIGGIE...
NO!
THAT'S NOT IT!
JUST LEAVE ME ALONE, OKAY?
GO TO THE GYM OR WHATEVER.
HE CAN'T SEE ME LIKE THIS!

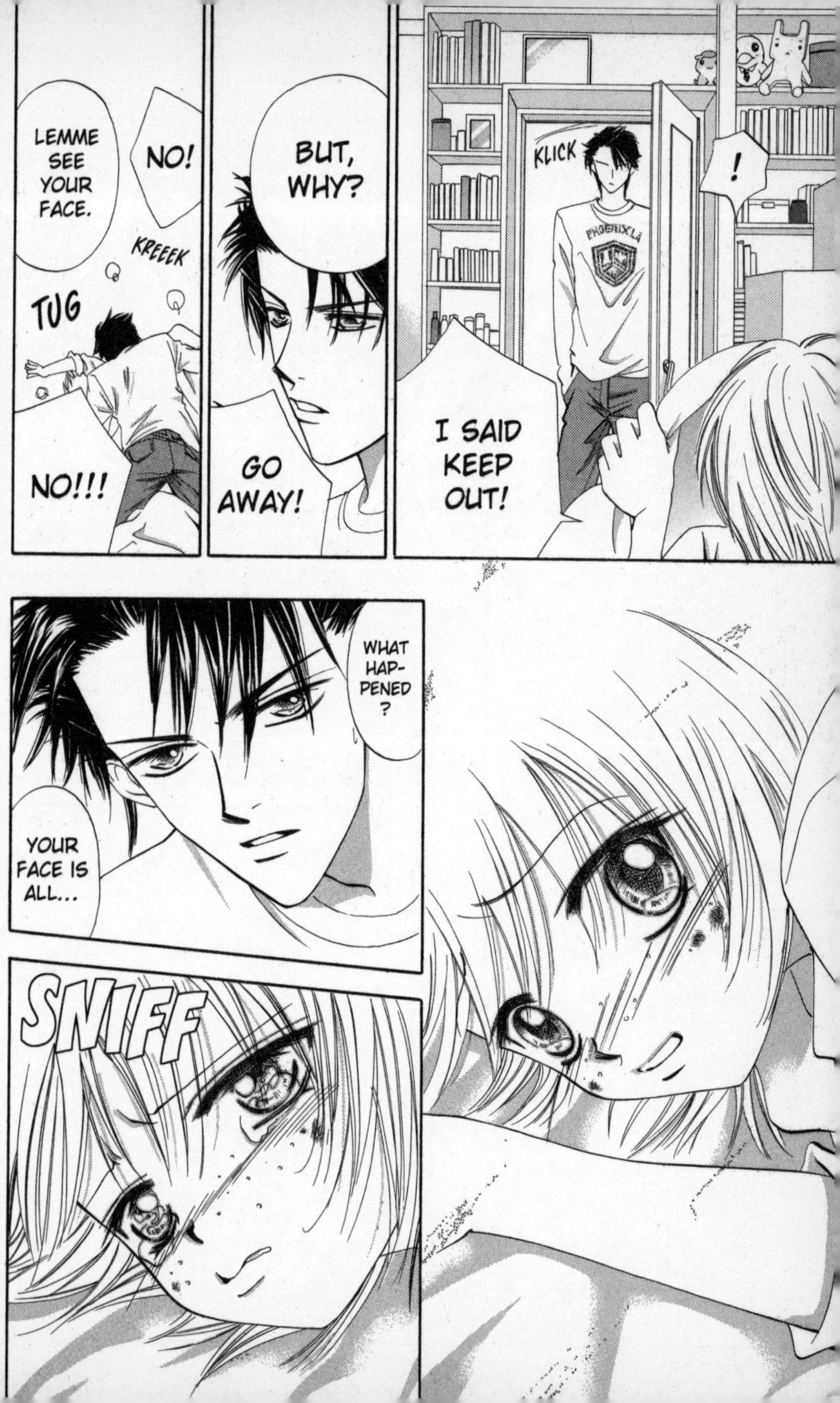
!
KLICK
I SAID KEEP OUT!
BUT, WHY?
GO AWAY!
LEMME SEE YOUR FACE.
NO!
KREEEK
TUG
NO!!!
WHAT HAP-PENED?
YOUR FACE IS ALL...
SNIFF

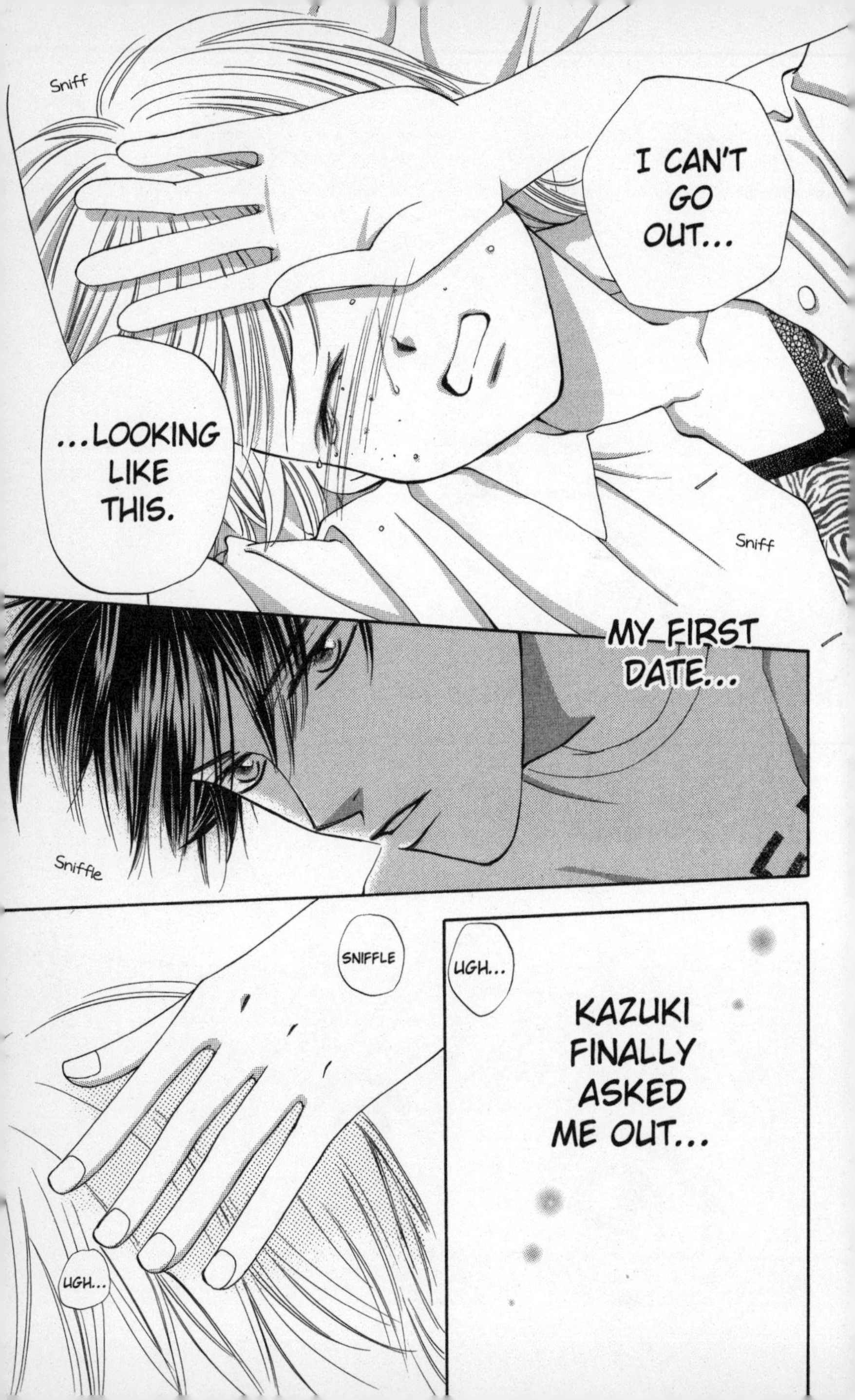
I CAN'T GO OUT...
Sniff
...LOOKING LIKE THIS.
Sniff
MY FIRST DATE...
Sniffle
UGH...
KAZUKI FINALLY ASKED ME OUT...
SNIFFLE
UGH...

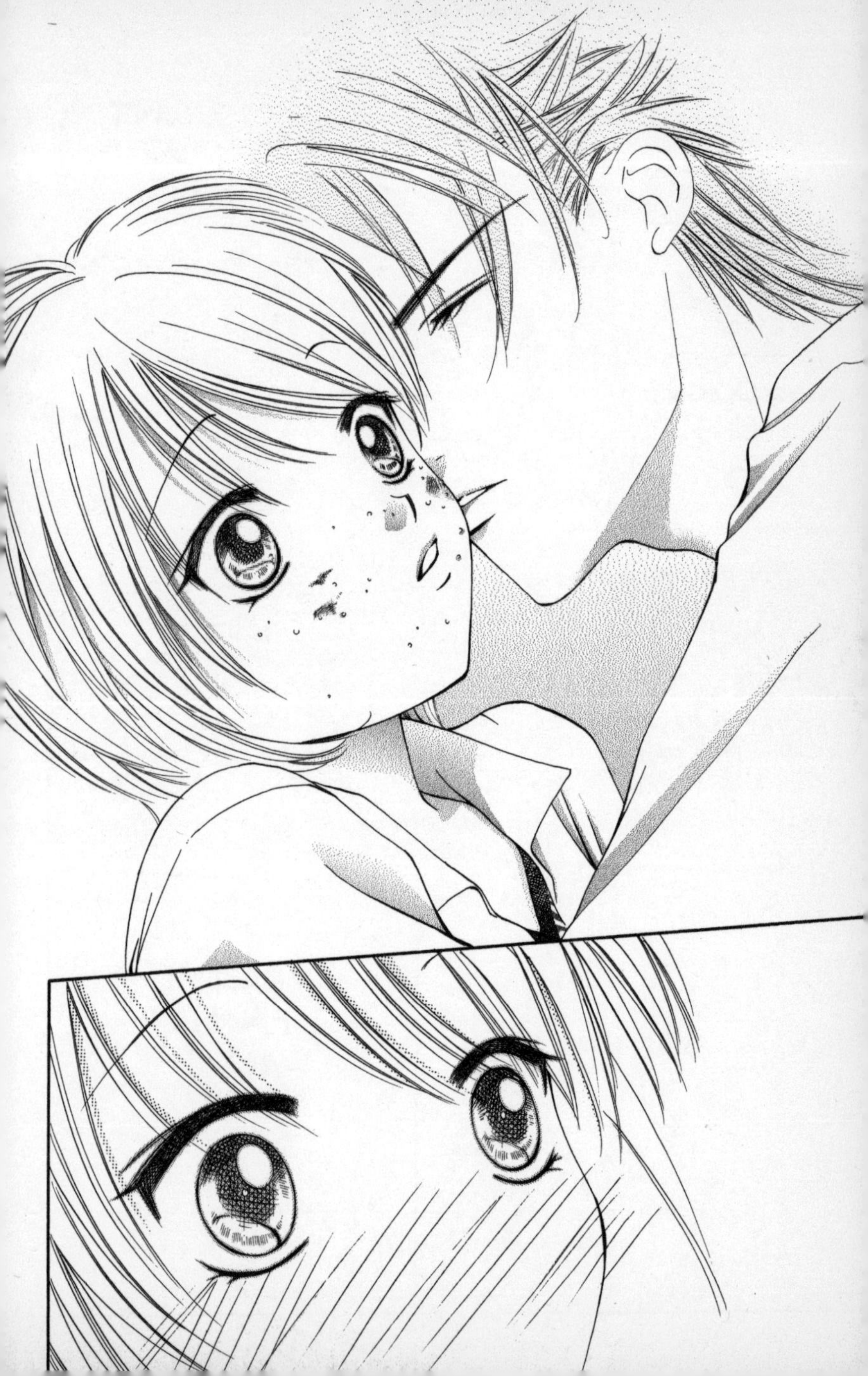

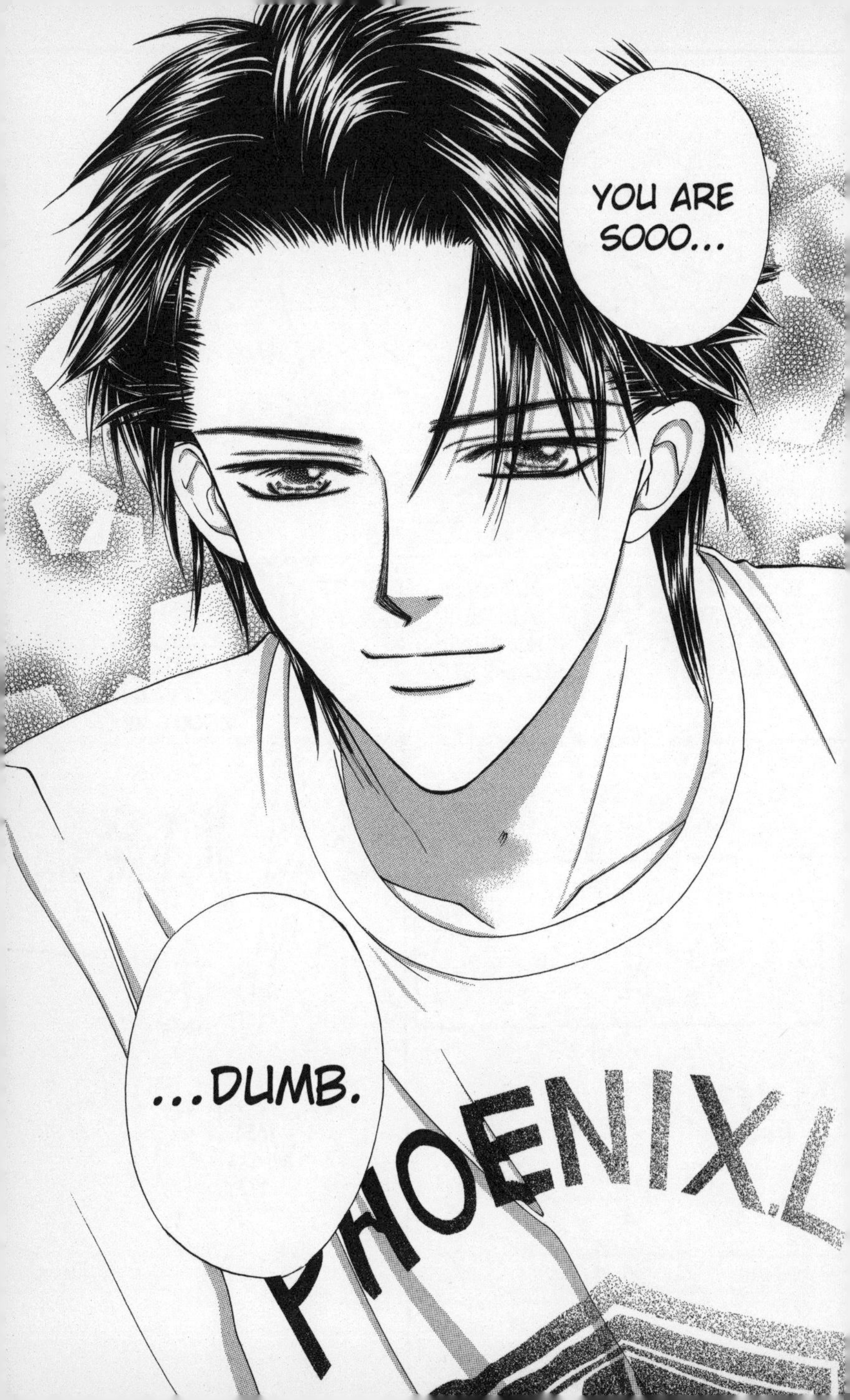
YOU ARE SOOO...
...DUMB.
PHOENIX.L

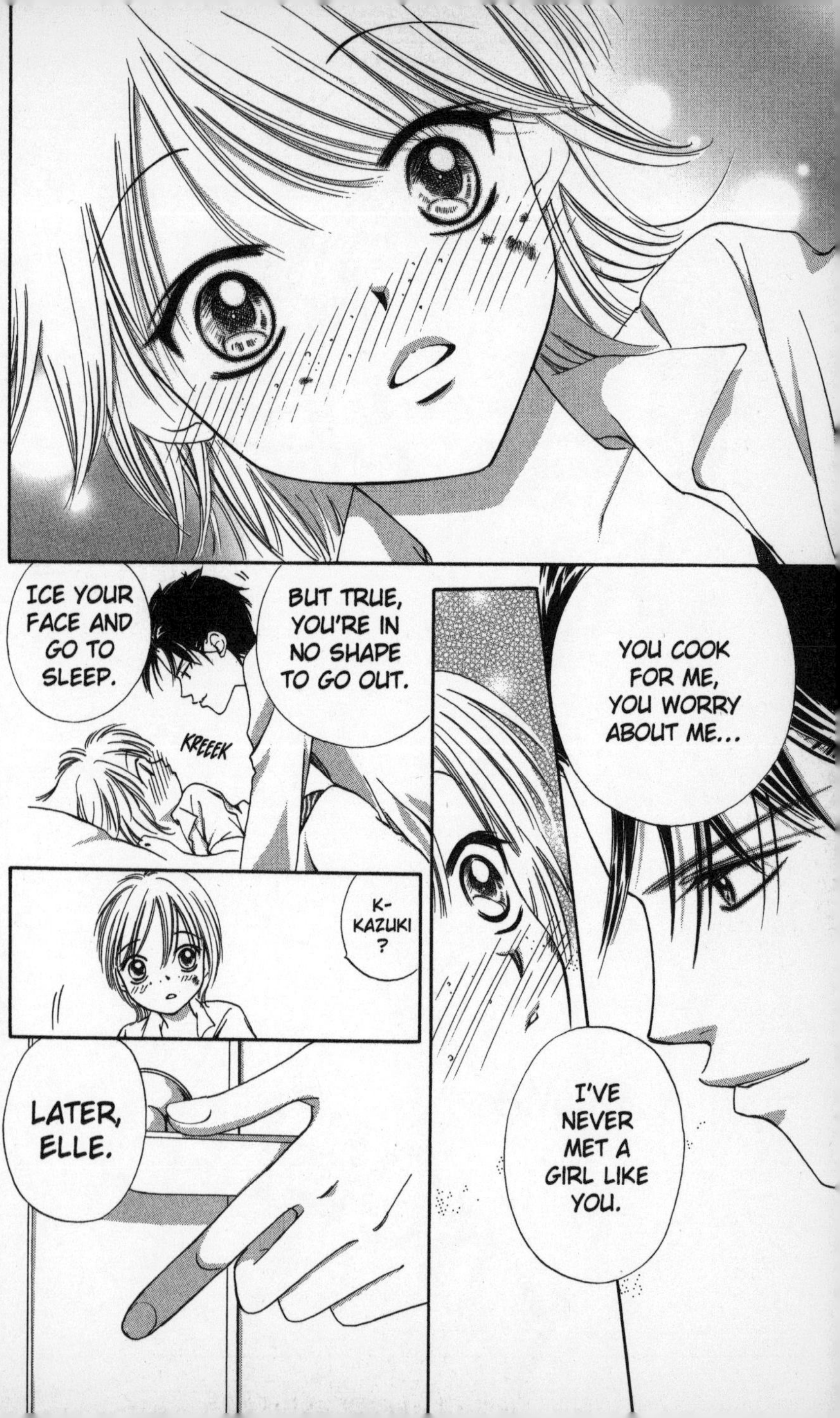
YOU COOK FOR ME, YOU WORRY ABOUT ME...
I'VE NEVER MET A GIRL LIKE YOU.
BUT TRUE, YOU'RE IN NO SHAPE TO GO OUT.
ICE YOUR FACE AND GO TO SLEEP.
KREEEK
K-KAZUKI?
LATER, ELLE.

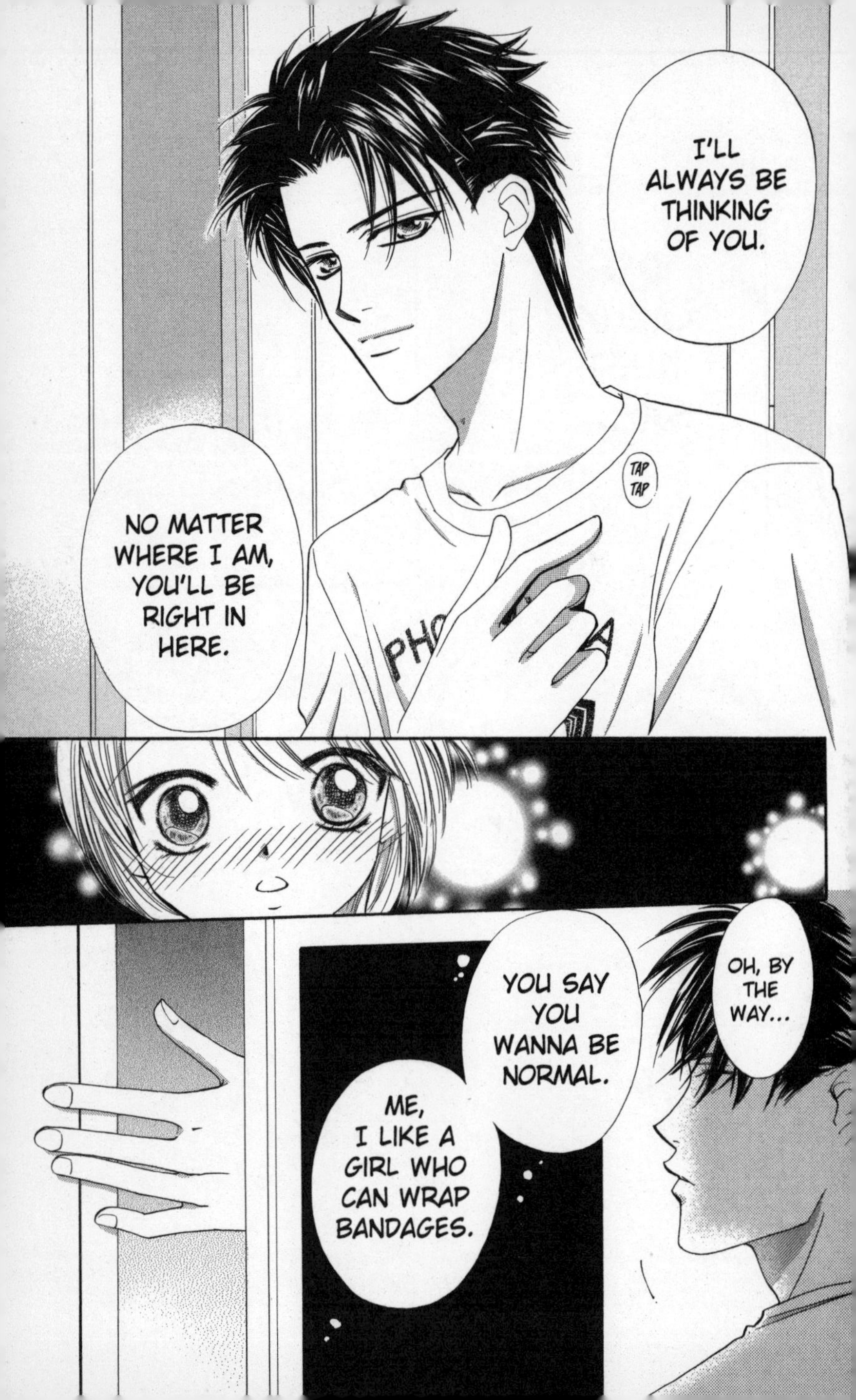
I'LL ALWAYS BE THINKING OF YOU.
TAP TAP
NO MATTER WHERE I AM, YOU'LL BE RIGHT IN HERE.
OH, BY THE WAY...
YOU SAY YOU WANNA BE NORMAL.
ME, I LIKE A GIRL WHO CAN WRAP BANDAGES.

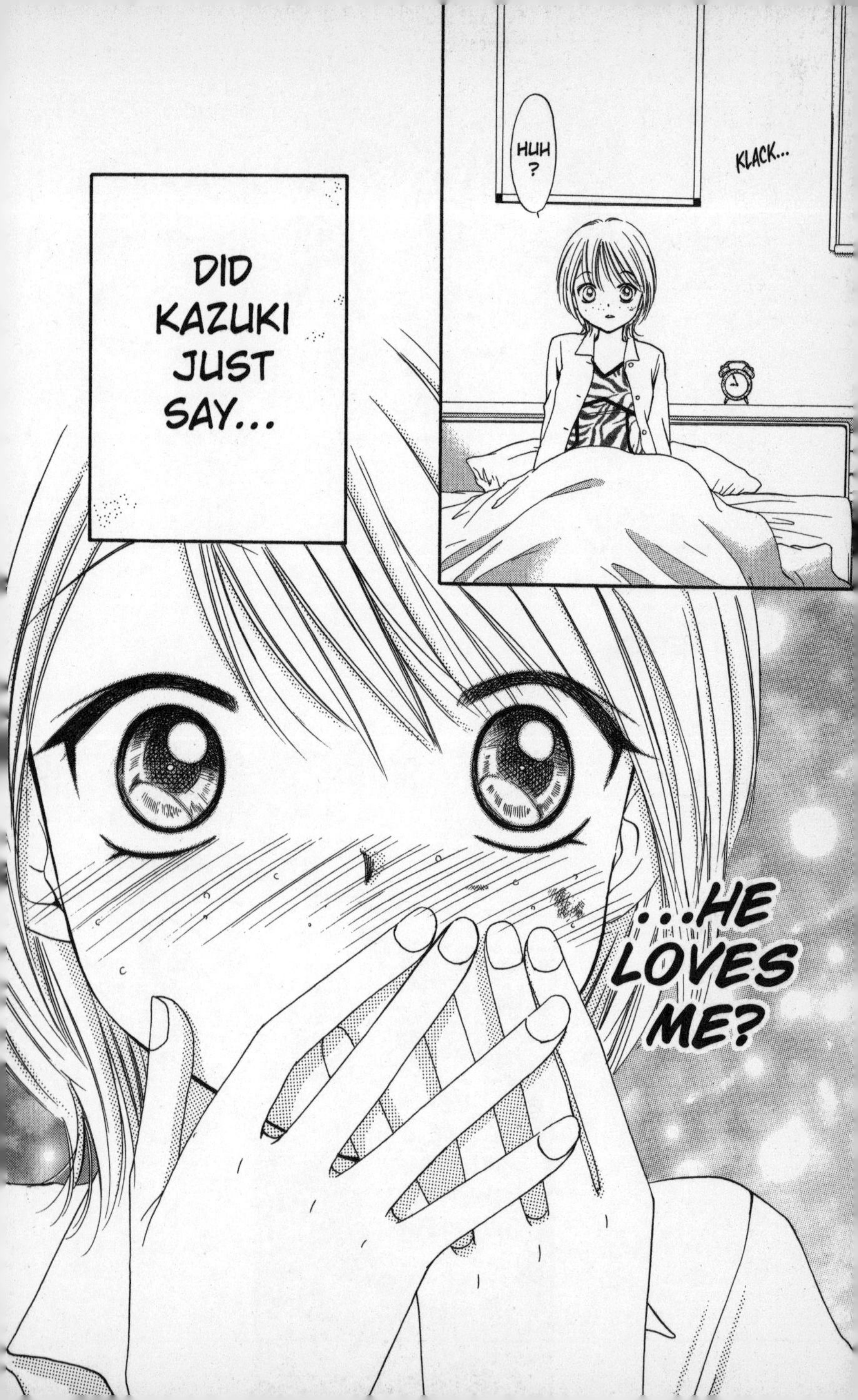
KLACK...
HUH?
DID KAZUKI JUST SAY...
...HE LOVES ME?

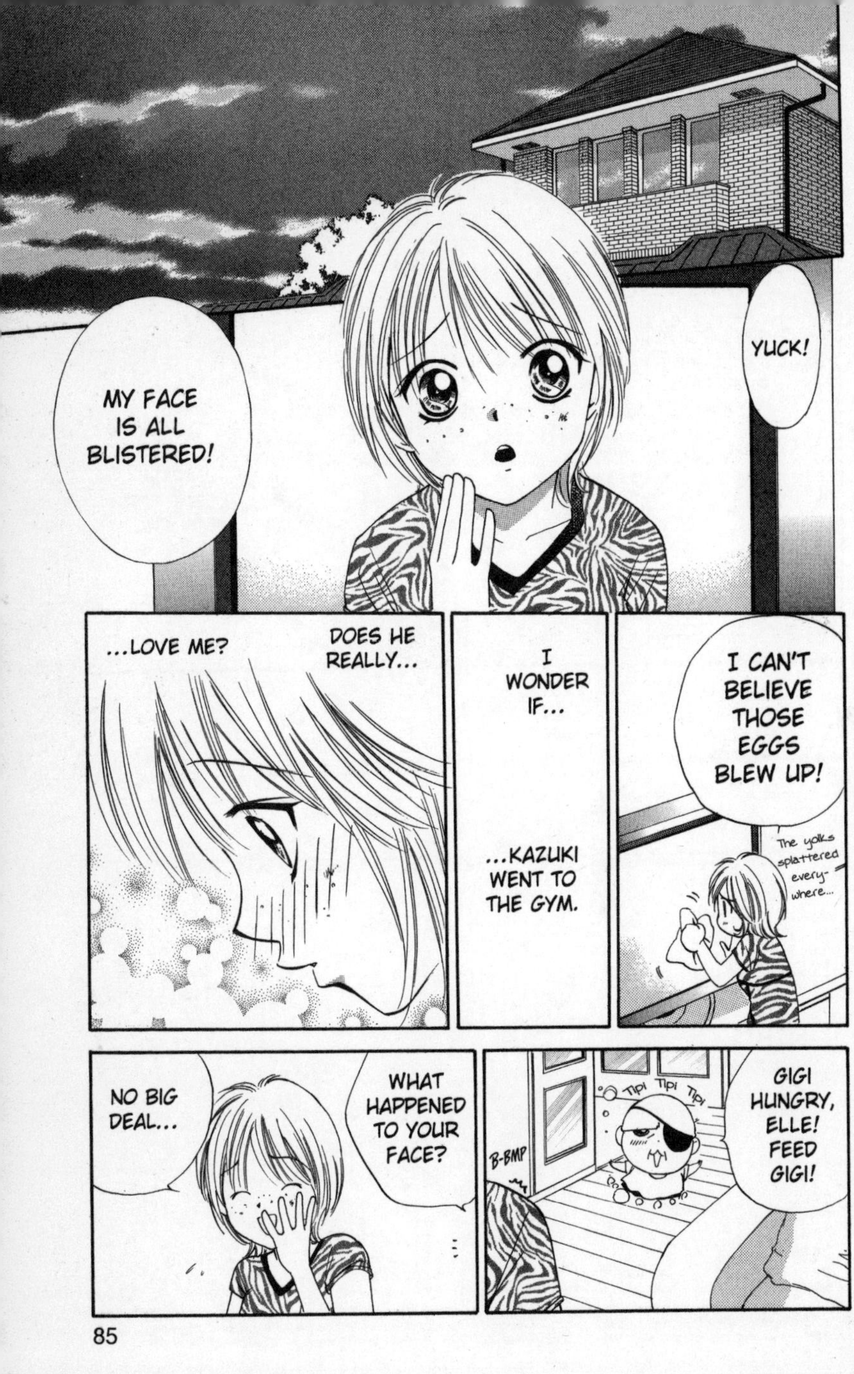
YUCK!
MY FACE IS ALL BLISTERED!
I CAN'T BELIEVE THOSE EGGS BLEW UP!
The yolks splattered every-where...
I WONDER IF...
...KAZUKI WENT TO THE GYM.
DOES HE REALLY...
...LOVE ME?
GIGI HUNGRY, ELLE! FEED GIGI!
Tipi Tipi Tipi
B-BMP
WHAT HAPPENED TO YOUR FACE?
NO BIG DEAL...

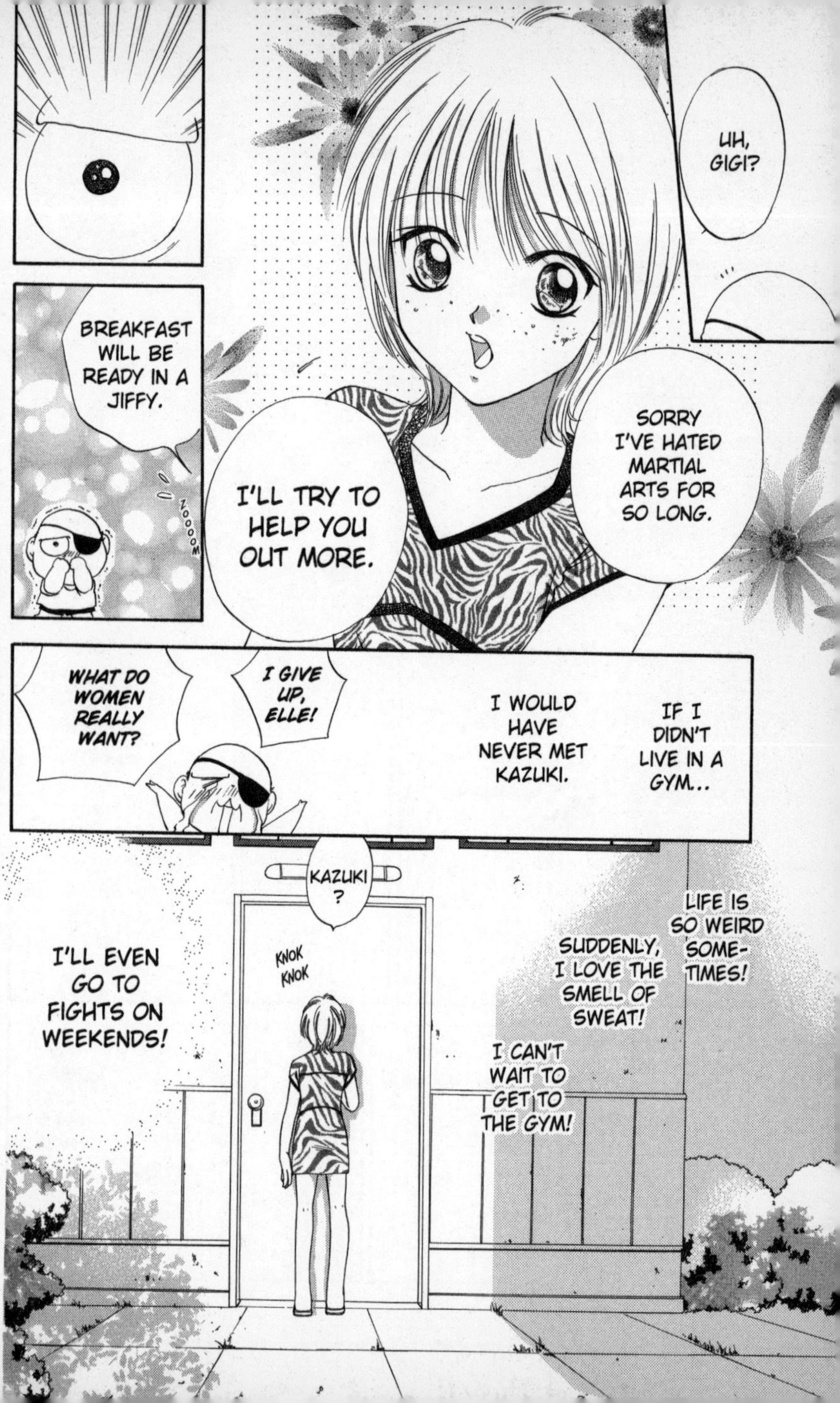
UH, GIGI?
SORRY I'VE HATED MARTIAL ARTS FOR SO LONG.
I'LL TRY TO HELP YOU OUT MORE.
BREAKFAST WILL BE READY IN A JIFFY.
ZOOOOM
IF I DIDN'T LIVE IN A GYM...
I WOULD HAVE NEVER MET KAZUKI.
I GIVE UP, ELLE!
WHAT DO WOMEN REALLY WANT?
KAZUKI?
LIFE IS SO WEIRD SOME-TIMES!
SUDDENLY, I LOVE THE SMELL OF SWEAT!
I CAN'T WAIT TO GET TO THE GYM!
KNOK KNOK
I'LL EVEN GO TO FIGHTS ON WEEKENDS!

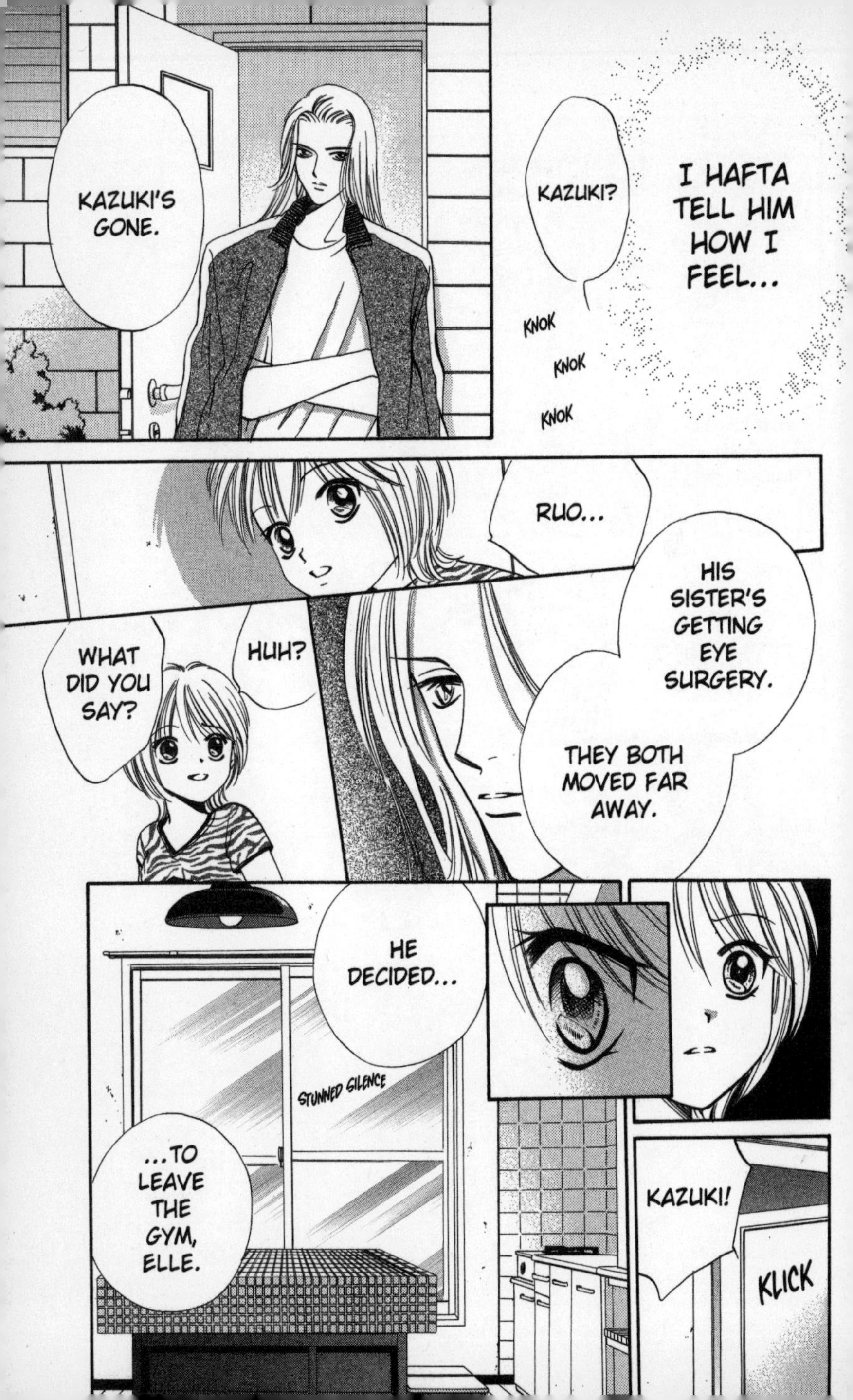
I HAFTA TELL HIM HOW I FEEL...
KAZUKI?
KNOK
KNOK
KNOK
KAZUKI'S GONE.
RUO...
HIS SISTER'S GETTING EYE SURGERY.
THEY BOTH MOVED FAR AWAY.
HUH?
WHAT DID YOU SAY?
HE DECIDED...
...TO LEAVE THE GYM, ELLE.
STUNNED SILENCE
KAZUKI!
KLICK

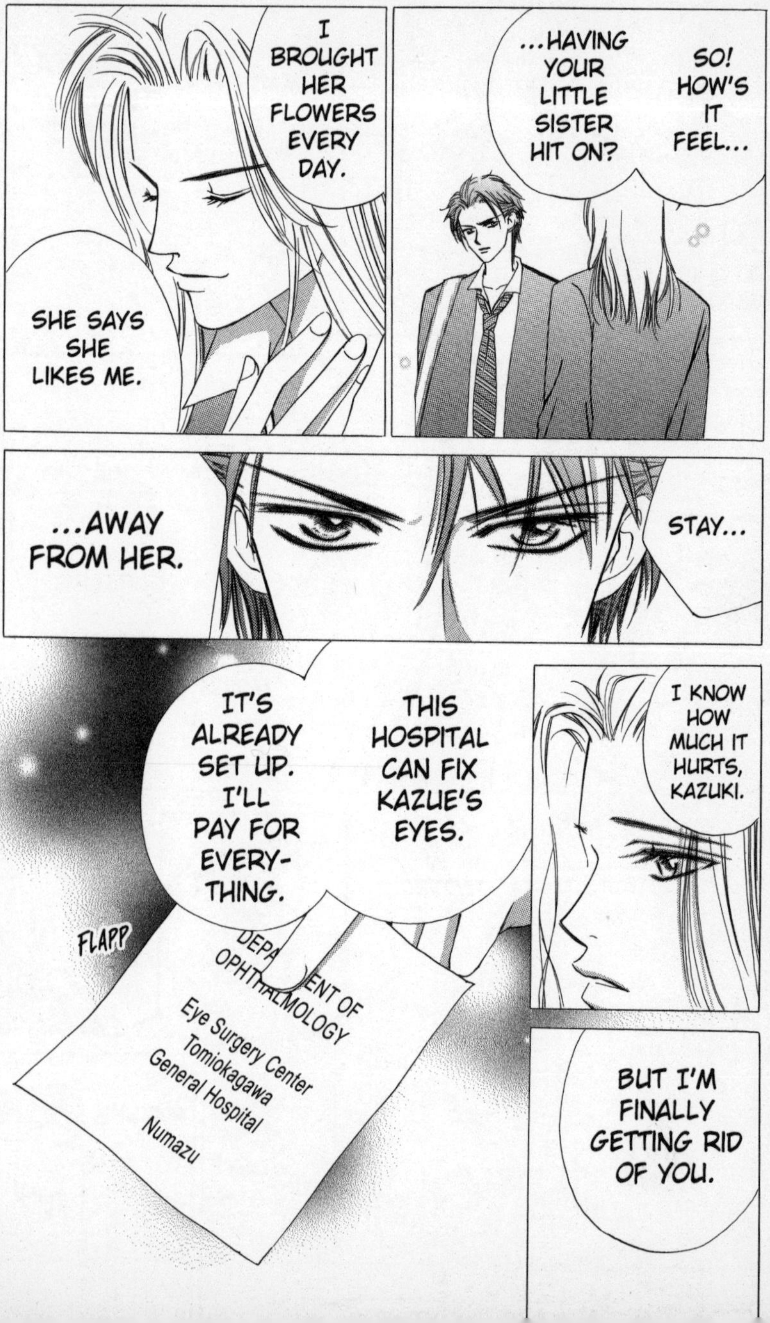
SO! HOW'S IT FEEL...
...HAVING YOUR LITTLE SISTER HIT ON?
I BROUGHT HER FLOWERS EVERY DAY.
SHE SAYS SHE LIKES ME.
STAY...
...AWAY FROM HER.
I KNOW HOW MUCH IT HURTS, KAZUKI.
BUT I'M FINALLY GETTING RID OF YOU.
THIS HOSPITAL CAN FIX KAZUE'S EYES.
IT'S ALREADY SET UP. I'LL PAY FOR EVERY-THING.
FLAPP
DEPA...ENT OF OPHTHALMOLOGY
Eye Surgery Center
Tomiokagawa
General Hospital
Numazu

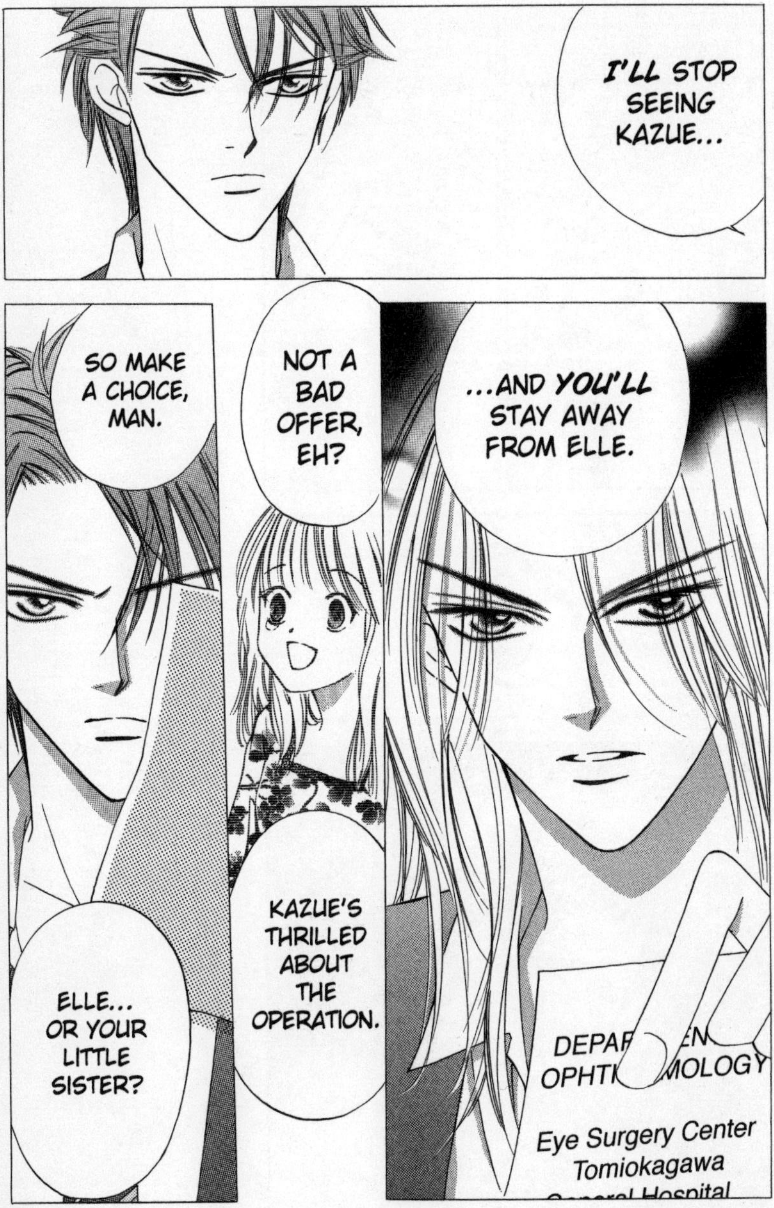
I'LL STOP SEEING KAZUE...
...AND *YOU'LL* STAY AWAY FROM ELLE.
Eye Surgery Center
Tomiokagawa
NOT A BAD OFFER, EH?
KAZUE'S THRILLED ABOUT THE OPERATION.
SO MAKE A CHOICE, MAN.
ELLE... OR YOUR LITTLE SISTER?

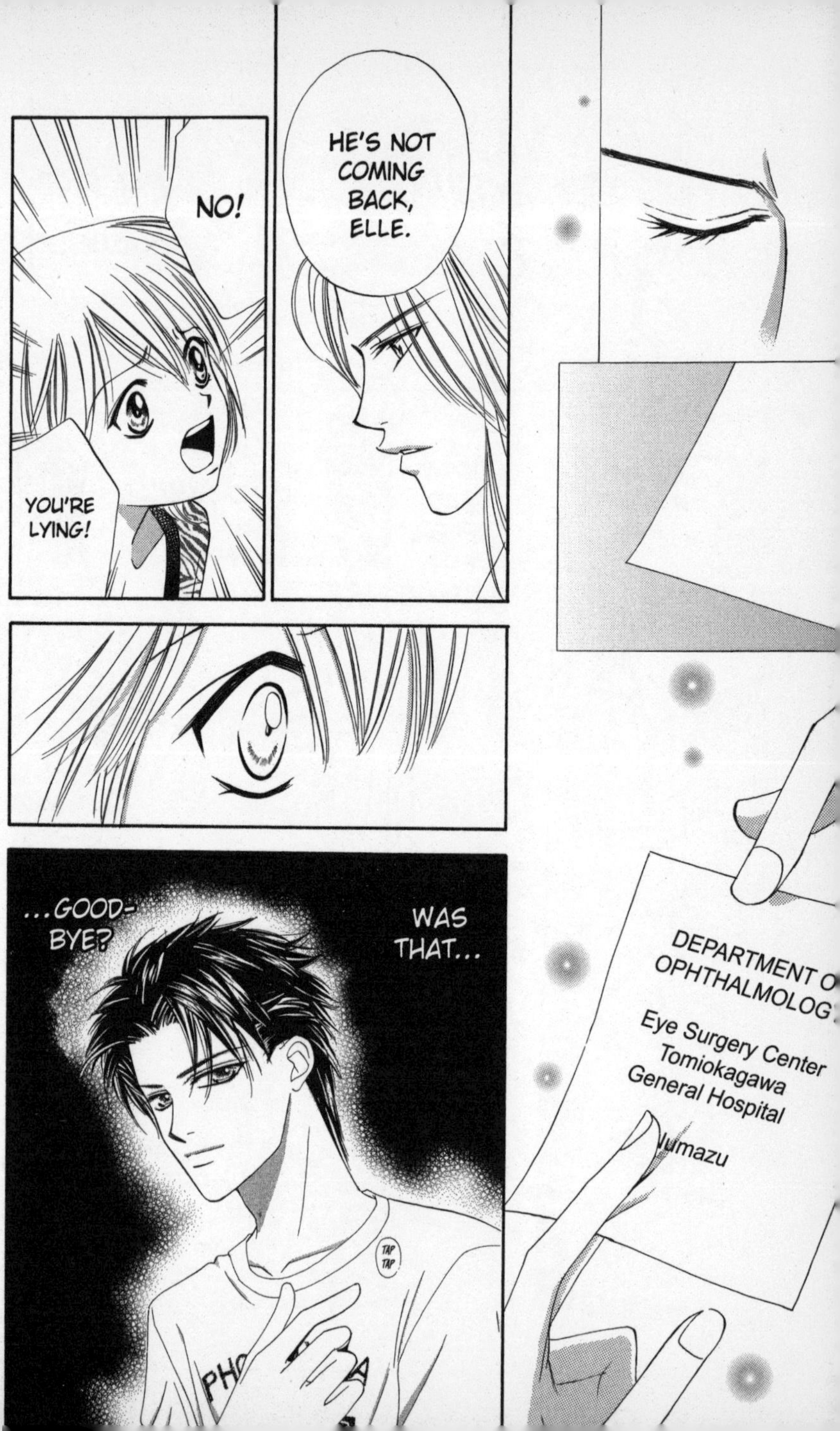
DEPARTMENT O
OPHTHALMOLOG
Eye Surgery Center
Tomiokagawa
General Hospital
umazu
HE'S NOT COMING BACK, ELLE.
NO!
YOU'RE LYING!
WAS THAT...
...GOOD-BYE?
TAP TAP

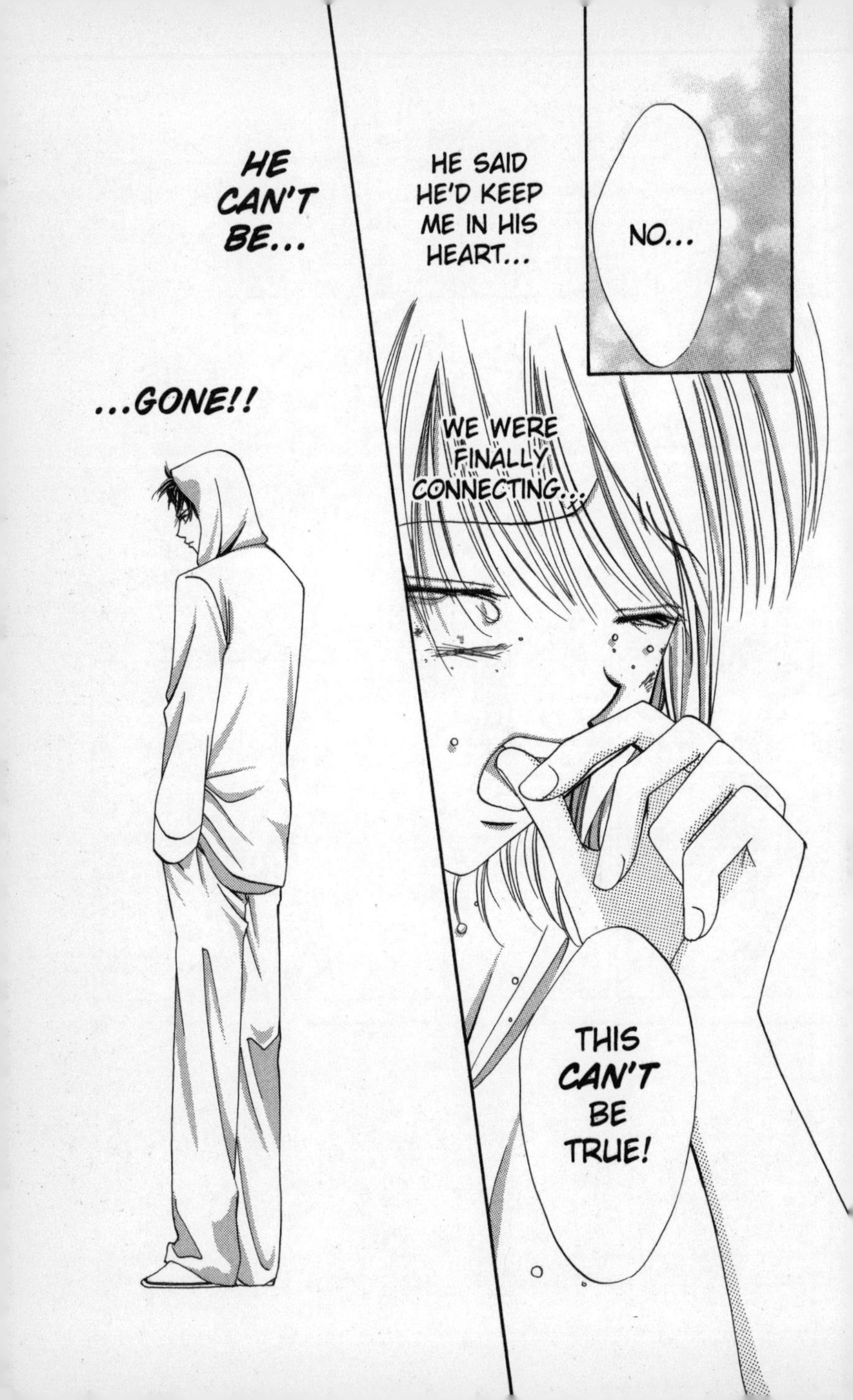
NO...
HE SAID HE'D KEEP ME IN HIS HEART...
WE WERE FINALLY CONNECTING...
THIS CAN'T BE TRUE!
HE CAN'T BE...
...GONE!!

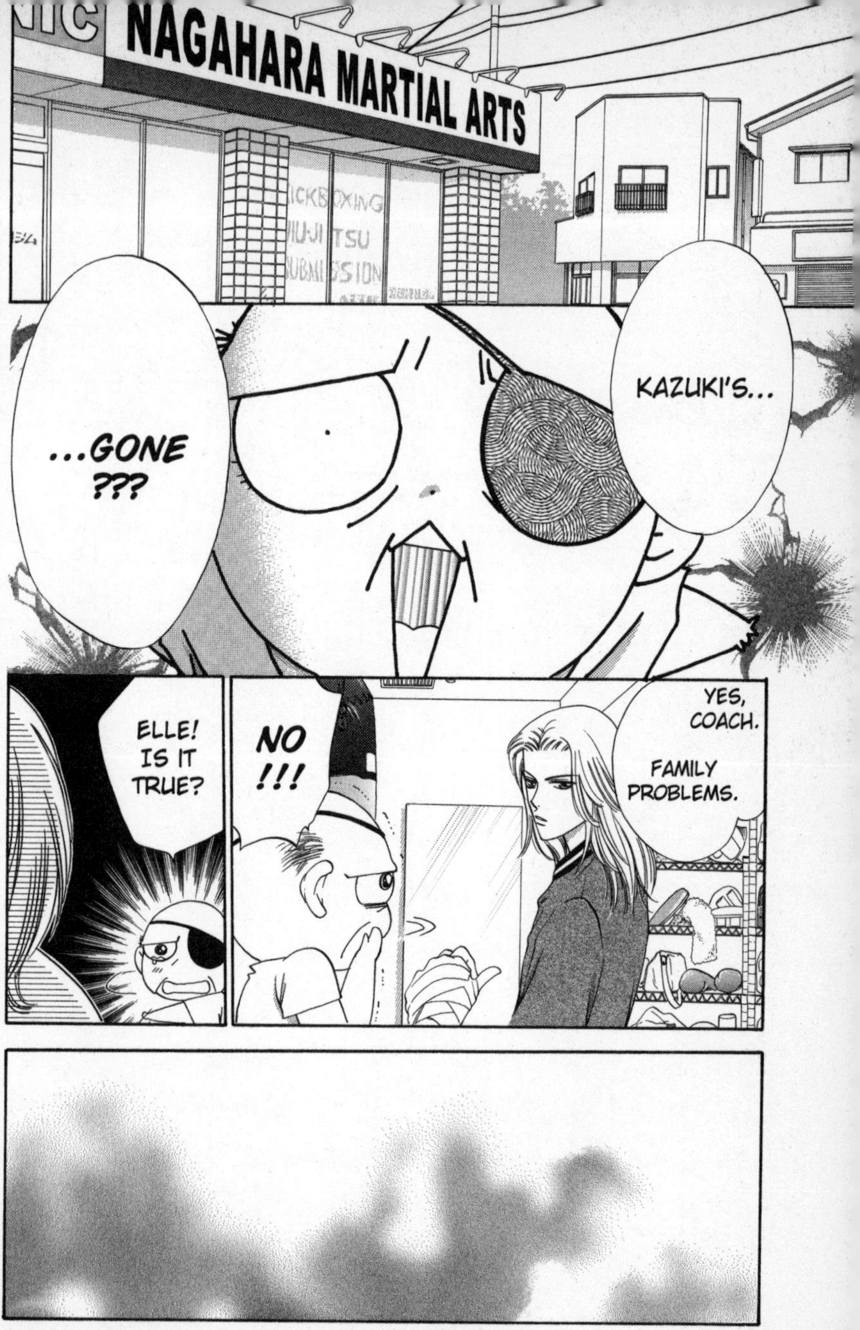

NAGAHARA MARTIAL ARTS
KAZUKI'S...
...GONE ???
YES, COACH.
FAMILY PROBLEMS.
NO !!!
ELLE! IS IT TRUE?

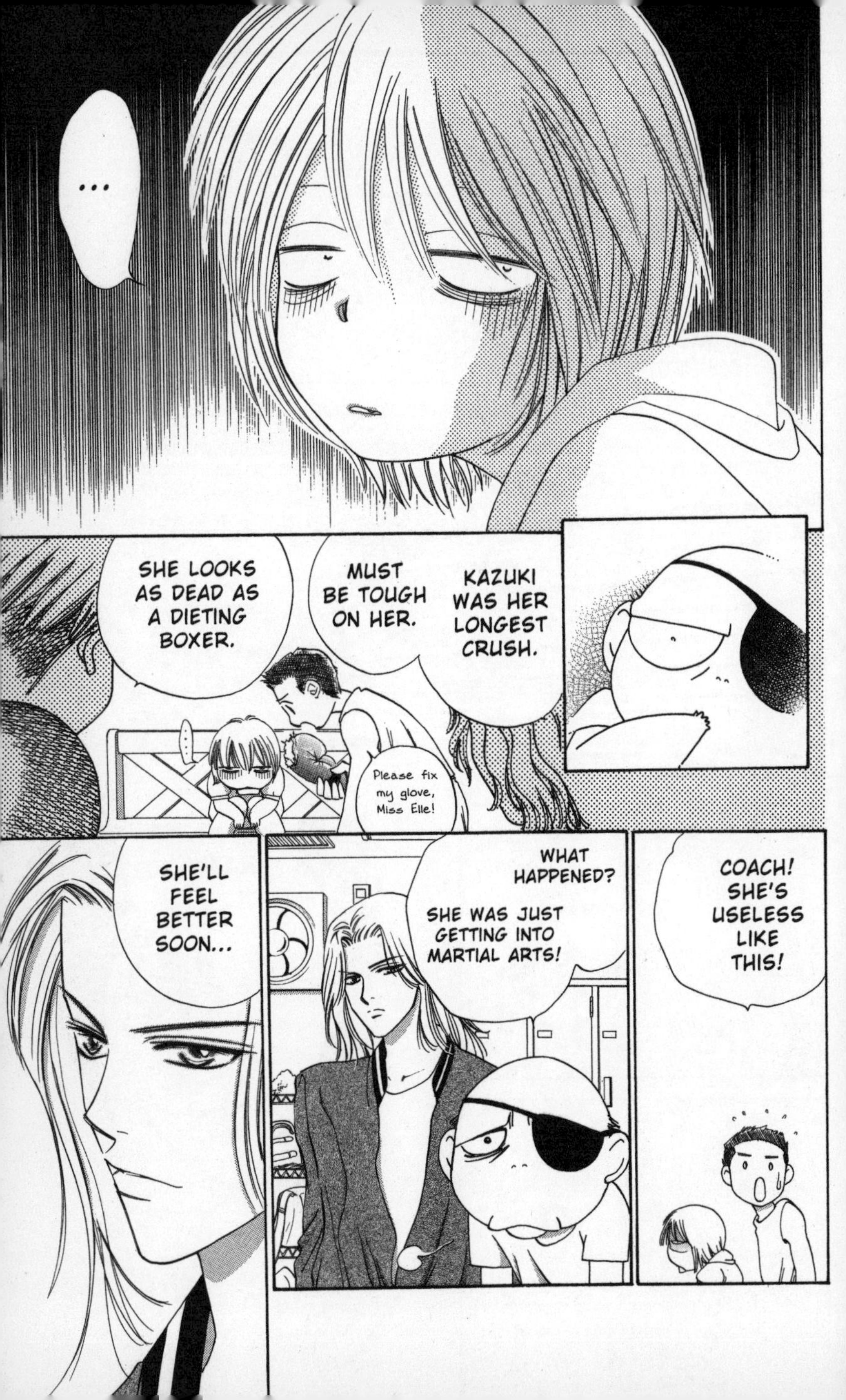
...
KAZUKI WAS HER LONGEST CRUSH.
MUST BE TOUGH ON HER.
SHE LOOKS AS DEAD AS A DIETING BOXER.
...
Please fix my glove, Miss Elle!
COACH! SHE'S USELESS LIKE THIS!
WHAT HAPPENED?
SHE WAS JUST GETTING INTO MARTIAL ARTS!
SHE'LL FEEL BETTER SOON...

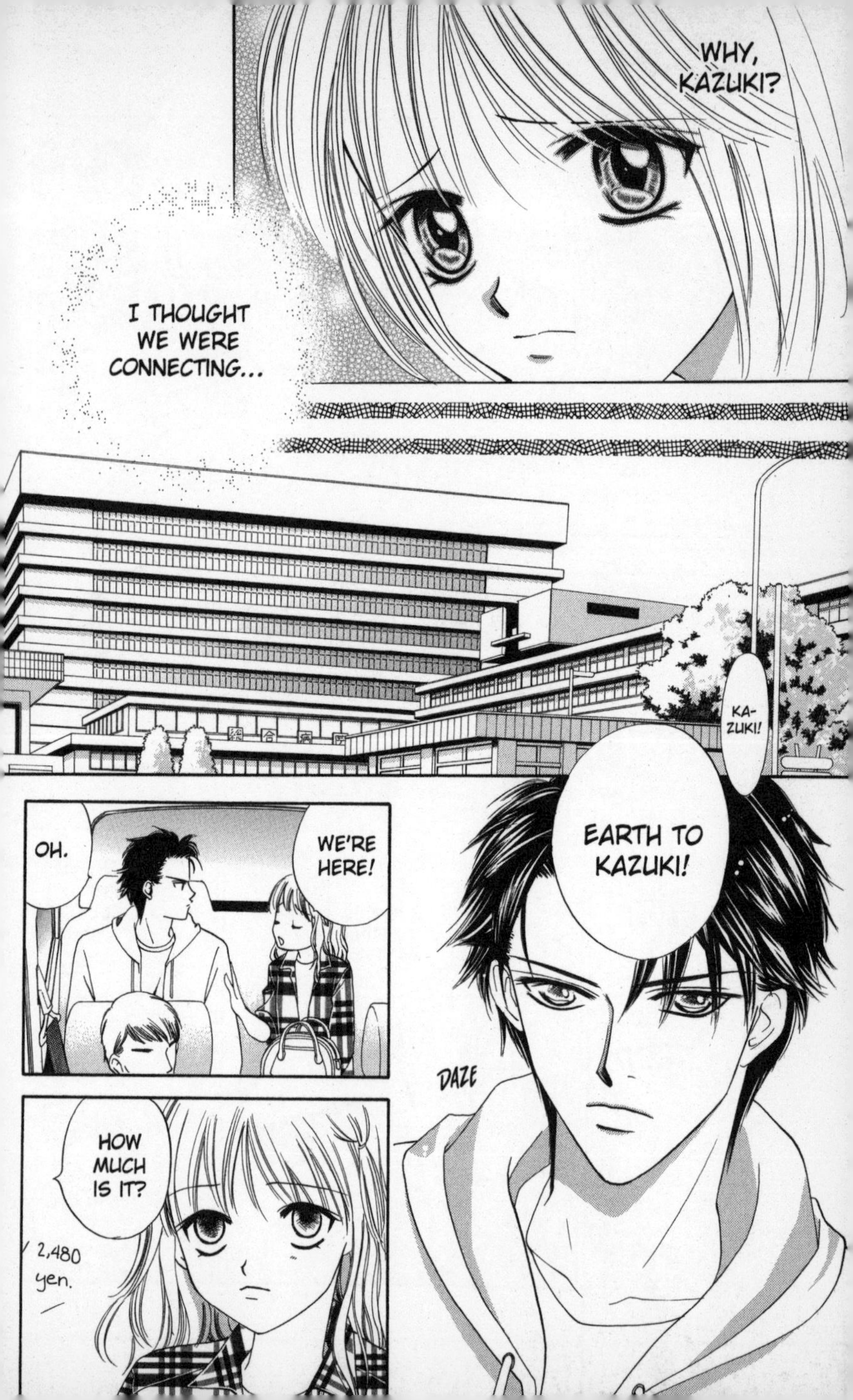
WHY, KAZUKI?
I THOUGHT WE WERE CONNECTING...
KA-ZUKI!
EARTH TO KAZUKI!
DAZE
WE'RE HERE!
OH.
HOW MUCH IS IT?
2,480 yen.

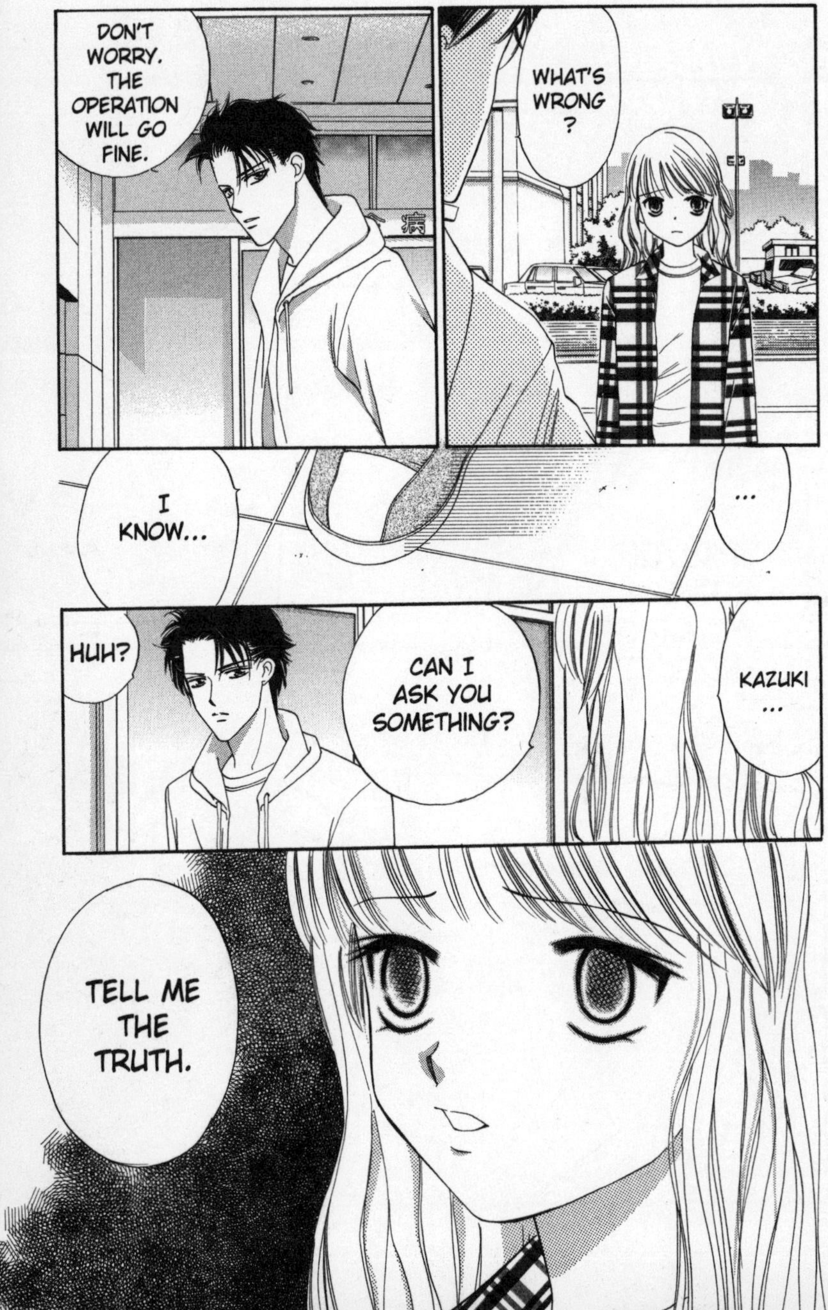
WHAT'S WRONG ?
DON'T WORRY. THE OPERATION WILL GO FINE.
...
I KNOW...
KAZUKI ...
CAN I ASK YOU SOMETHING?
HUH?
TELL ME THE TRUTH.

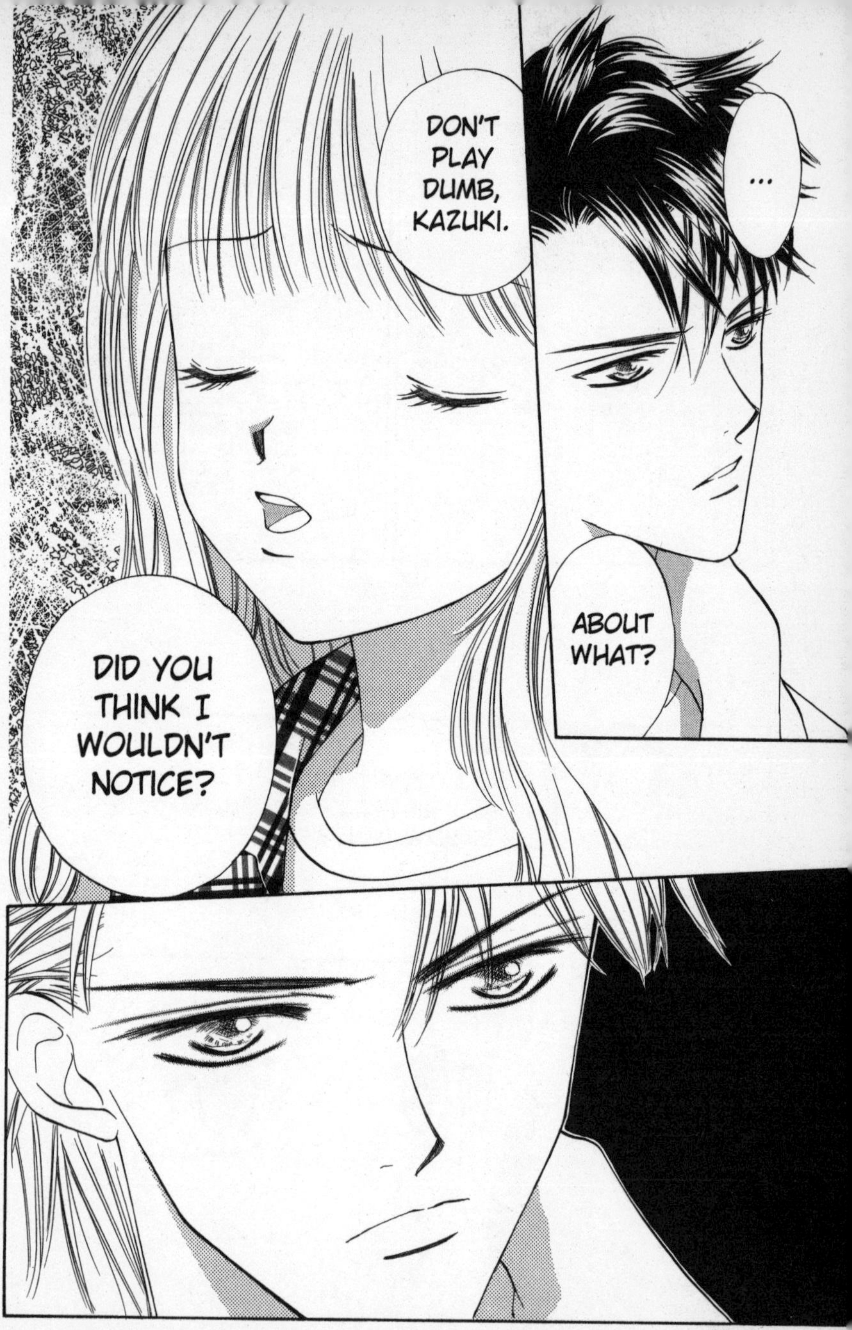
...
ABOUT WHAT?
DON'T PLAY DUMB, KAZUKI.
DID YOU THINK I WOULDN'T NOTICE?

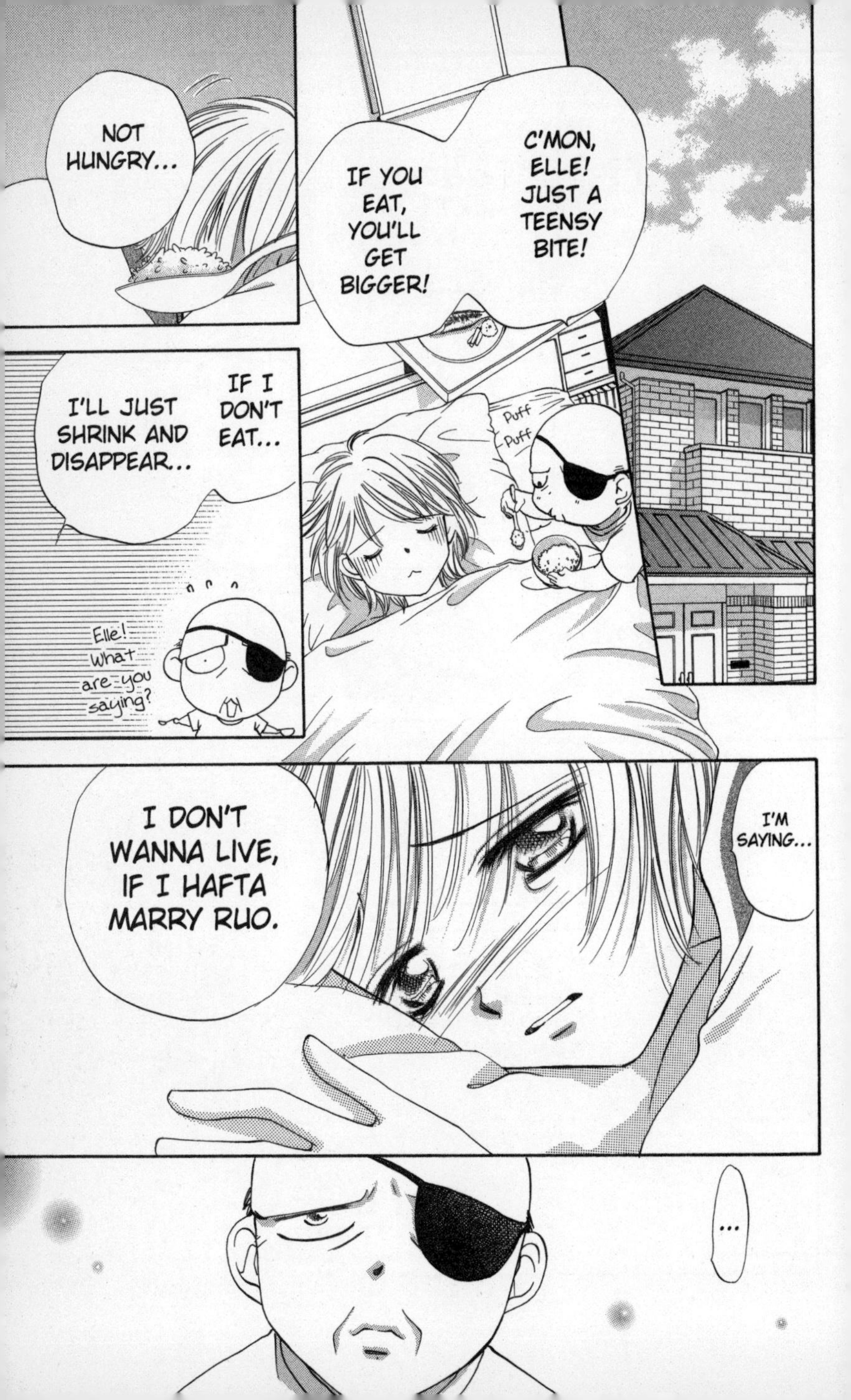
C'MON, ELLE! JUST A TEENSY BITE!
IF YOU EAT, YOU'LL GET BIGGER!
Puff Puff
NOT HUNGRY...
IF I DON'T EAT...
I'LL JUST SHRINK AND DISAPPEAR...
Elle! What are you saying?
I'M SAYING...
I DON'T WANNA LIVE, IF I HAFTA MARRY RUO.
...

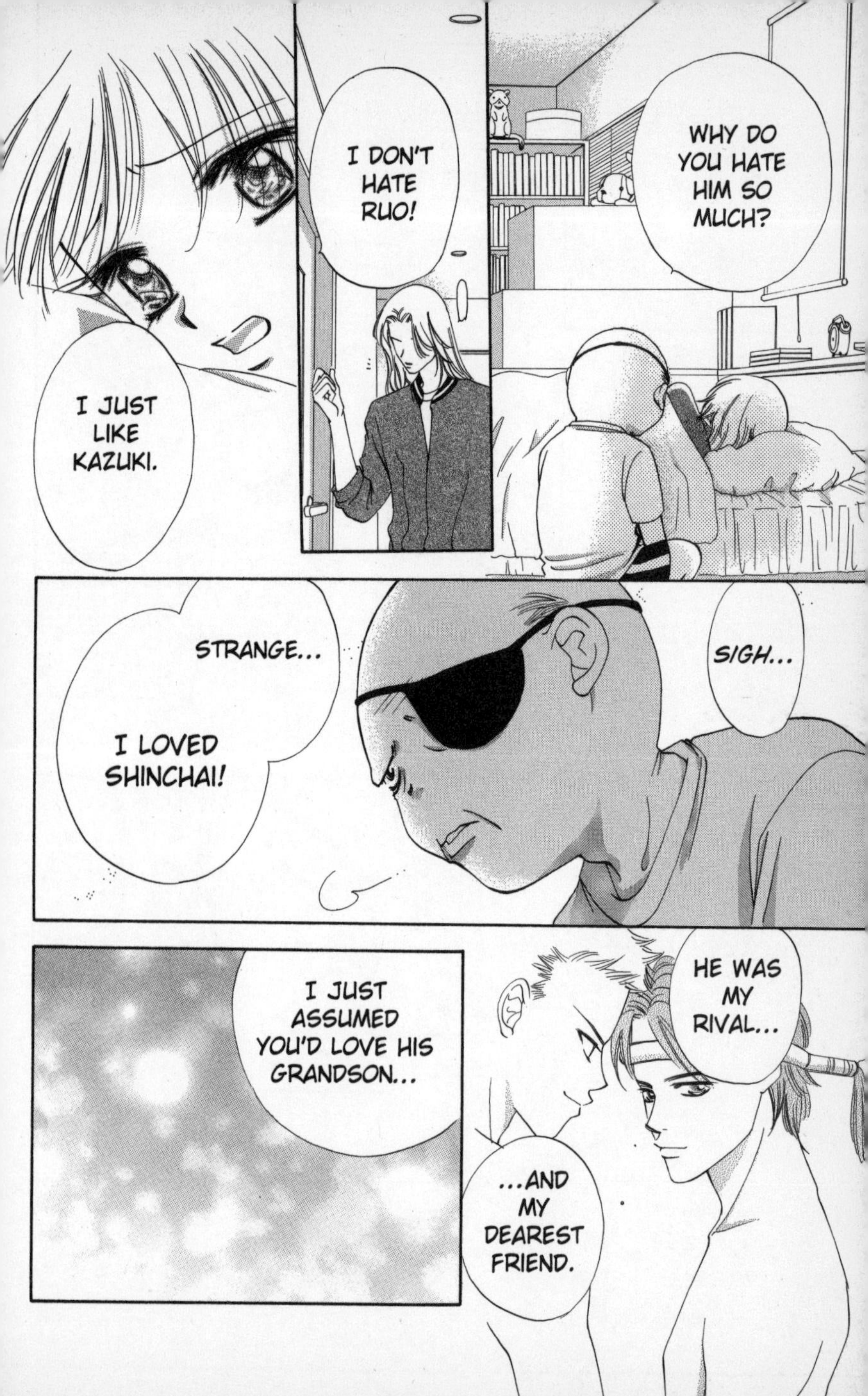
WHY DO YOU HATE HIM SO MUCH?
I DON'T HATE RUO!
I JUST LIKE KAZUKI.
SIGH...
STRANGE...
I LOVED SHINCHAI!
HE WAS MY RIVAL...
...AND MY DEAREST FRIEND.
I JUST ASSUMED YOU'D LOVE HIS GRANDSON...

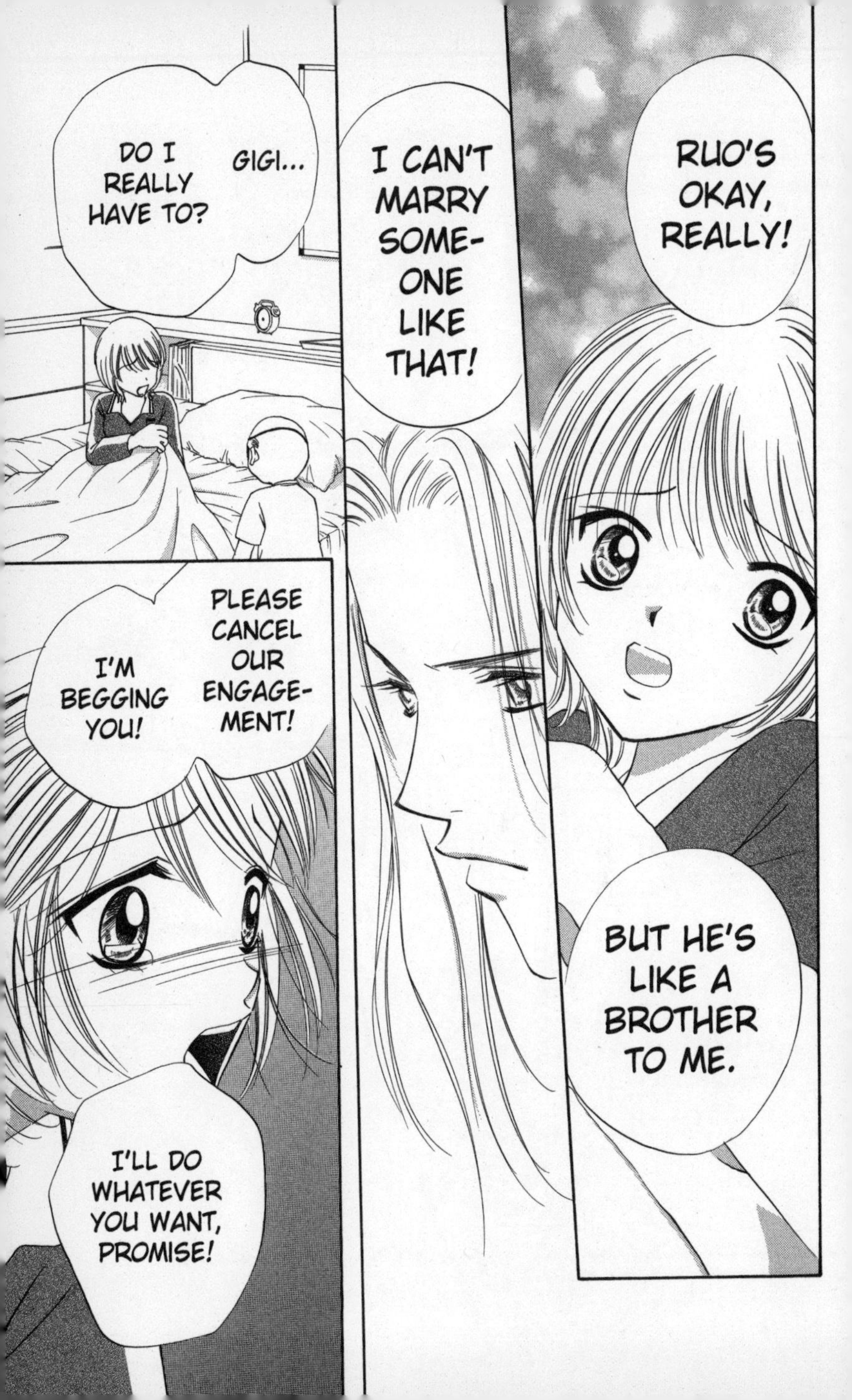
RUO'S OKAY, REALLY!
BUT HE'S LIKE A BROTHER TO ME.
I CAN'T MARRY SOME-ONE LIKE THAT!
GIGI...
DO I REALLY HAVE TO?
PLEASE CANCEL OUR ENGAGE-MENT!
I'M BEGGING YOU!
I'LL DO WHATEVER YOU WANT, PROMISE!

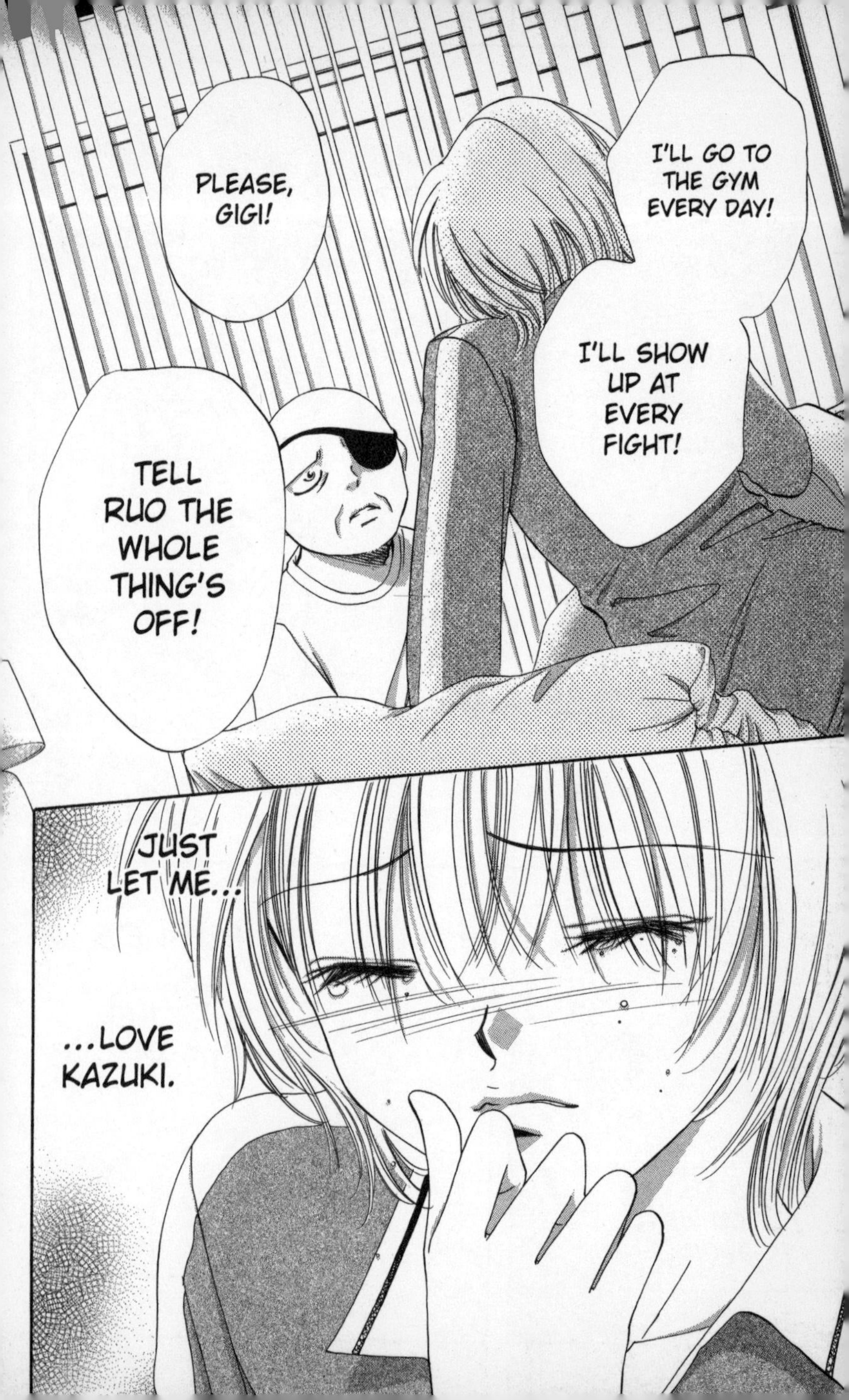
I'LL GO TO THE GYM EVERY DAY!
I'LL SHOW UP AT EVERY FIGHT!
PLEASE, GIGI!
TELL RUO THE WHOLE THING'S OFF!
JUST LET ME...
...LOVE KAZUKI.

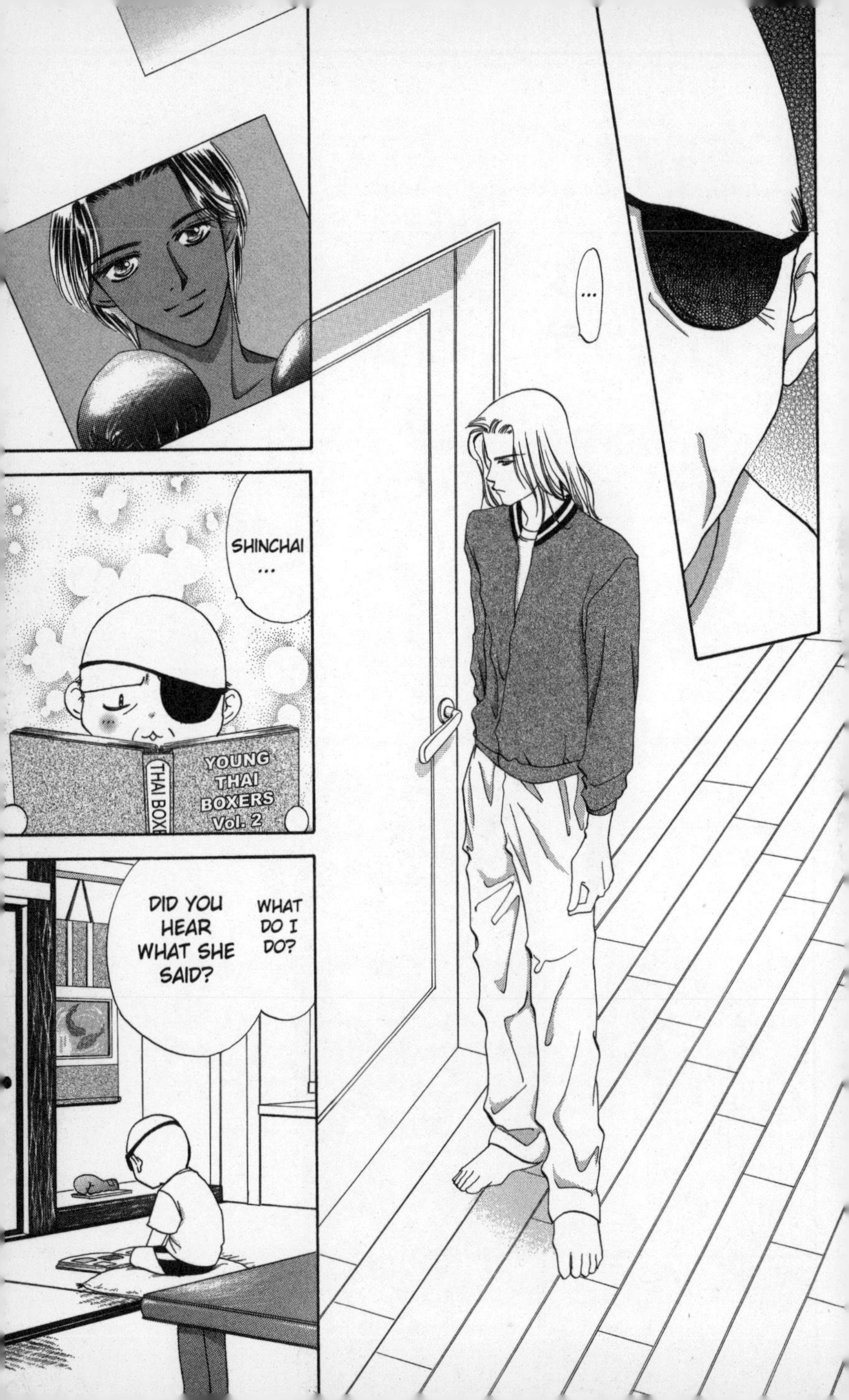
...
SHINCHAI ...
THAI BOXE
YOUNG THAI BOXERS Vol. 2
DID YOU HEAR WHAT SHE SAID?
WHAT DO I DO?

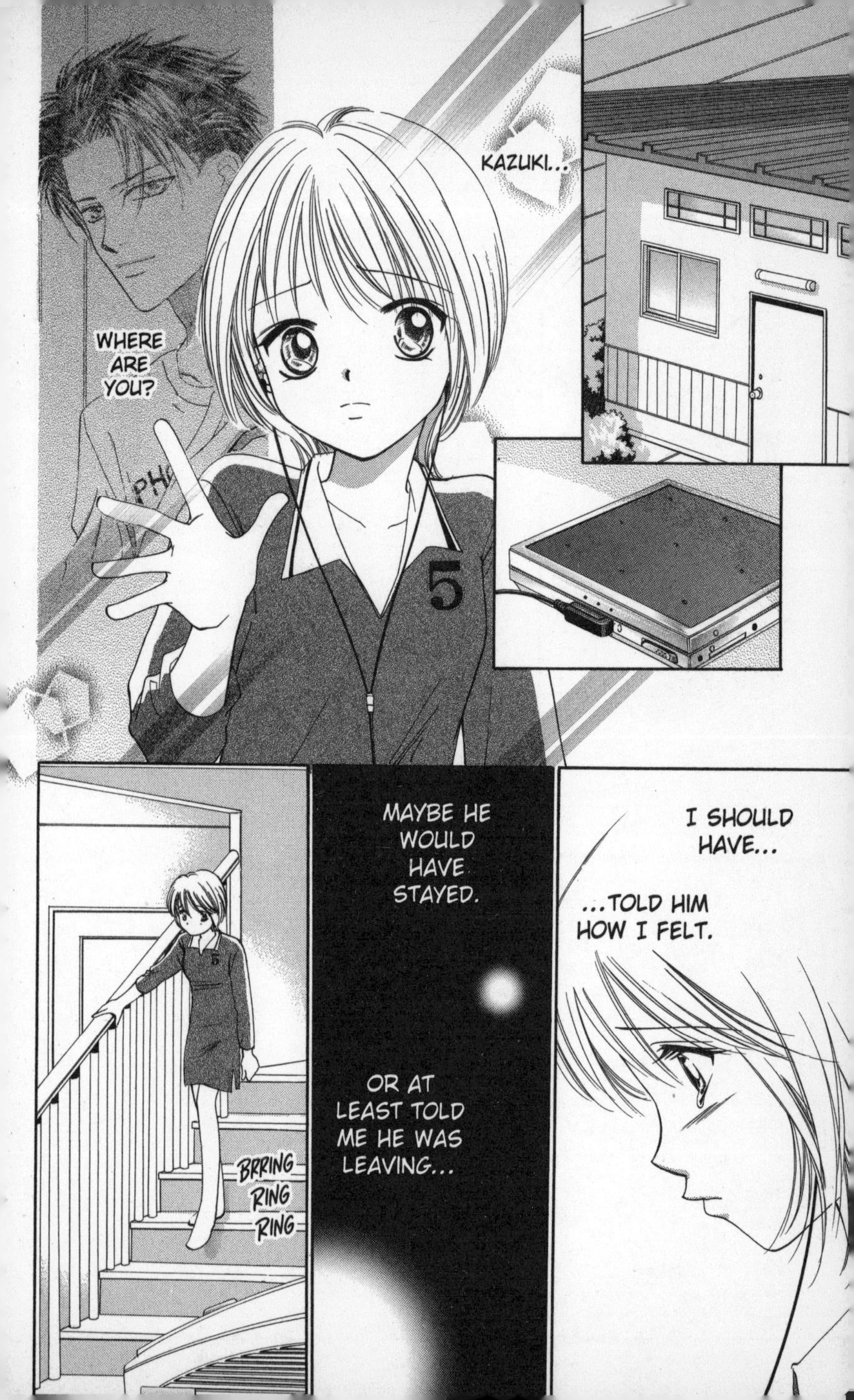
KAZUKI...
WHERE ARE YOU?
I SHOULD HAVE...
...TOLD HIM HOW I FELT.
MAYBE HE WOULD HAVE STAYED.
OR AT LEAST TOLD ME HE WAS LEAVING...
BRRING RING RING

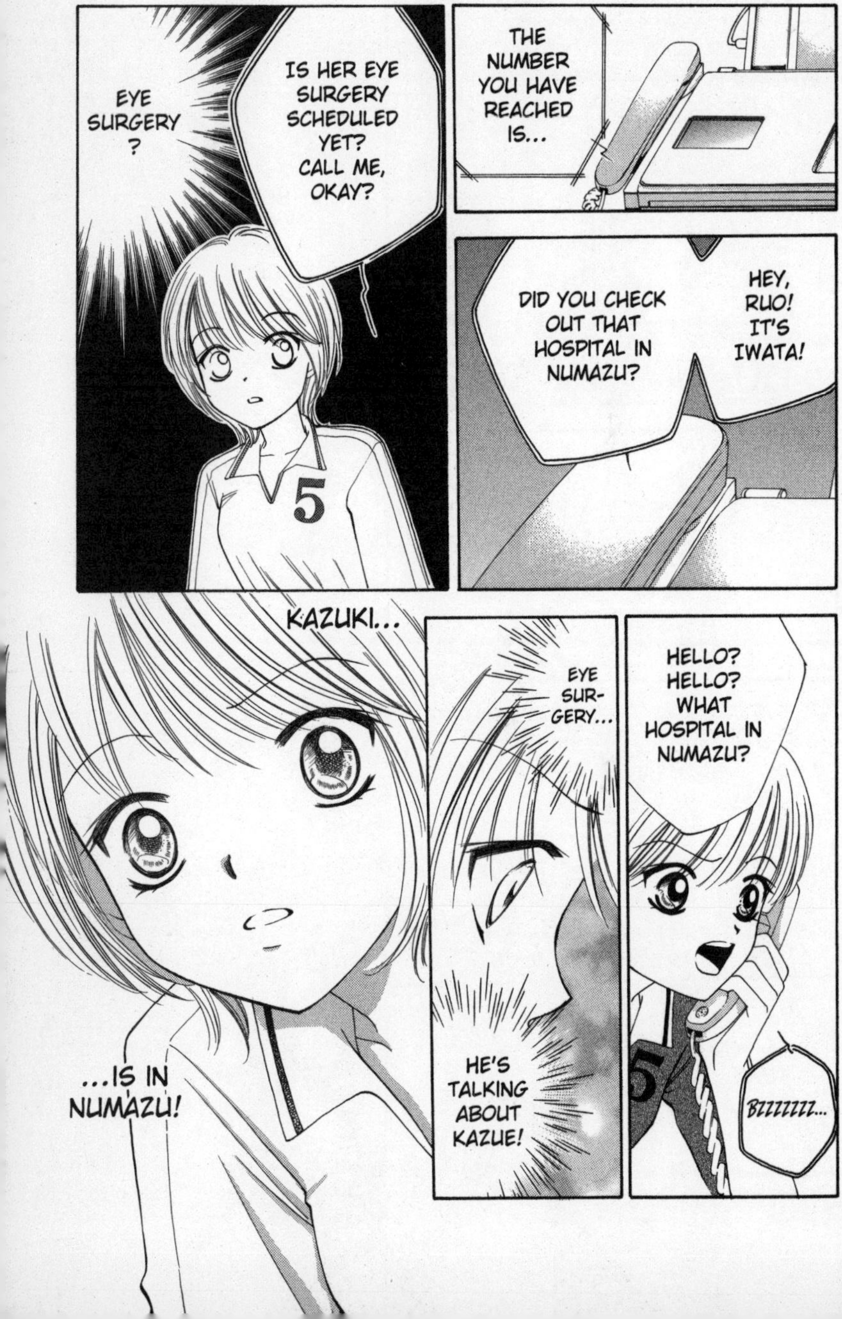
THE NUMBER YOU HAVE REACHED IS...
HEY, RUO! IT'S IWATA!
DID YOU CHECK OUT THAT HOSPITAL IN NUMAZU?
IS HER EYE SURGERY SCHEDULED YET? CALL ME, OKAY?
EYE SURGERY ?
HELLO? HELLO? WHAT HOSPITAL IN NUMAZU?
BZZZZZZZ...
EYE SURGERY...
HE'S TALKING ABOUT KAZUE!
KAZUKI...
...IS IN NUMAZU!

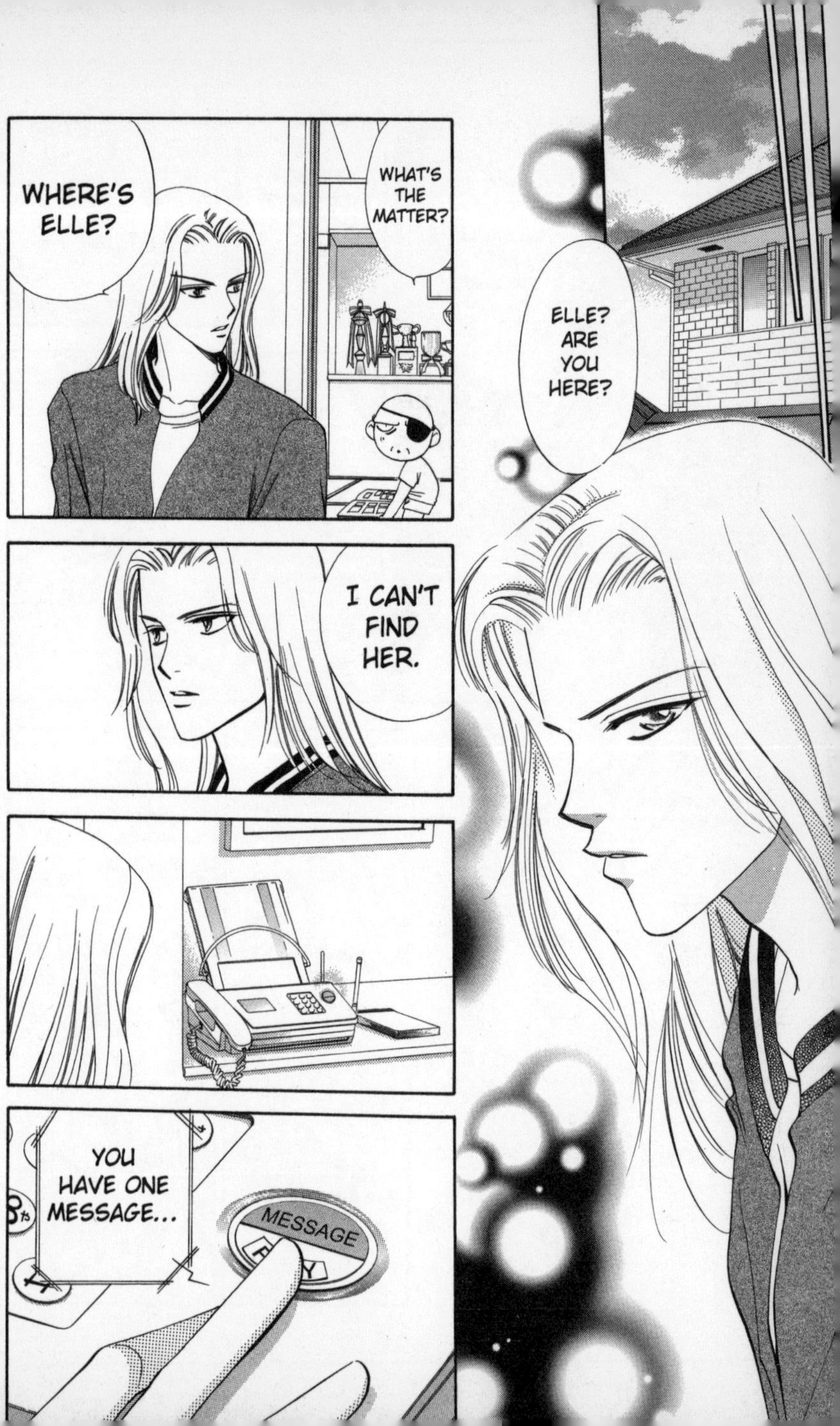
ELLE? ARE YOU HERE?
WHAT'S THE MATTER?
WHERE'S ELLE?
I CAN'T FIND HER.
YOU HAVE ONE MESSAGE...
MESSAGE

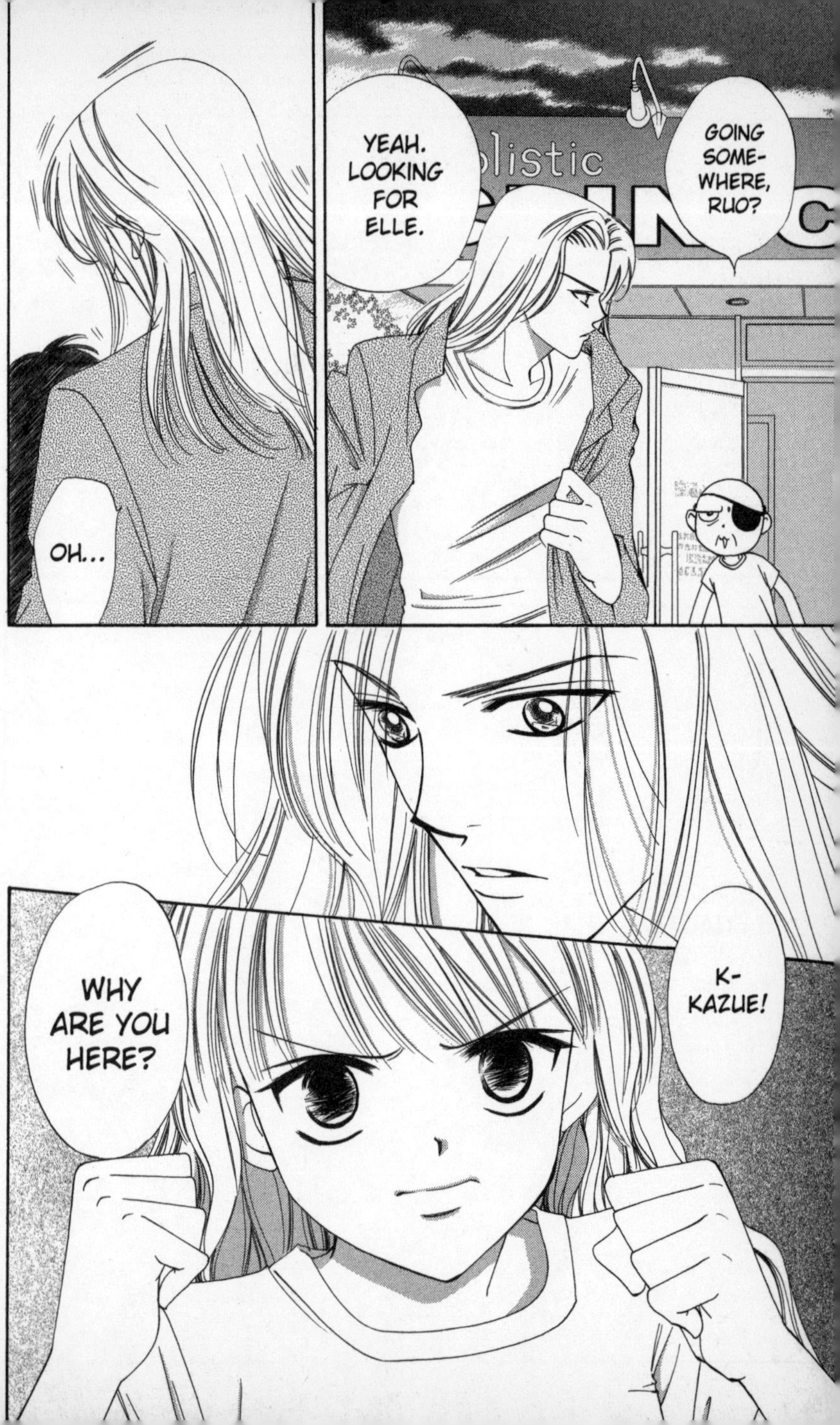
GOING SOME-WHERE, RUO?
YEAH. LOOKING FOR ELLE.
OH...
K-KAZUE!
WHY ARE YOU HERE?

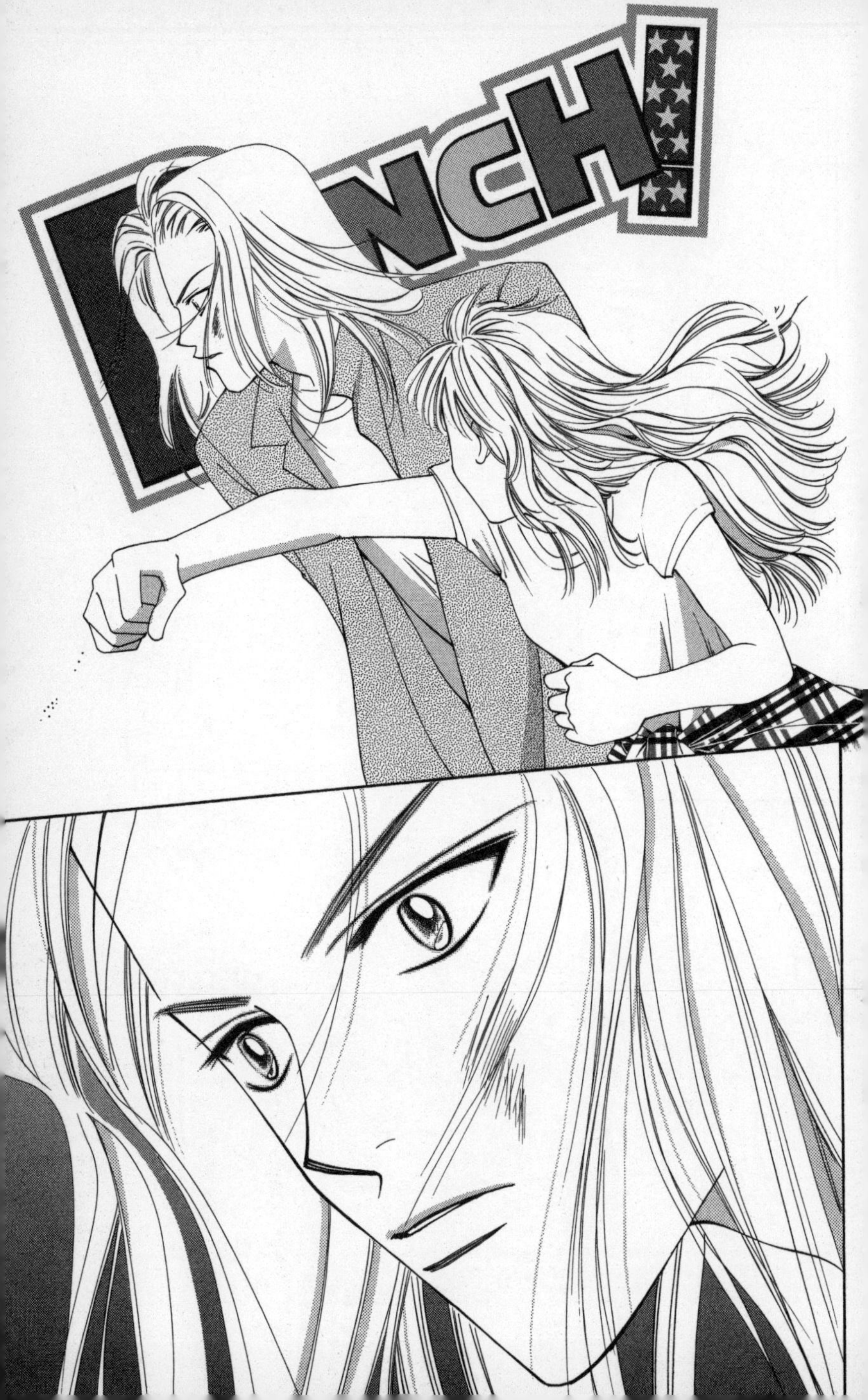
NCH!

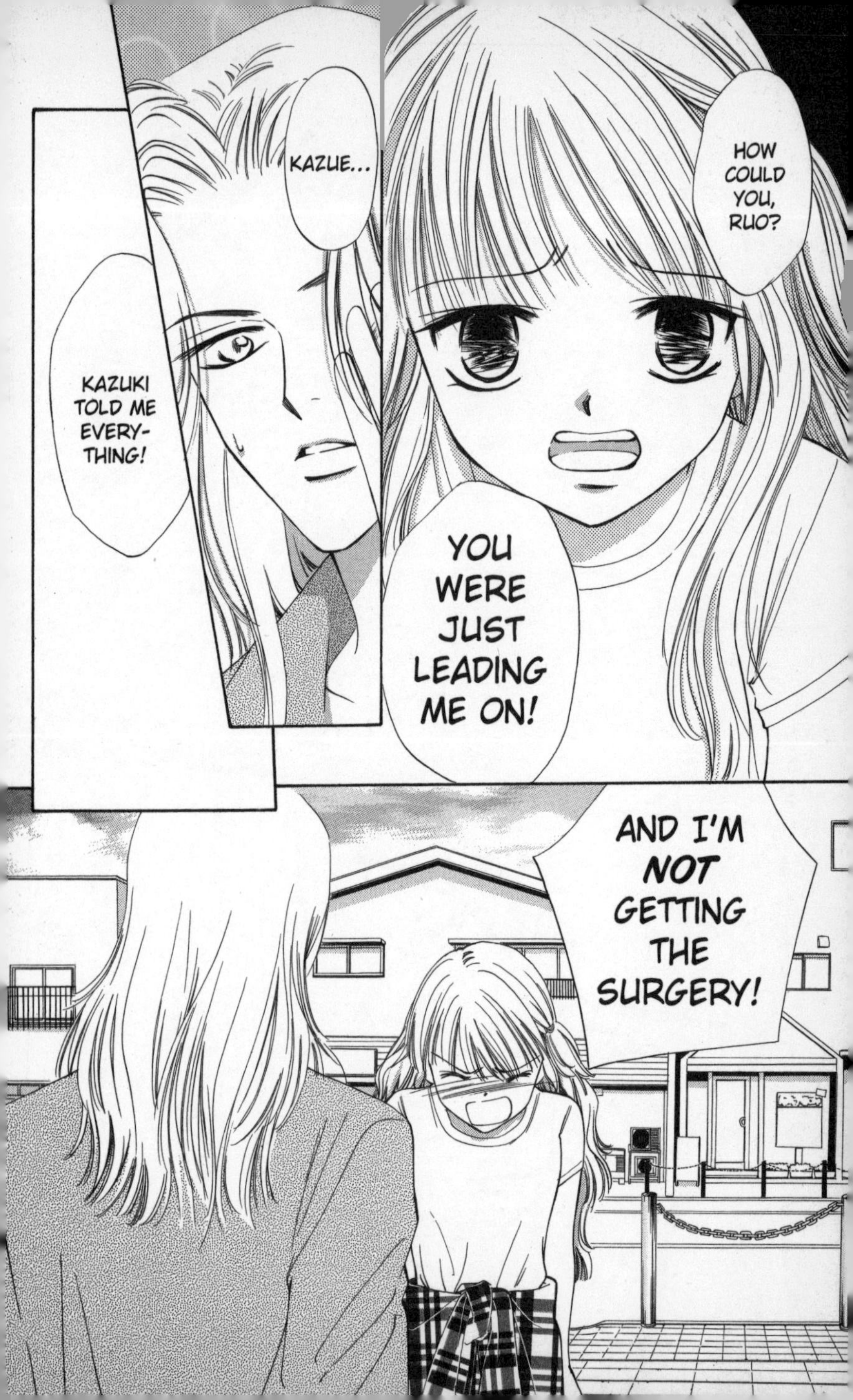
HOW COULD YOU, RUO?
YOU WERE JUST LEADING ME ON!
KAZUE...
KAZUKI TOLD ME EVERY-THING!
AND I'M NOT GETTING THE SURGERY!

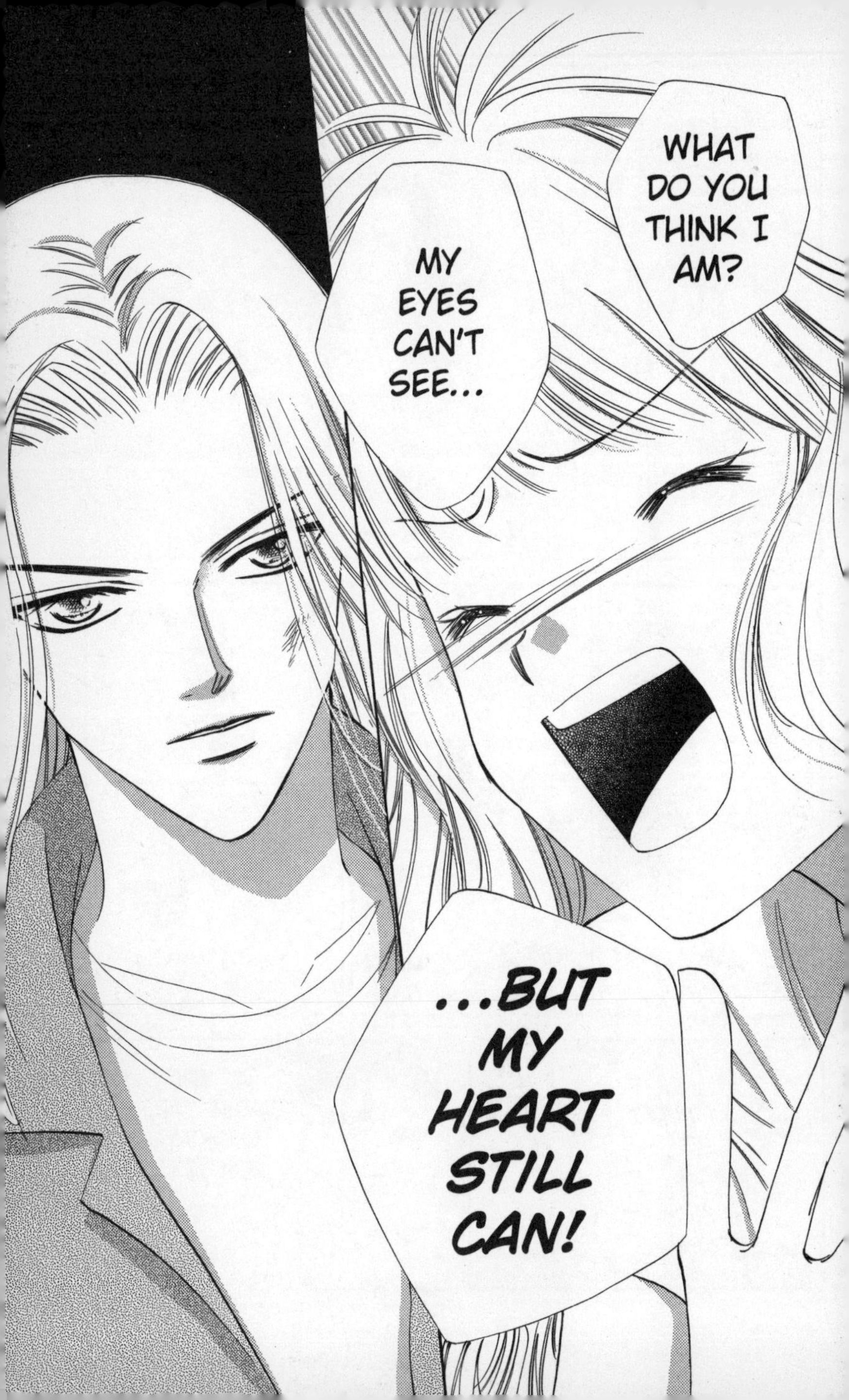
WHAT DO YOU THINK I AM?
MY EYES CAN'T SEE...
...BUT MY HEART STILL CAN!

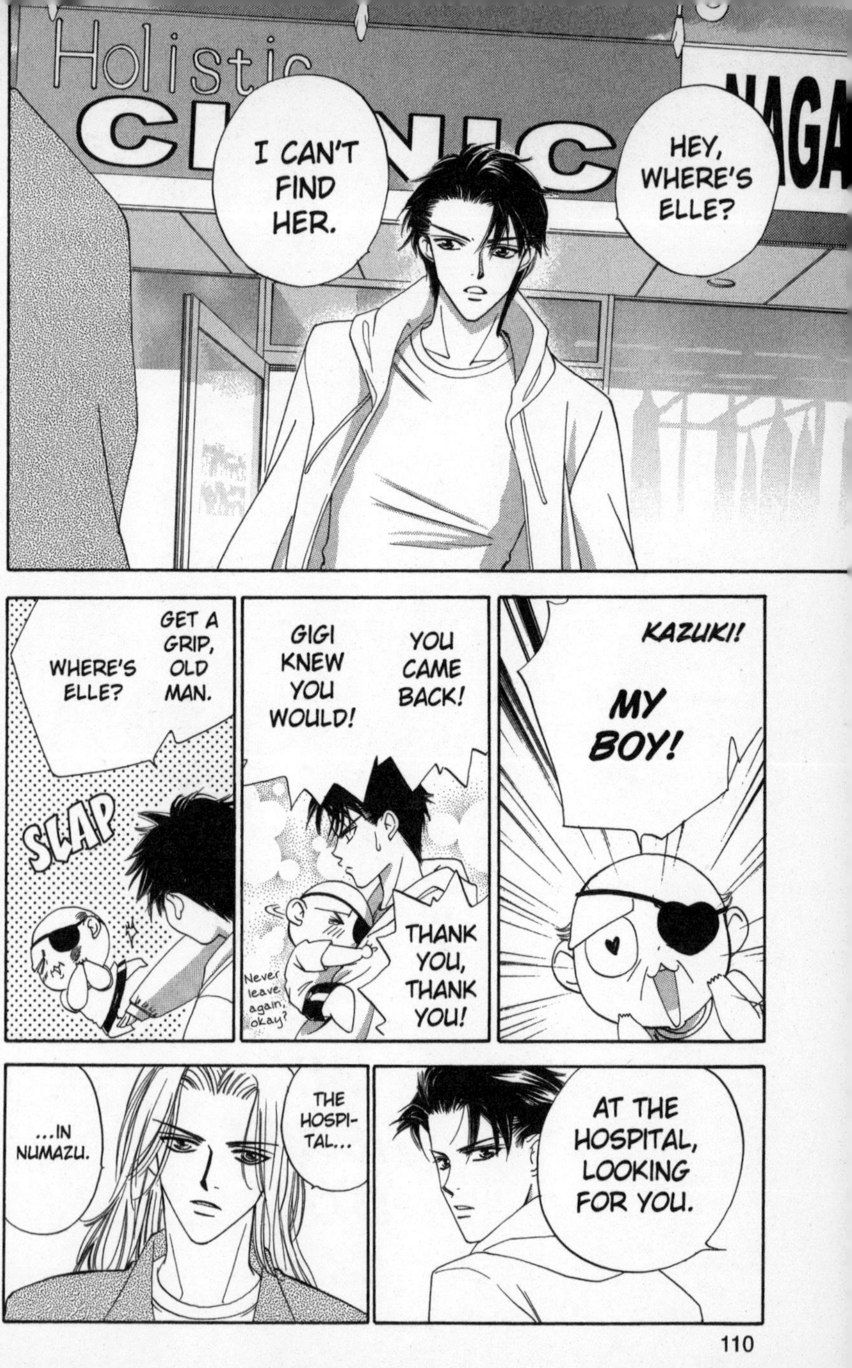
Holistic
HEY, WHERE'S ELLE?
I CAN'T FIND HER.
KAZUKI!
MY BOY!
YOU CAME BACK!
GIGI KNEW YOU WOULD!
THANK YOU, THANK YOU!
Never leave again, okay?
GET A GRIP, OLD MAN.
WHERE'S ELLE?
SLAP
AT THE HOSPITAL, LOOKING FOR YOU.
THE HOSPI-TAL...
...IN NUMAZU.

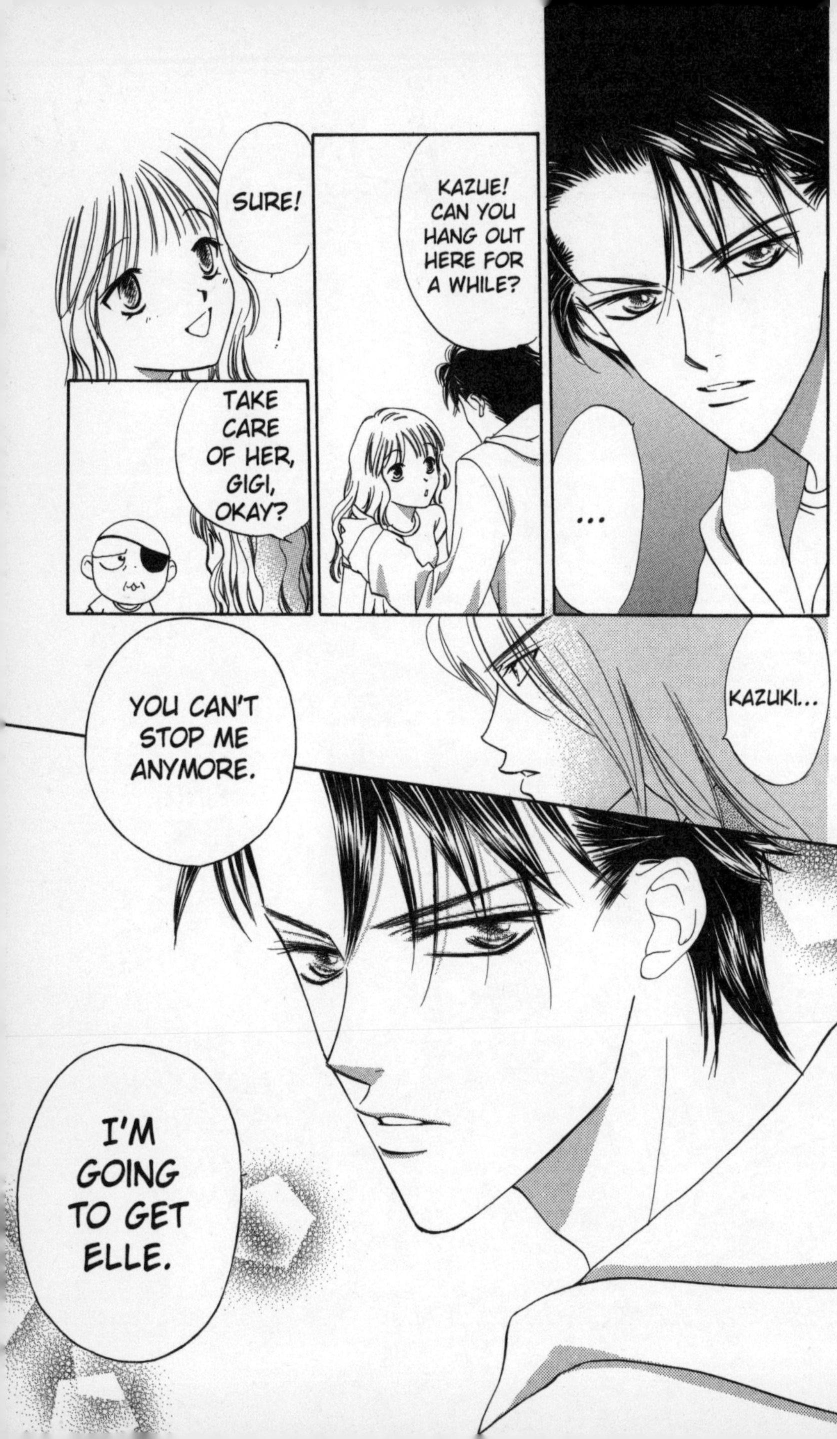
...
KAZUE! CAN YOU HANG OUT HERE FOR A WHILE?
SURE!
TAKE CARE OF HER, GIGI, OKAY?
KAZUKI...
YOU CAN'T STOP ME ANYMORE.
I'M GOING TO GET ELLE.

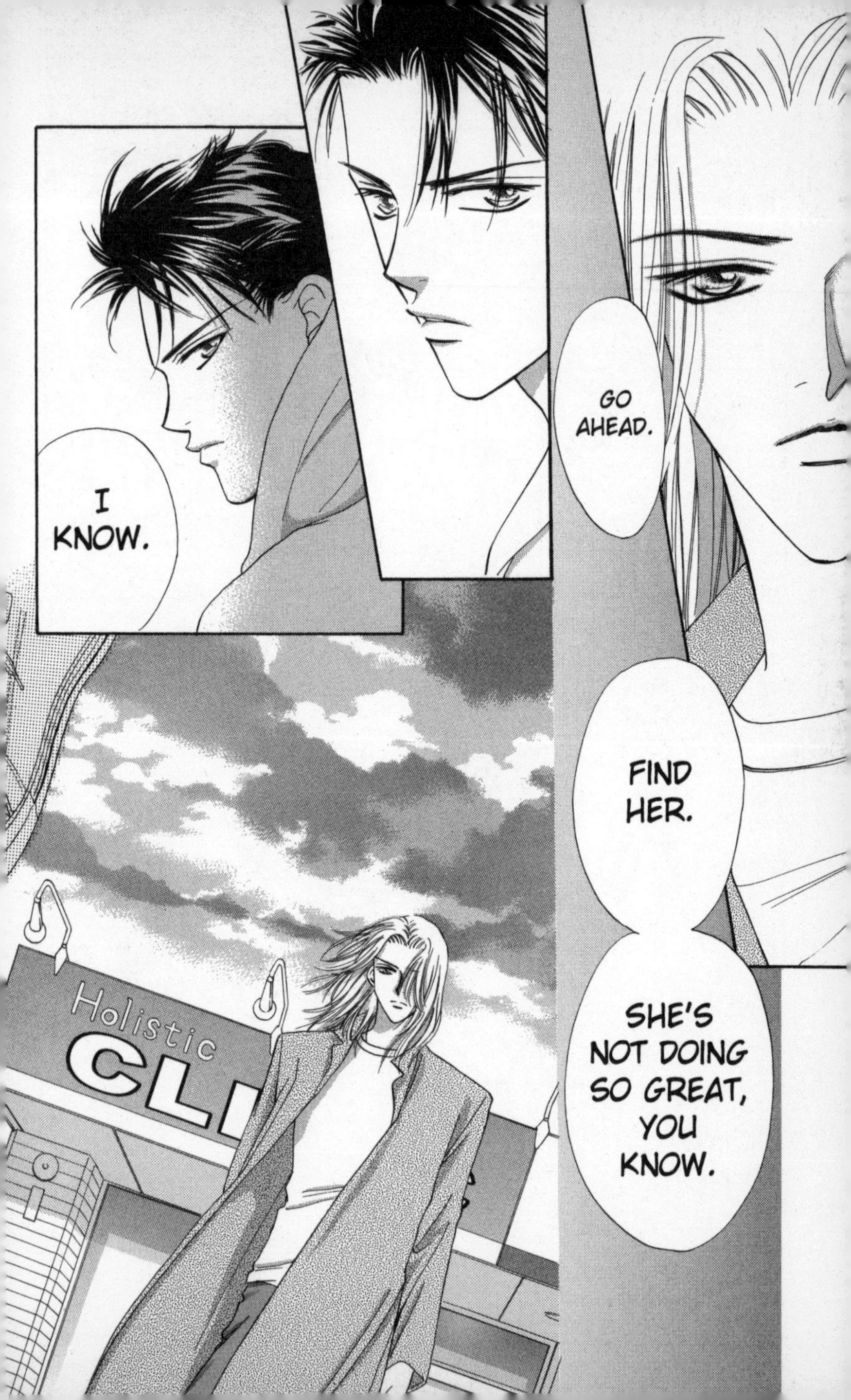
GO AHEAD.
FIND HER.
SHE'S NOT DOING SO GREAT, YOU KNOW.
I KNOW.
Holistic
CLI

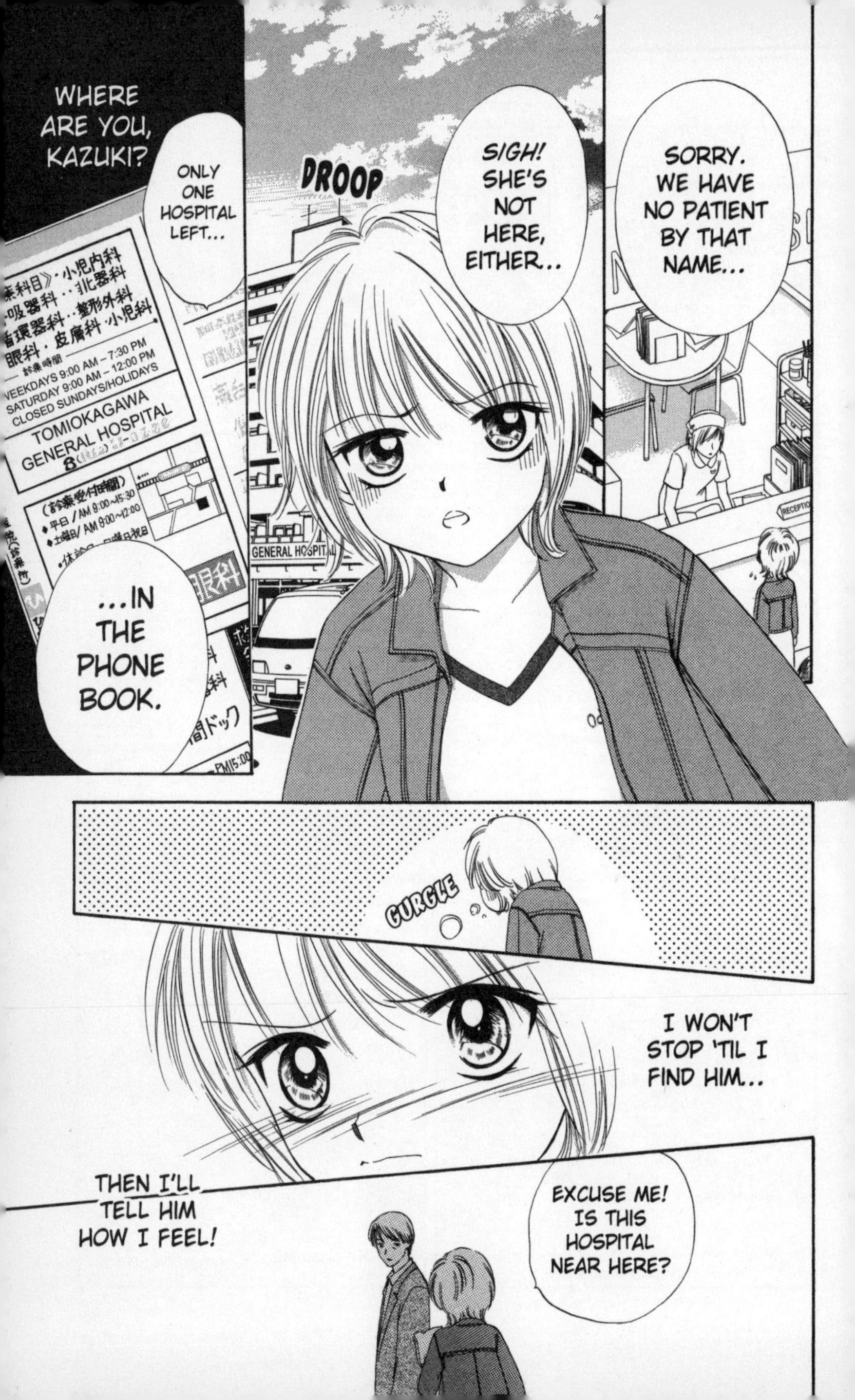
SORRY. WE HAVE NO PATIENT BY THAT NAME...
RECEPTION
DROOP
SIGH! SHE'S NOT HERE, EITHER...
GENERAL HOSPITAL
WHERE ARE YOU, KAZUKI?
ONLY ONE HOSPITAL LEFT...
WEEKDAYS 9:00 AM – 7:30 PM
SATURDAY 9:00 AM – 12:00 PM
CLOSED SUNDAYS/HOLIDAYS
TOMIOKAGAWA GENERAL HOSPITAL
...IN THE PHONE BOOK.
GURGLE
I WON'T STOP 'TIL I FIND HIM...
THEN I'LL TELL HIM HOW I FEEL!
EXCUSE ME! IS THIS HOSPITAL NEAR HERE?

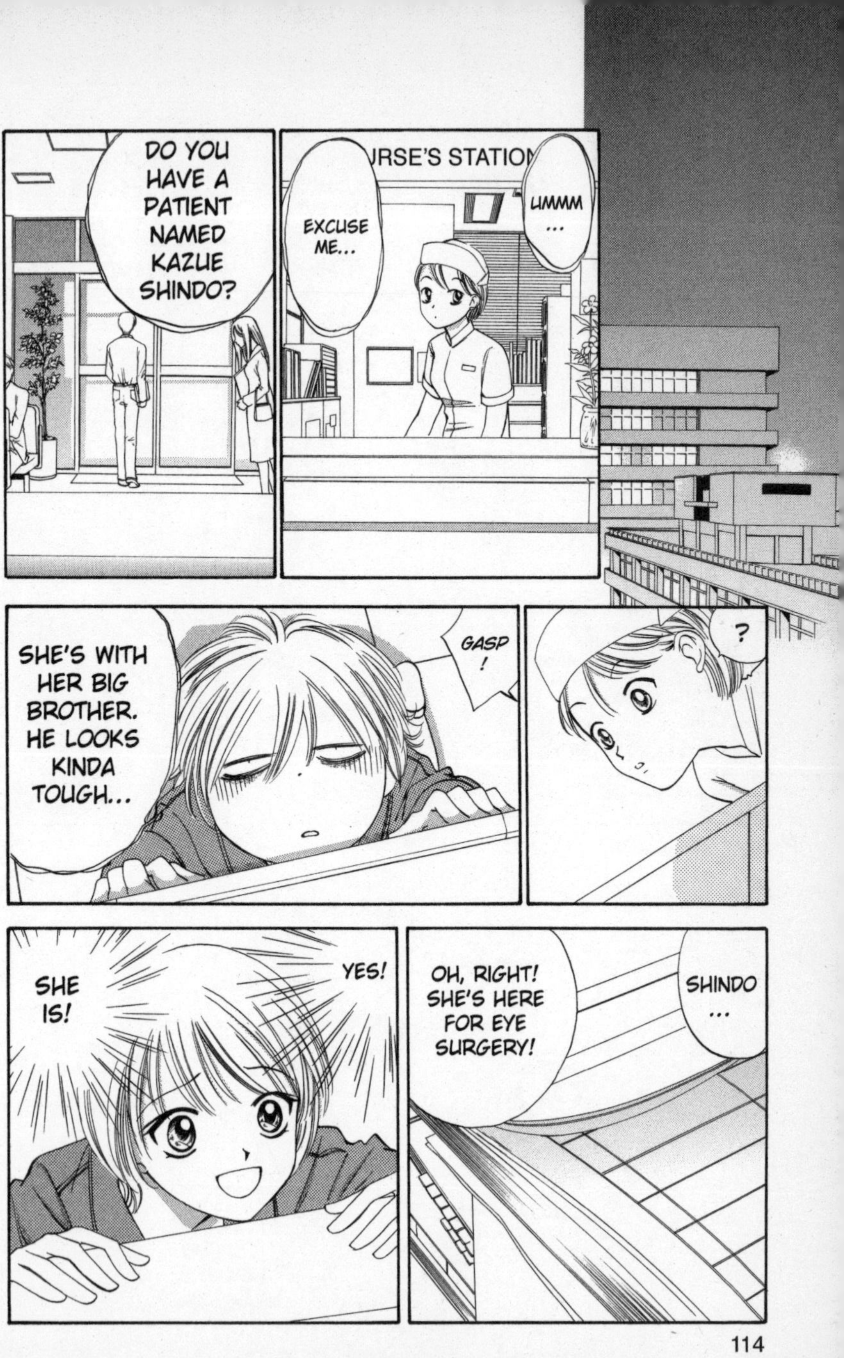
URSE'S STATION
UMMM ...
EXCUSE ME...
DO YOU HAVE A PATIENT NAMED KAZUE SHINDO?
?
GASP !
SHE'S WITH HER BIG BROTHER. HE LOOKS KINDA TOUGH...
SHINDO ...
OH, RIGHT! SHE'S HERE FOR EYE SURGERY!
YES!
SHE IS!

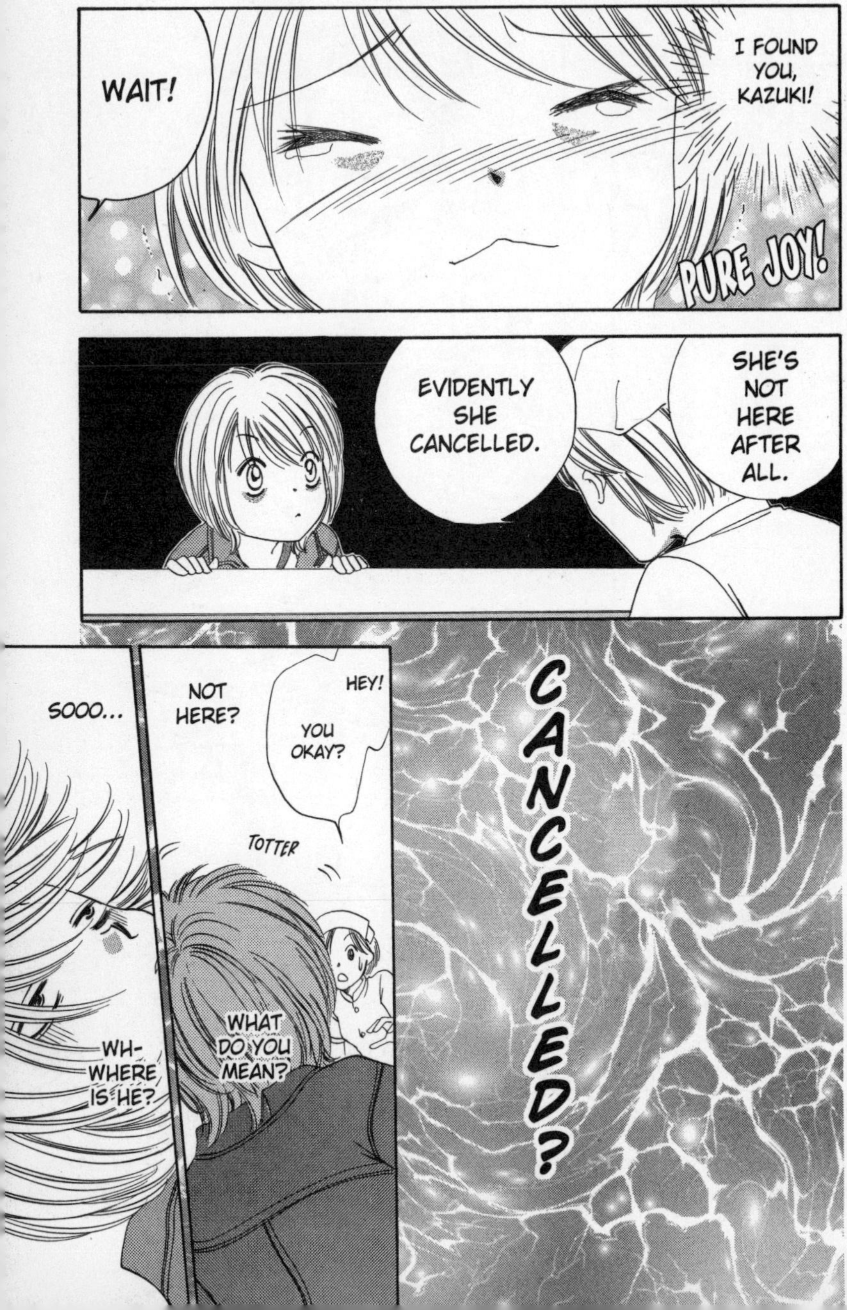
I FOUND YOU, KAZUKI!
PURE JOY!
WAIT!
SHE'S NOT HERE AFTER ALL.
EVIDENTLY SHE CANCELLED.
CANCELLED?
HEY!
YOU OKAY?
NOT HERE?
TOTTER
WHAT DO YOU MEAN?
SOOO...
WH-WHERE IS HE?

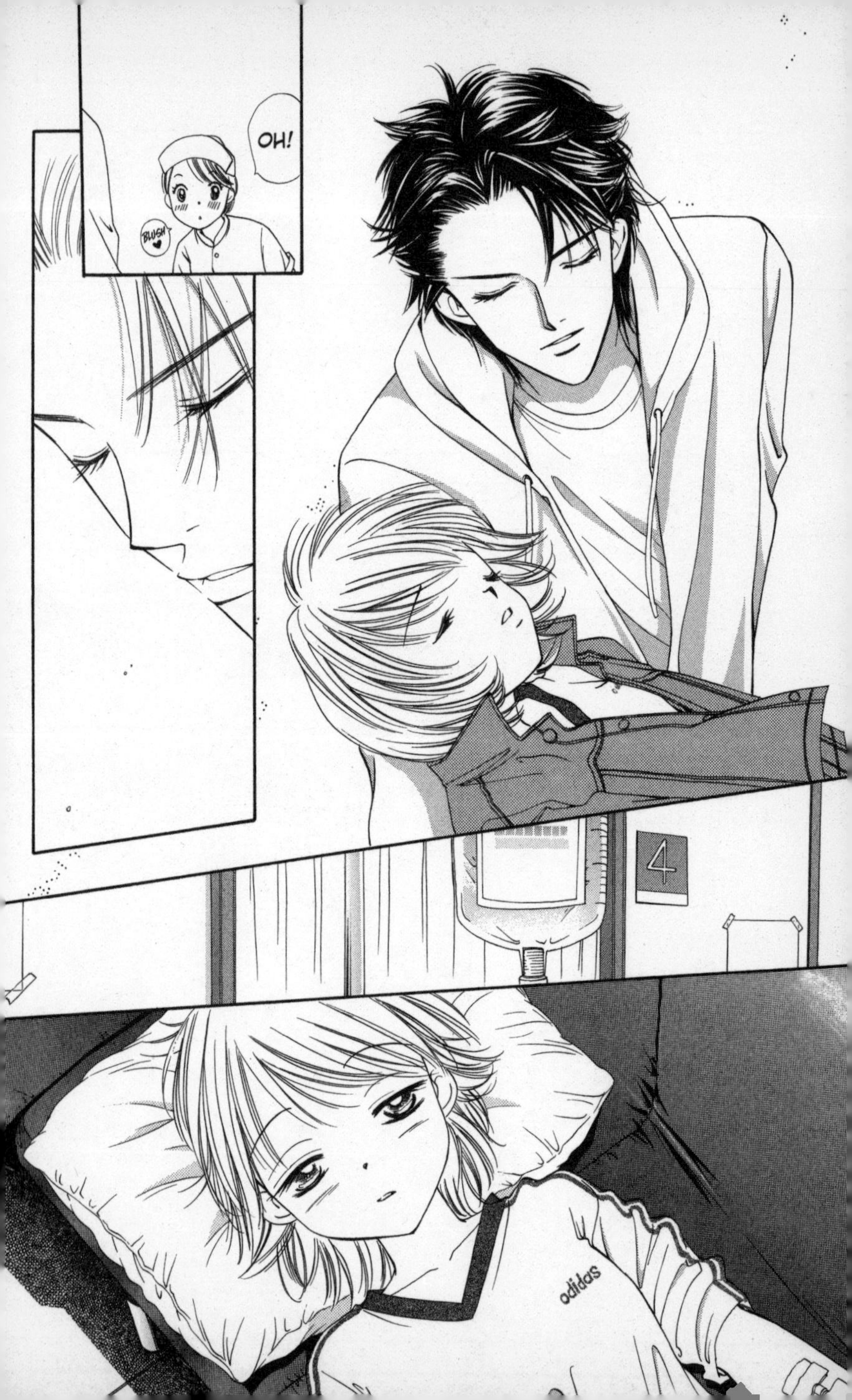
OH!
BLUSH ♥
adidas

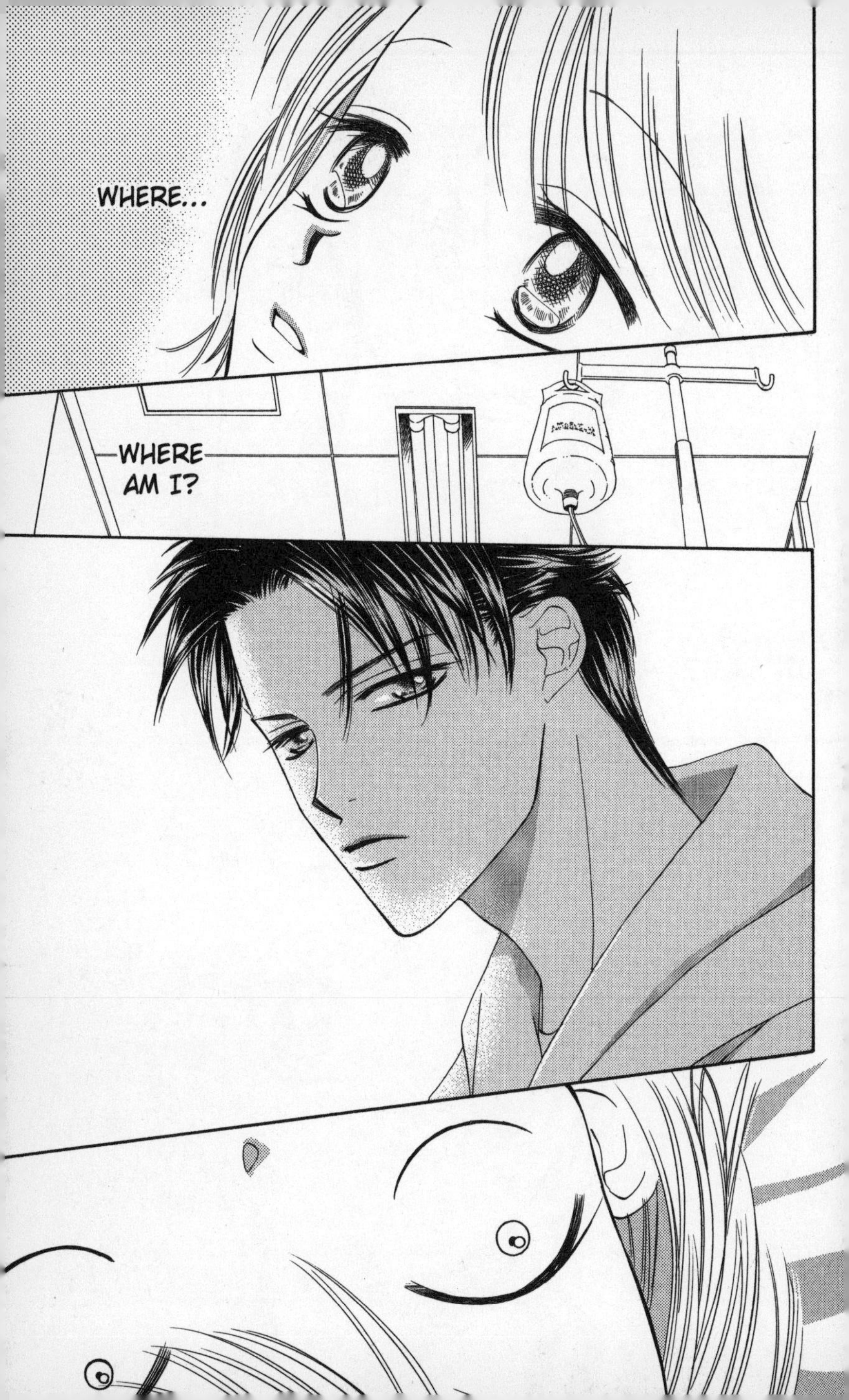
WHERE...
WHERE AM I?

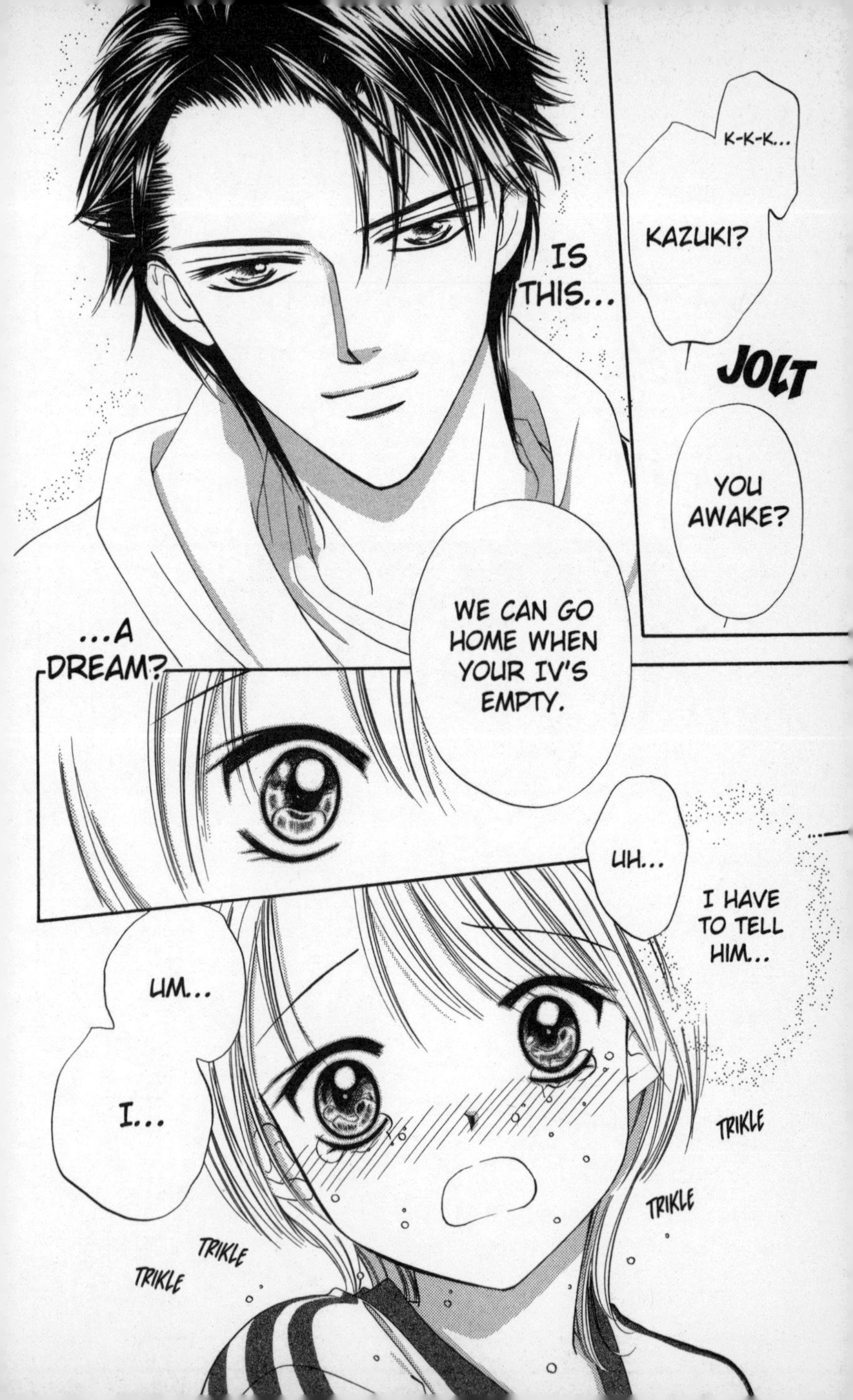
K-K-K...
KAZUKI?
JOLT
YOU AWAKE?
IS THIS...
WE CAN GO HOME WHEN YOUR IV'S EMPTY.
...A DREAM?
UH...
I HAVE TO TELL HIM...
TRIKLE
TRIKLE
UM...
I...
TRIKLE
TRIKLE

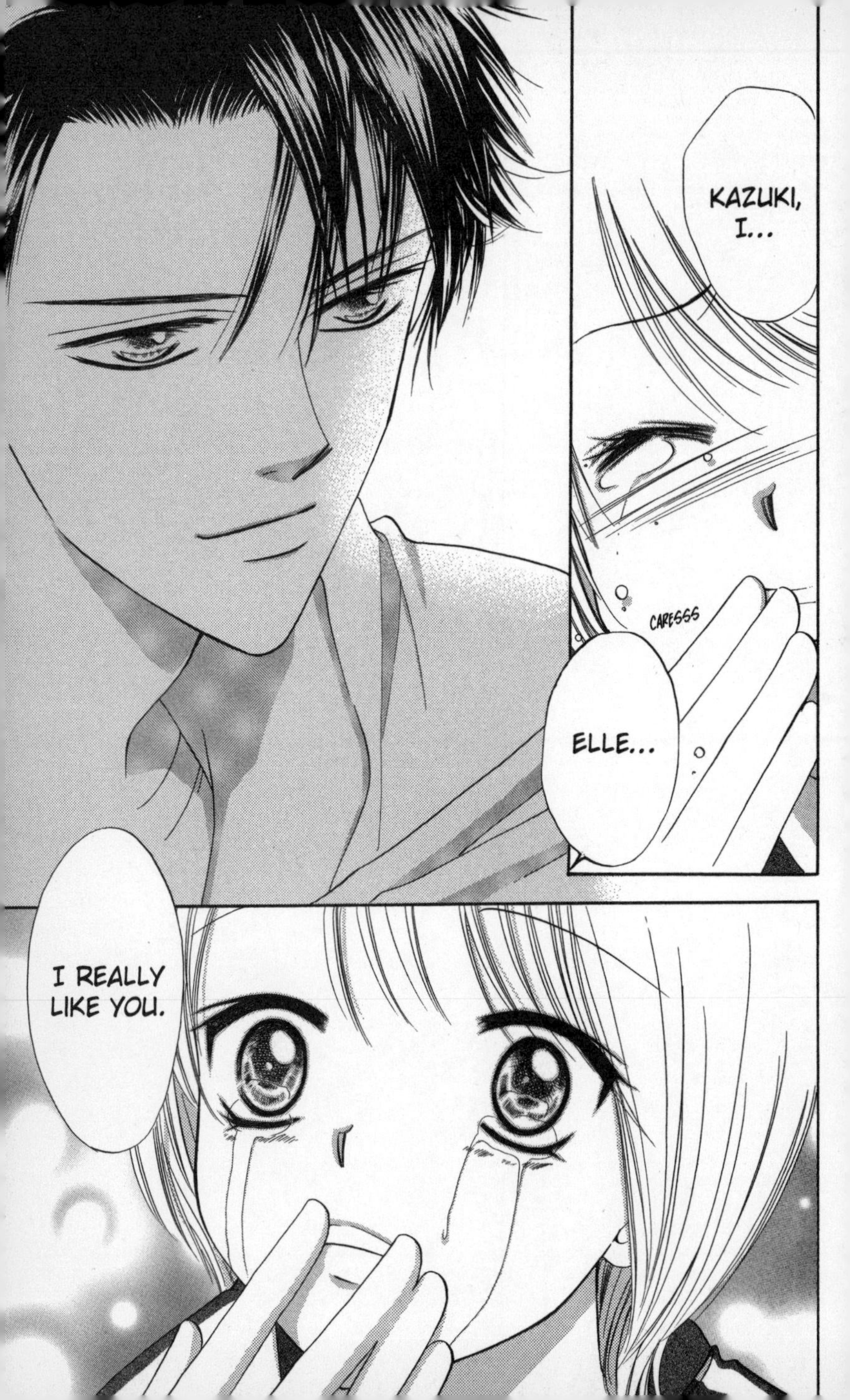
KAZUKI, I...
CARESSS
ELLE...
I REALLY LIKE YOU.

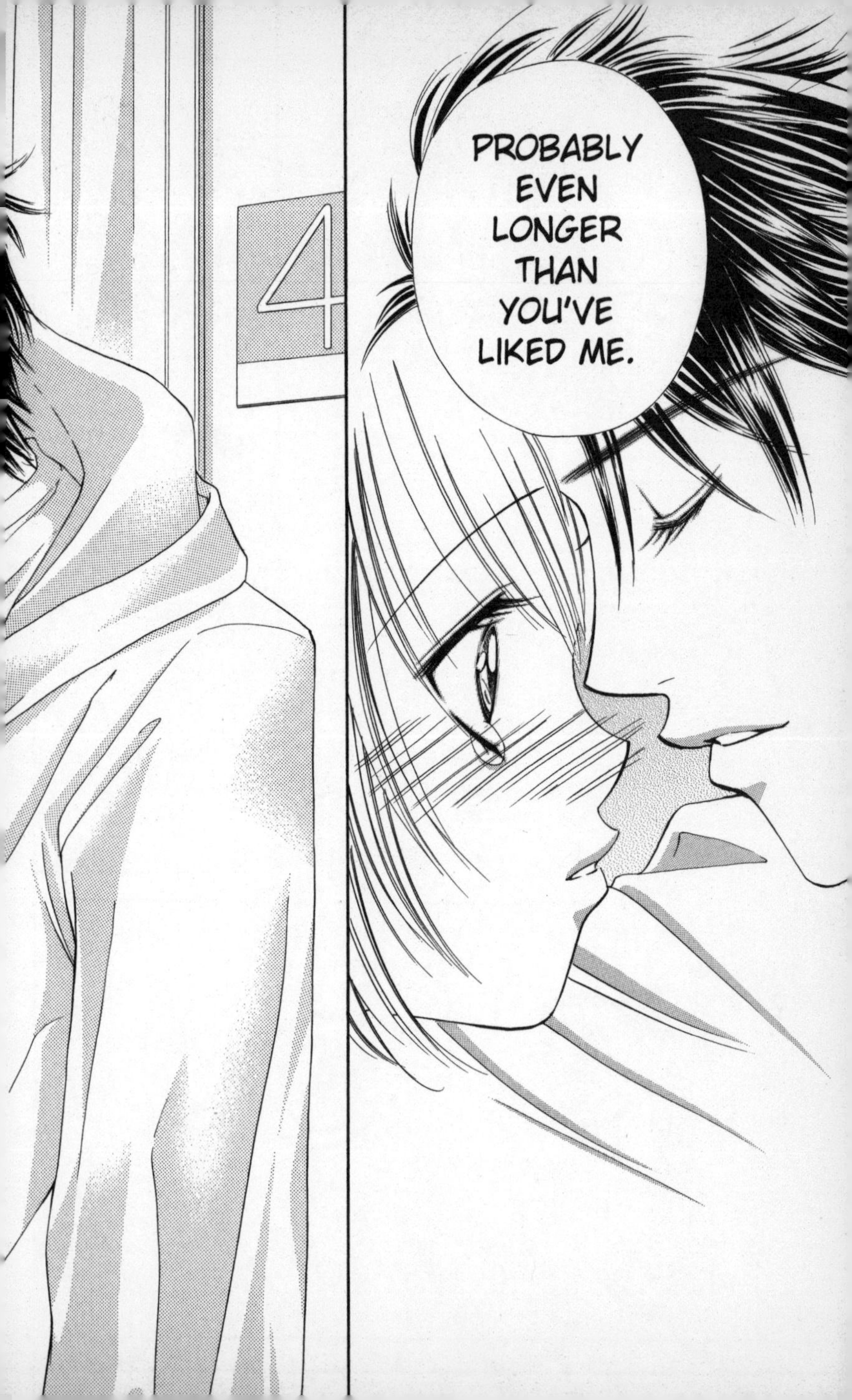
PROBABLY EVEN LONGER THAN YOU'VE LIKED ME.

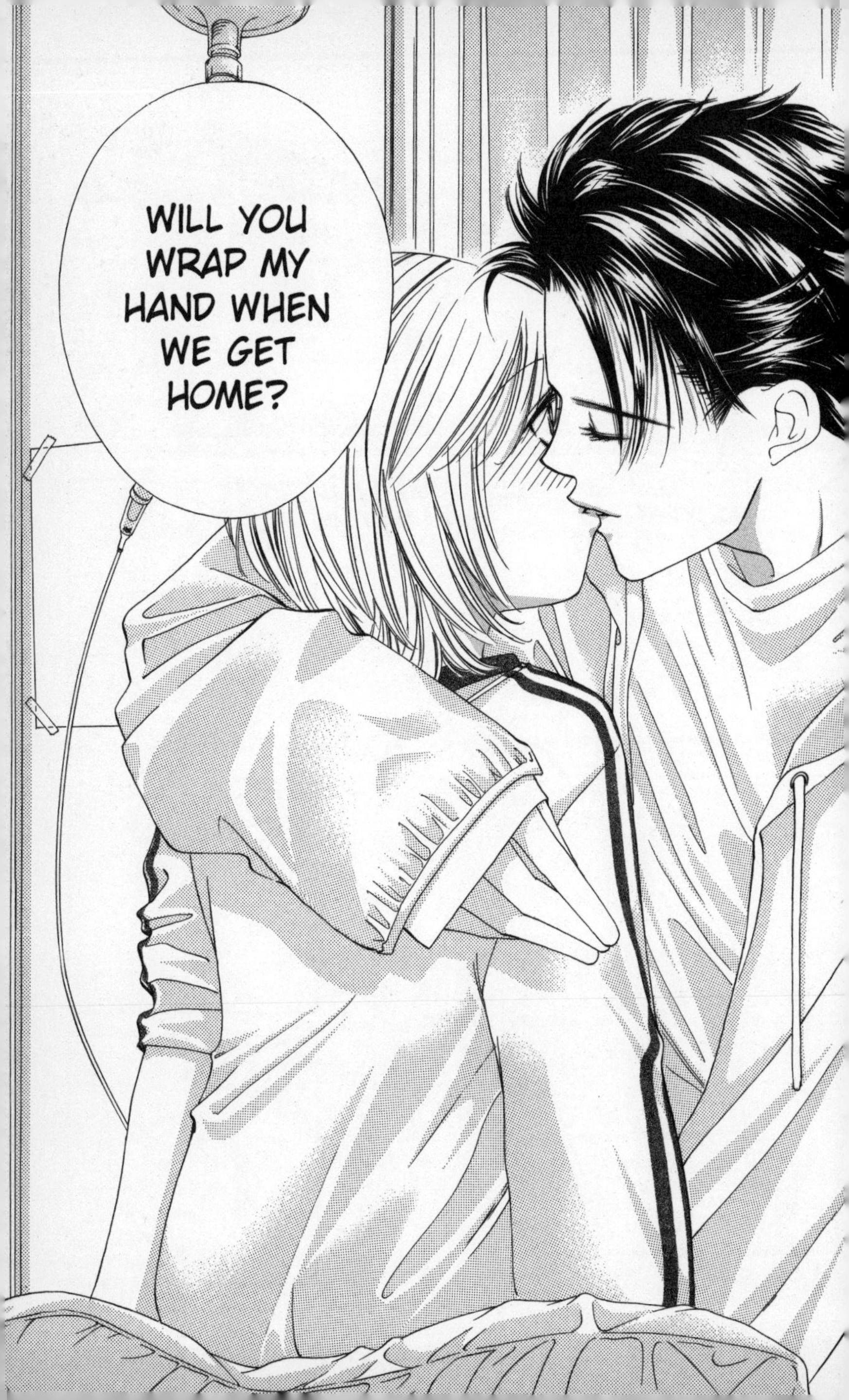
WILL YOU WRAP MY HAND WHEN WE GET HOME?

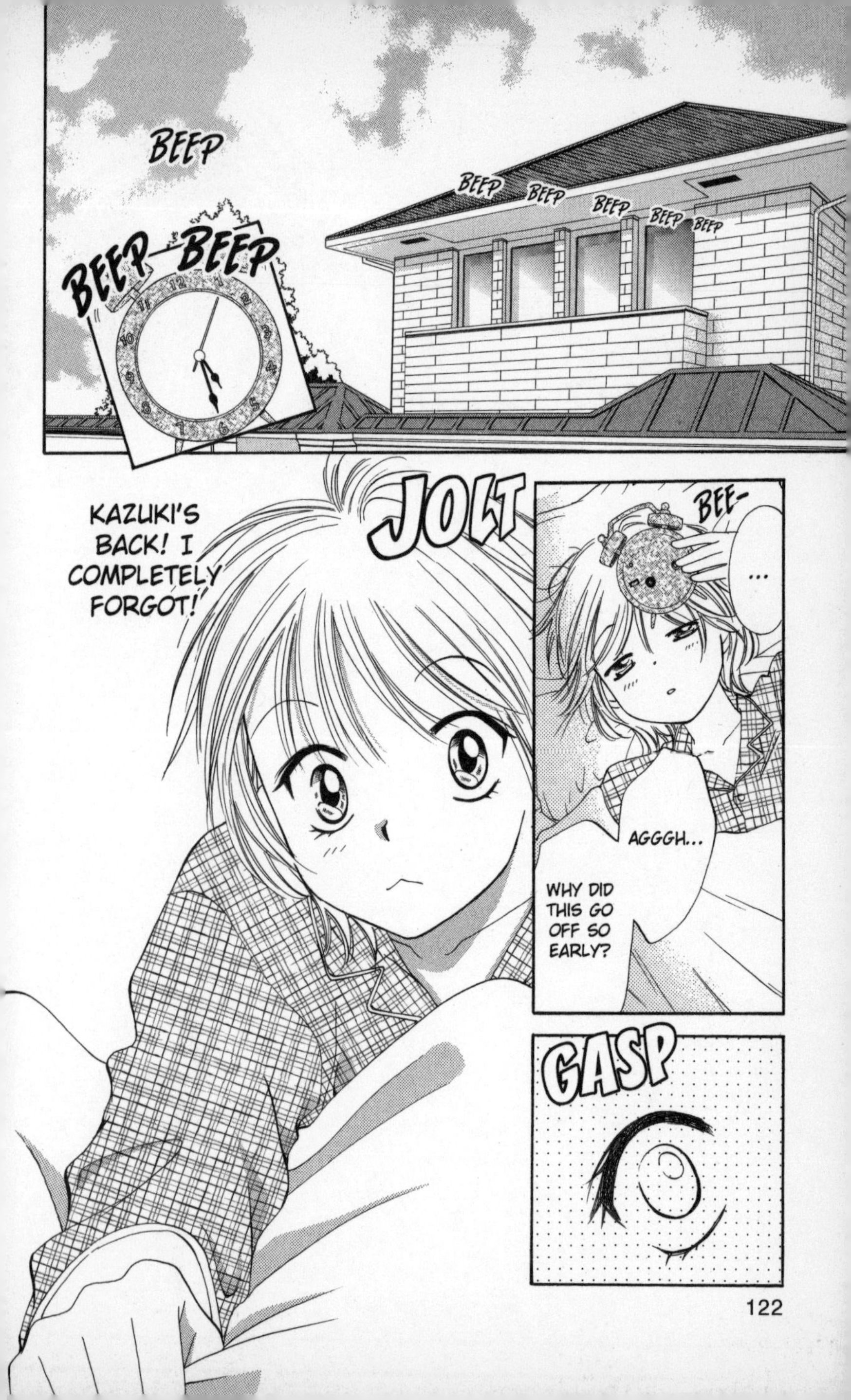
BEEP
BEEP BEEP BEEP BEEP BEEP
BEEP-BEEP
BEE-
...
AGGGH...
WHY DID THIS GO OFF SO EARLY?
GASP
JOLT
KAZUKI'S BACK! I COMPLETELY FORGOT!

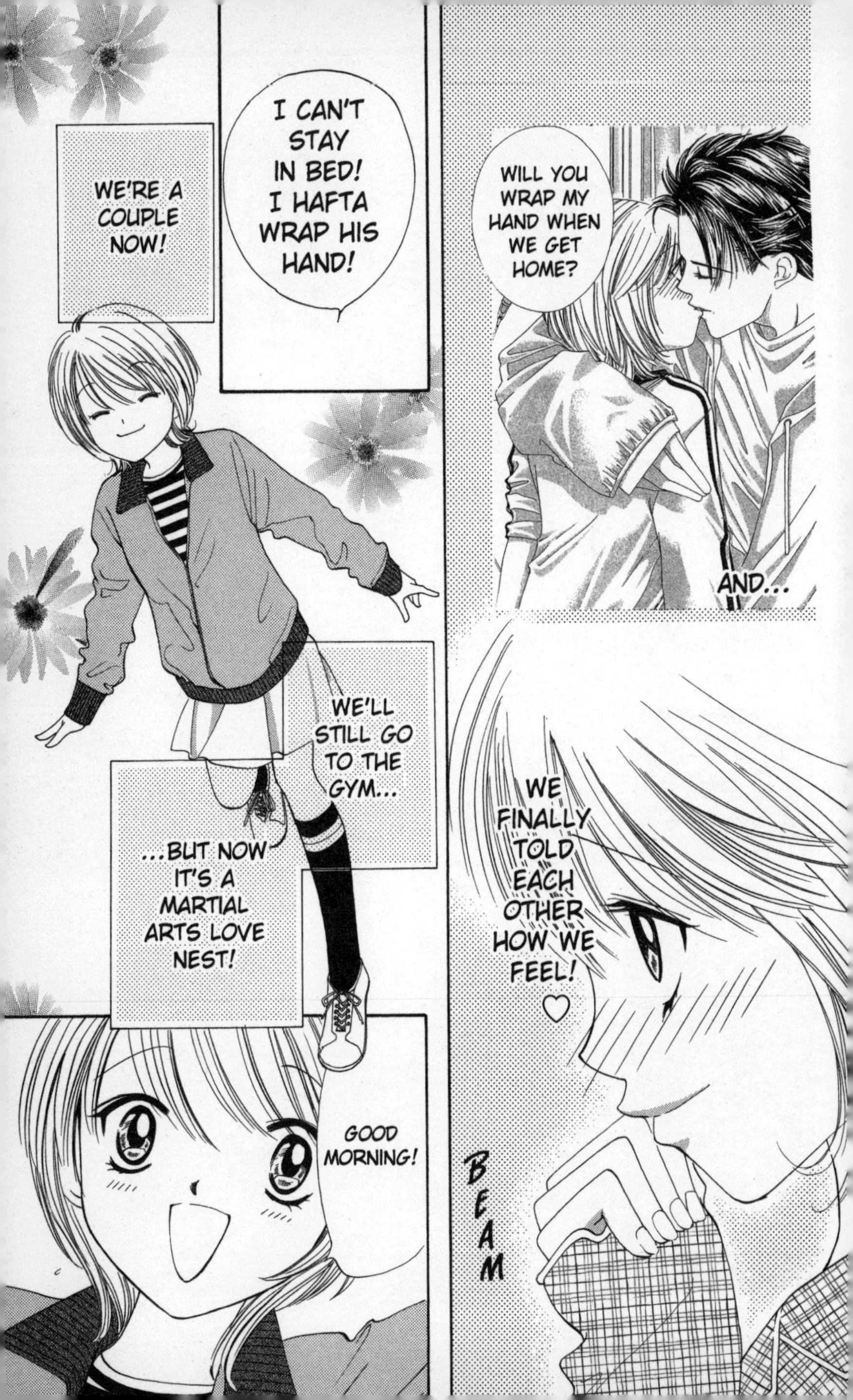
WILL YOU WRAP MY HAND WHEN WE GET HOME?
AND...
WE FINALLY TOLD EACH OTHER HOW WE FEEL! ♡
BEAM
I CAN'T STAY IN BED! I HAFTA WRAP HIS HAND!
WE'RE A COUPLE NOW!
WE'LL STILL GO TO THE GYM...
...BUT NOW IT'S A MARTIAL ARTS LOVE NEST!
GOOD MORNING!

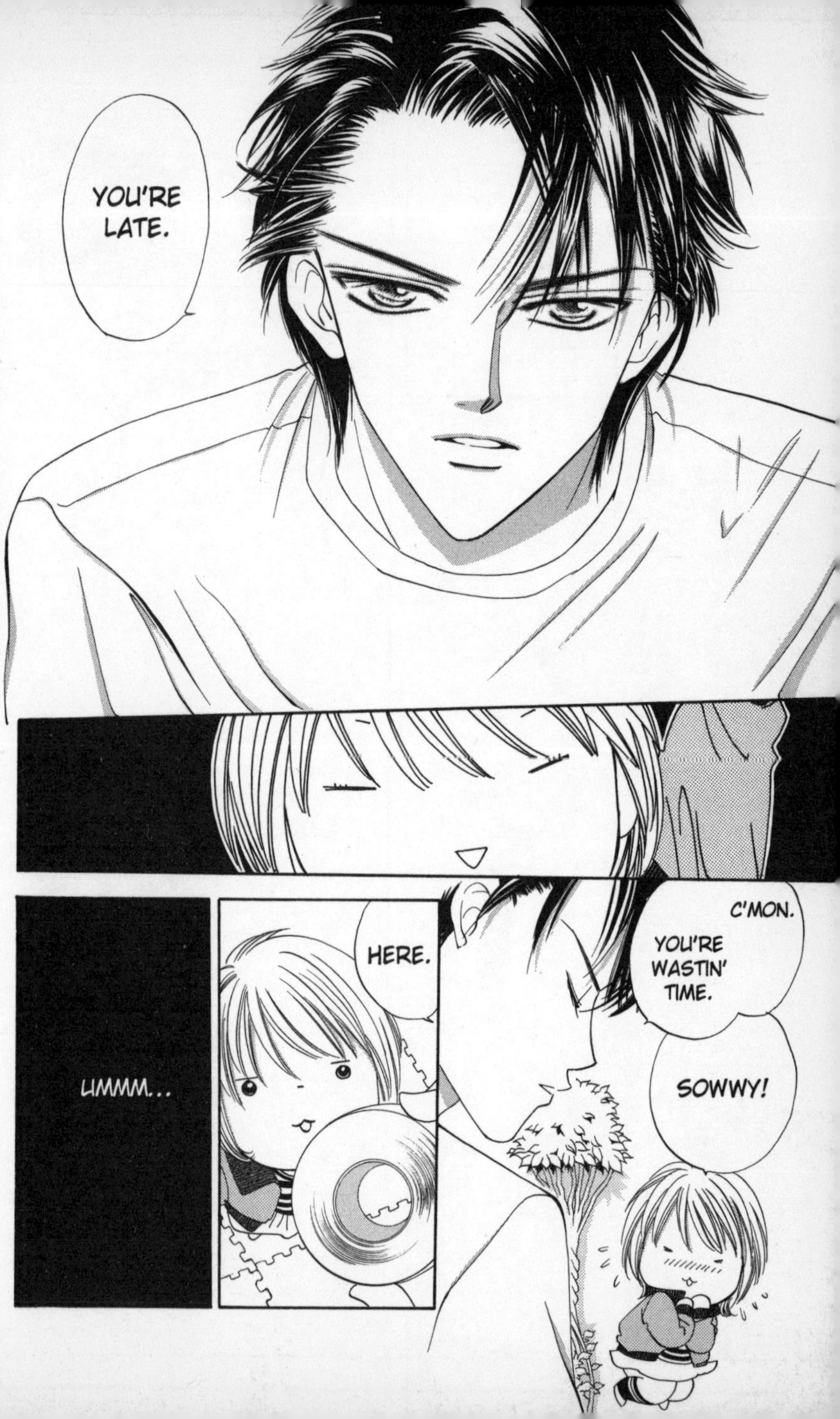
YOU'RE LATE.
C'MON.
YOU'RE WASTIN' TIME.
SOWWY!
HERE.
UMMM...

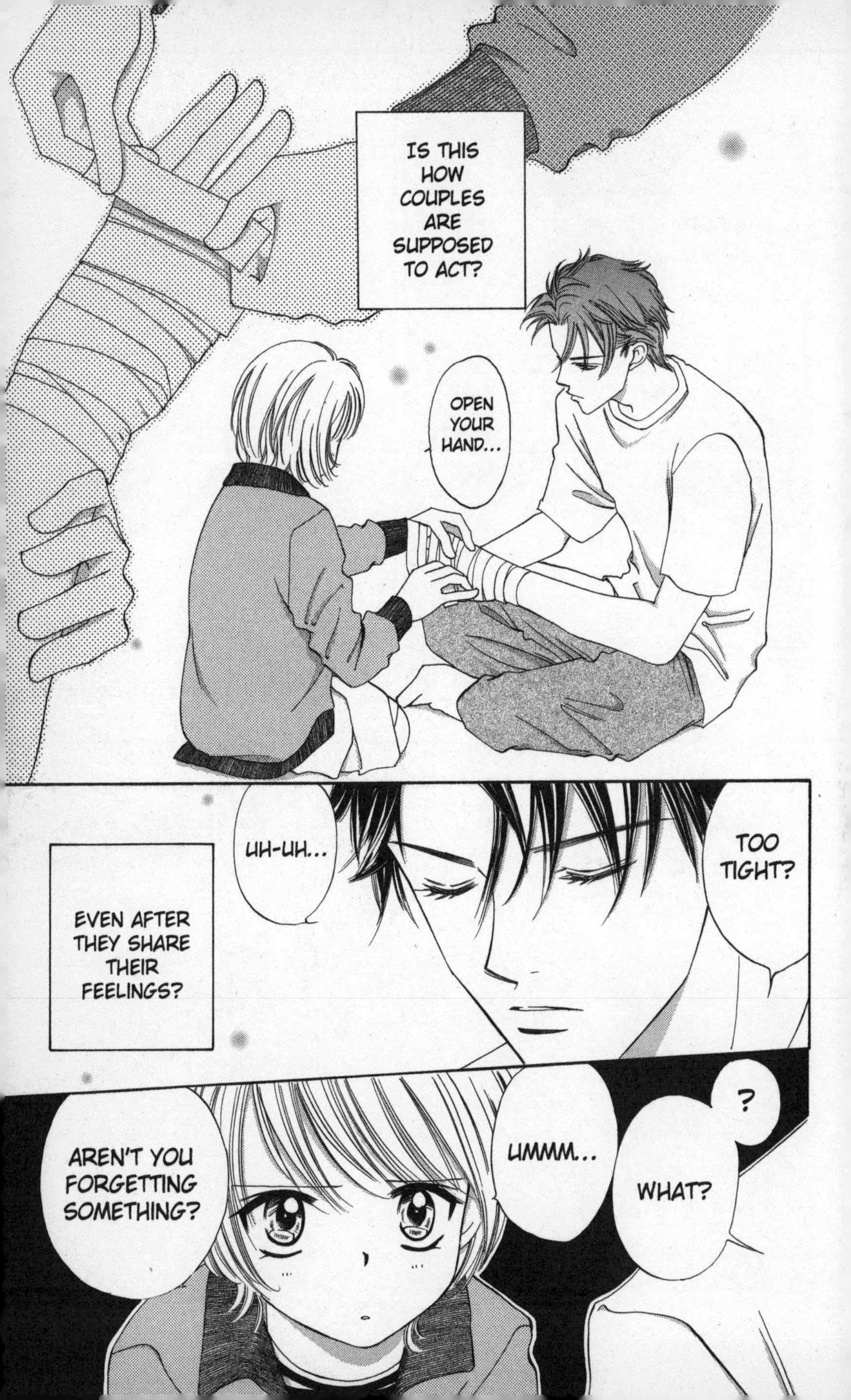
IS THIS HOW COUPLES ARE SUPPOSED TO ACT?
OPEN YOUR HAND...
TOO TIGHT?
UH-UH...
EVEN AFTER THEY SHARE THEIR FEELINGS?
?
WHAT?
UMMM...
AREN'T YOU FORGETTING SOMETHING?

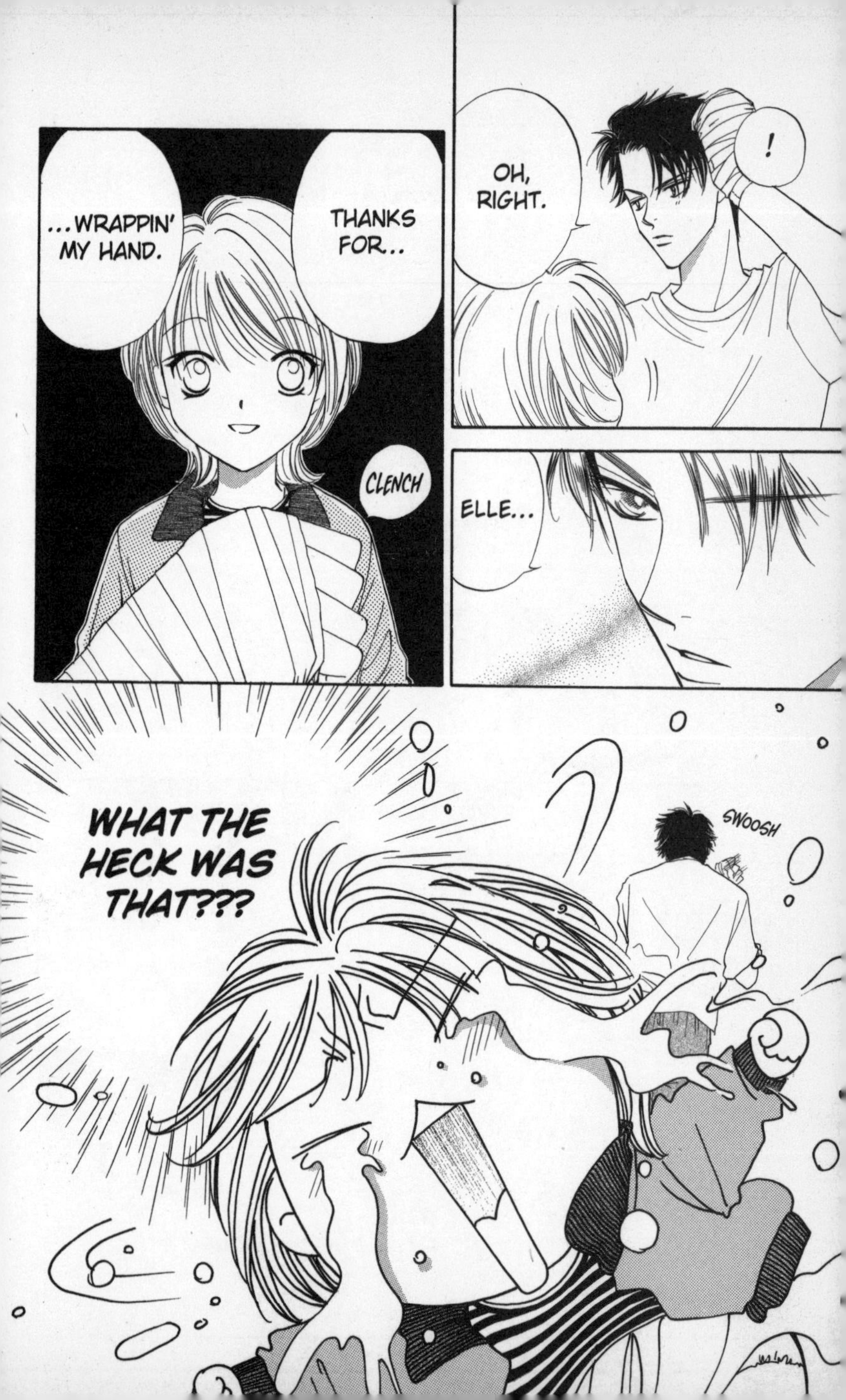
!
OH, RIGHT.
ELLE...
THANKS FOR...
...WRAPPIN' MY HAND.
CLENCH
SWOOSH
WHAT THE HECK WAS THAT???

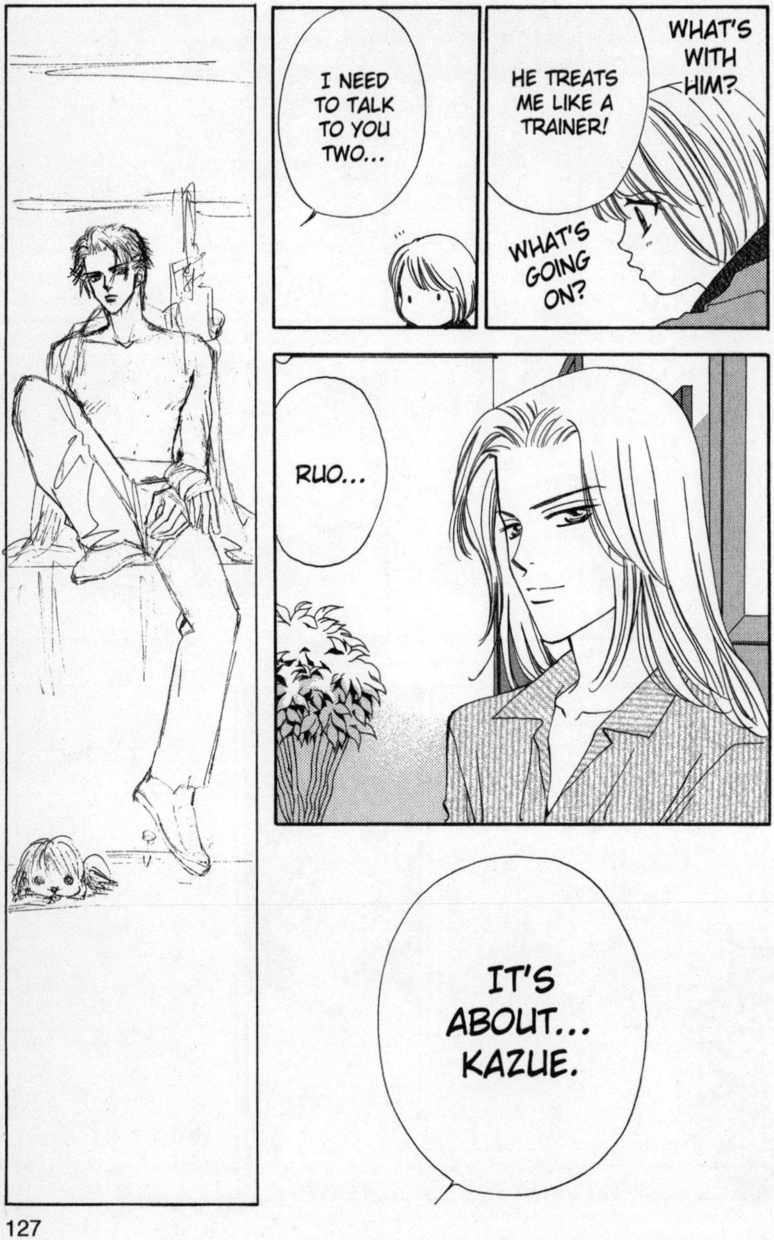
WHAT'S WITH HIM?
HE TREATS ME LIKE A TRAINER!
WHAT'S GOING ON?
I NEED TO TALK TO YOU TWO...
RUO...
IT'S ABOUT... KAZUE.

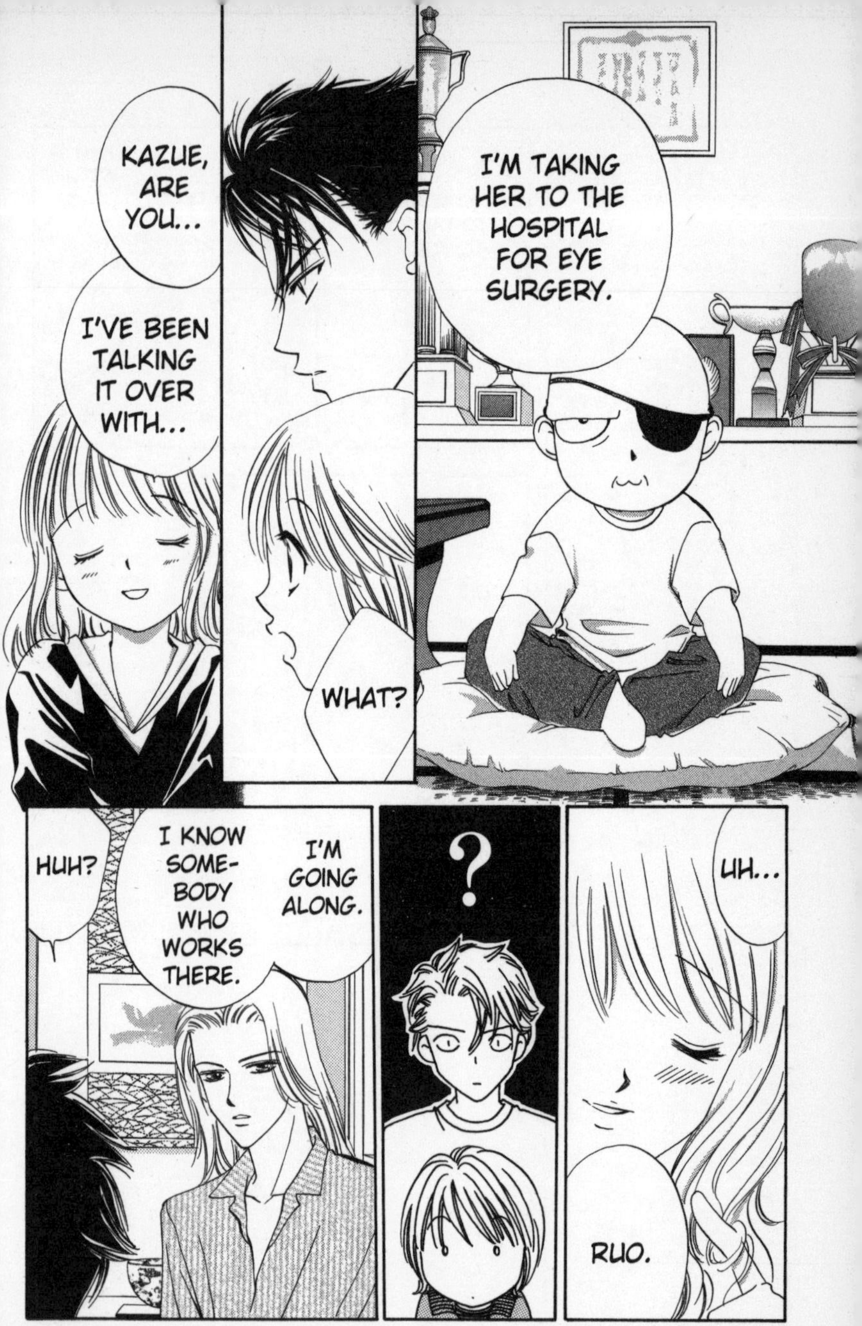
I'M TAKING HER TO THE HOSPITAL FOR EYE SURGERY.
WHAT?
KAZUE, ARE YOU...
I'VE BEEN TALKING IT OVER WITH...
UH...
RUO.
?
I'M GOING ALONG.
I KNOW SOME-BODY WHO WORKS THERE.
HUH?

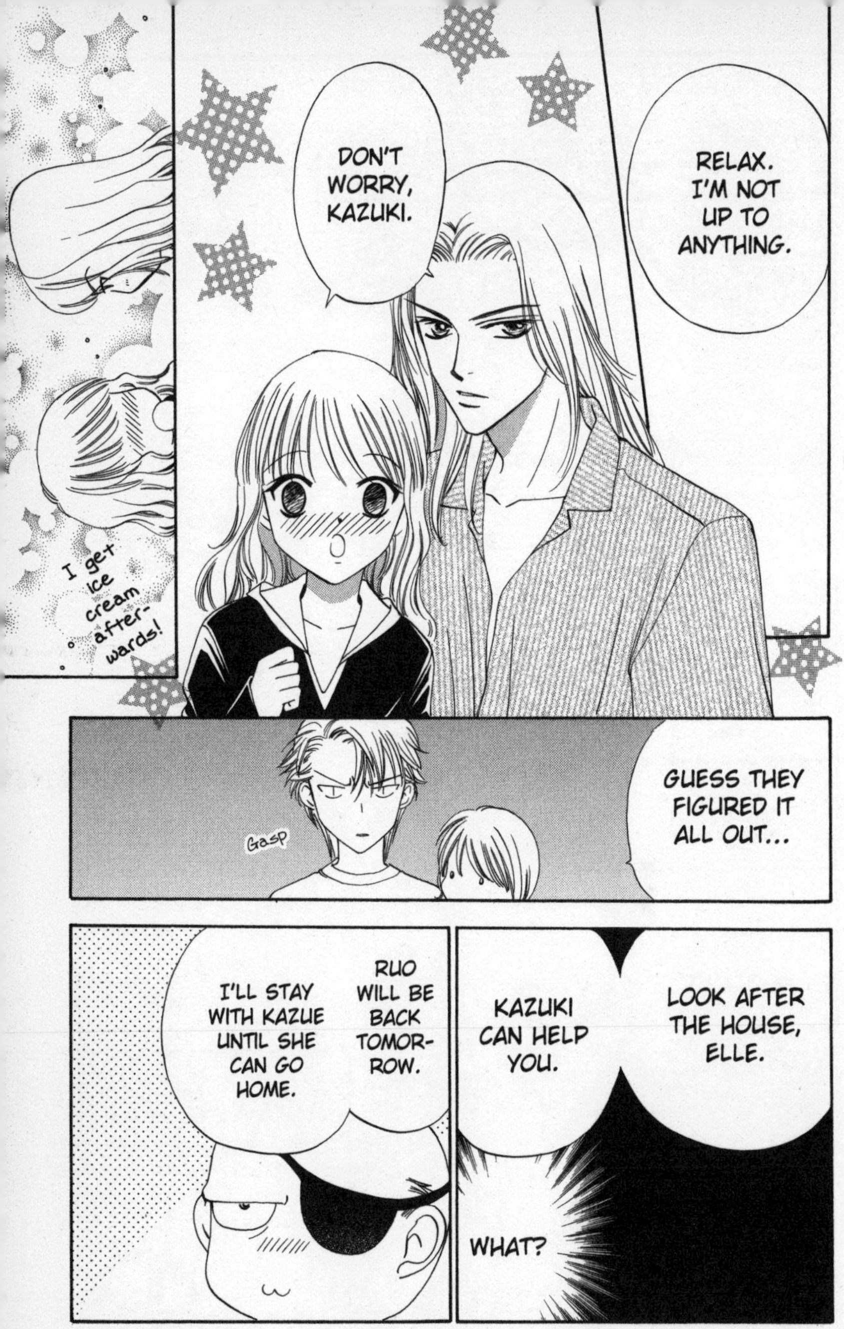
RELAX. I'M NOT UP TO ANYTHING.
DON'T WORRY, KAZUKI.
I get ice cream after-wards!
GUESS THEY FIGURED IT ALL OUT...
Gasp
LOOK AFTER THE HOUSE, ELLE.
KAZUKI CAN HELP YOU.
WHAT?
RUO WILL BE BACK TOMOR-ROW.
I'LL STAY WITH KAZUE UNTIL SHE CAN GO HOME.

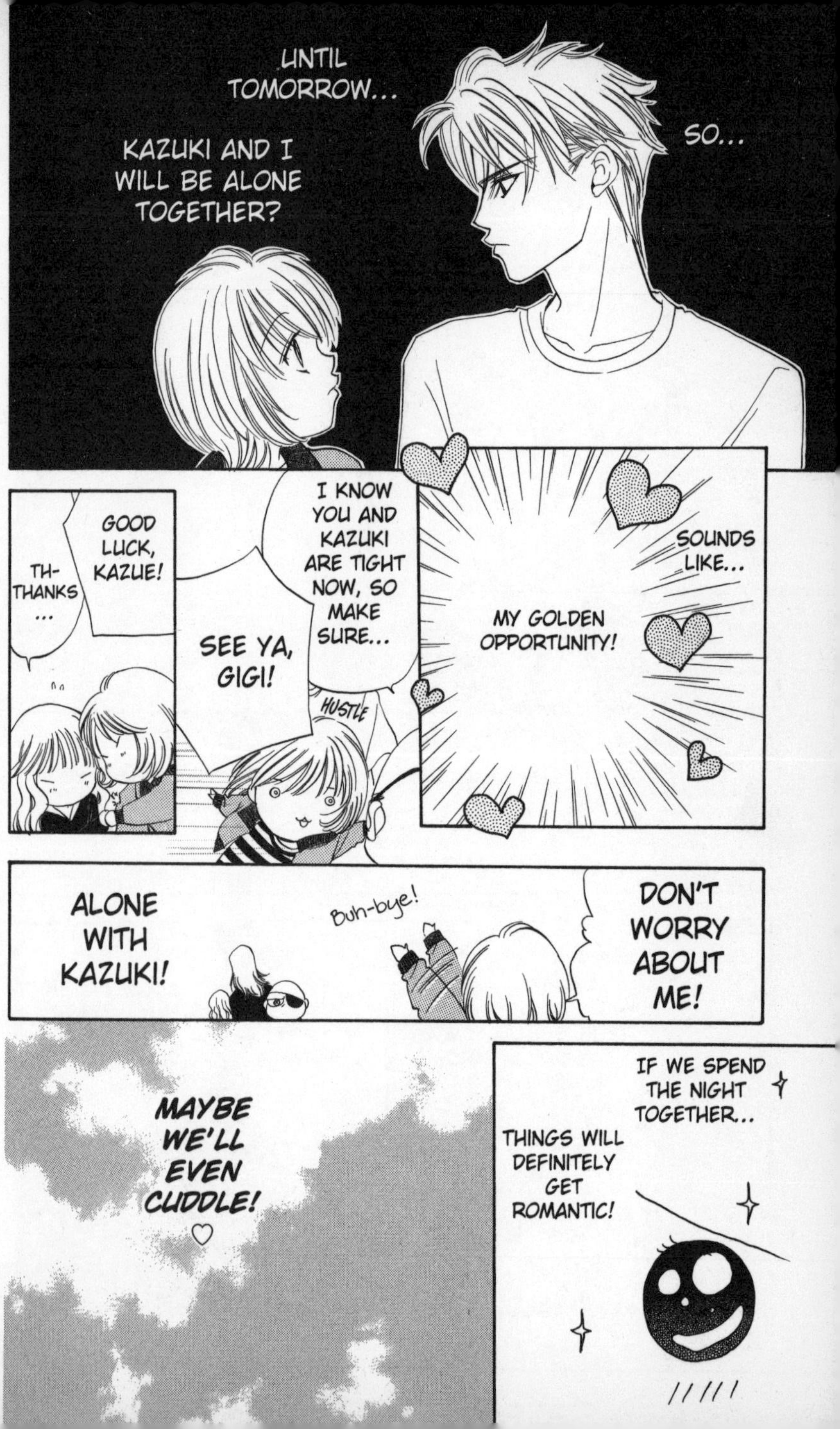
SO...
UNTIL TOMORROW...
KAZUKI AND I WILL BE ALONE TOGETHER?
SOUNDS LIKE...
MY GOLDEN OPPORTUNITY!
I KNOW YOU AND KAZUKI ARE TIGHT NOW, SO MAKE SURE...
HUSTLE
SEE YA, GIGI!
GOOD LUCK, KAZUE!
TH-THANKS ...
DON'T WORRY ABOUT ME!
Buh-bye!
ALONE WITH KAZUKI!
IF WE SPEND THE NIGHT TOGETHER...
THINGS WILL DEFINITELY GET ROMANTIC!
MAYBE WE'LL EVEN CUDDLE! ♡

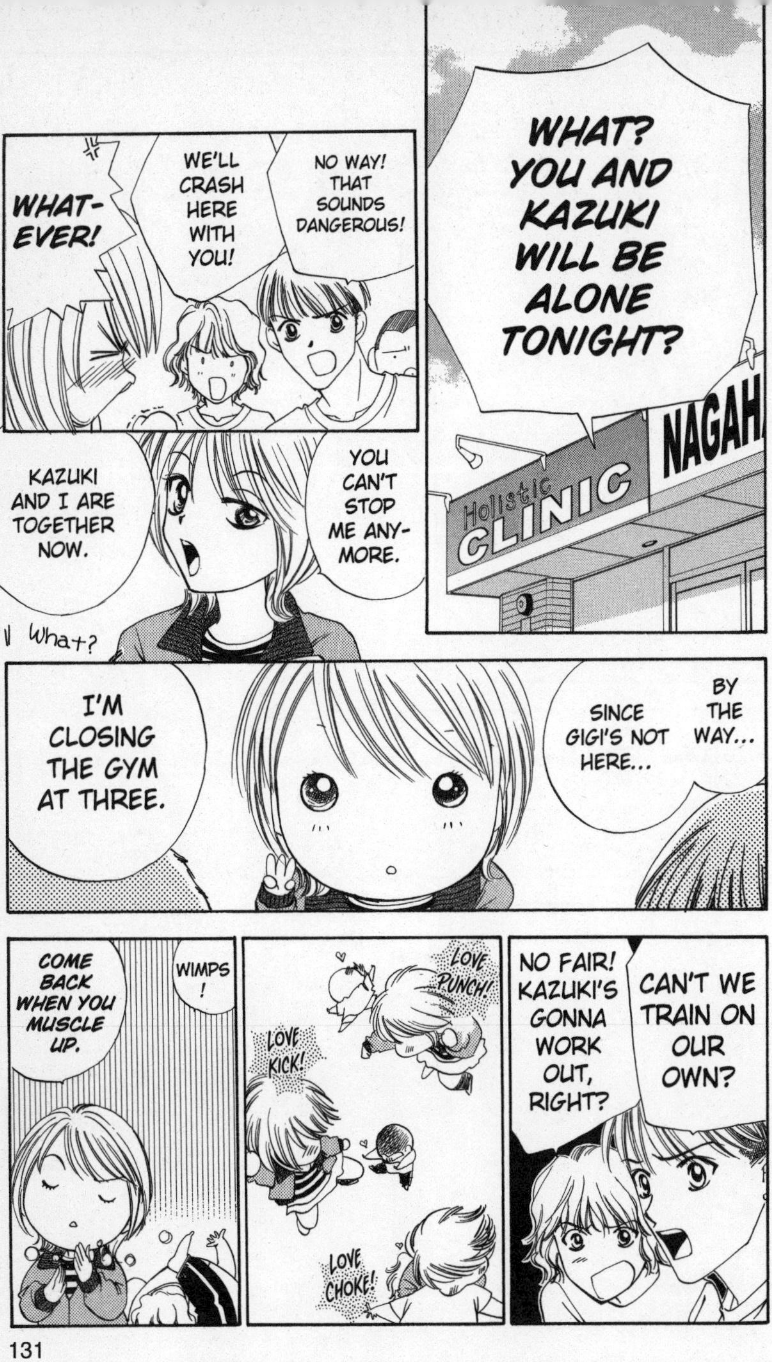
WHAT? YOU AND KAZUKI WILL BE ALONE TONIGHT?
Holistic CLINIC
NAGAH
NO WAY! THAT SOUNDS DANGEROUS!
WE'LL CRASH HERE WITH YOU!
WHAT-EVER!
YOU CAN'T STOP ME ANY-MORE.
KAZUKI AND I ARE TOGETHER NOW.
What?
BY THE WAY...
SINCE GIGI'S NOT HERE...
I'M CLOSING THE GYM AT THREE.
CAN'T WE TRAIN ON OUR OWN?
NO FAIR! KAZUKI'S GONNA WORK OUT, RIGHT?
LOVE PUNCH!
LOVE KICK!
LOVE CHOKE!
WIMPS!
COME BACK WHEN YOU MUSCLE UP.

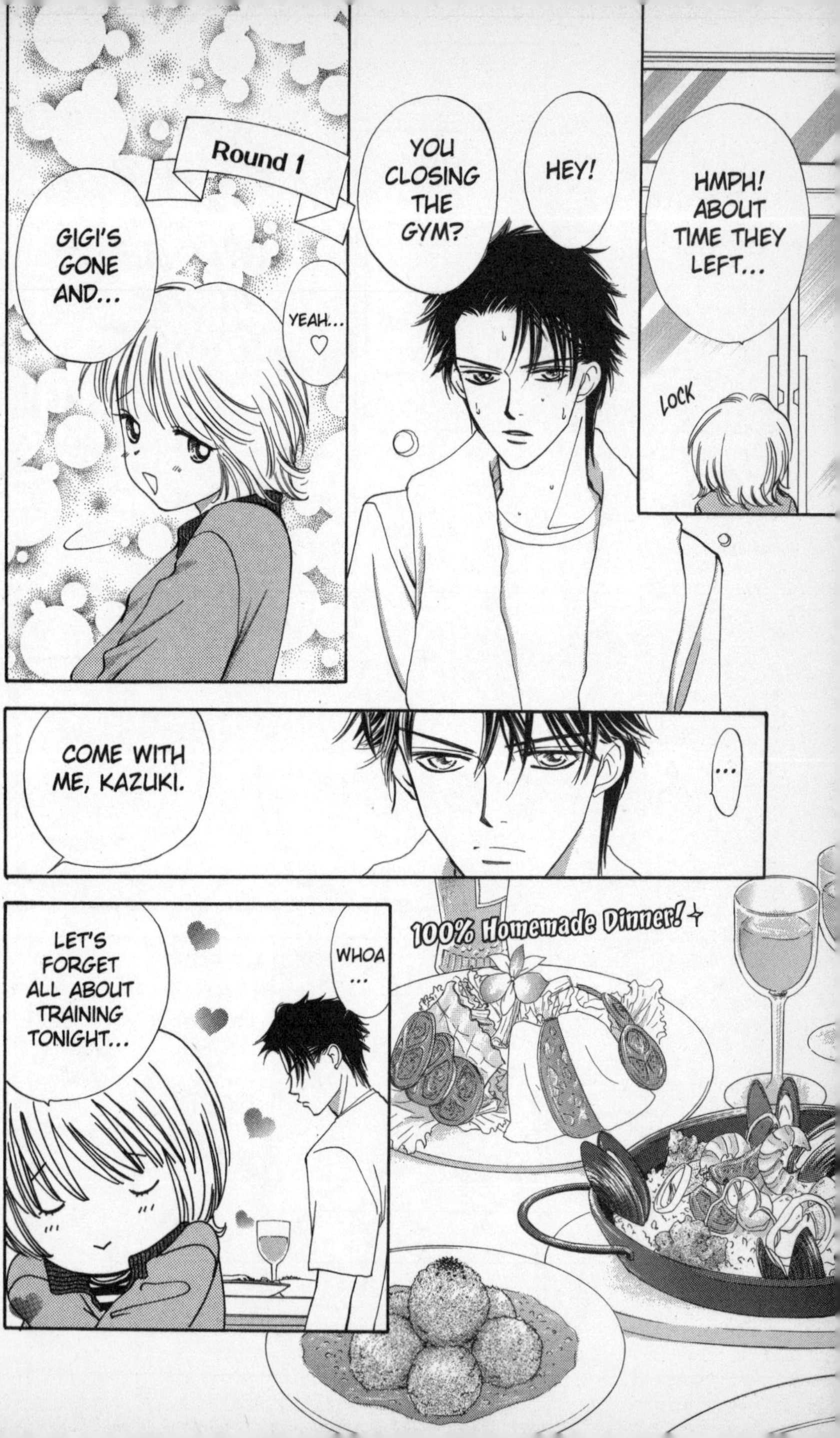
HMPH! ABOUT TIME THEY LEFT...
LOCK
HEY!
YOU CLOSING THE GYM?
Round 1
GIGI'S GONE AND...
YEAH... ♡
...
COME WITH ME, KAZUKI.
100% Homemade Dinner!
WHOA ...
LET'S FORGET ALL ABOUT TRAINING TONIGHT...

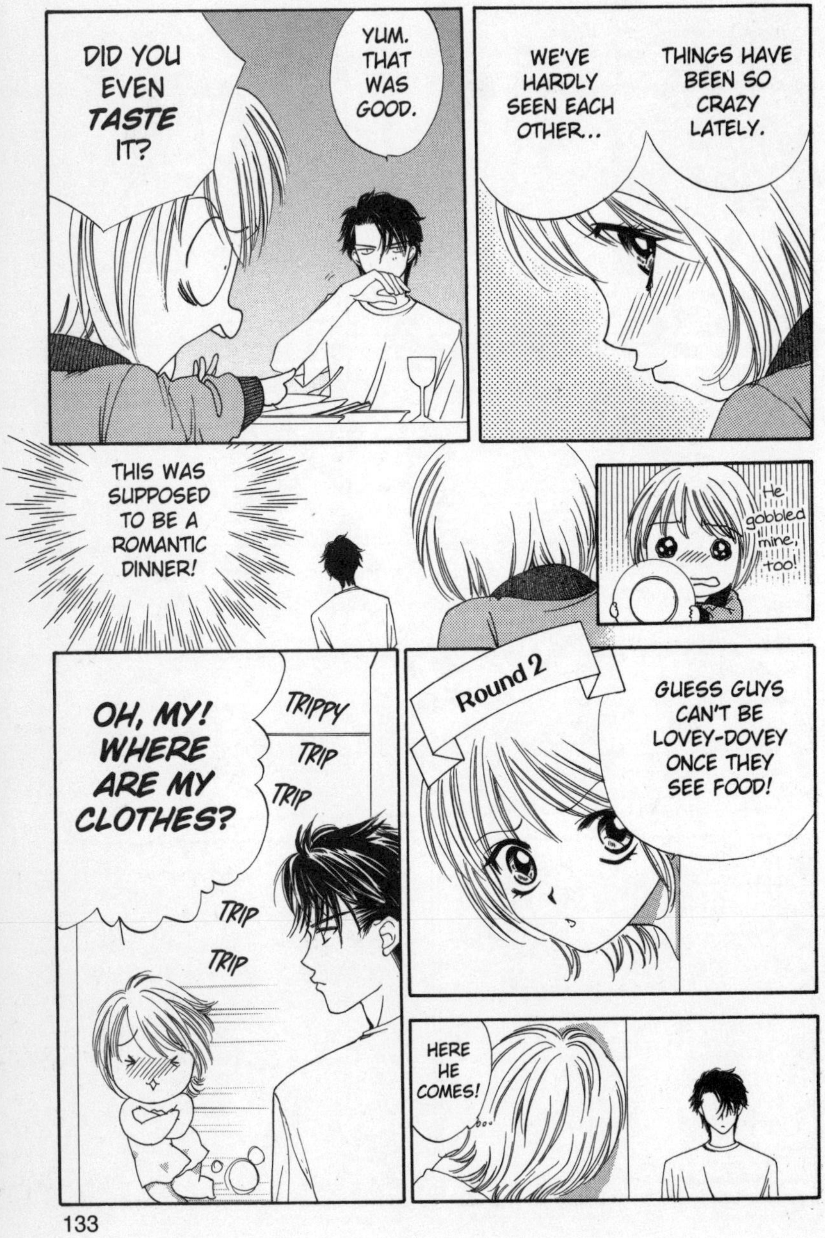
THINGS HAVE BEEN SO CRAZY LATELY.
WE'VE HARDLY SEEN EACH OTHER...
YUM. THAT WAS GOOD.
DID YOU EVEN TASTE IT?
He gobbled mine, too!
THIS WAS SUPPOSED TO BE A ROMANTIC DINNER!
Round 2
GUESS GUYS CAN'T BE LOVEY-DOVEY ONCE THEY SEE FOOD!
HERE HE COMES!
OH, MY! WHERE ARE MY CLOTHES?
TRIPPY
TRIP
TRIP
TRIP
TRIP

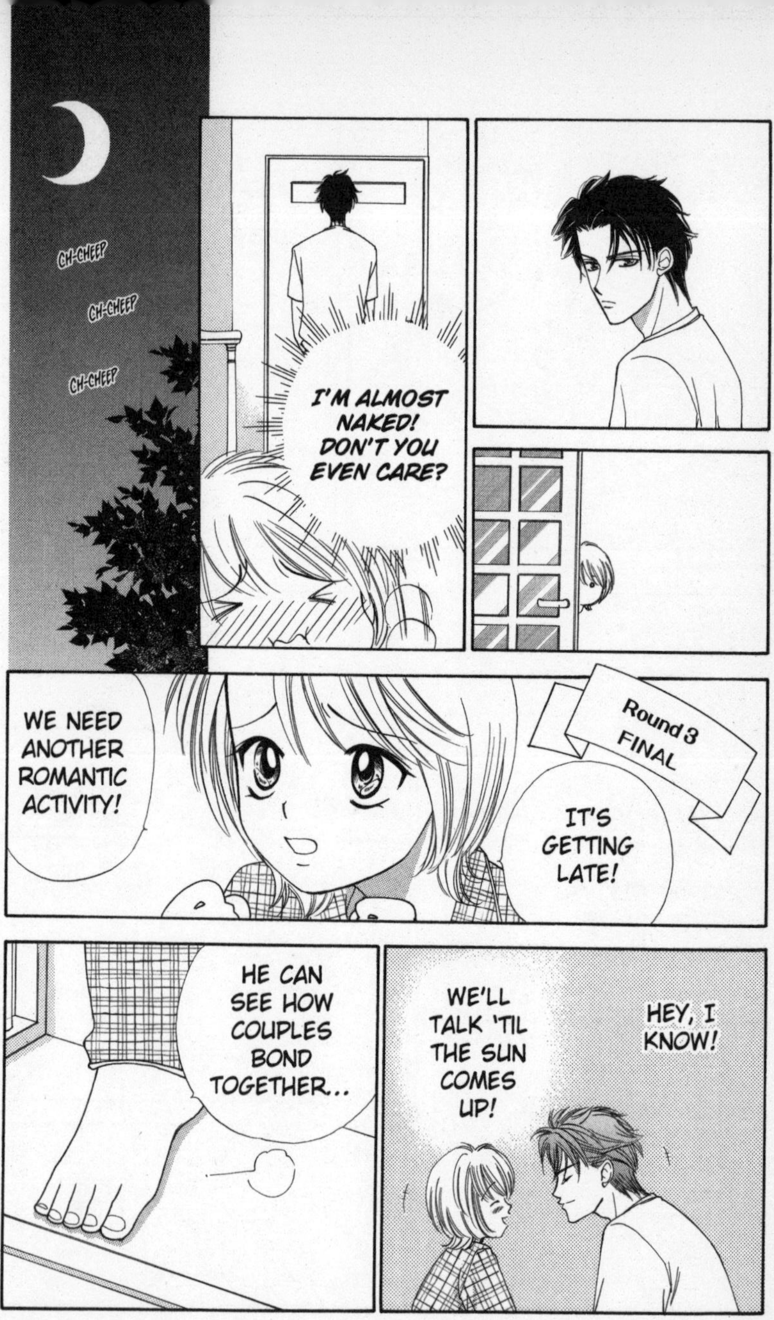
I'M ALMOST NAKED! DON'T YOU EVEN CARE?
CH-CHEEP
CH-CHEEP
CH-CHEEP
Round 3 FINAL
IT'S GETTING LATE!
WE NEED ANOTHER ROMANTIC ACTIVITY!
HEY, I KNOW!
WE'LL TALK 'TIL THE SUN COMES UP!
HE CAN SEE HOW COUPLES BOND TOGETHER...

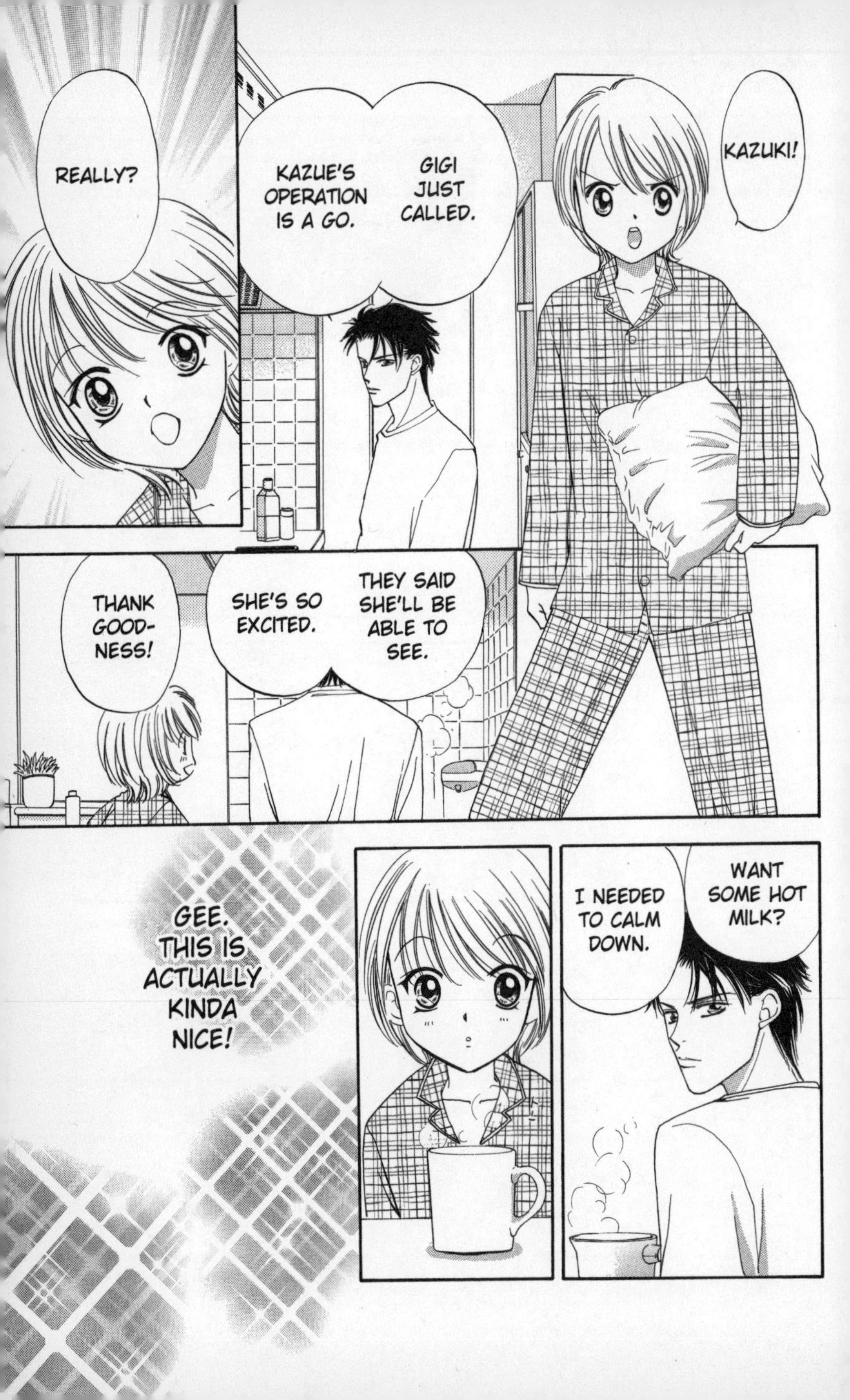
KAZUKI!
GIGI JUST CALLED.
KAZUE'S OPERATION IS A GO.
REALLY?
THEY SAID SHE'LL BE ABLE TO SEE.
SHE'S SO EXCITED.
THANK GOOD-NESS!
WANT SOME HOT MILK?
I NEEDED TO CALM DOWN.
GEE. THIS IS ACTUALLY KINDA NICE!

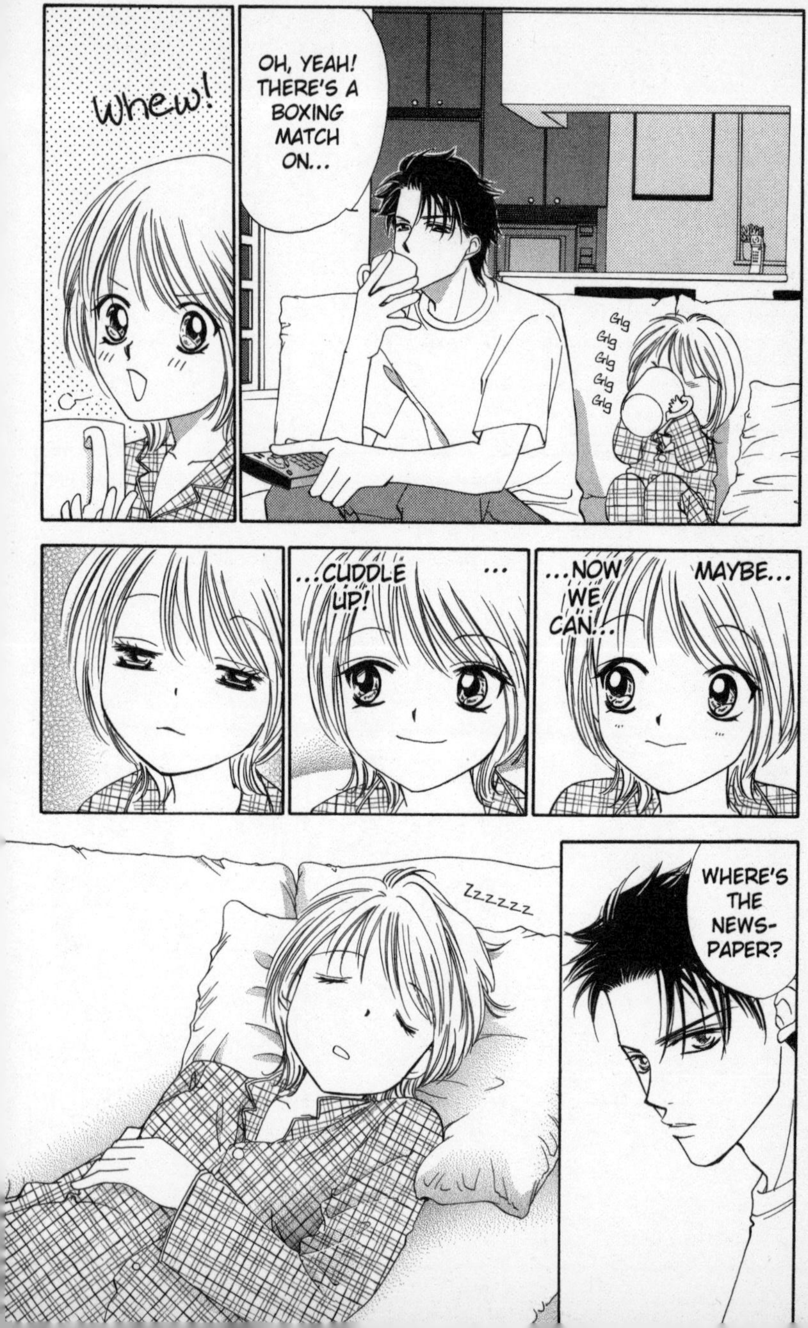
OH, YEAH! THERE'S A BOXING MATCH ON...
Grlg Grlg Grlg Grlg Grlg
Whew!
MAYBE...
...NOW WE CAN...
...
...CUDDLE UP!
WHERE'S THE NEWS-PAPER?
Zzzzzz

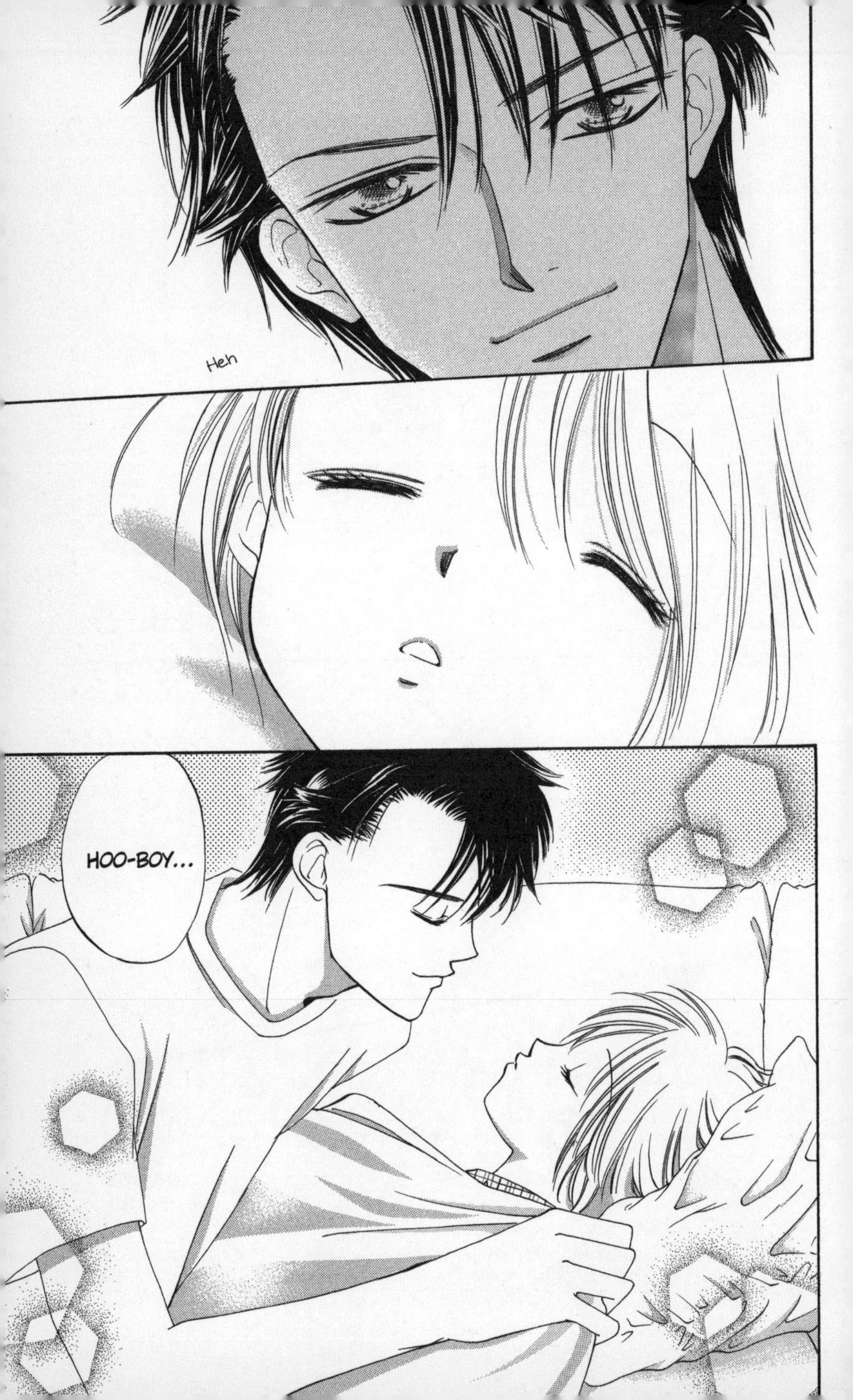
Heh
HOO-BOY...

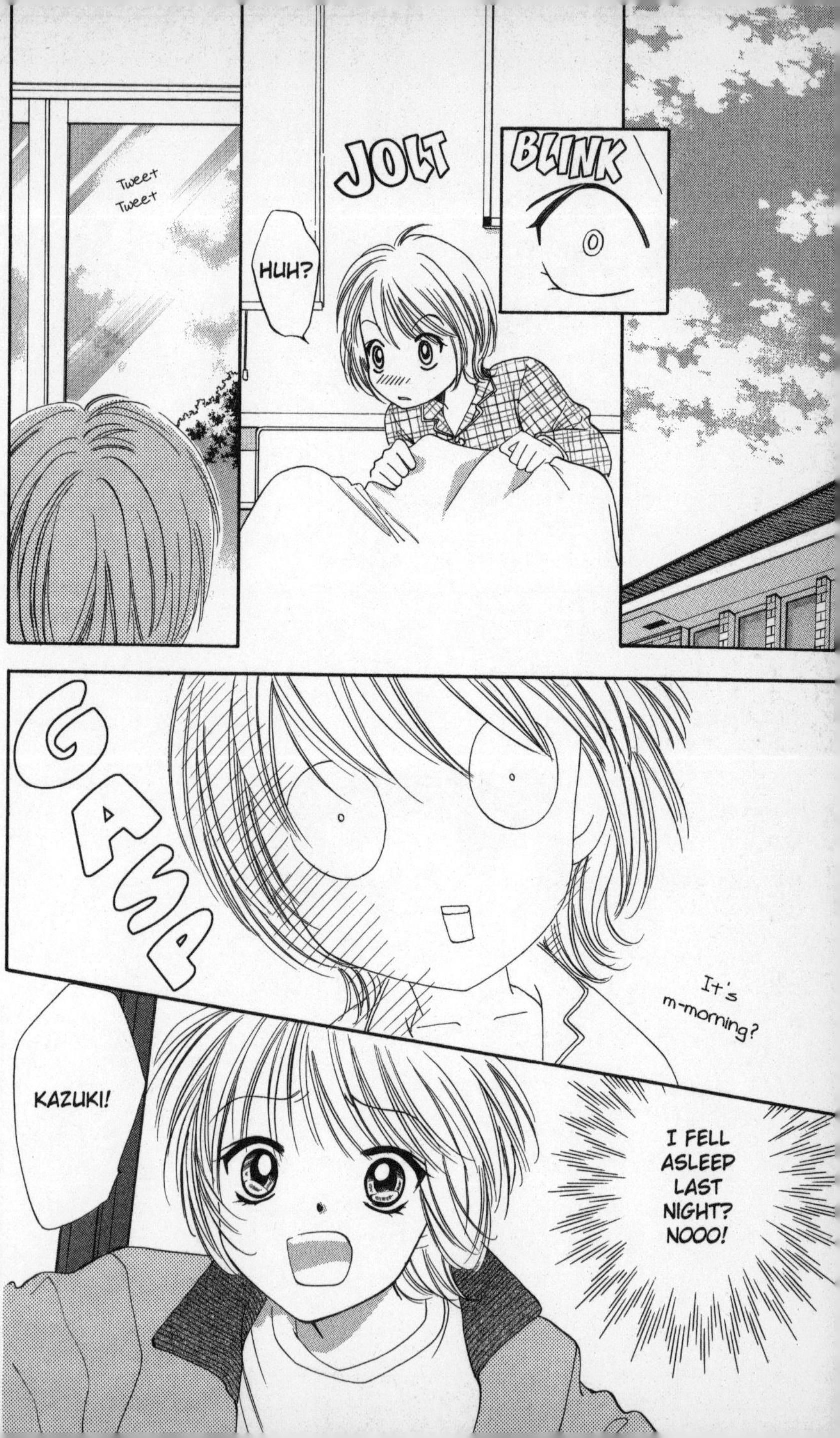
BLINK
JOLT
HUH?
Tweet Tweet
GAWA
It's m-morning?
I FELL ASLEEP LAST NIGHT? NOOO!
KAZUKI!

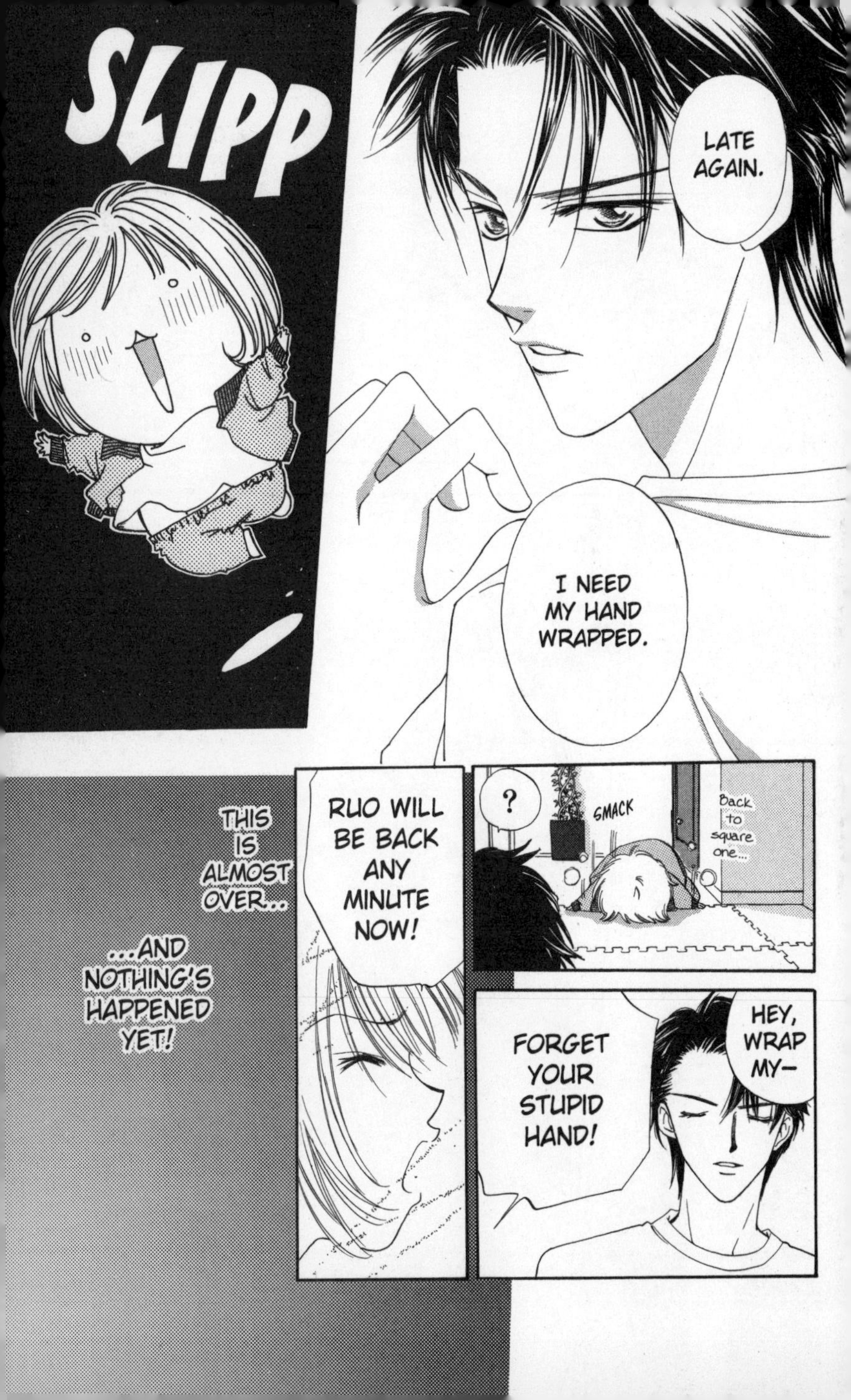
LATE AGAIN.
I NEED MY HAND WRAPPED.
SLIPP
?
SMACK
Back to square one...
HEY, WRAP MY—
FORGET YOUR STUPID HAND!
RUO WILL BE BACK ANY MINUTE NOW!
THIS IS ALMOST OVER...
...AND NOTHING'S HAPPENED YET!

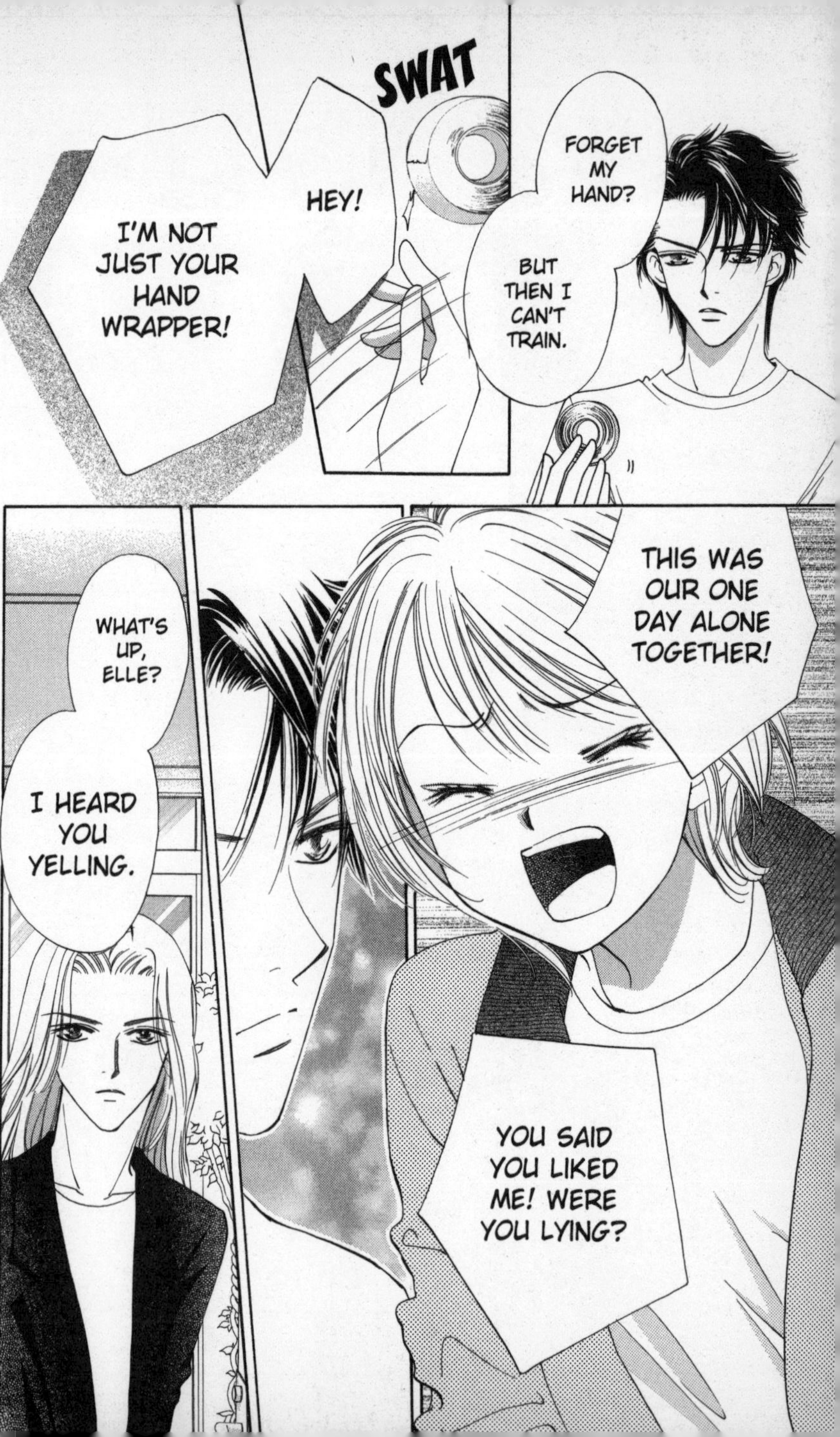
FORGET MY HAND?
BUT THEN I CAN'T TRAIN.
SWAT
HEY!
I'M NOT JUST YOUR HAND WRAPPER!
THIS WAS OUR ONE DAY ALONE TOGETHER!
YOU SAID YOU LIKED ME! WERE YOU LYING?
WHAT'S UP, ELLE?
I HEARD YOU YELLING.

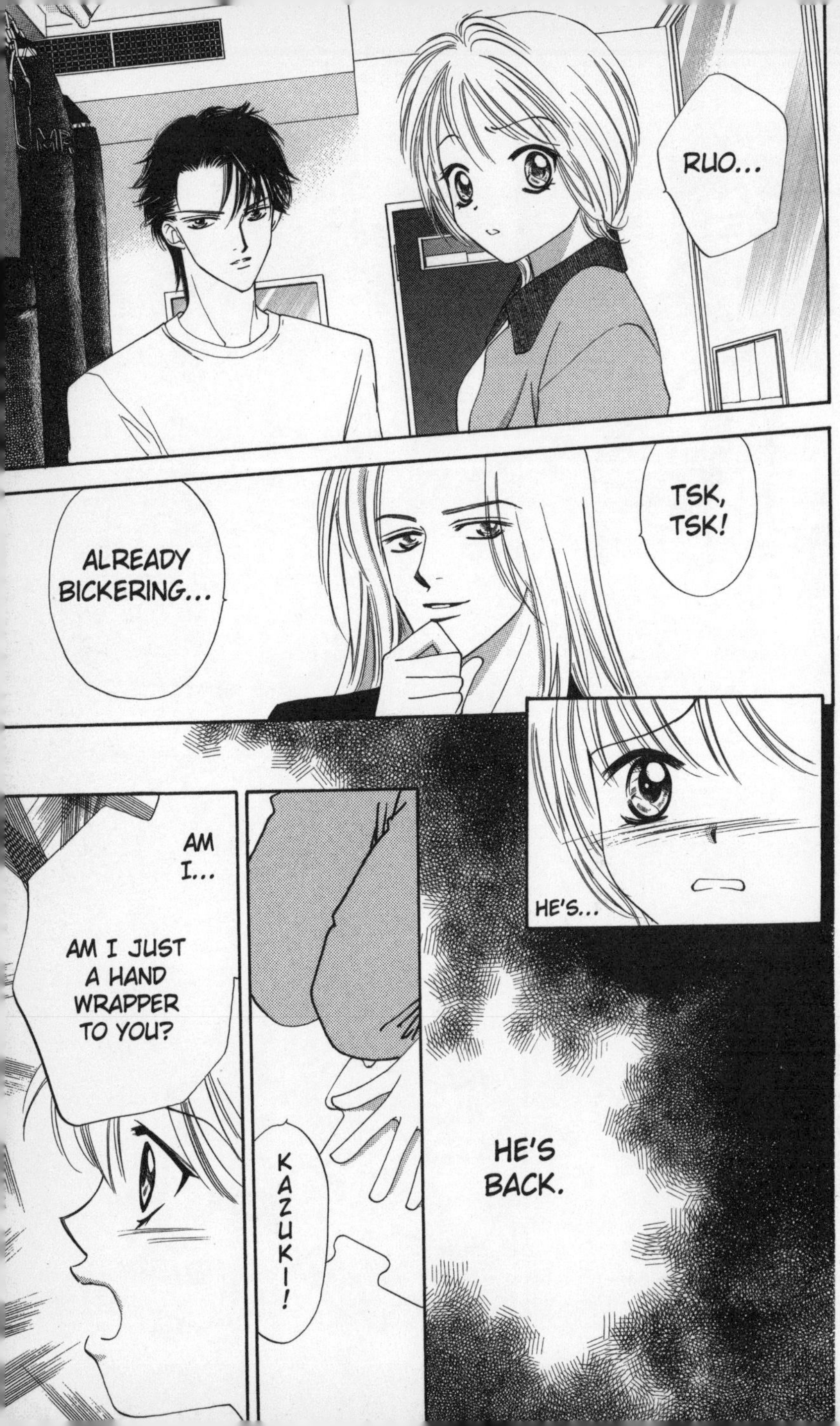
RUO...
TSK, TSK!
ALREADY BICKERING...
HE'S...
HE'S BACK.
KAZUKI!
AM I...
AM I JUST A HAND WRAPPER TO YOU?

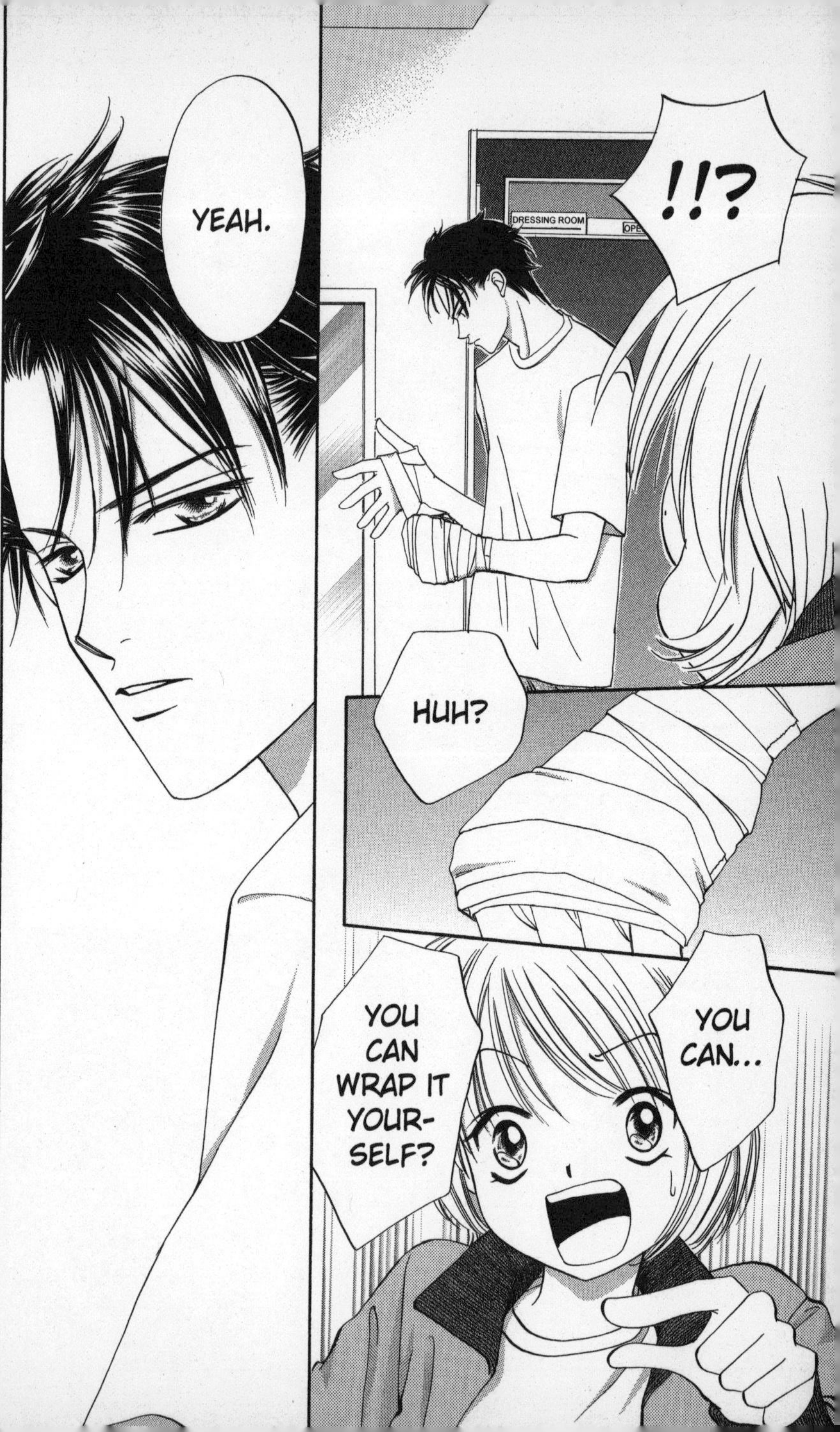
!!?
DRESSING ROOM
HUH?
YOU CAN...
YOU CAN WRAP IT YOUR-SELF?
YEAH.

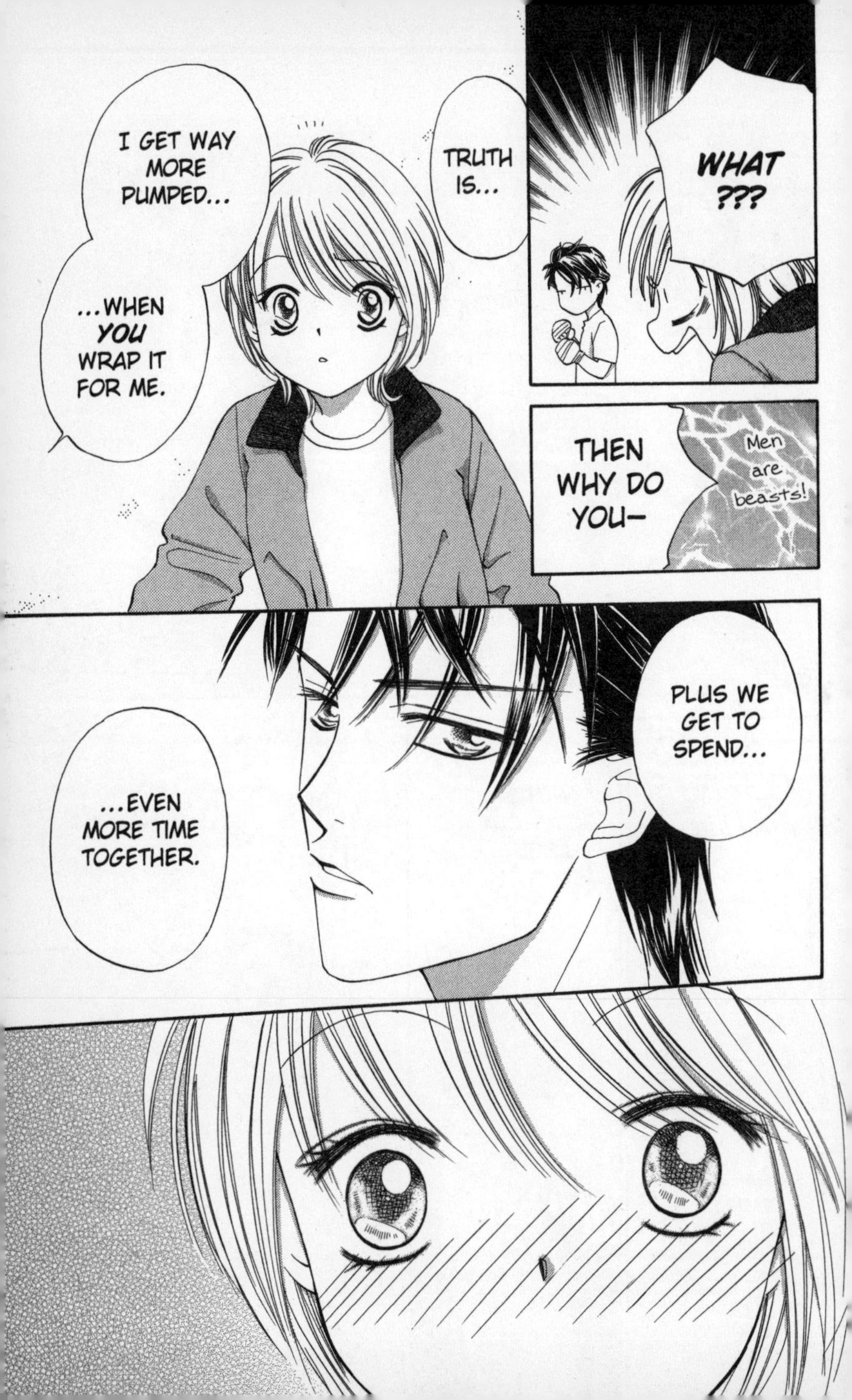
WHAT ???
Men are beasts!
THEN WHY DO YOU–
TRUTH IS...
I GET WAY MORE PUMPED...
...WHEN YOU WRAP IT FOR ME.
PLUS WE GET TO SPEND...
...EVEN MORE TIME TOGETHER.

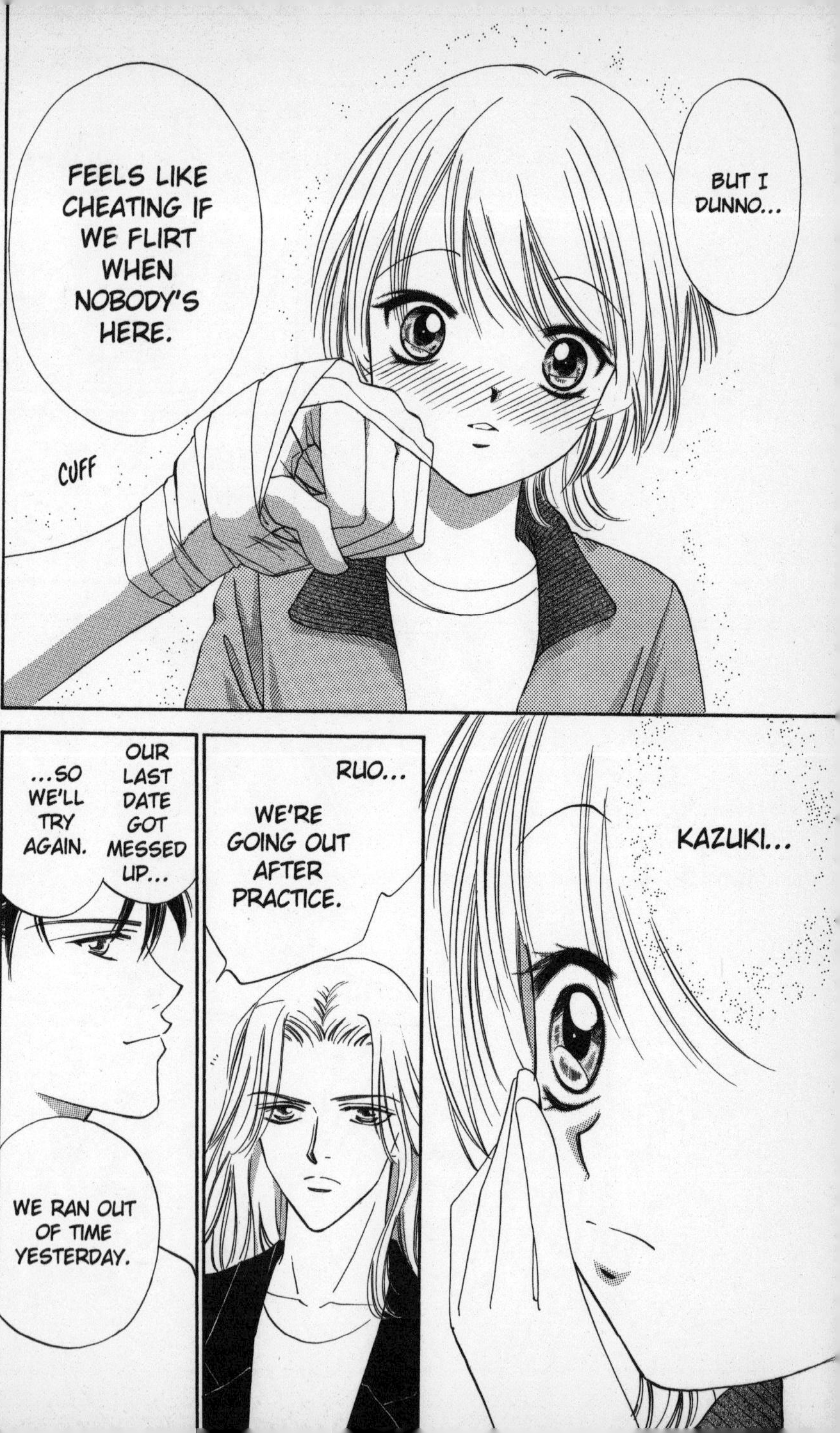
BUT I DUNNO...
FEELS LIKE CHEATING IF WE FLIRT WHEN NOBODY'S HERE.
CUFF
KAZUKI...
RUO...
WE'RE GOING OUT AFTER PRACTICE.
OUR LAST DATE GOT MESSED UP...
...SO WE'LL TRY AGAIN.
WE RAN OUT OF TIME YESTERDAY.

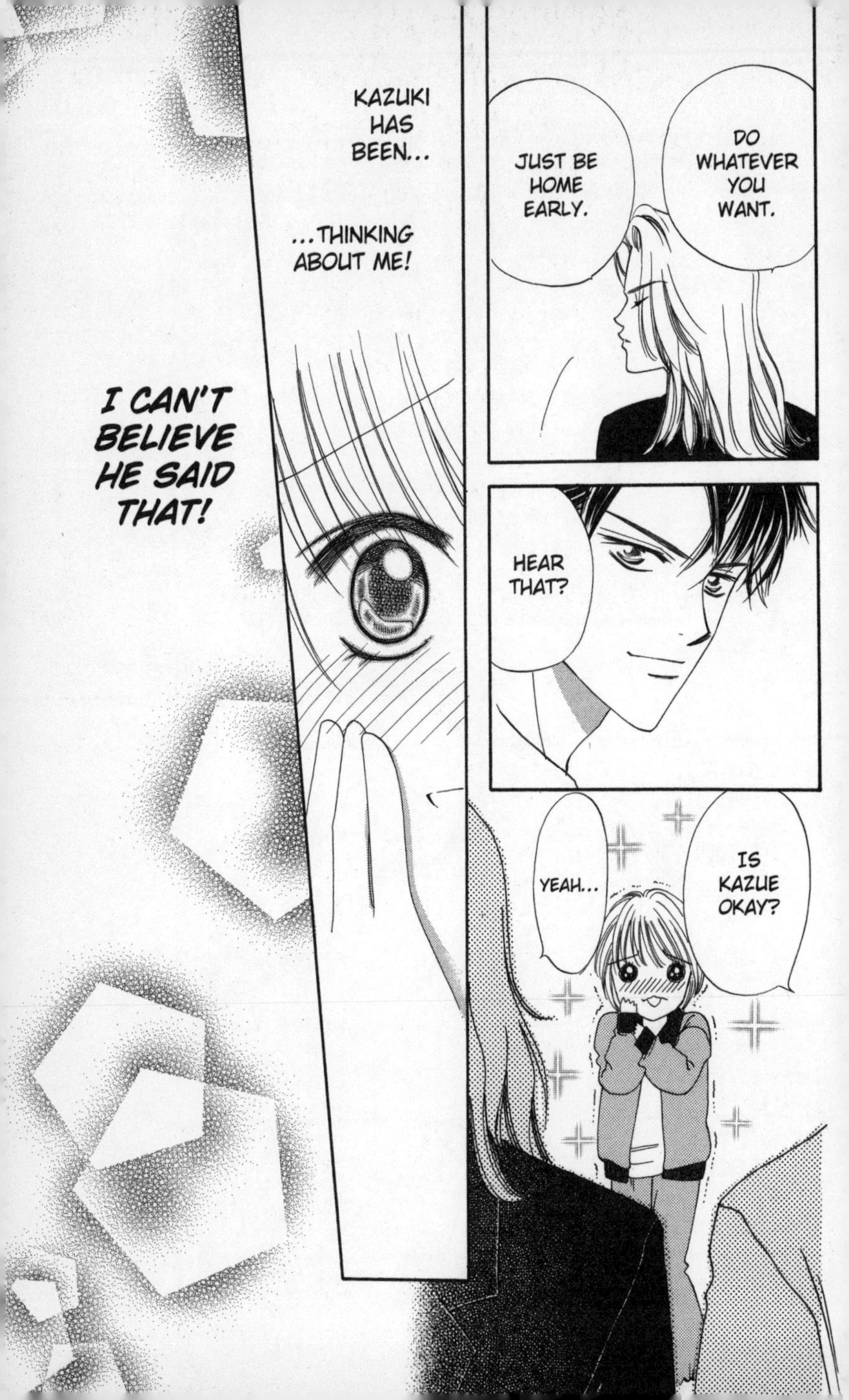
DO WHATEVER YOU WANT.
JUST BE HOME EARLY.
HEAR THAT?
IS KAZUE OKAY?
YEAH...
KAZUKI HAS BEEN...
...THINKING ABOUT ME!
I CAN'T BELIEVE HE SAID THAT!

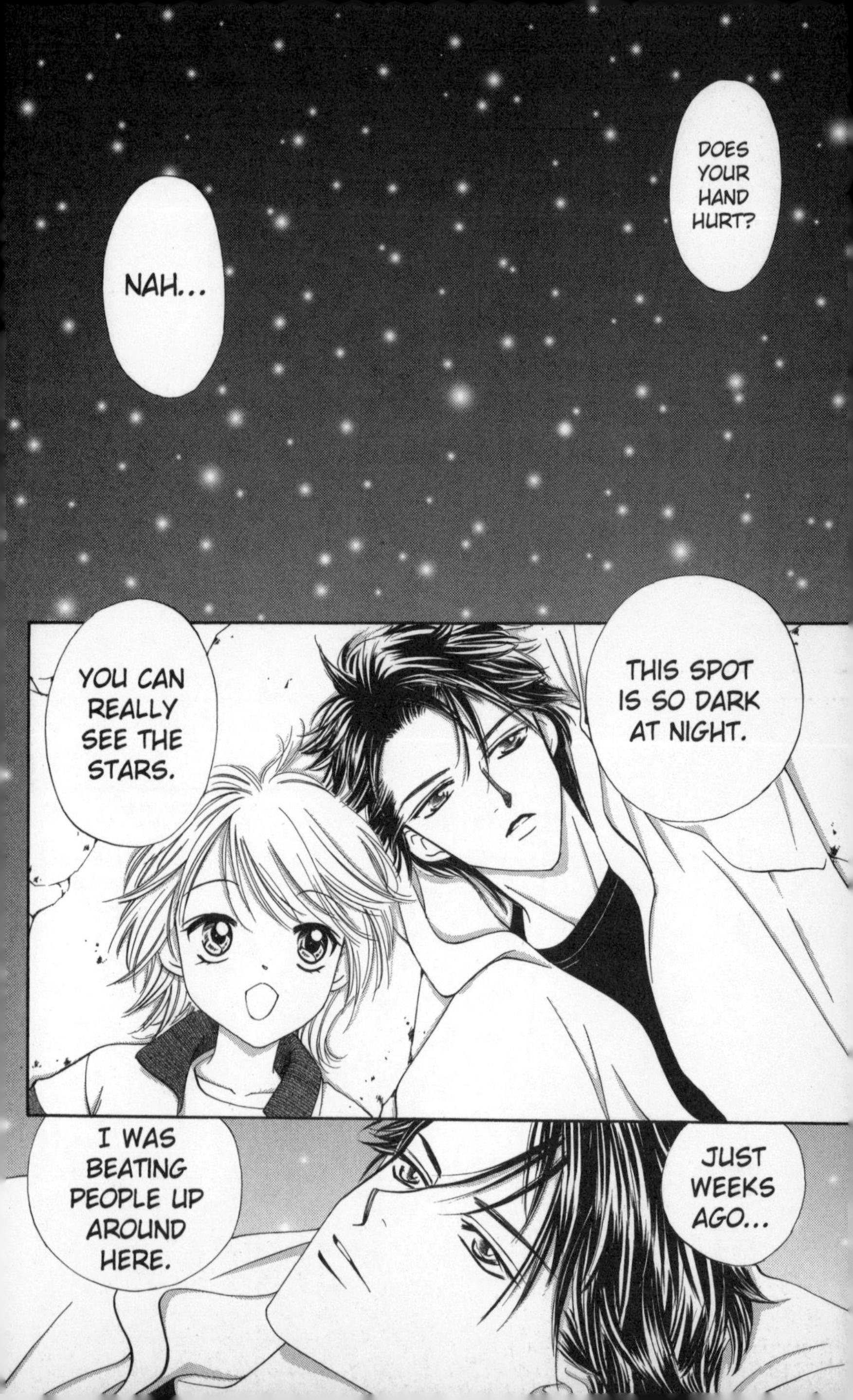
DOES YOUR HAND HURT?
NAH...
THIS SPOT IS SO DARK AT NIGHT.
YOU CAN REALLY SEE THE STARS.
JUST WEEKS AGO...
I WAS BEATING PEOPLE UP AROUND HERE.

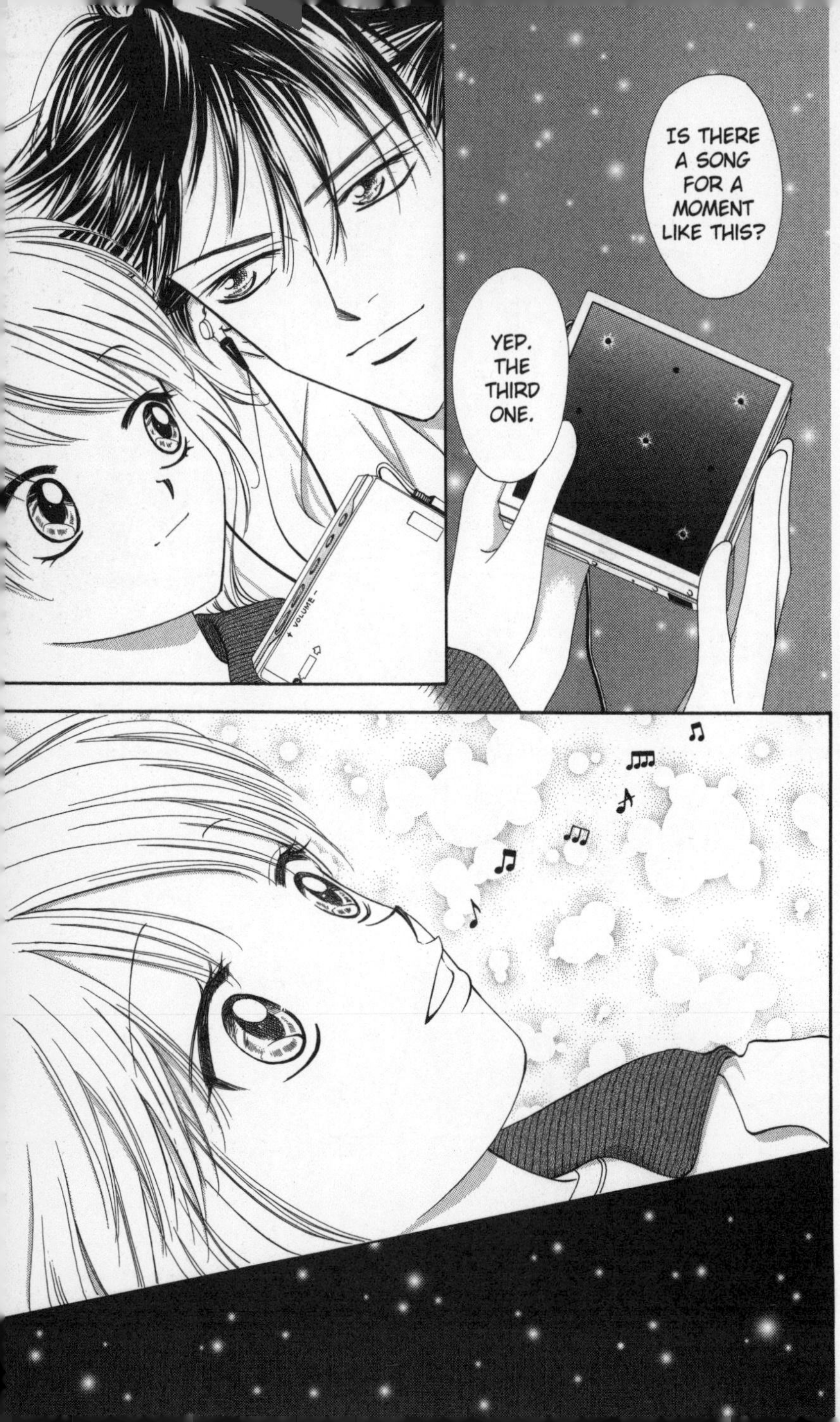
IS THERE A SONG FOR A MOMENT LIKE THIS?
YEP. THE THIRD ONE.
+ VOLUME -

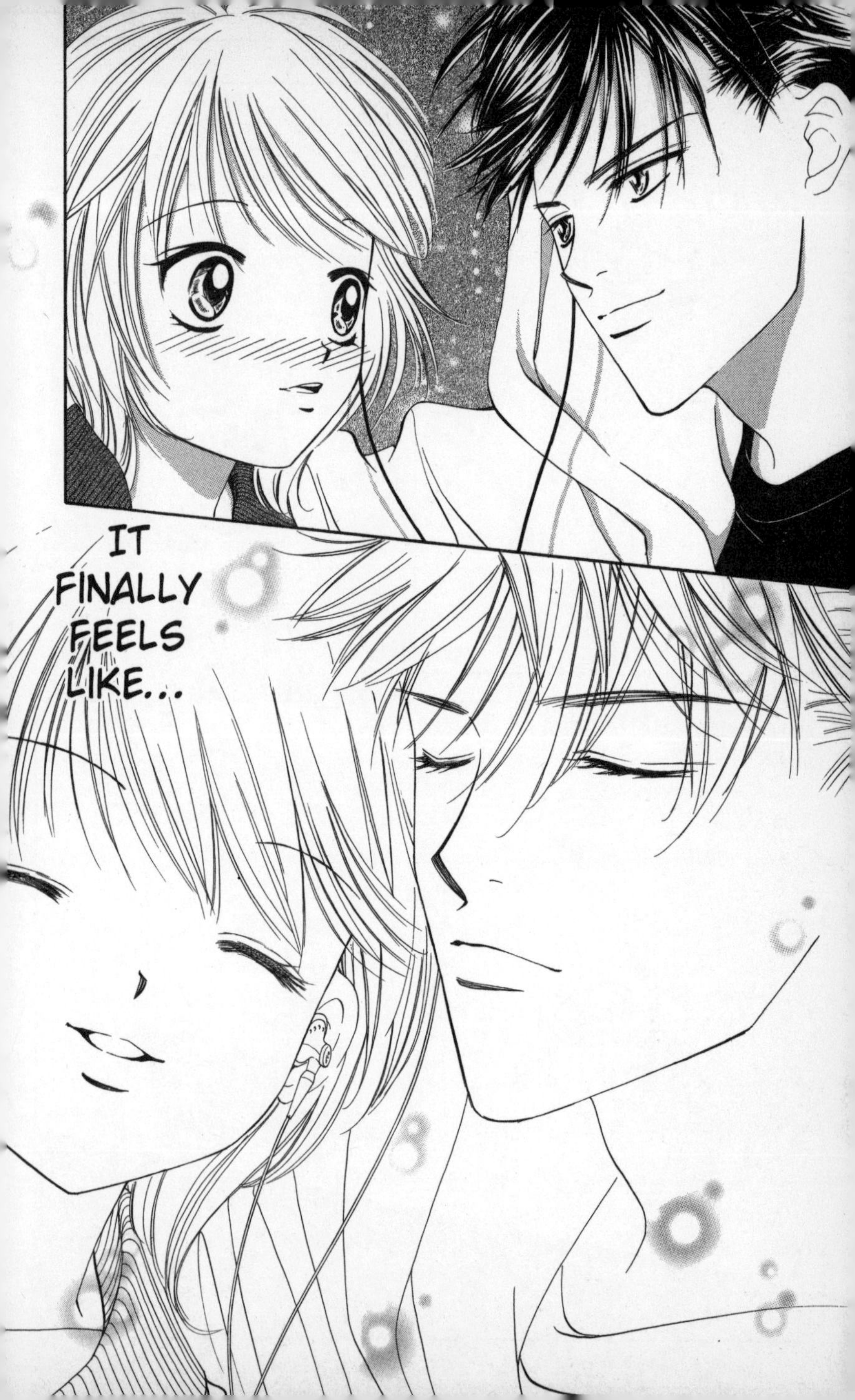
IT FINALLY FEELS LIKE...

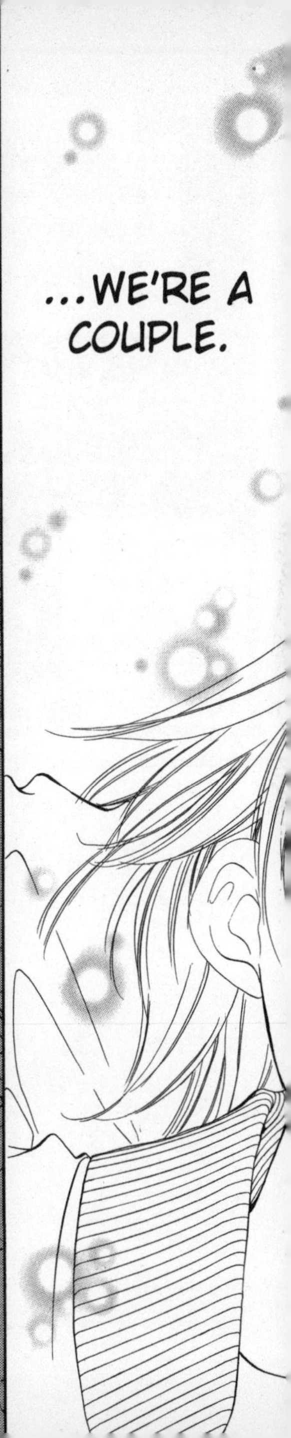
...WE'RE A COUPLE.

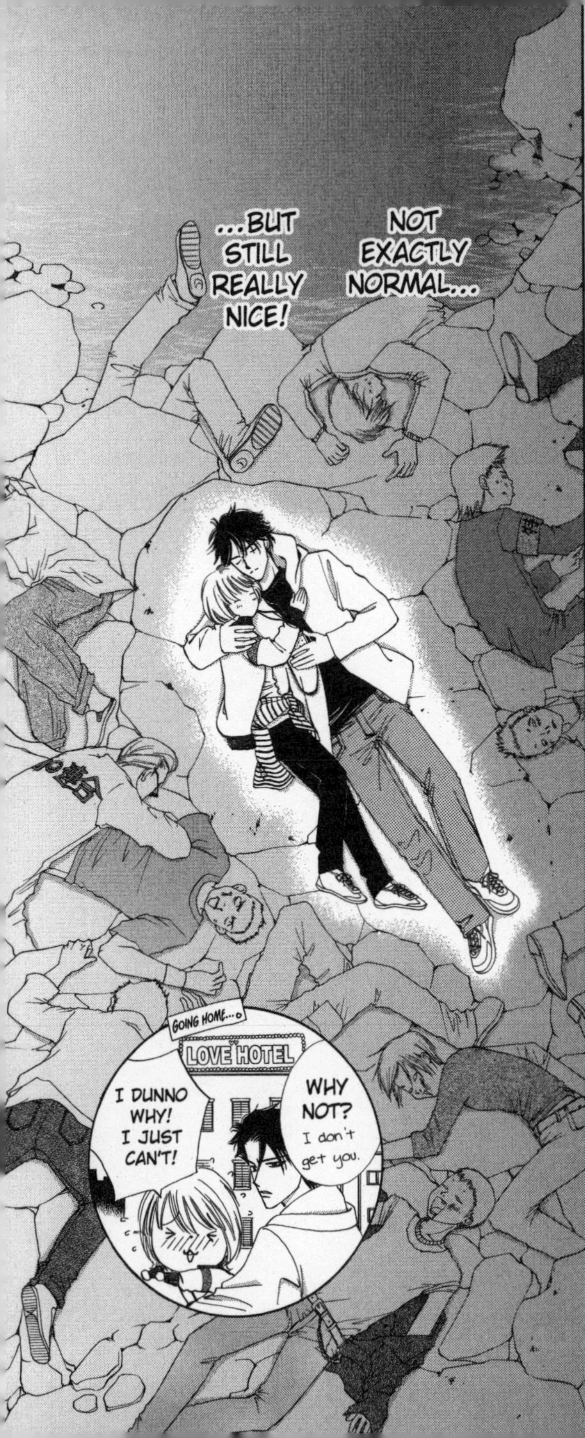
NOT EXACTLY NORMAL...
...BUT STILL REALLY NICE!
GOING HOME...
LOVE HOTEL
WHY NOT? I don't get you.
I DUNNO WHY! I JUST CAN'T!

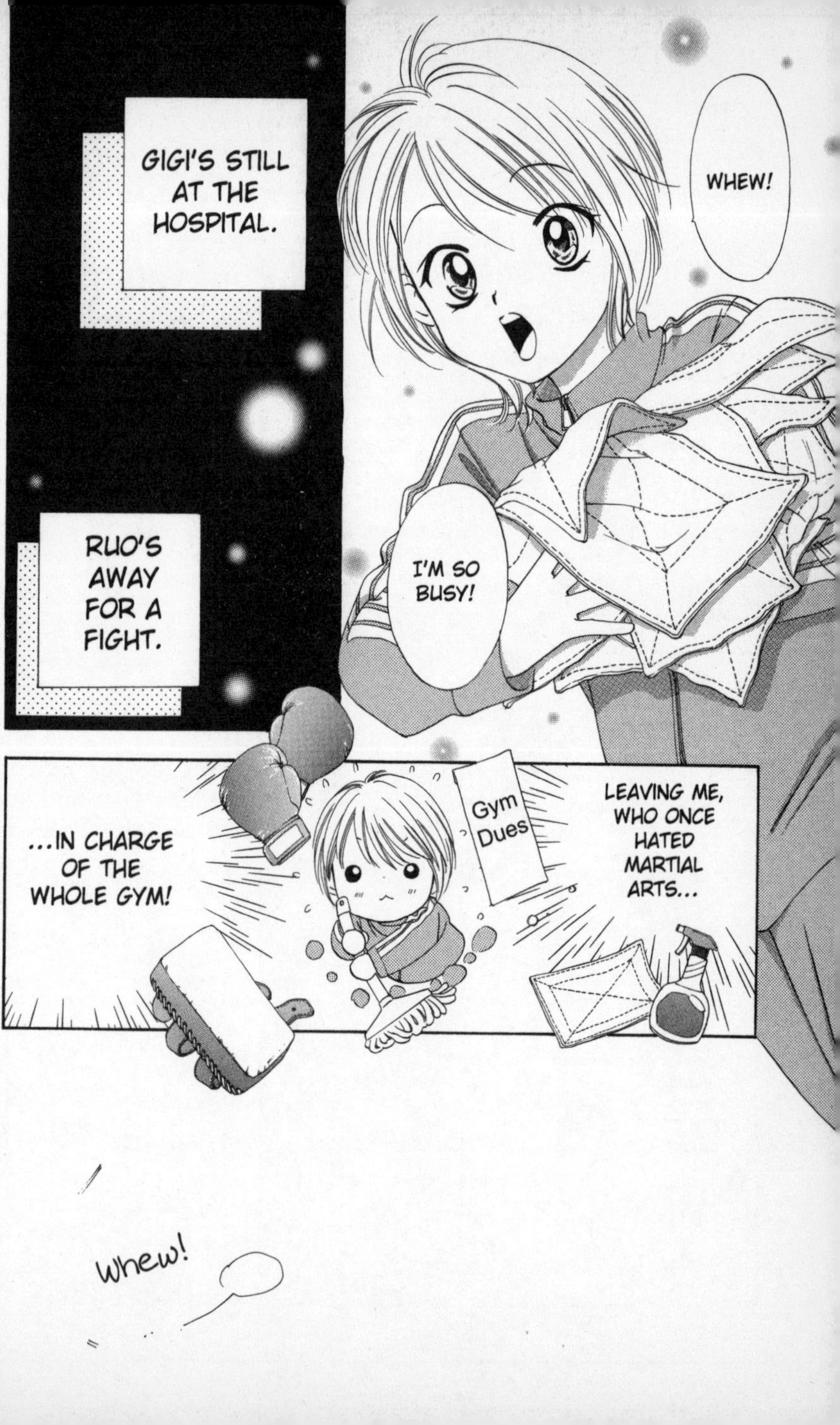
WHEW!
I'M SO BUSY!
GIGI'S STILL AT THE HOSPITAL.
RUO'S AWAY FOR A FIGHT.
LEAVING ME, WHO ONCE HATED MARTIAL ARTS...
Gym Dues
...IN CHARGE OF THE WHOLE GYM!
Whew!

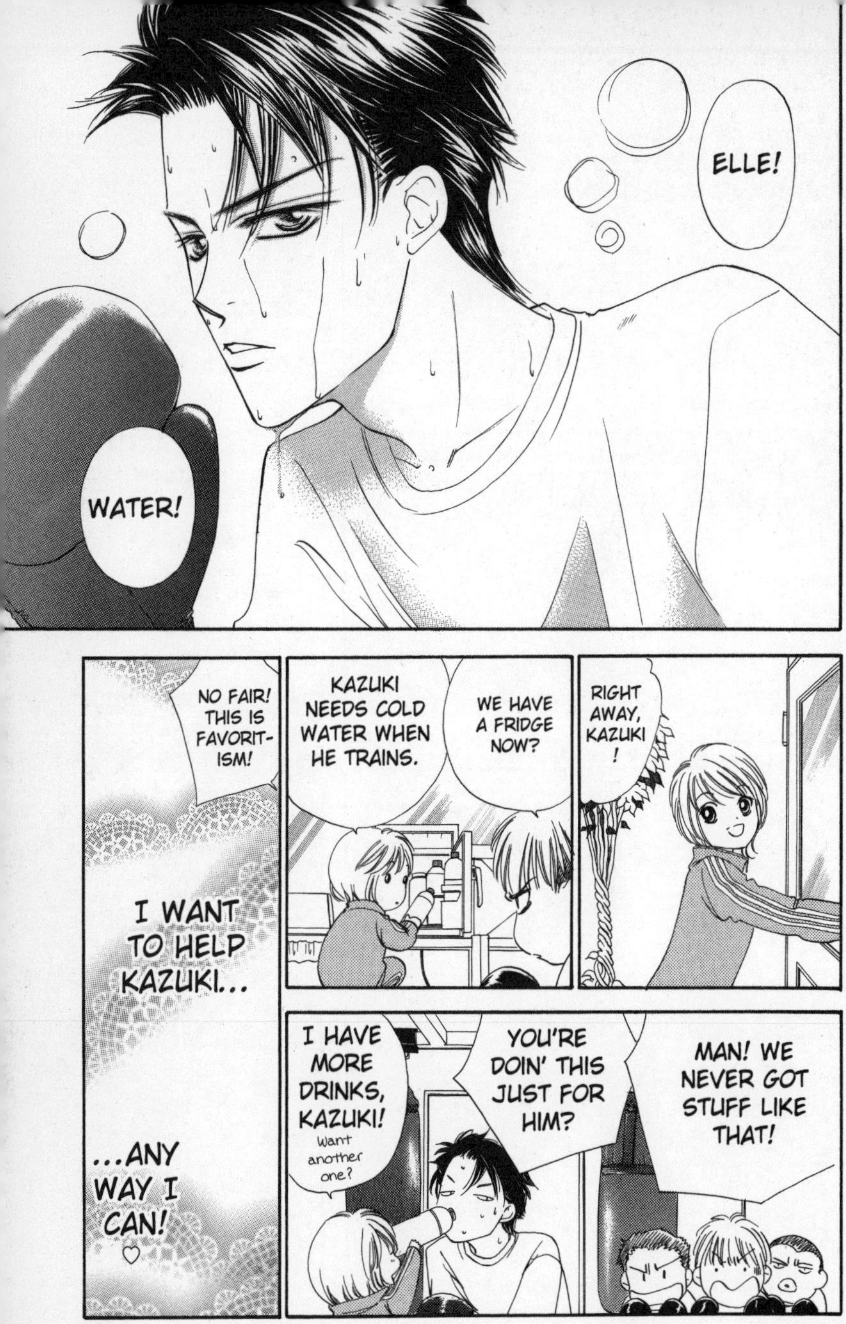
ELLE!
WATER!
RIGHT AWAY, KAZUKI!
WE HAVE A FRIDGE NOW?
KAZUKI NEEDS COLD WATER WHEN HE TRAINS.
MAN! WE NEVER GOT STUFF LIKE THAT!
YOU'RE DOIN' THIS JUST FOR HIM?
I HAVE MORE DRINKS, KAZUKI!
Want another one?
NO FAIR! THIS IS FAVORIT-ISM!
I WANT TO HELP KAZUKI...
...ANY WAY I CAN! ♡

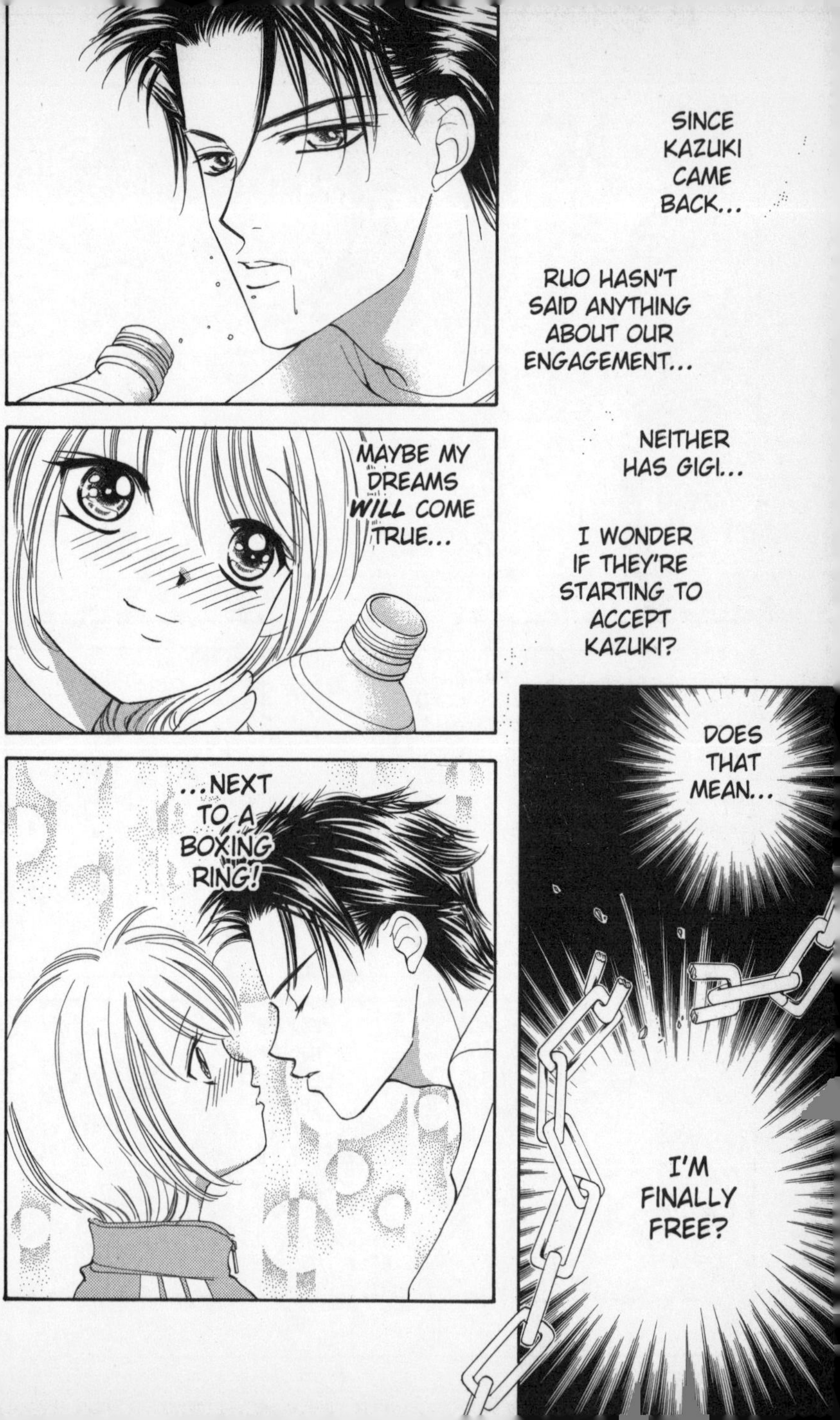
SINCE KAZUKI CAME BACK...
RUO HASN'T SAID ANYTHING ABOUT OUR ENGAGEMENT...
NEITHER HAS GIGI...
MAYBE MY DREAMS WILL COME TRUE...
I WONDER IF THEY'RE STARTING TO ACCEPT KAZUKI?
DOES THAT MEAN...
I'M FINALLY FREE?
...NEXT TO A BOXING RING!

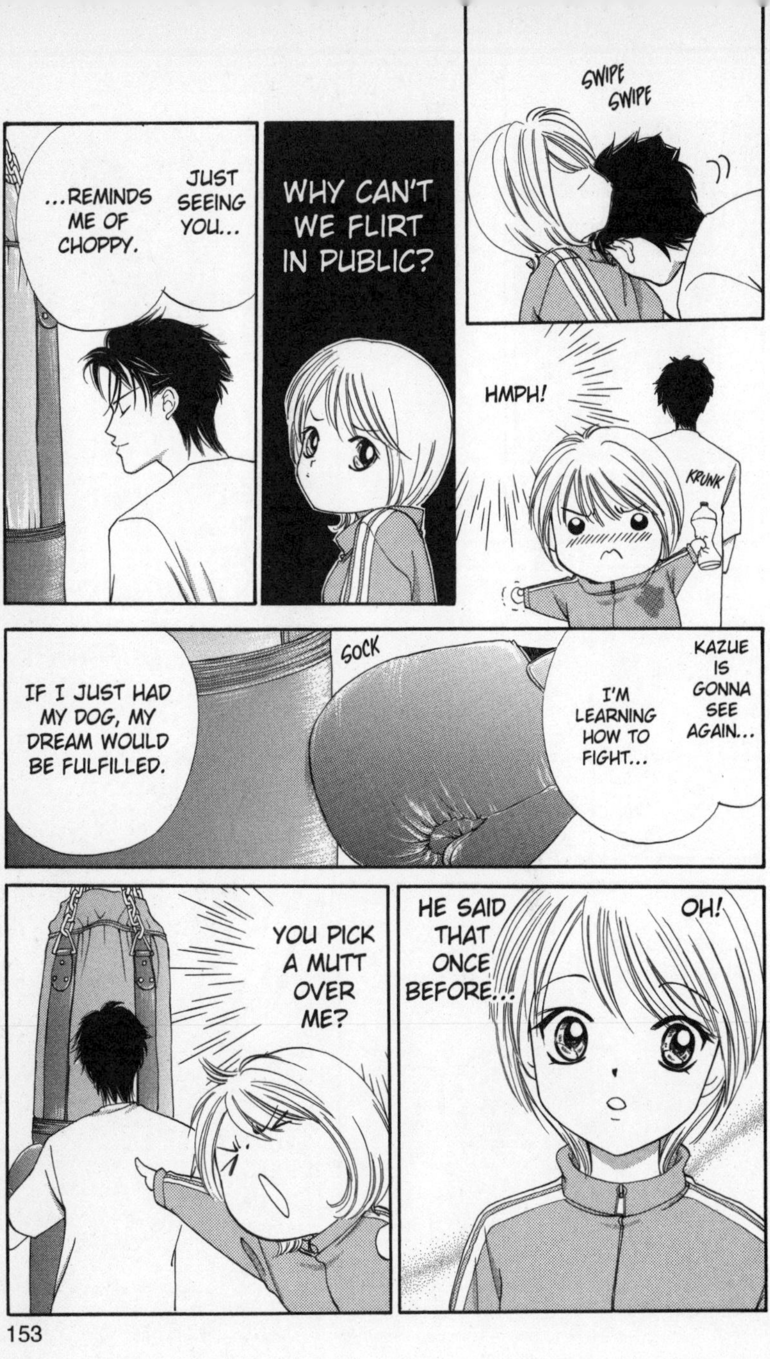
SWIPE SWIPE
HMPH!
KRUNK
WHY CAN'T WE FLIRT IN PUBLIC?
JUST SEEING YOU...
...REMINDS ME OF CHOPPY.
KAZUE IS GONNA SEE AGAIN...
I'M LEARNING HOW TO FIGHT...
SOCK
IF I JUST HAD MY DOG, MY DREAM WOULD BE FULFILLED.
OH!
HE SAID THAT ONCE BEFORE...
YOU PICK A MUTT OVER ME?

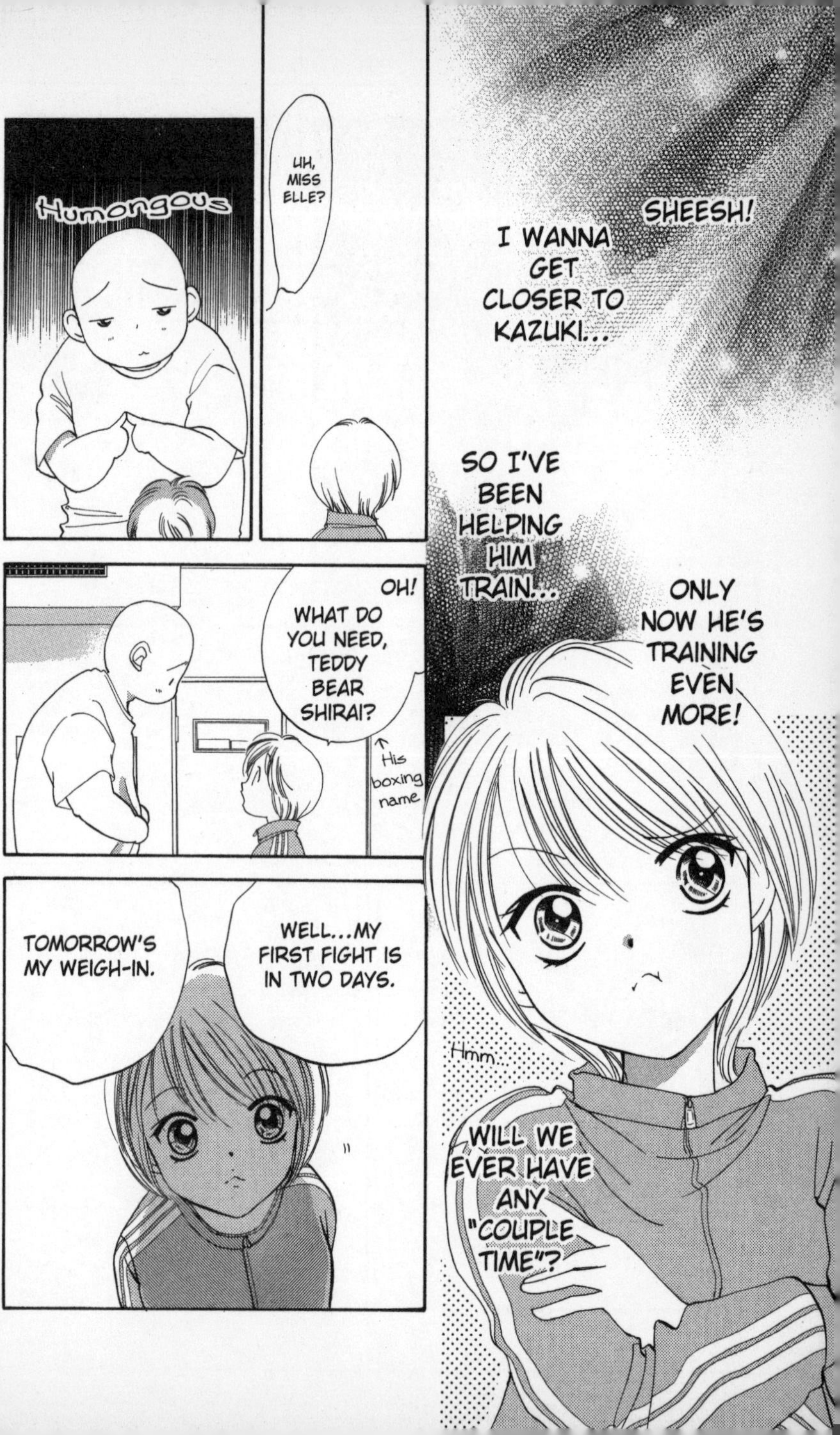
SHEESH!
I WANNA GET CLOSER TO KAZUKI...
SO I'VE BEEN HELPING HIM TRAIN...
ONLY NOW HE'S TRAINING EVEN MORE!
Hmm
WILL WE EVER HAVE ANY "COUPLE TIME"?
UH, MISS ELLE?
Humongous
OH!
WHAT DO YOU NEED, TEDDY BEAR SHIRAI?
↑ His boxing name
WELL...MY FIRST FIGHT IS IN TWO DAYS.
TOMORROW'S MY WEIGH-IN.

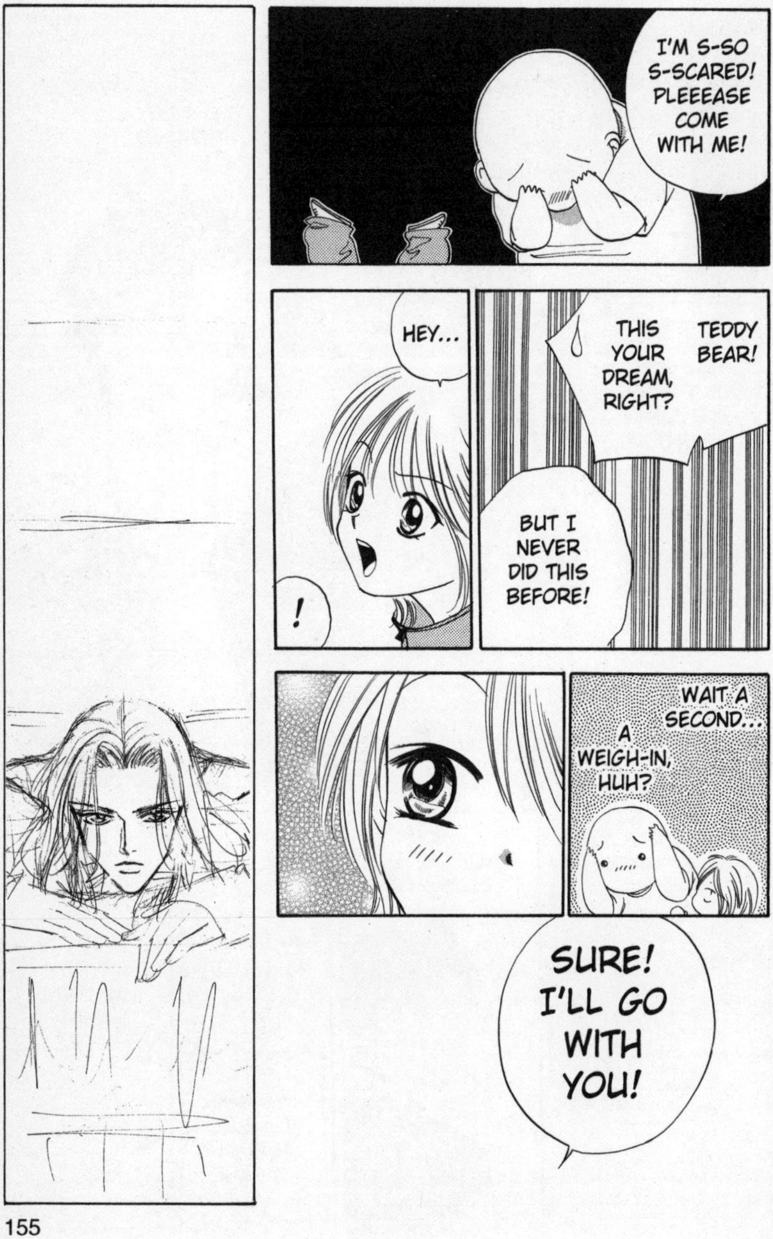
I'M S-SO S-SCARED! PLEEEASE COME WITH ME!
TEDDY BEAR!
THIS YOUR DREAM, RIGHT?
BUT I NEVER DID THIS BEFORE!
HEY...
!
WAIT A SECOND...
A WEIGH-IN, HUH?
SURE! I'LL GO WITH YOU!

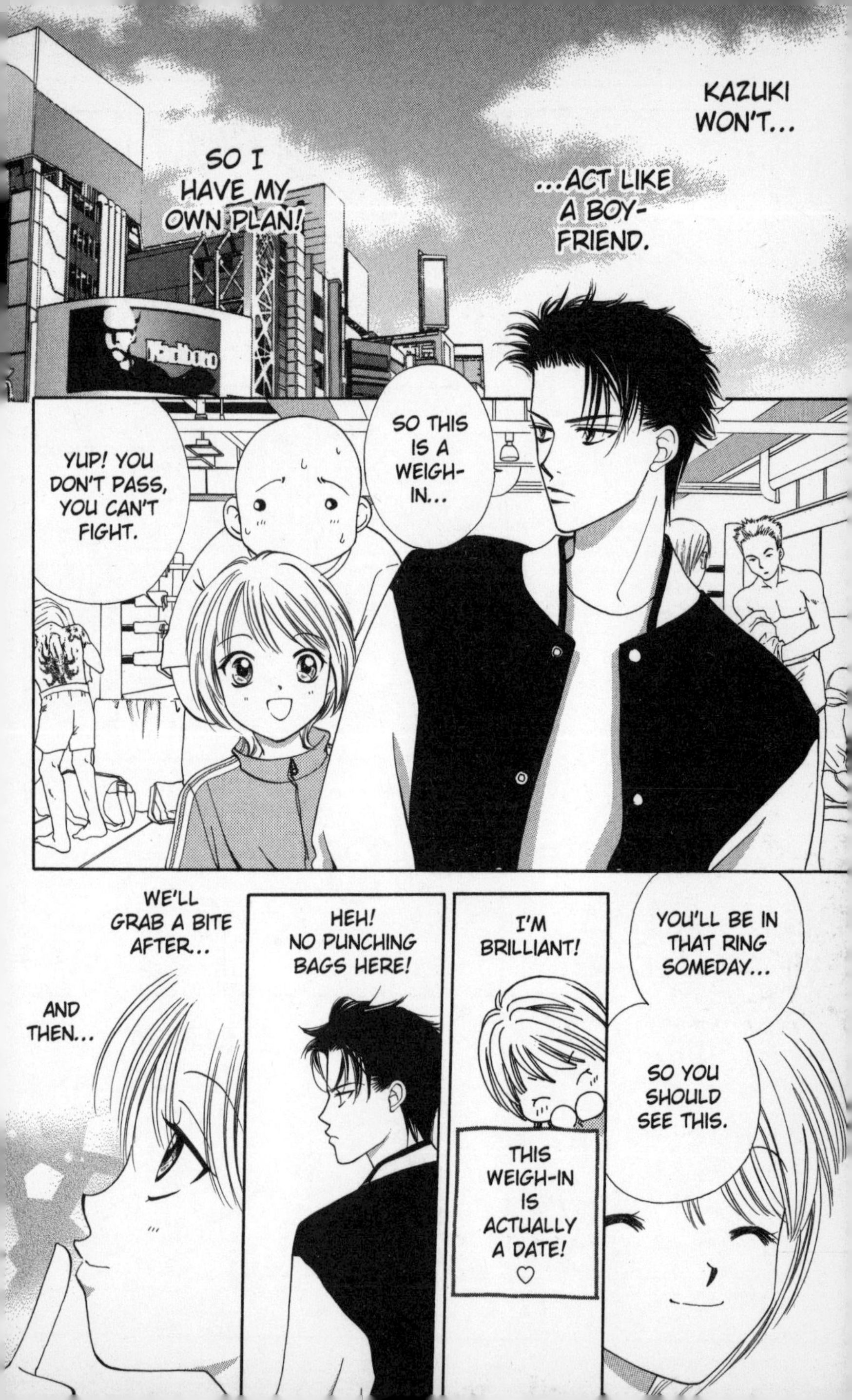
KAZUKI WON'T...
...ACT LIKE A BOY-FRIEND.
SO I HAVE MY OWN PLAN!
SO THIS IS A WEIGH-IN...
YUP! YOU DON'T PASS, YOU CAN'T FIGHT.
YOU'LL BE IN THAT RING SOMEDAY...
SO YOU SHOULD SEE THIS.
I'M BRILLIANT!
THIS WEIGH-IN IS ACTUALLY A DATE! ♡
HEH! NO PUNCHING BAGS HERE!
WE'LL GRAB A BITE AFTER...
AND THEN...

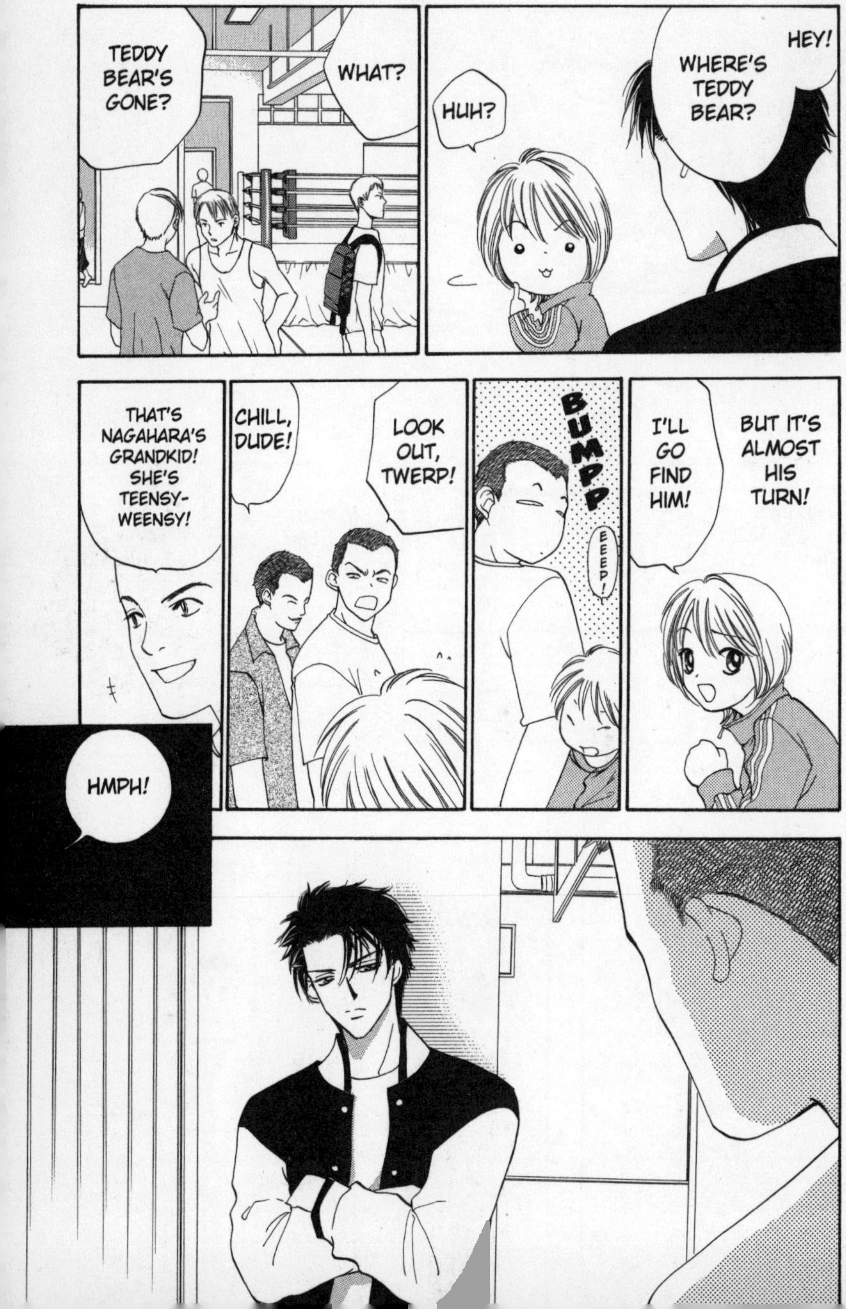
HEY!
WHERE'S TEDDY BEAR?
HUH?
WHAT?
TEDDY BEAR'S GONE?
BUT IT'S ALMOST HIS TURN!
I'LL GO FIND HIM!
BUMPP
EEEEP!
LOOK OUT, TWERP!
CHILL, DUDE!
THAT'S NAGAHARA'S GRANDKID! SHE'S TEENSY-WEENSY!
HMPH!

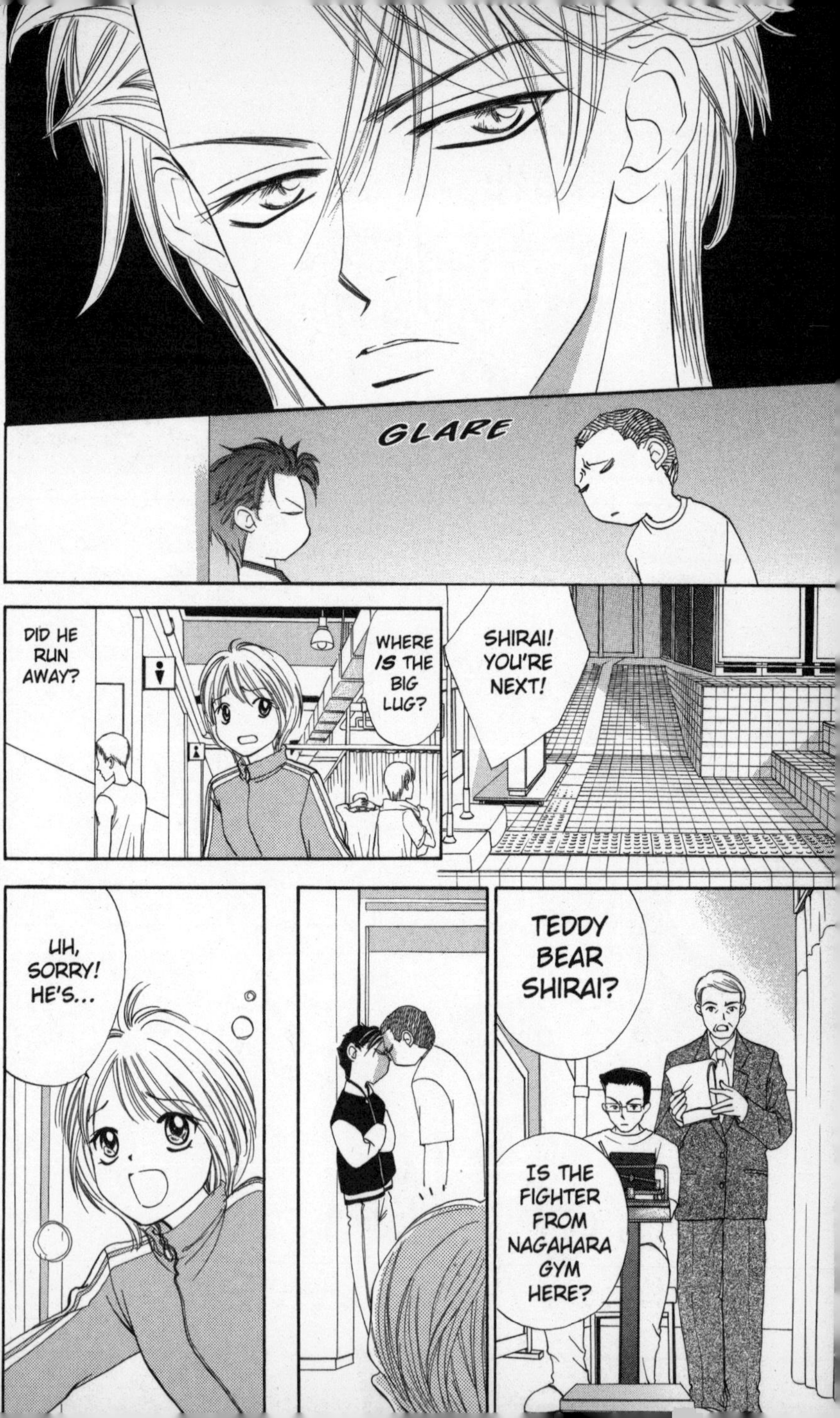
GLARE
SHIRAI! YOU'RE NEXT!
WHERE IS THE BIG LUG?
DID HE RUN AWAY?
TEDDY BEAR SHIRAI?
IS THE FIGHTER FROM NAGAHARA GYM HERE?
UH, SORRY! HE'S...

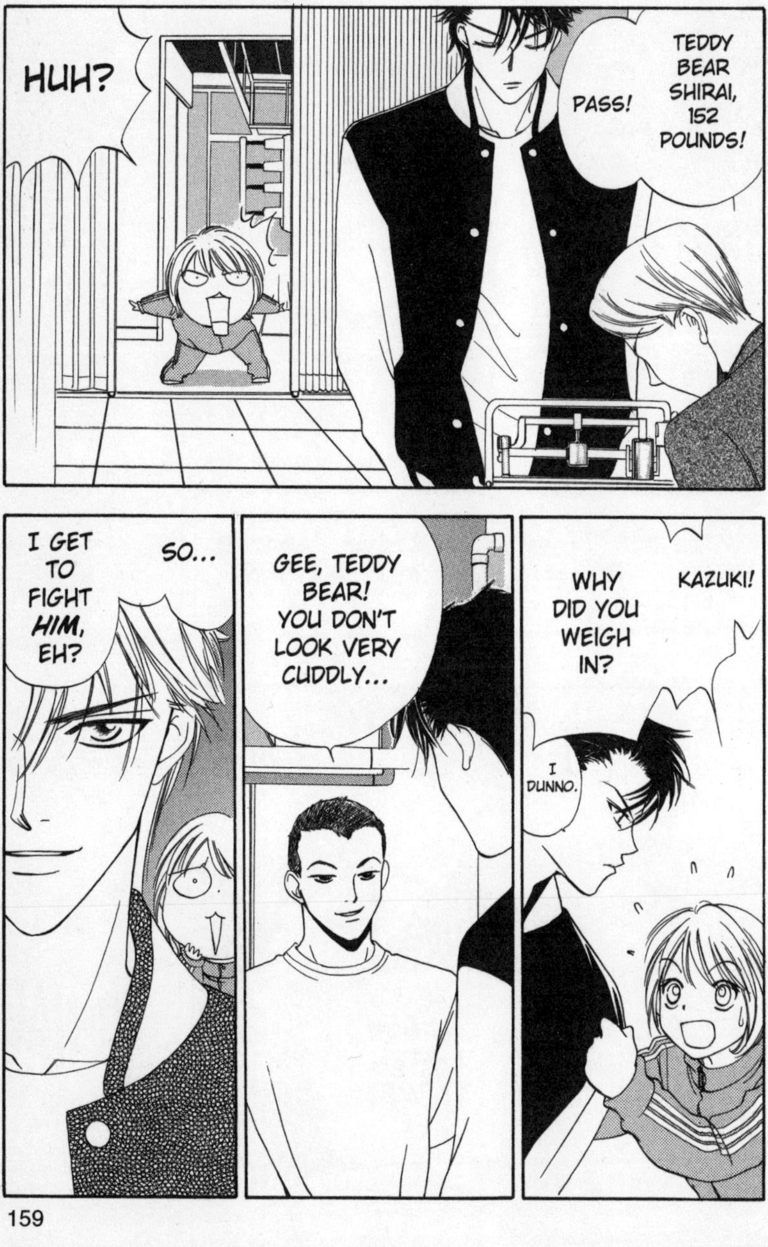
TEDDY BEAR SHIRAI, 152 POUNDS!
PASS!
HUH?
KAZUKI!
WHY DID YOU WEIGH IN?
I DUNNO.
GEE, TEDDY BEAR! YOU DON'T LOOK VERY CUDDLY...
SO...
I GET TO FIGHT *HIM*, EH?

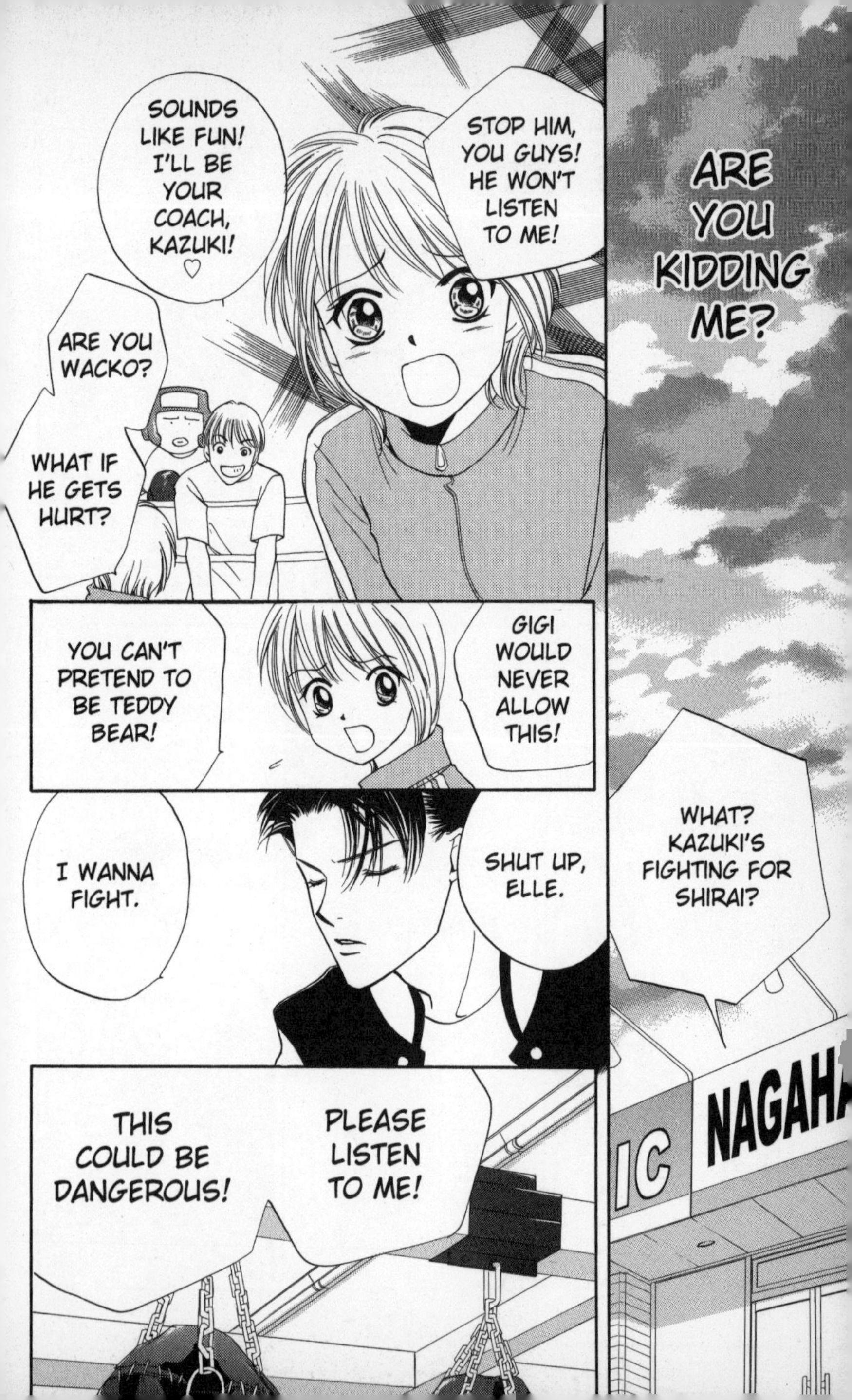
ARE YOU KIDDING ME?
WHAT? KAZUKI'S FIGHTING FOR SHIRAI?
STOP HIM, YOU GUYS! HE WON'T LISTEN TO ME!
SOUNDS LIKE FUN! I'LL BE YOUR COACH, KAZUKI! ♡
ARE YOU WACKO?
WHAT IF HE GETS HURT?
GIGI WOULD NEVER ALLOW THIS!
YOU CAN'T PRETEND TO BE TEDDY BEAR!
SHUT UP, ELLE.
I WANNA FIGHT.
PLEASE LISTEN TO ME!
THIS COULD BE DANGEROUS!

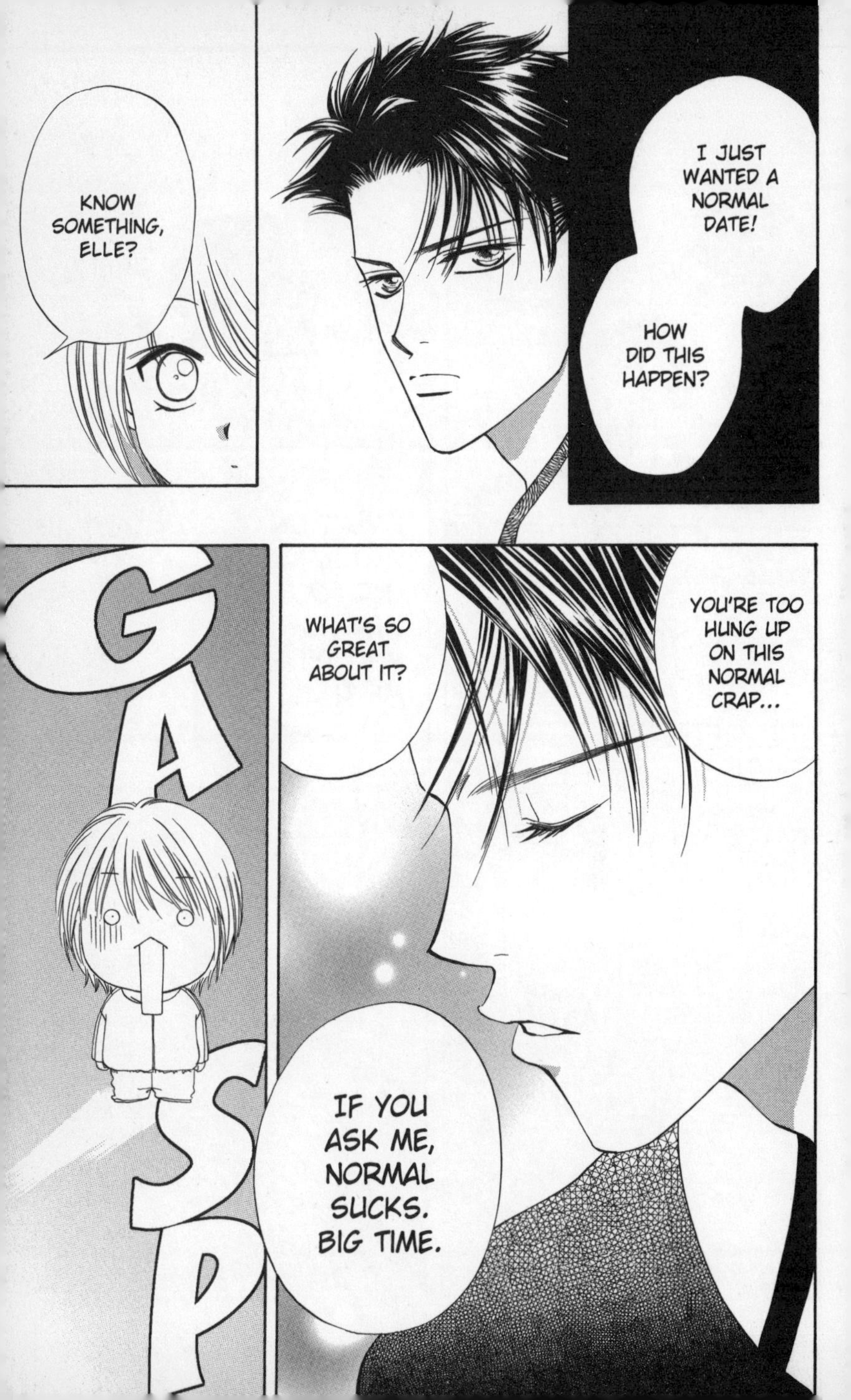
I JUST WANTED A NORMAL DATE!
HOW DID THIS HAPPEN?
KNOW SOMETHING, ELLE?
YOU'RE TOO HUNG UP ON THIS NORMAL CRAP...
WHAT'S SO GREAT ABOUT IT?
IF YOU ASK ME, NORMAL SUCKS. BIG TIME.
GASP

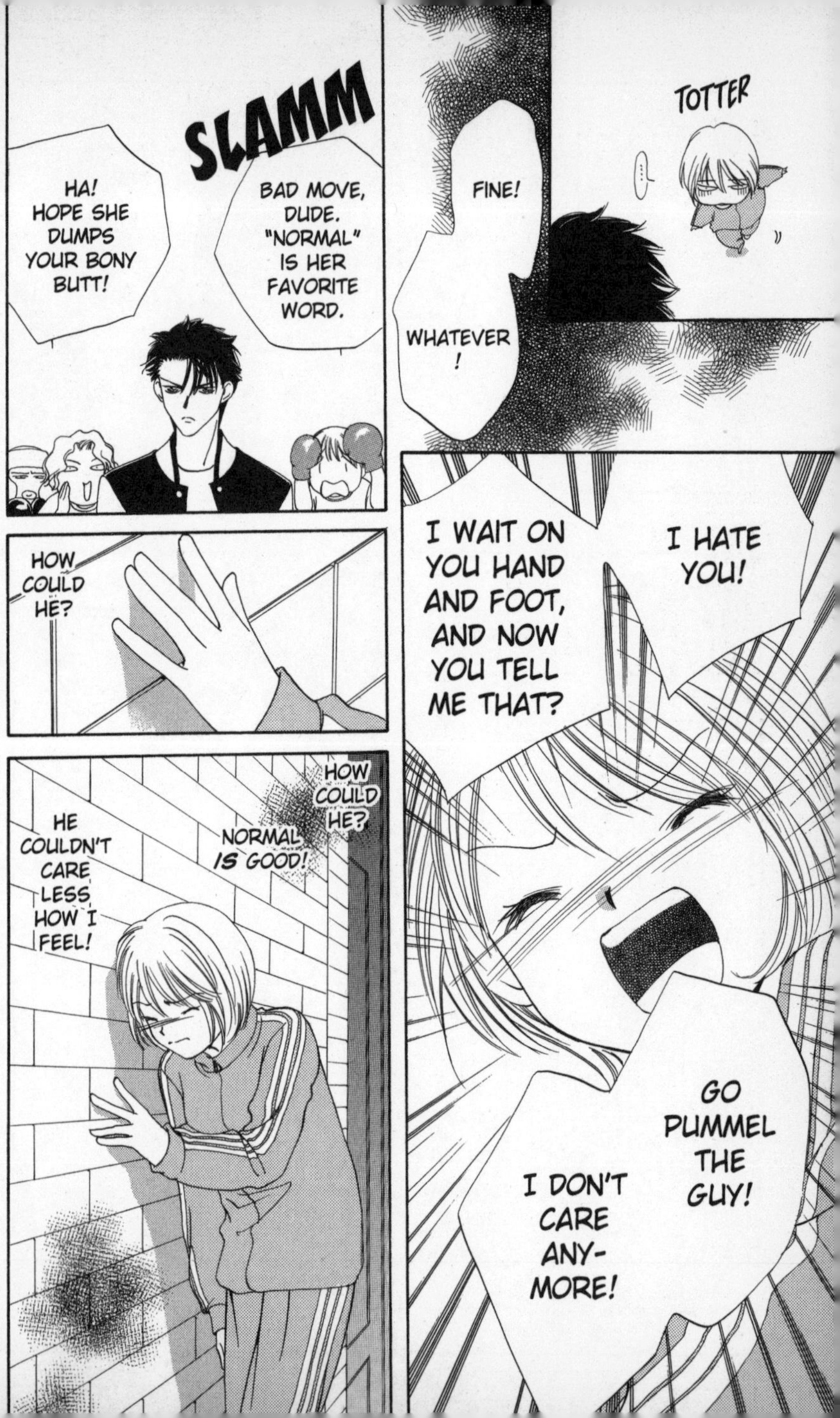
TOTTER
...
FINE!
WHATEVER!
SLAMM
BAD MOVE, DUDE. "NORMAL" IS HER FAVORITE WORD.
HA! HOPE SHE DUMPS YOUR BONY BUTT!
I HATE YOU!
I WAIT ON YOU HAND AND FOOT, AND NOW YOU TELL ME THAT?
GO PUMMEL THE GUY!
I DON'T CARE ANY-MORE!
HOW COULD HE?
HOW COULD HE?
NORMAL IS GOOD!
HE COULDN'T CARE LESS HOW I FEEL!

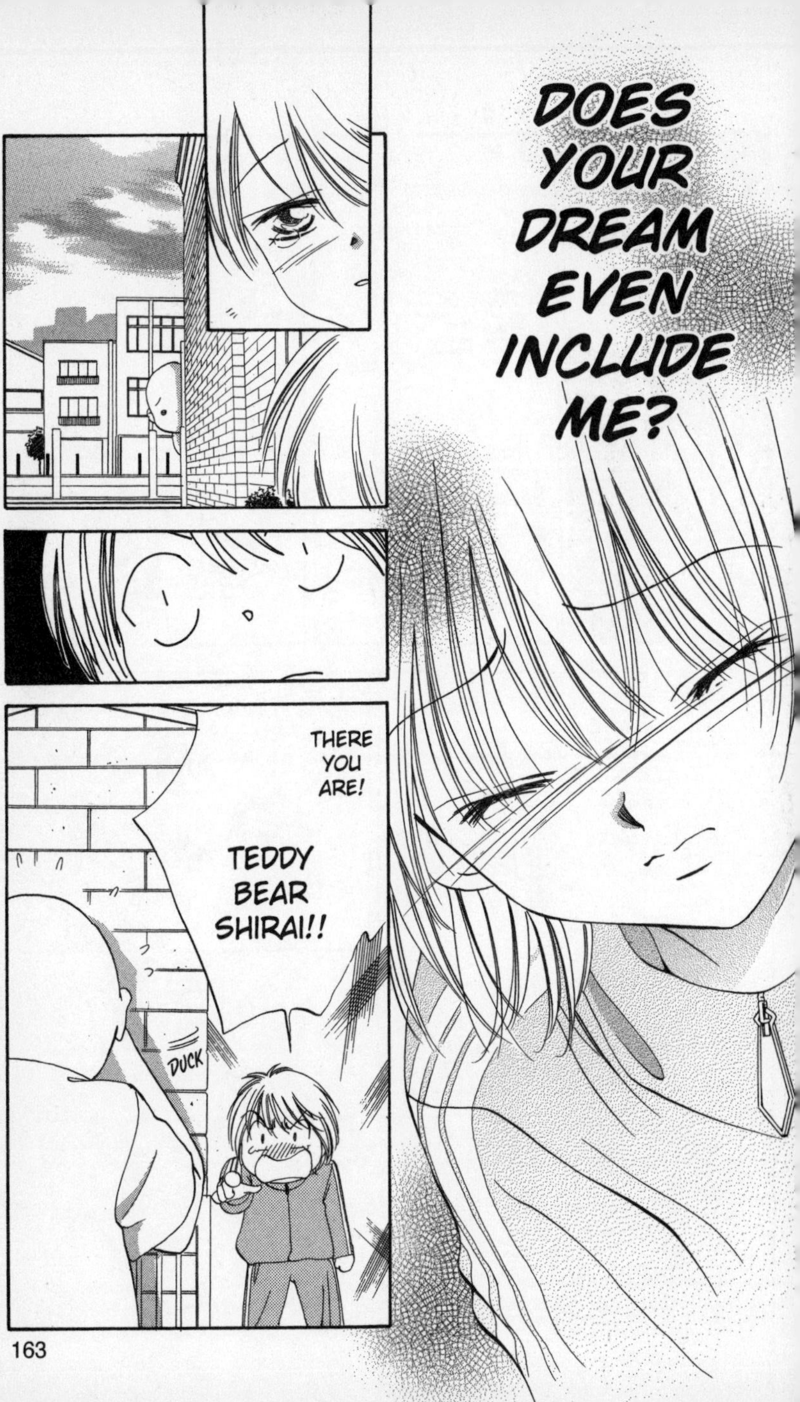
DOES YOUR DREAM EVEN INCLUDE ME?
THERE YOU ARE!
TEDDY BEAR SHIRAI!!
DUCK

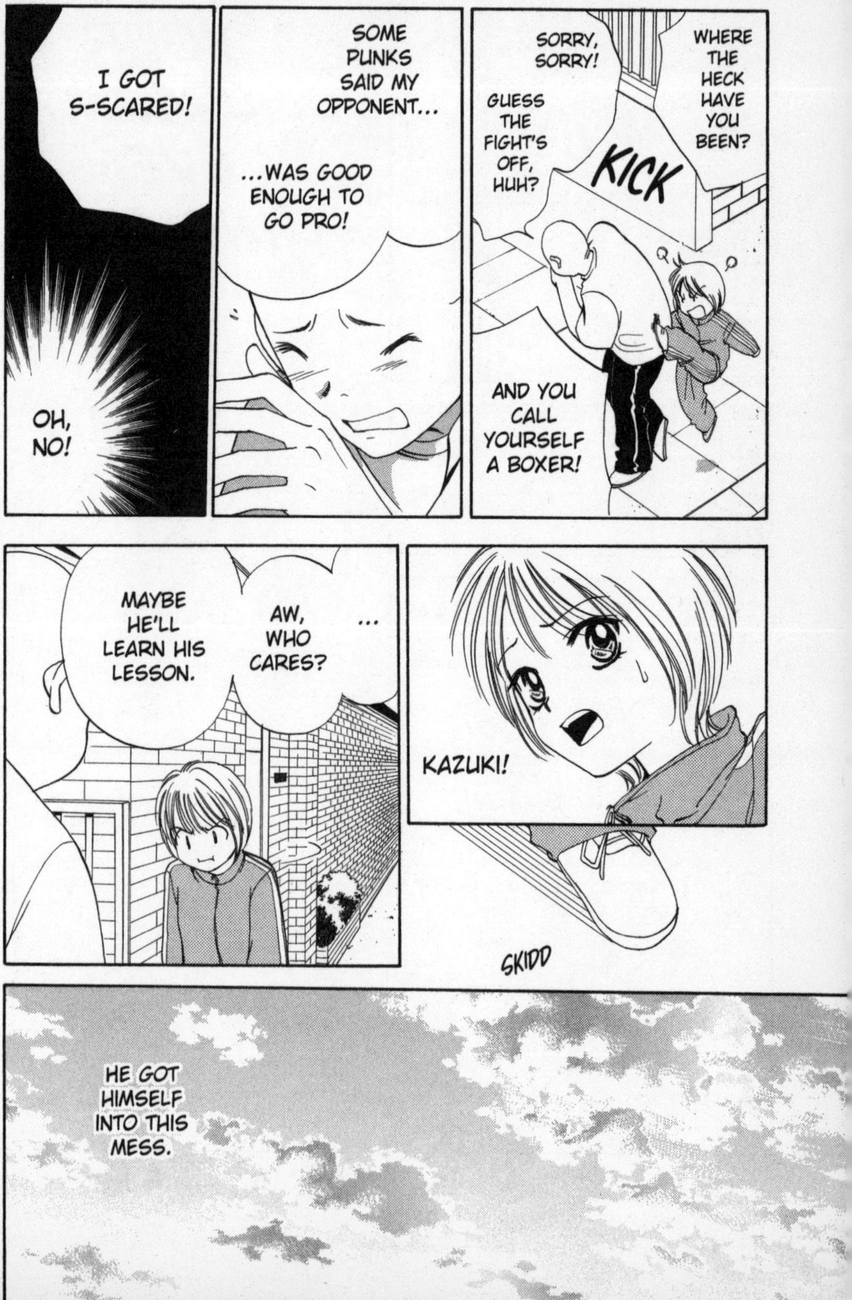
WHERE THE HECK HAVE YOU BEEN?
SORRY, SORRY!
GUESS THE FIGHT'S OFF, HUH?
KICK
AND YOU CALL YOURSELF A BOXER!
SOME PUNKS SAID MY OPPONENT...
...WAS GOOD ENOUGH TO GO PRO!
I GOT S-SCARED!
OH, NO!
KAZUKI!
SKIDD
...
AW, WHO CARES?
MAYBE HE'LL LEARN HIS LESSON.
HE GOT HIMSELF INTO THIS MESS.

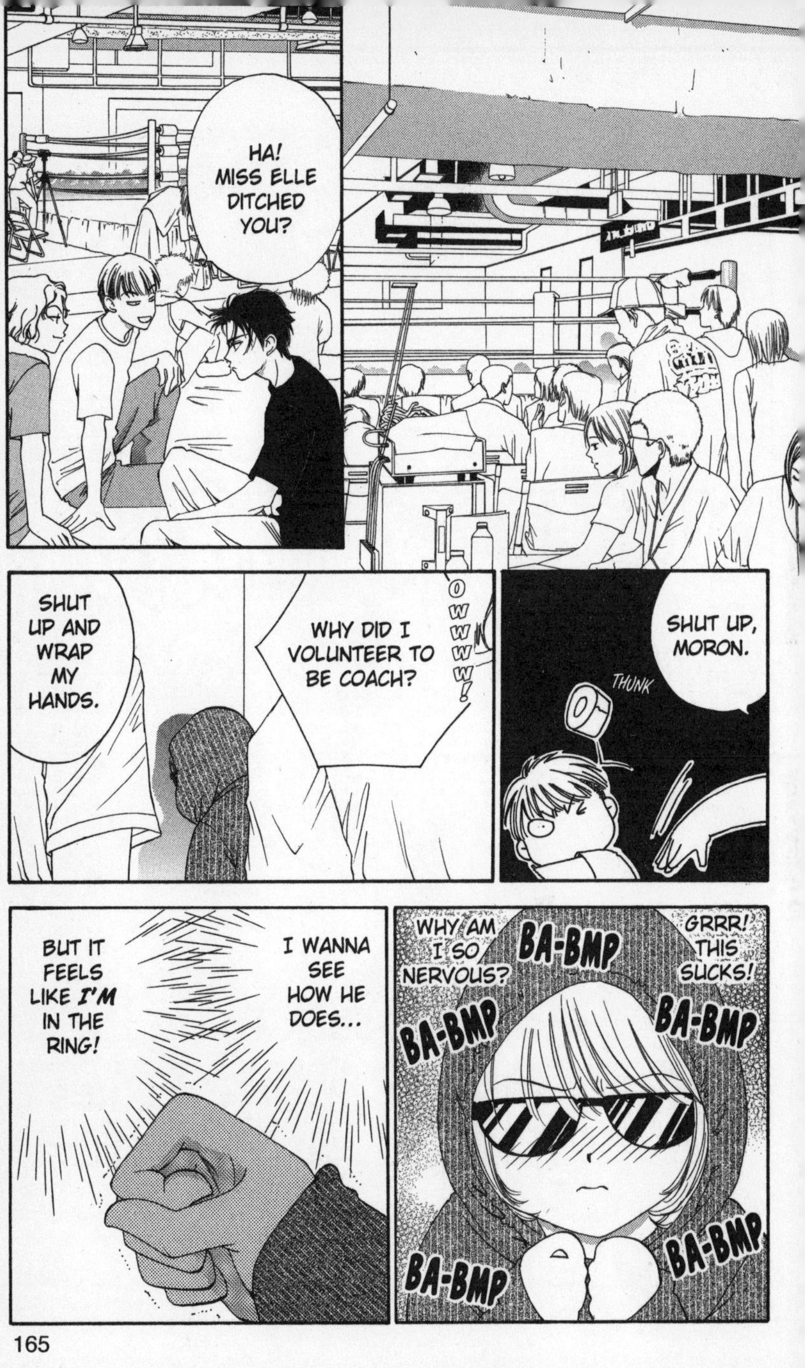
HA! MISS ELLE DITCHED YOU?
SHUT UP, MORON.
THUNK
OWWWWW!
WHY DID I VOLUNTEER TO BE COACH?
SHUT UP AND WRAP MY HANDS.
GRRR! THIS SUCKS!
BA-BMP
WHY AM I SO NERVOUS?
BA-BMP
BA-BMP
BA-BMP
BA-BMP
I WANNA SEE HOW HE DOES...
BUT IT FEELS LIKE *I'M* IN THE RING!

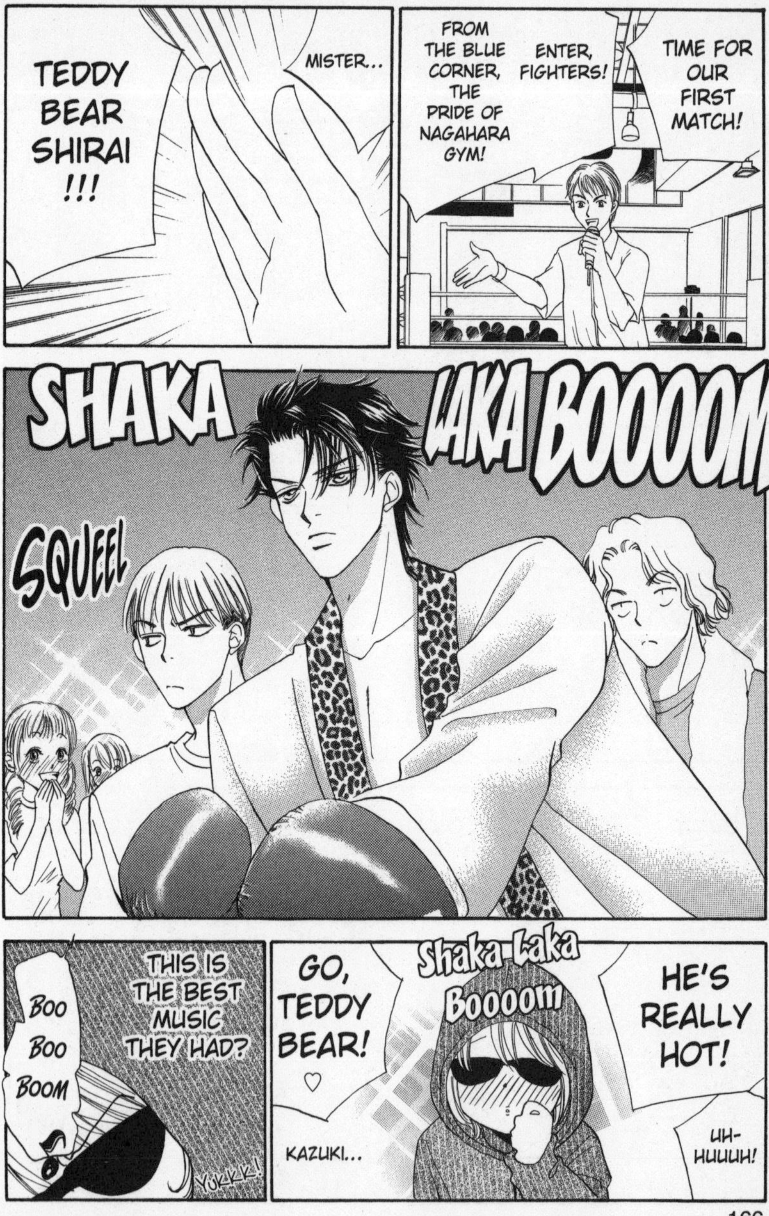
TIME FOR OUR FIRST MATCH!
ENTER, FIGHTERS!
FROM THE BLUE CORNER, THE PRIDE OF NAGAHARA GYM!
MISTER...
TEDDY BEAR SHIRAI!!!
SHAKA LAKA BOOOOM
SQUEEL
HE'S REALLY HOT!
Shaka Laka Booooom
GO, TEDDY BEAR! ♡
UH-HUUUH!
KAZUKI...
THIS IS THE BEST MUSIC THEY HAD?
Boo Boo Boom
YUKKK!

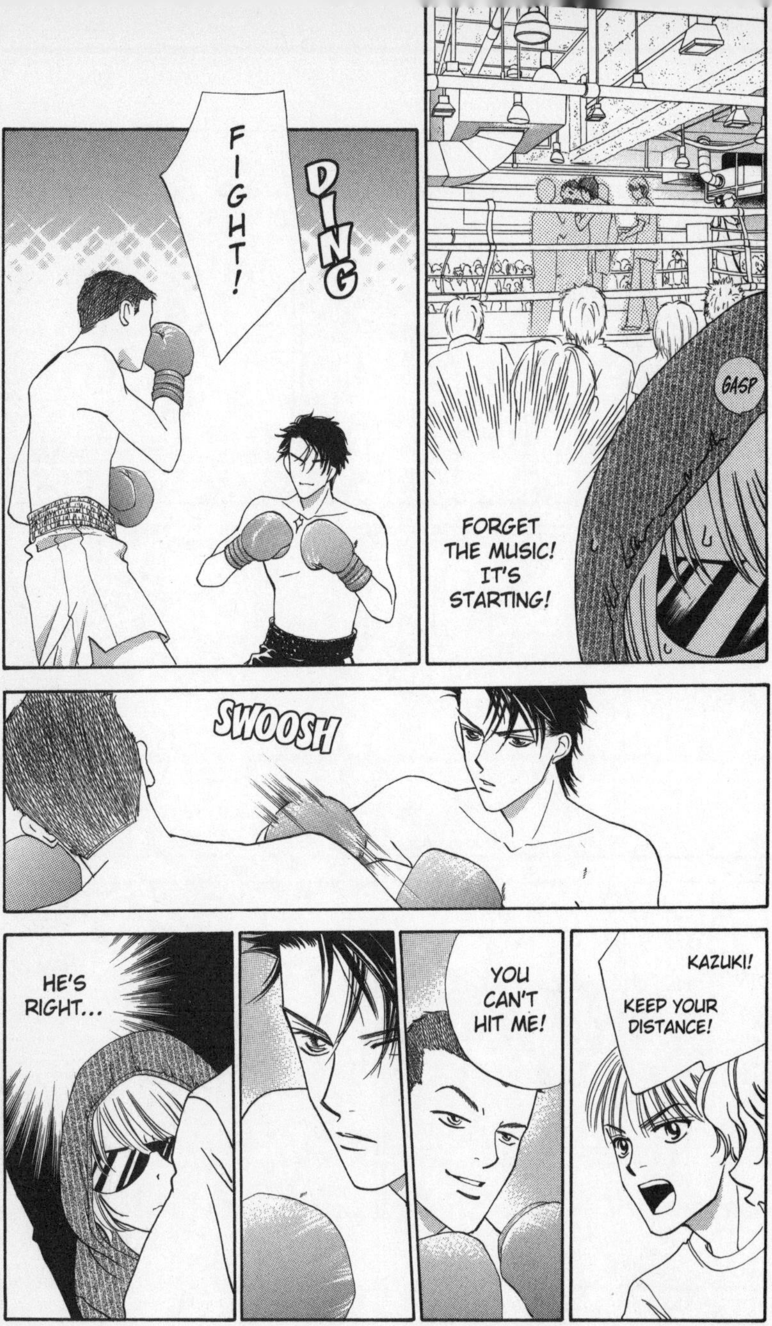
GASP
FORGET THE MUSIC! IT'S STARTING!
FIGHT!
DING
SWOOSH
KAZUKI!
KEEP YOUR DISTANCE!
YOU CAN'T HIT ME!
HE'S RIGHT...

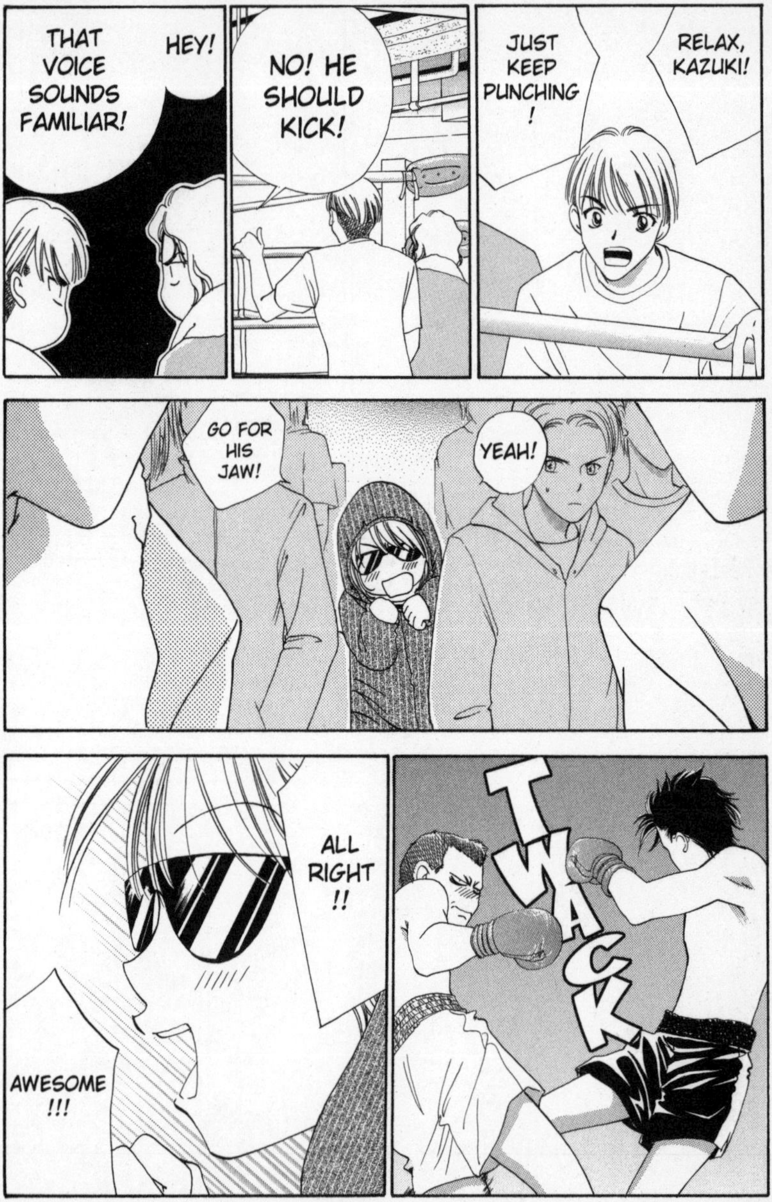
RELAX, KAZUKI!
JUST KEEP PUNCHING!
NO! HE SHOULD KICK!
HEY!
THAT VOICE SOUNDS FAMILIAR!
YEAH!
GO FOR HIS JAW!
TWACK
ALL RIGHT!!
AWESOME!!!

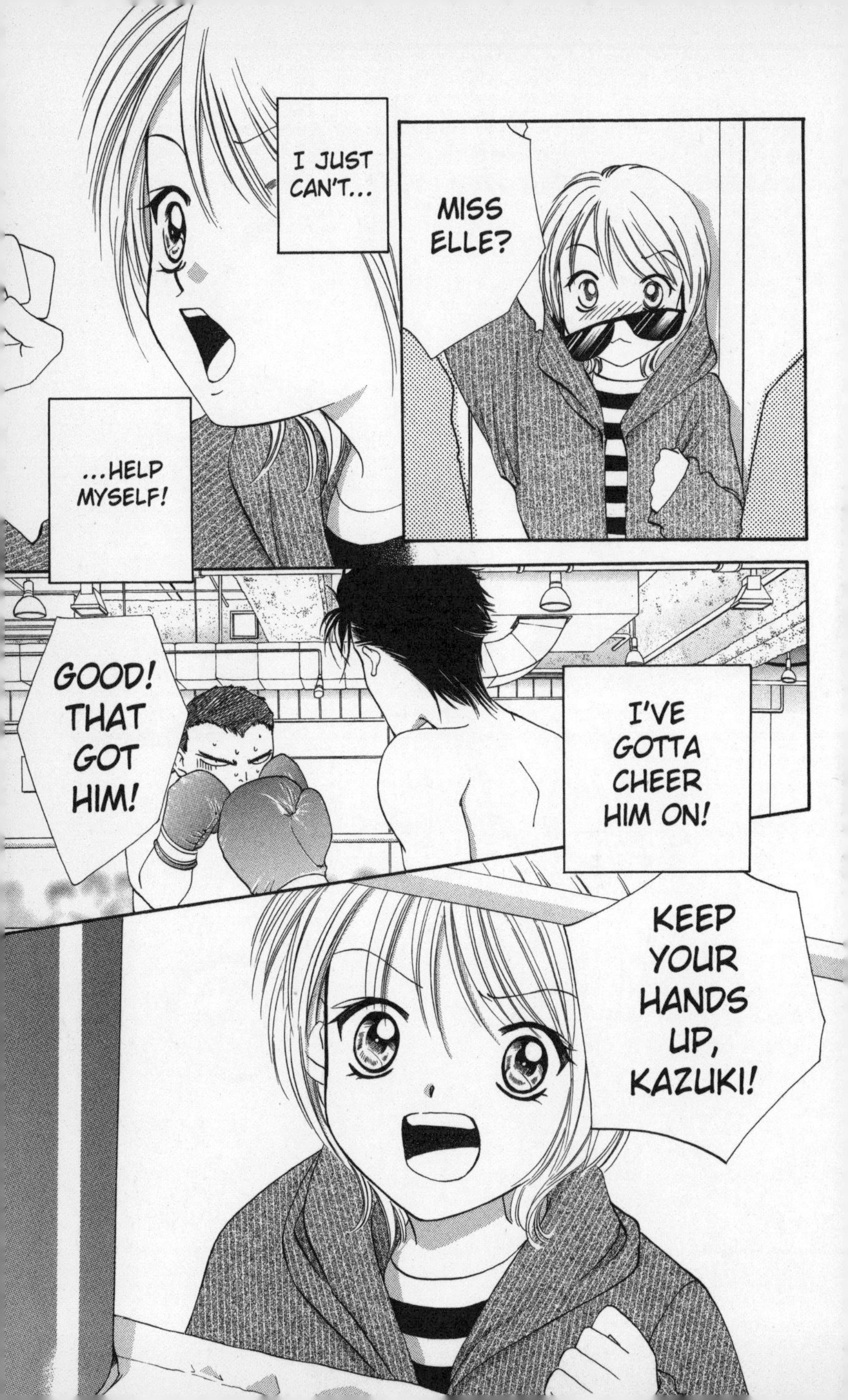
MISS ELLE?
I JUST CAN'T...
...HELP MYSELF!
I'VE GOTTA CHEER HIM ON!
GOOD! THAT GOT HIM!
KEEP YOUR HANDS UP, KAZUKI!

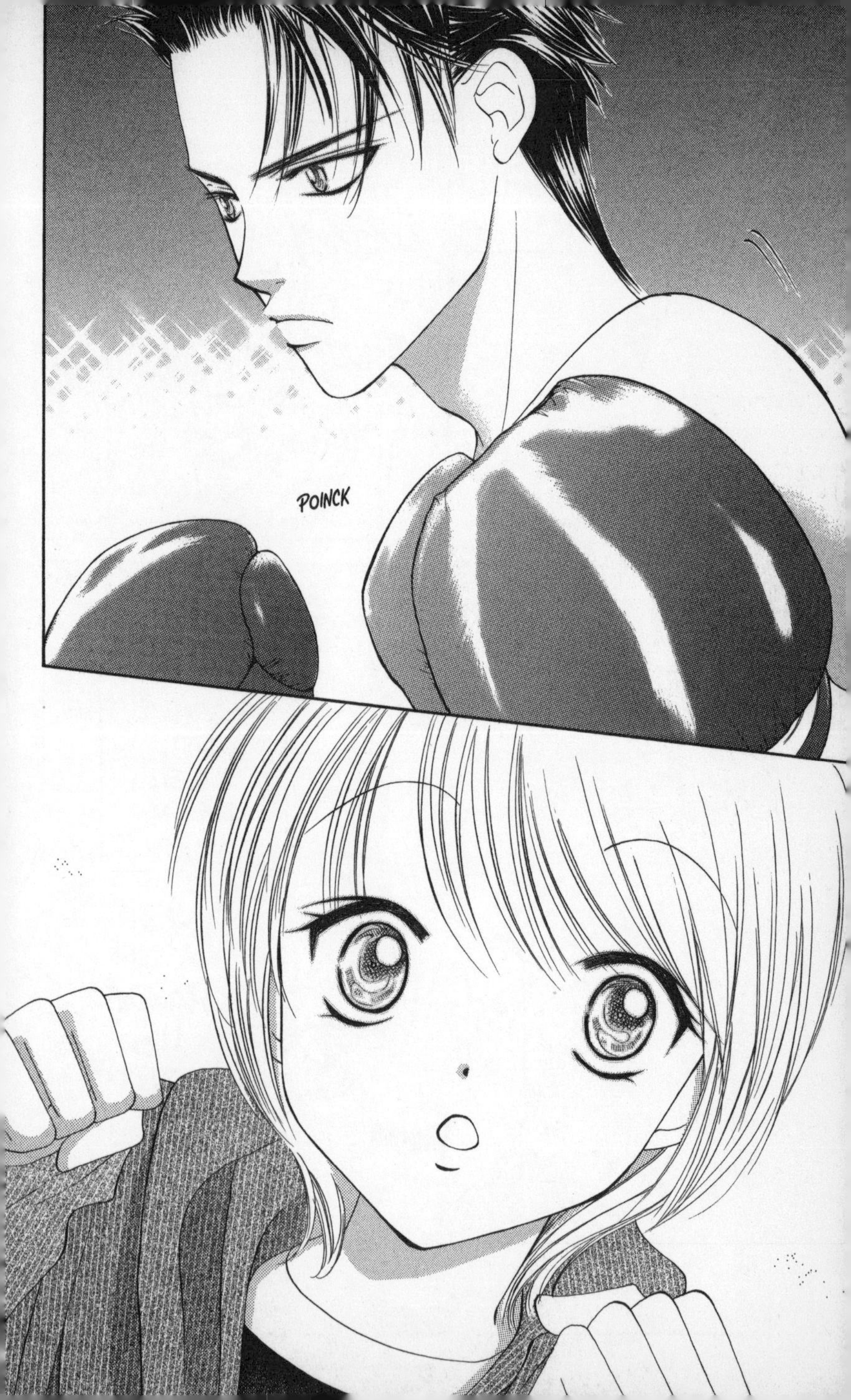
POINCK

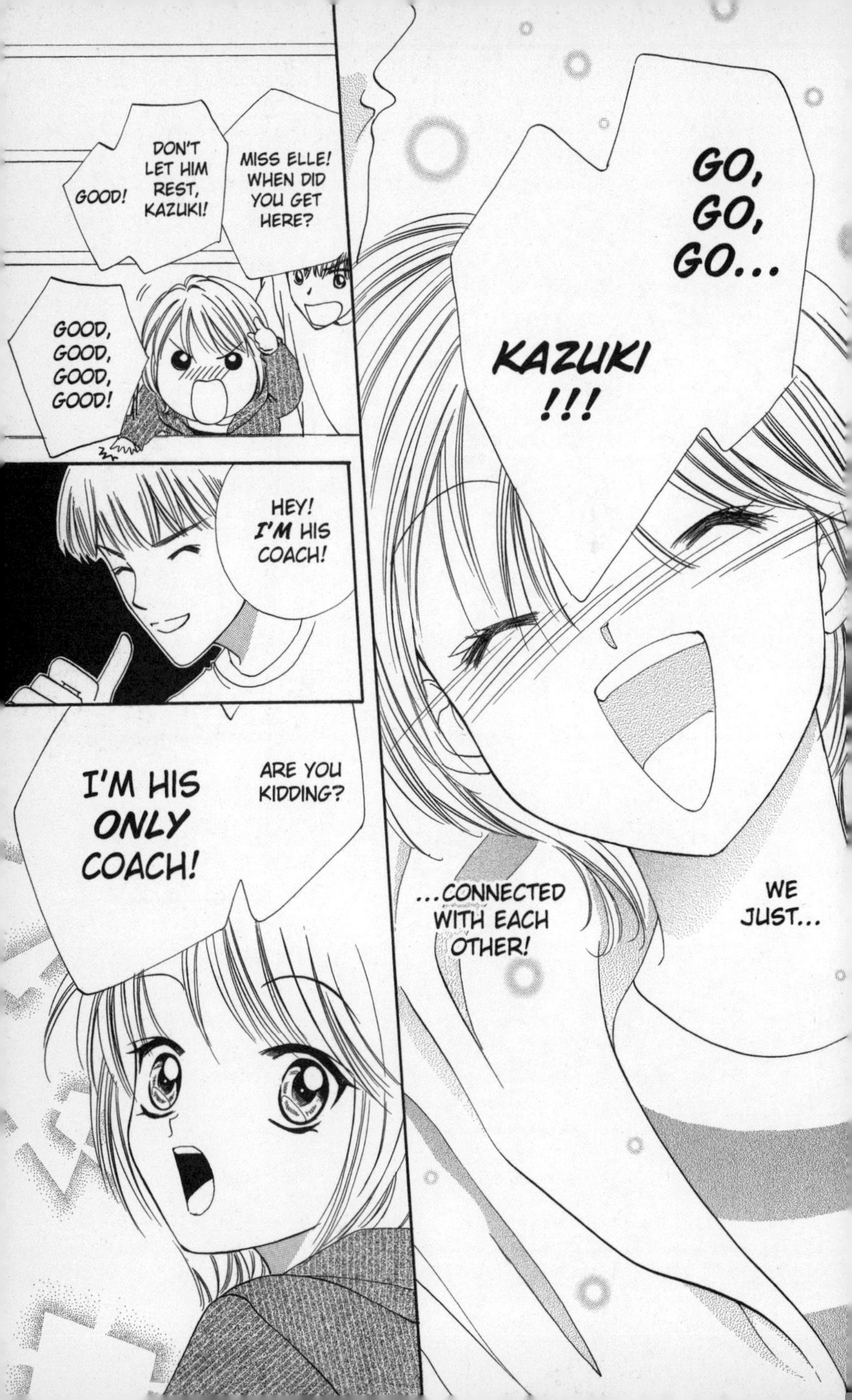
GO, GO, GO...
KAZUKI !!!
WE JUST...
...CONNECTED WITH EACH OTHER!
MISS ELLE! WHEN DID YOU GET HERE?
DON'T LET HIM REST, KAZUKI!
GOOD!
GOOD, GOOD, GOOD, GOOD!
HEY! *I'M* HIS COACH!
ARE YOU KIDDING?
I'M HIS *ONLY* COACH!

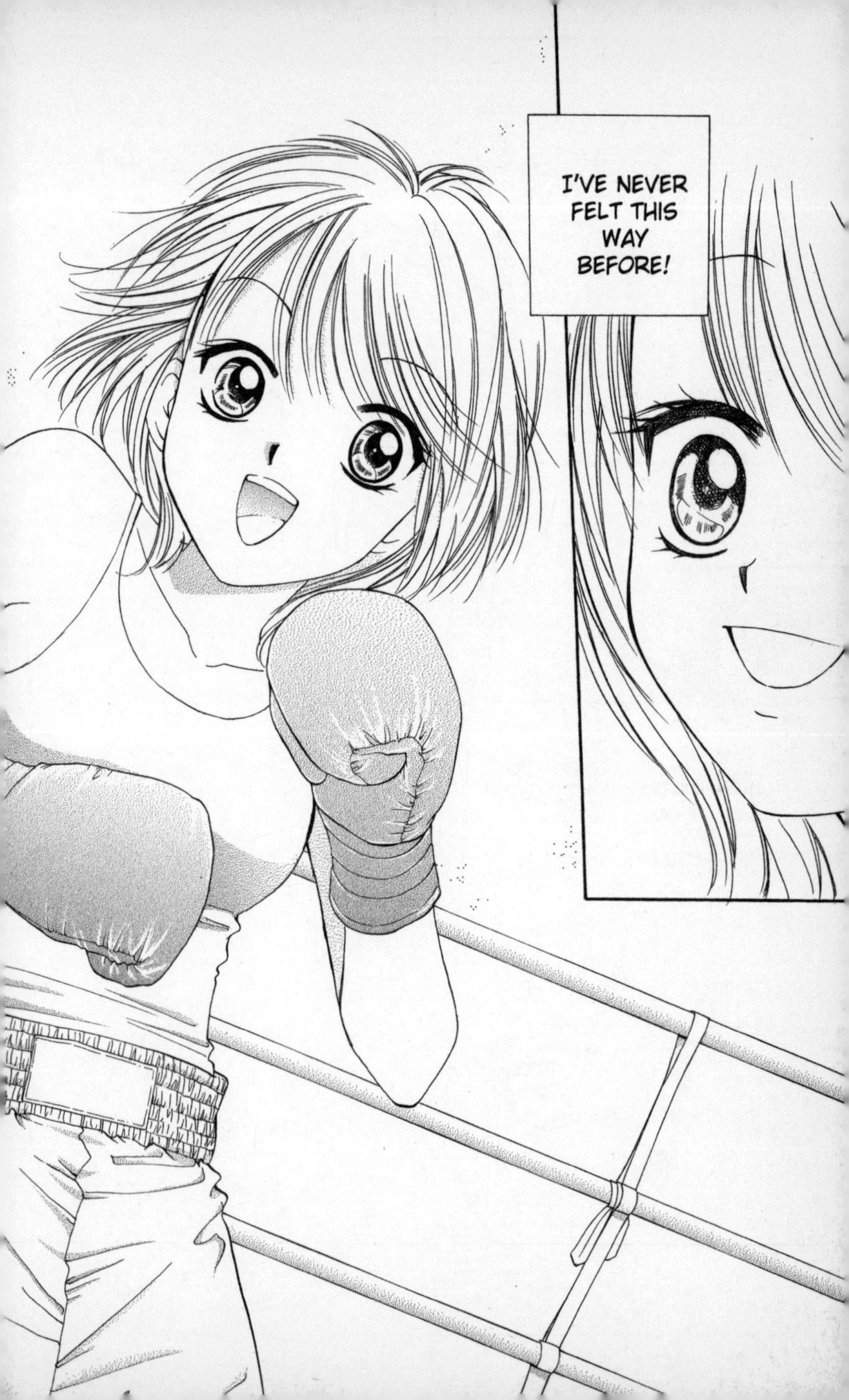
I'VE NEVER FELT THIS WAY BEFORE!

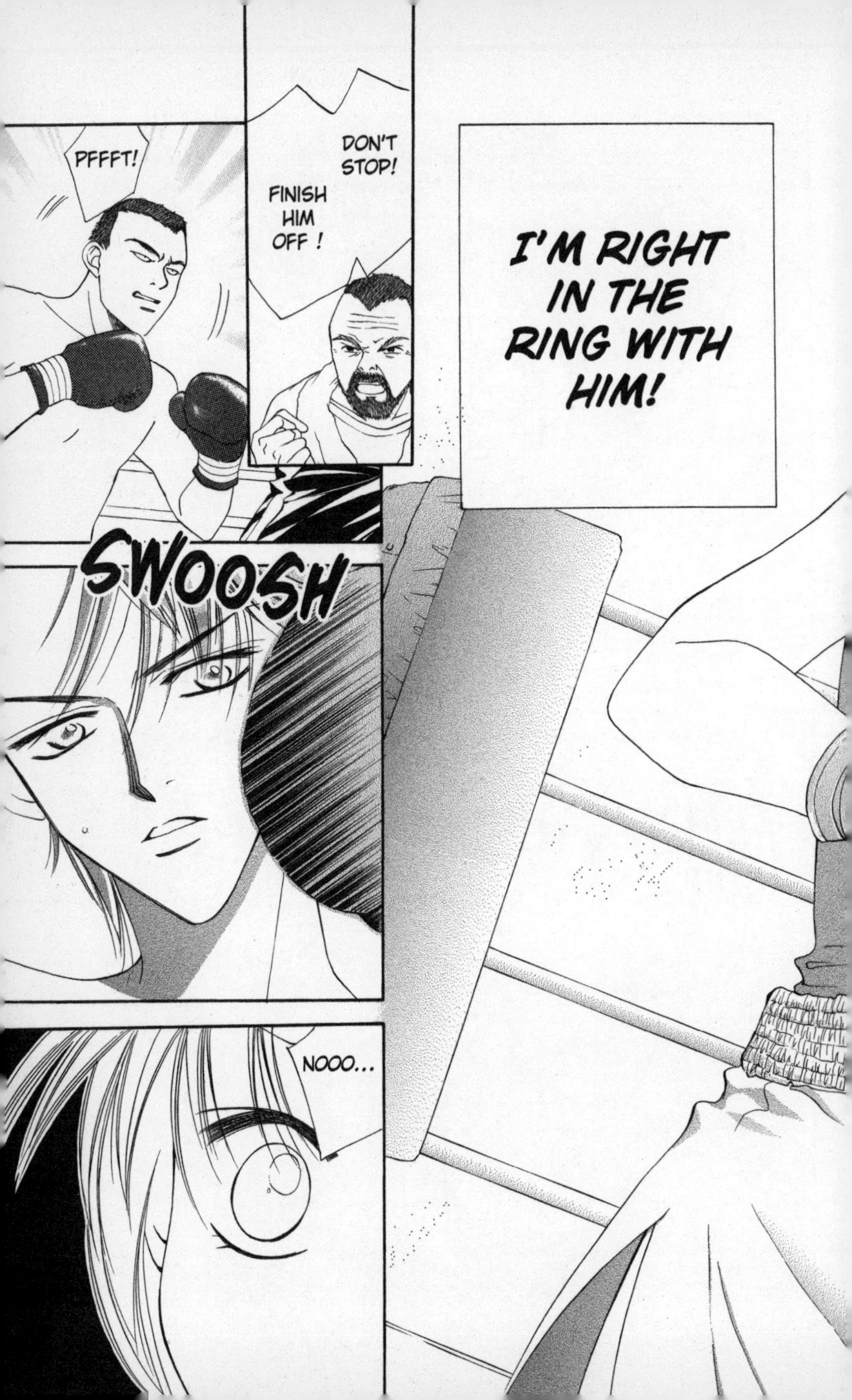
DON'T STOP!
FINISH HIM OFF !
I'M RIGHT IN THE RING WITH HIM!
PFFFT!
SWOOSH
NOOO...

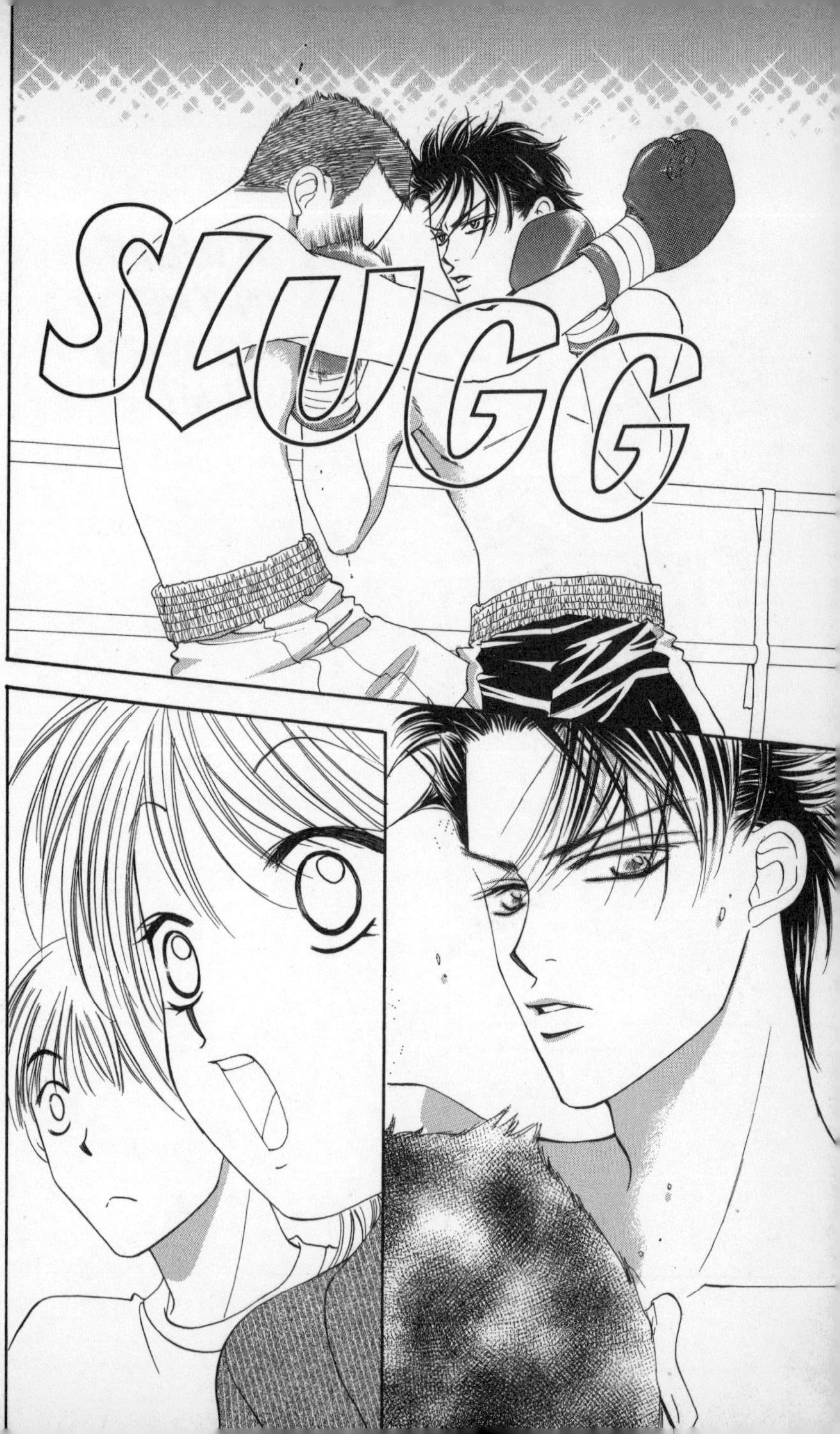
SLUGG

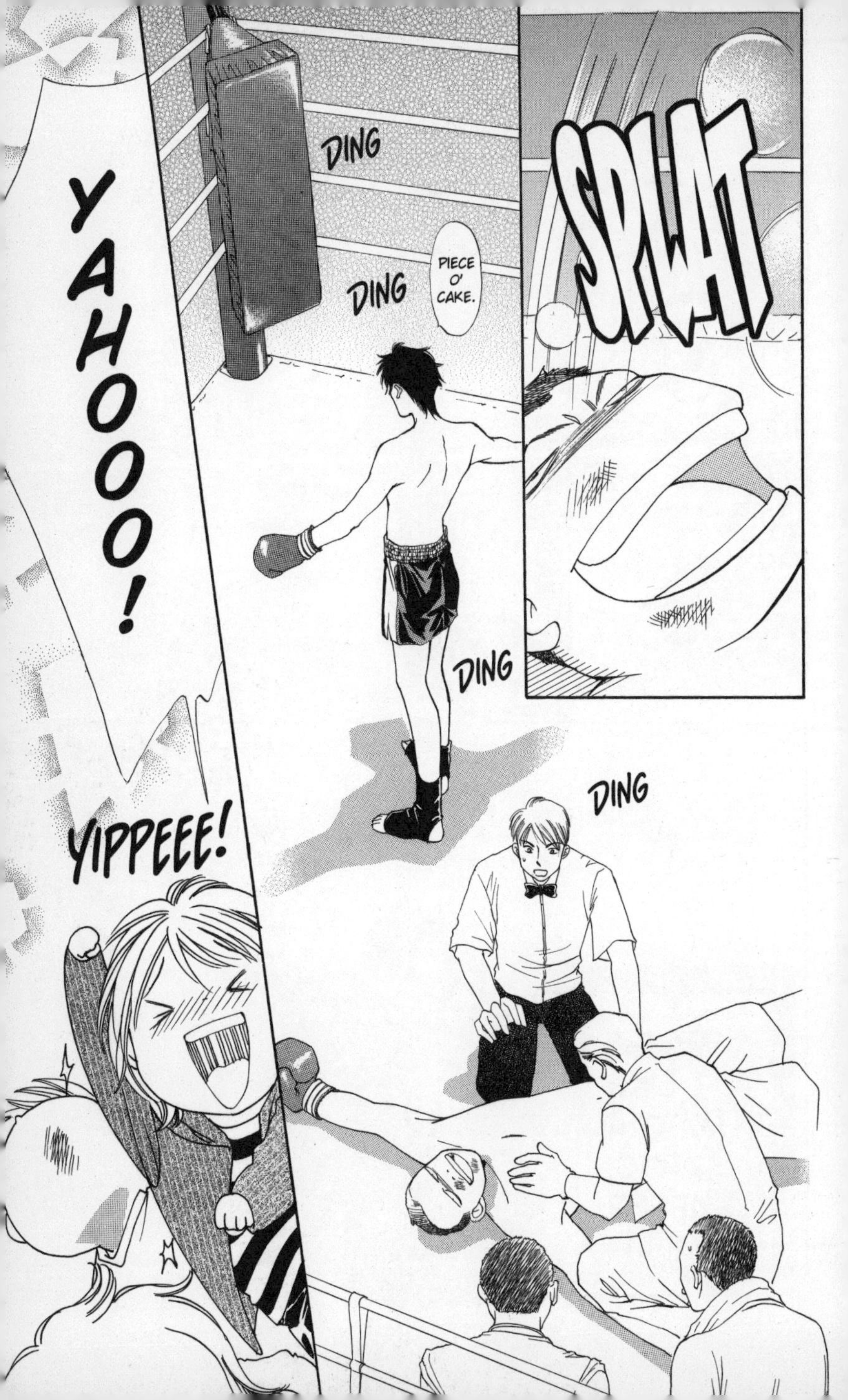

SPLAT
DING
PIECE O' CAKE.
DING
DING
DING
YAHOOO!
YIPPEEE!

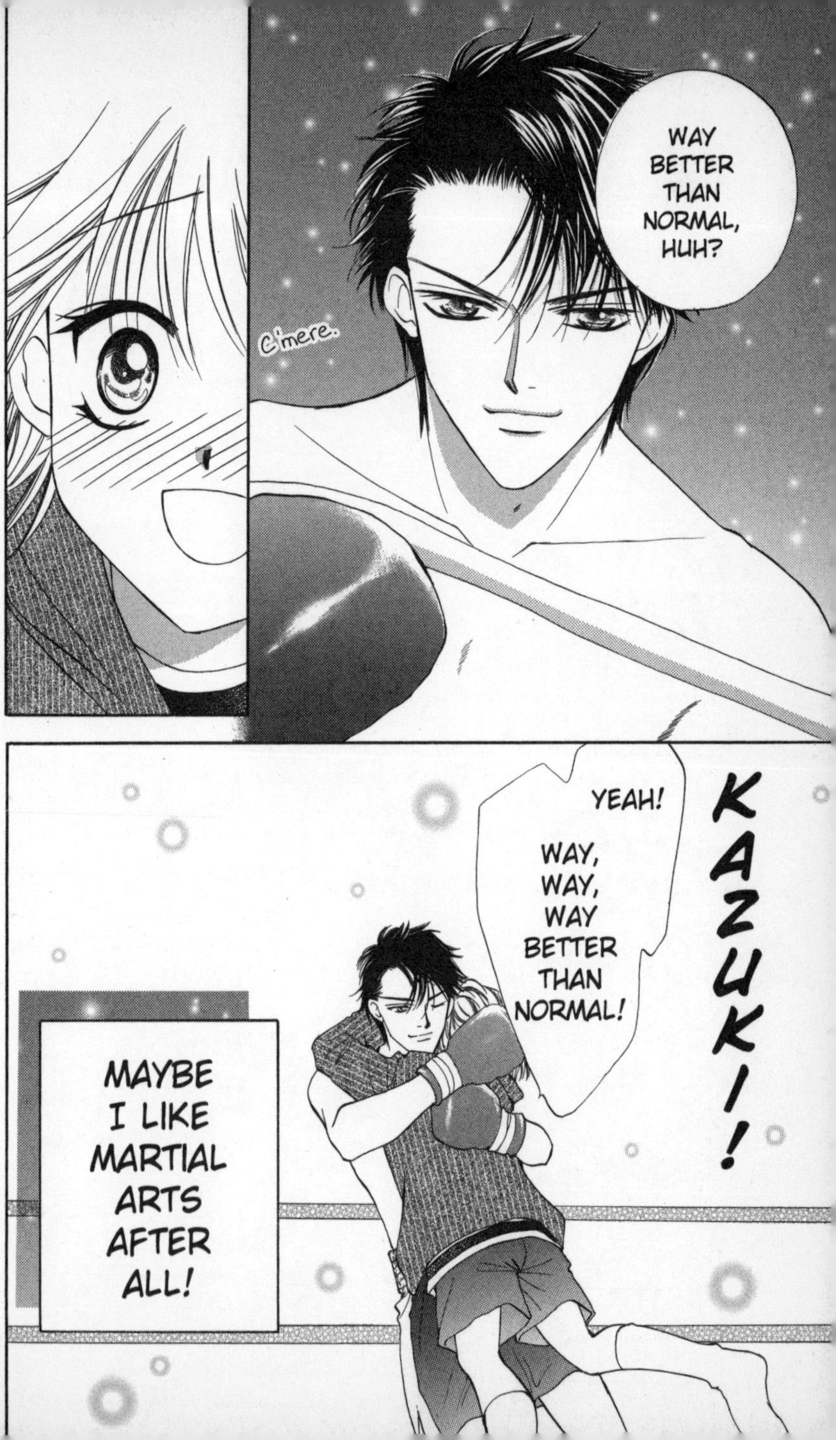

WAY BETTER THAN NORMAL, HUH?
C'mere.
KAZUKI!
YEAH!
WAY, WAY, WAY BETTER THAN NORMAL!
MAYBE I LIKE MARTIAL ARTS AFTER ALL!

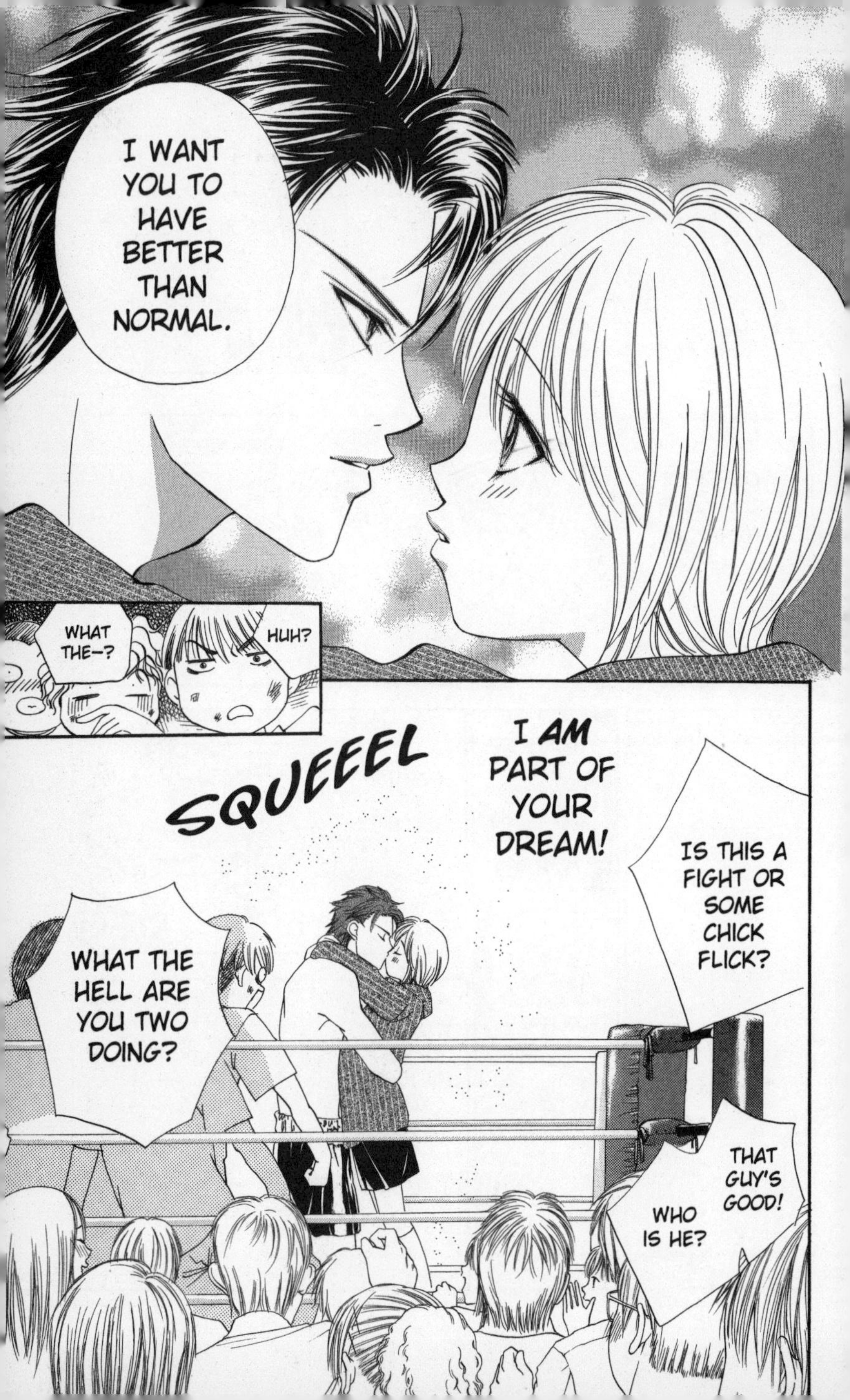
I WANT YOU TO HAVE BETTER THAN NORMAL.
HUH?
WHAT THE-?
I AM PART OF YOUR DREAM!
SQUEEEL
IS THIS A FIGHT OR SOME CHICK FLICK?
WHAT THE HELL ARE YOU TWO DOING?
THAT GUY'S GOOD!
WHO IS HE?

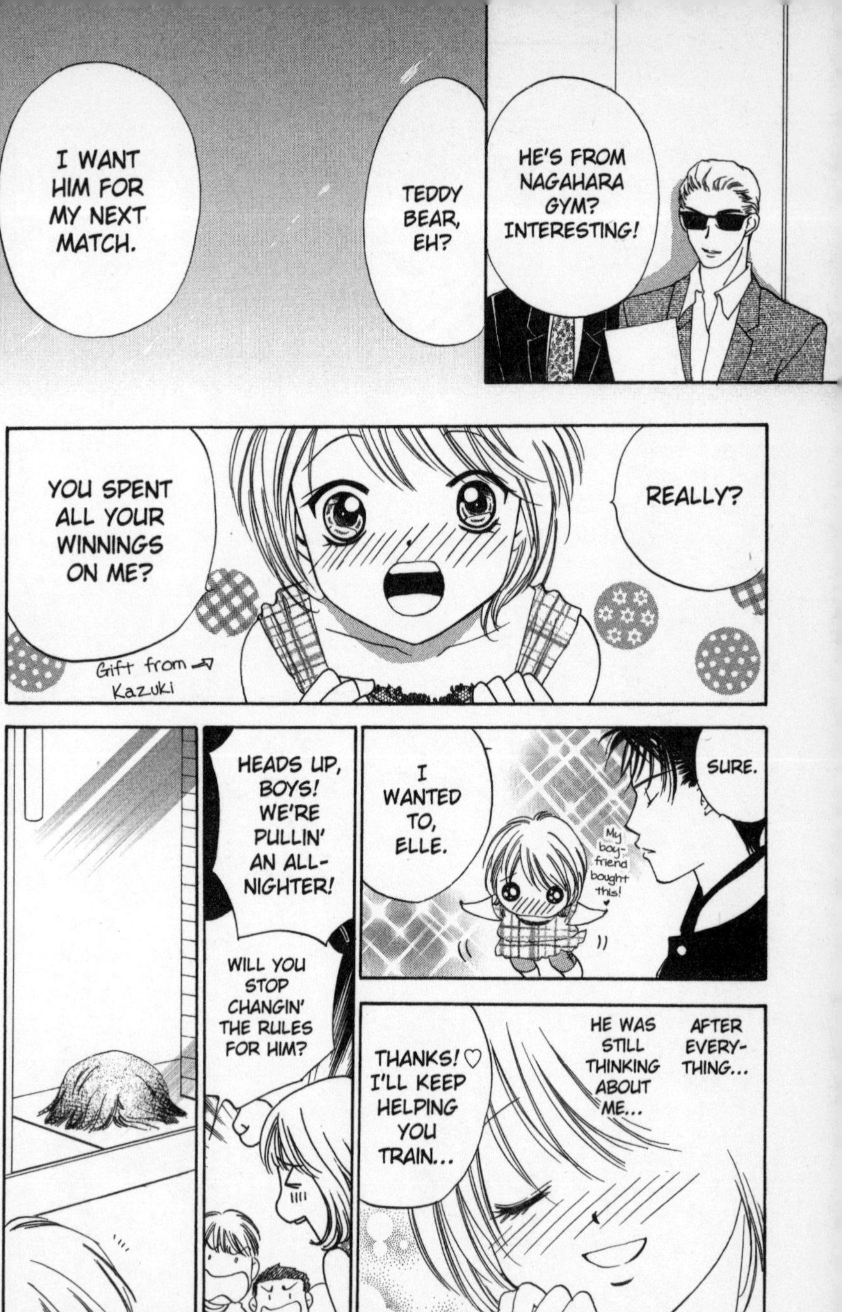
HE'S FROM NAGAHARA GYM? INTERESTING!
TEDDY BEAR, EH?
I WANT HIM FOR MY NEXT MATCH.
REALLY?
YOU SPENT ALL YOUR WINNINGS ON ME?
Gift from Kazuki
SURE.
My boyfriend bought this! ♥
I WANTED TO, ELLE.
AFTER EVERYTHING...
HE WAS STILL THINKING ABOUT ME...
THANKS! ♡ I'LL KEEP HELPING YOU TRAIN...
HEADS UP, BOYS! WE'RE PULLIN' AN ALL-NIGHTER!
WILL YOU STOP CHANGIN' THE RULES FOR HIM?

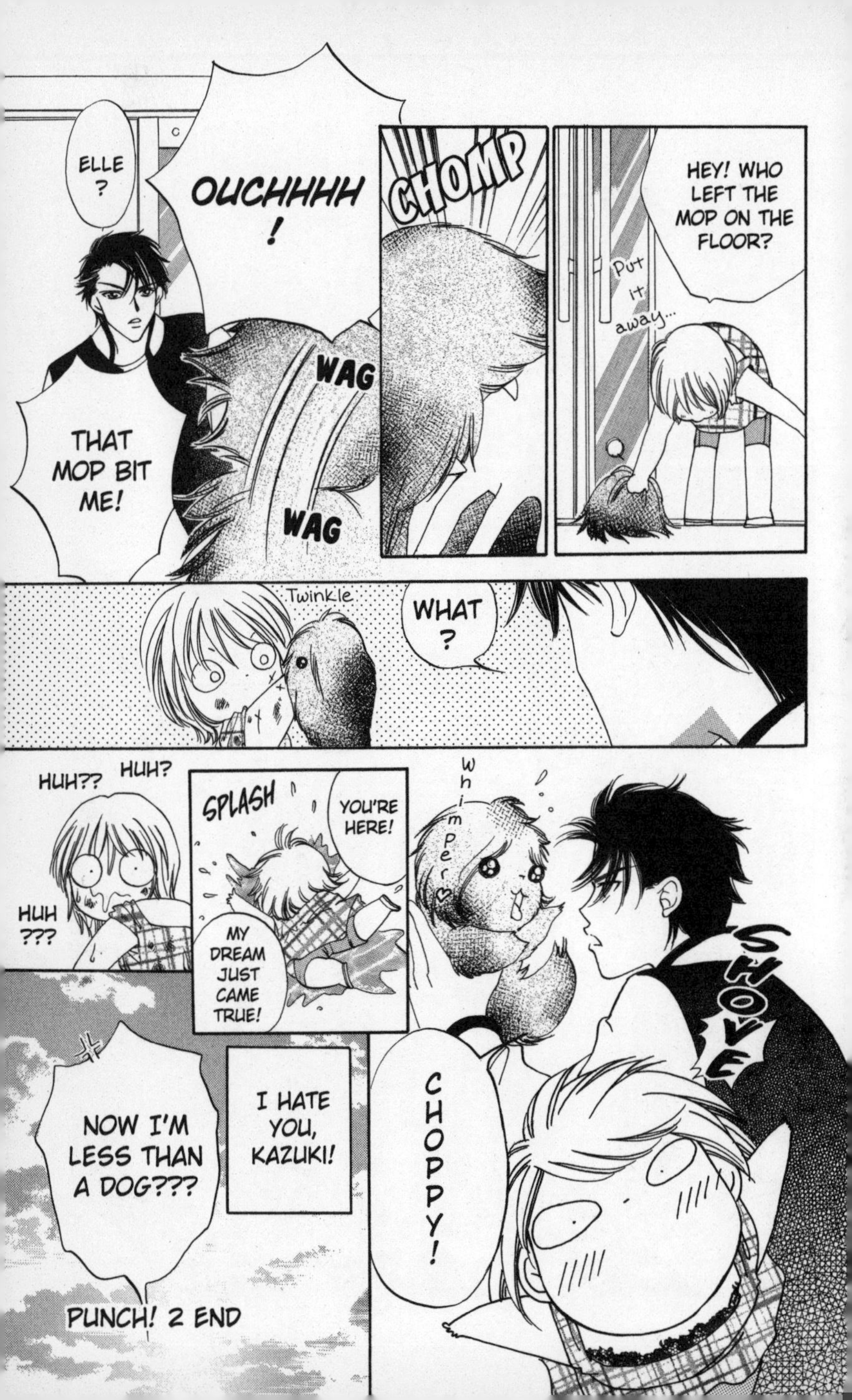
HEY! WHO LEFT THE MOP ON THE FLOOR?
Put it away...
CHOMP
OUCHHHH!
ELLE?
WAG
WAG
THAT MOP BIT ME!
WHAT?
Twinkle
Whimper
SHOVE
CHOPPY!
YOU'RE HERE!
SPLASH
MY DREAM JUST CAME TRUE!
HUH?
HUH??
HUH ???
I HATE YOU, KAZUKI!
NOW I'M LESS THAN A DOG???
PUNCH! 2 END

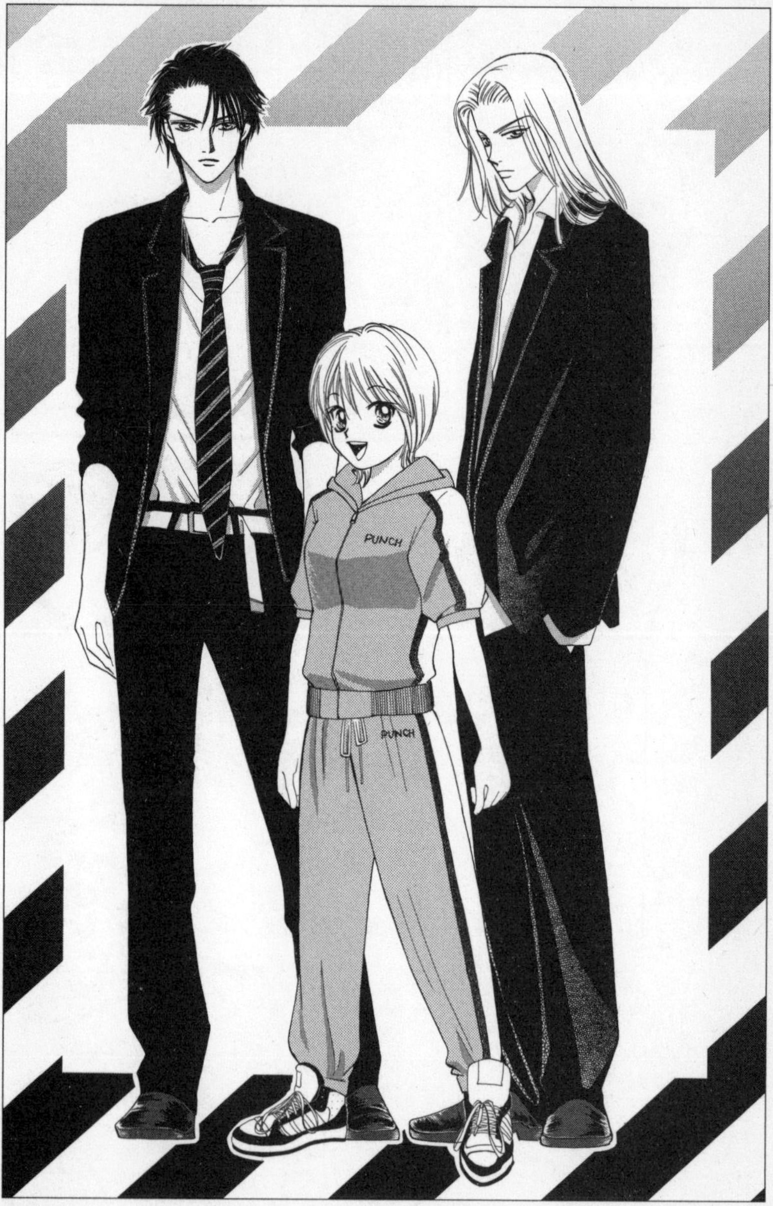
PUNCH
PUNCH

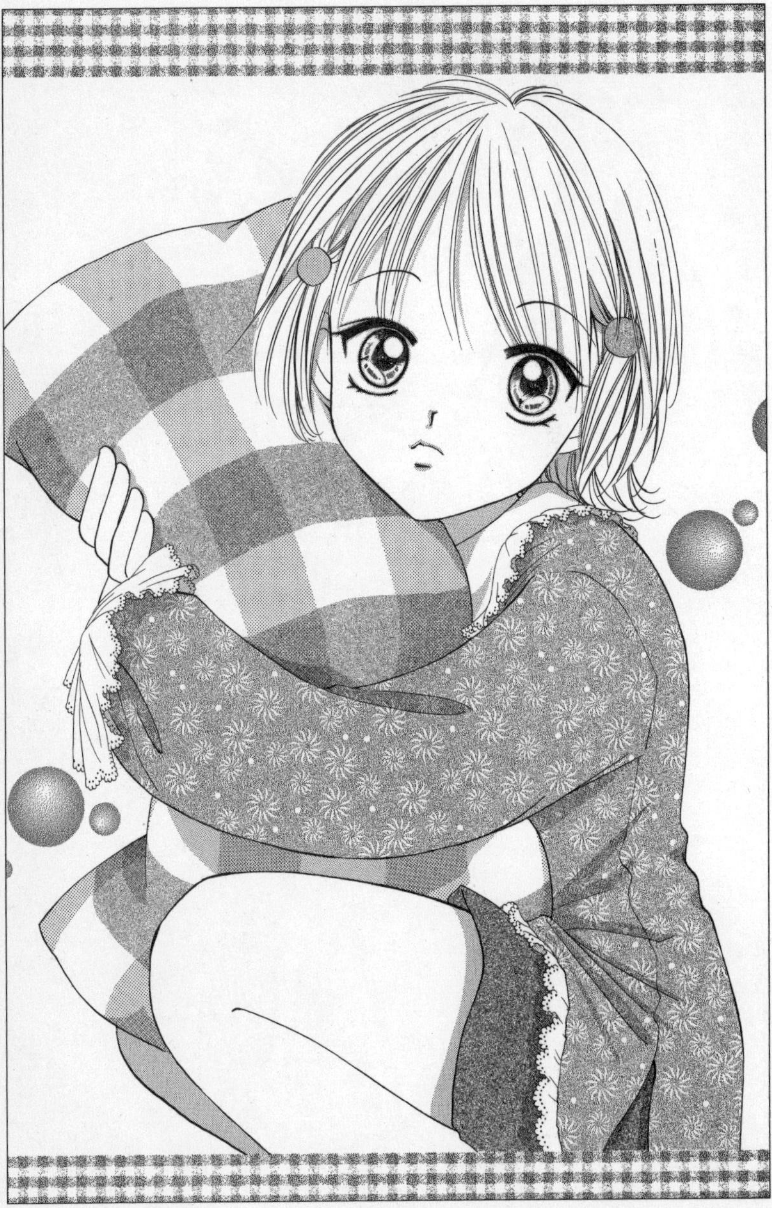

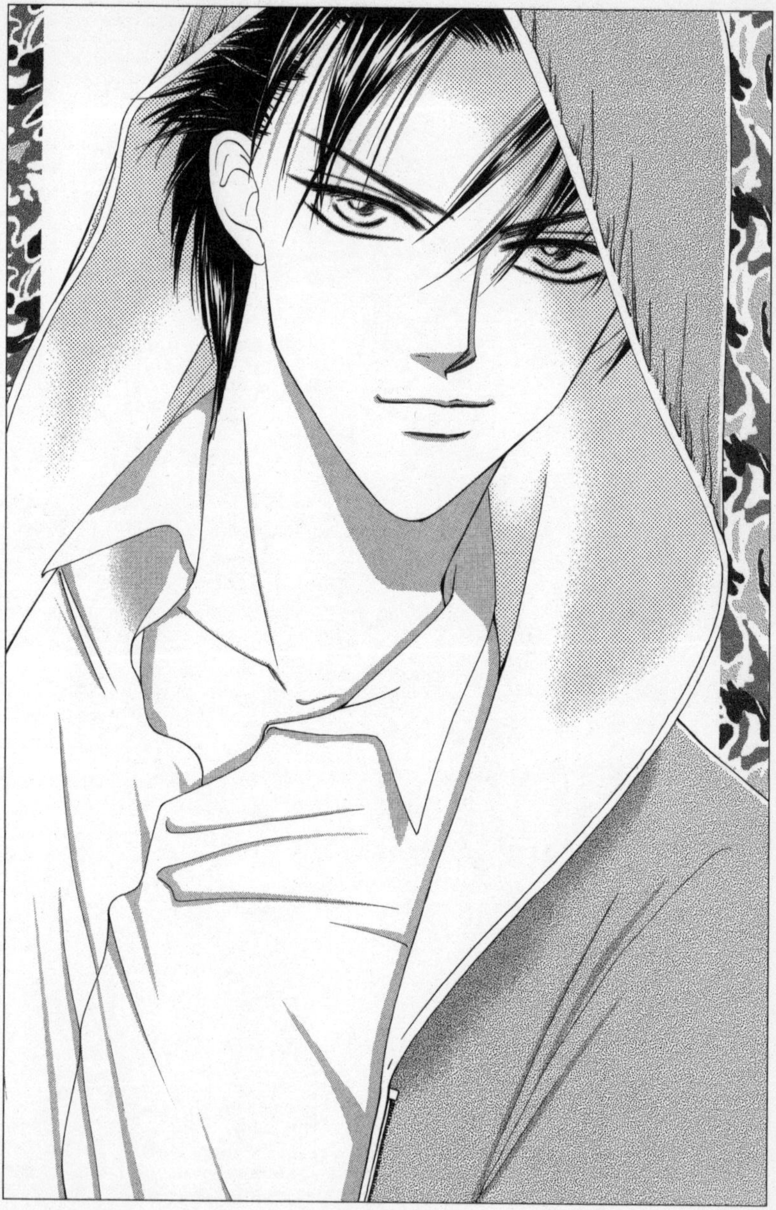

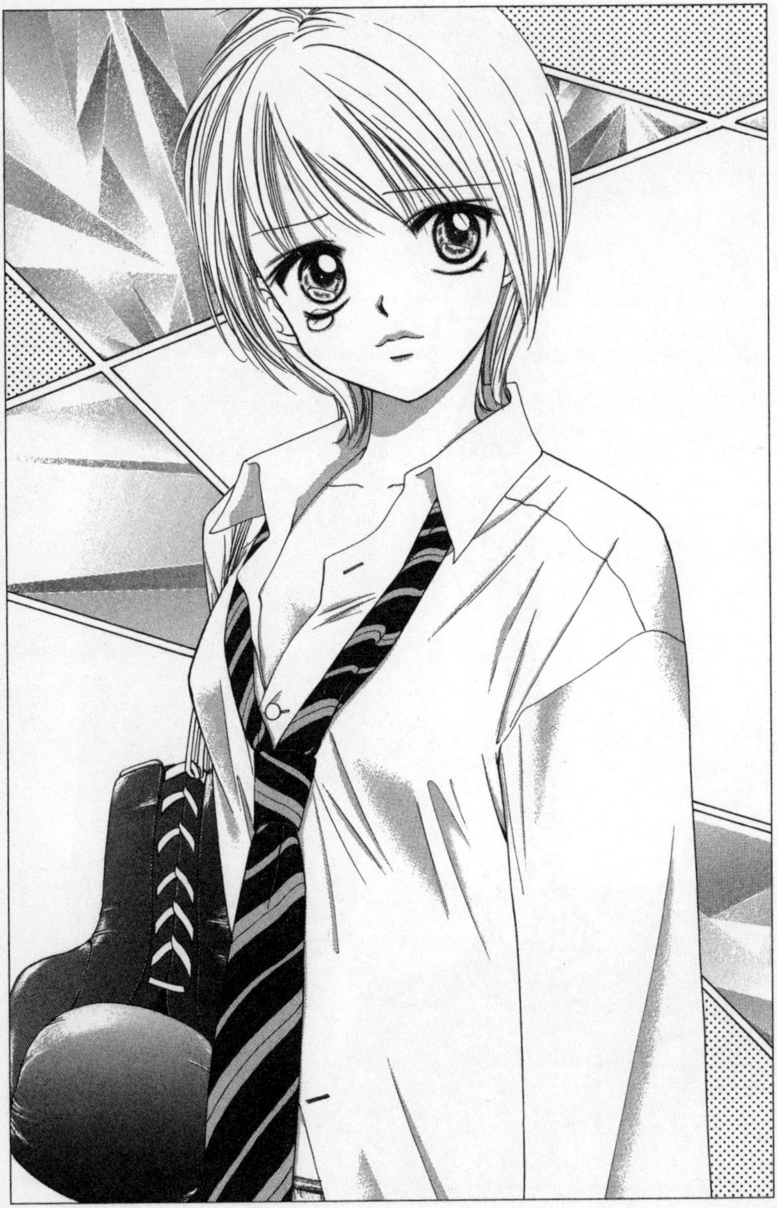

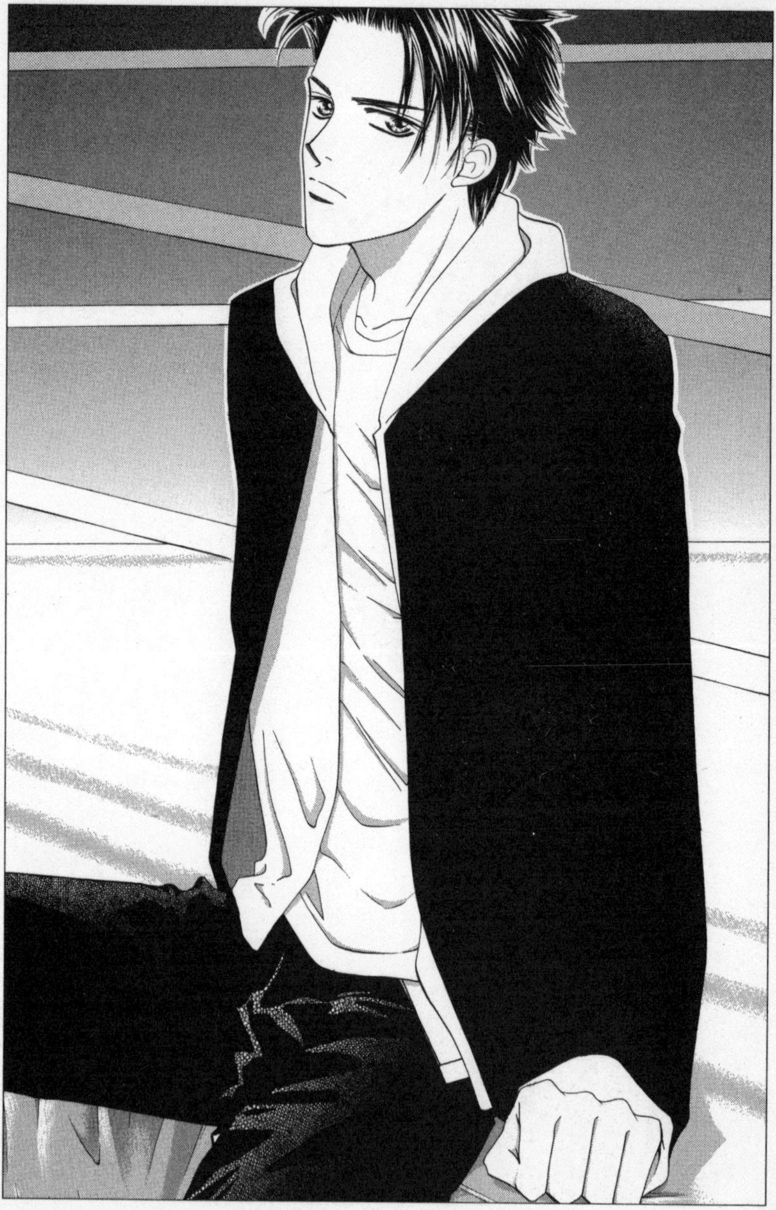

PUNCH! 2

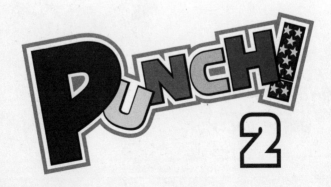

FINALLY THE CLIMAX!

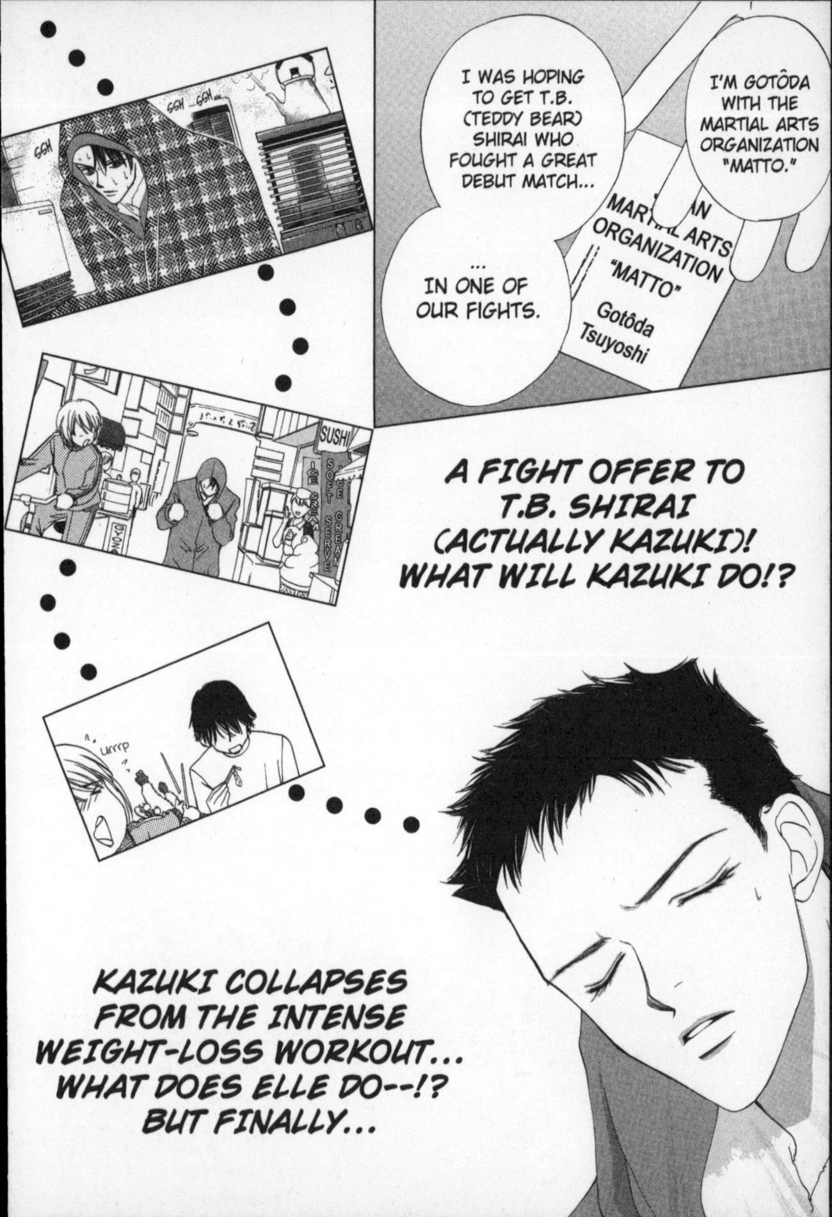
I'M GOTÔDA WITH THE MARTIAL ARTS ORGANIZATION "MATTO."
I WAS HOPING TO GET T.B. (TEDDY BEAR) SHIRAI WHO FOUGHT A GREAT DEBUT MATCH...
... IN ONE OF OUR FIGHTS.
MARTIAL ARTS ORGANIZATION "MATTO"
Gotôda Tsuyoshi
GGH
GGH GGH
SUSHI
SOFT SERVE
urrrp
A FIGHT OFFER TO T.B. SHIRAI (ACTUALLY KAZUKI)! WHAT WILL KAZUKI DO!?
KAZUKI COLLAPSES FROM THE INTENSE WEIGHT-LOSS WORKOUT... WHAT DOES ELLE DO--!? BUT FINALLY...

HE'S A HIGH SCHOOLER CALLED KAZUKI SHINDO. HE FAKED HIS IDENTITY TO FIGHT THE OTHER DAY.

THAT GUY AIN'T TEDDY BEAR SHIRAI.

THEY FIND OUT!?

NO...

KAZUKI AND NAGAHARA GYM PERMANENTLY BANNED FROM THE MARTIAL-ARTS WORLD!?

PUNCH! CONCLUSION VOLUME 3

ON SALE MARCH 2007!

RIE TAKADA

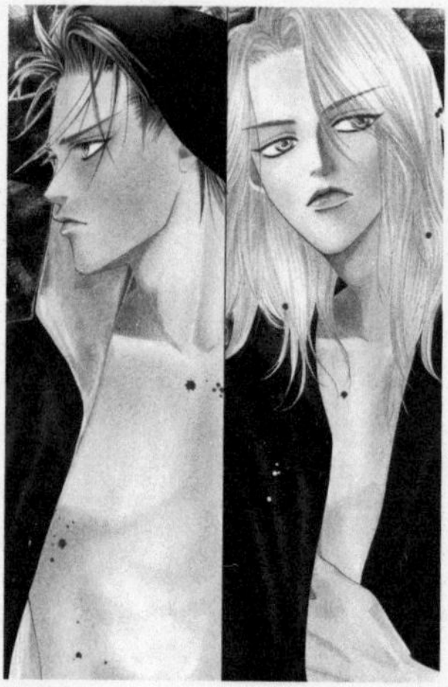

★Born August 10th in Hokkaido. Leo. Blood type O.
★Made her debut with *SP Girl* in 1990's *Shojo Comic* issue 17.
★Currently publishing in *Shojo Comic.*

I rode an airplane the other day and saw a circular rainbow. There were many rainbows like sliced Baumkuchen [round sweet cake from Germany] spread out all over the sky. It was so beautiful I was totally amazed. I can't believe they were circular. By the way fireworks seen from the sky are round too.

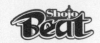

PUNCH!
VOL. 2
The Shojo Beat Manga Edition

STORY & ART BY
RIE TAKADA

English Adaptation/Janet Gilbert
Translation/Joe Yamazaki
Touch-up Art & Lettering/Primary Graphix
Design/Izumi Hirayama
Editor/Urian Brown

Editor in Chief, Books/Alvin Lu
Editor in Chief, Magazines/Marc Weidenbaum
VP of Publishing Licensing/Rika Inouye
VP of Sales/Gonzalo Ferreyra
Sr. VP of Marketing/Liza Coppola
Publisher/Hyoe Narita

Printed in Canada

Published by VIZ Media, LLC
P.O. Box 77010
San Francisco, CA 94107

Shojo Beat Manga Edition
10 9 8 7 6 5 4 3 2
First printing, January 2007
Second printing, March 2007

store.viz.com

PARENTAL ADVISORY
PUNCH! is rated T+ for Older Teen and is recommended for ages 16 and up. This volume contains strong language and sexual themes.

Tell us what you think about Shojo Beat Manga!

Our survey is now available online. Go to:

shojobeat.com/mangasurvey

Help us make our product offerings better!

Love. Laugh. Live.

In addition to hundreds of pages of manga each month, *Shojo Beat* will bring you the latest in Japanese fashion, music, art, and culture—plus shopping, how-tos, industry updates, interviews, and much more!

DON'T YOU WANT TO HAVE THIS MUCH FUN?

NANA
by AI YAZAWA

Subscribe Now!
Fill out the coupon on the other side

Or go to:
www.shojobeat.com

Or call toll-free
800-541-7876

by MITSUBA TAKANASHI   by KANOKO SAKURAKOJI   by MATSURI HINO   by MARIMO RAGAWA   by YUU WATASE